Dr. Stephen Beall

Macmillan Teach Yourself
Latin

in 24 hours

Pearson Education Macmillan USA
201 West 103rd Street
Indianapolis, IN 46290

D1412573

MACMILLAN TEACH YOURSELF LATIN IN 24 HOURS

International Standard Book Number: 0-02-863932-4
Library of Congress Catalog Card Number: Available upon request.

Printed in the United States of America

First printing: 2000

03 02 01 00   4   3   2   1

Trademarks

ACQUISITIONS EDITOR
Mike Sanders
Susan Zingraf

DEVELOPMENT EDITOR
Alana Morgan

PRODUCTION EDITOR
JoAnna Kremer

COPY EDITOR
Krista Hansing

INDEXER
Lisa Wilson

PROOFREADER
John Etchison

PRODUCTION
Darin Crone

COVER DESIGNER
Alan Clements

BOOK DESIGNER
Gary Adair

MANAGING EDITOR
Cari Luna

PRODUCT MANAGER
Phil Kitchel

PUBLISHER
Marie Butler-Knight

Overview

Contents

Introduction

WHAT IS LATIN?

Latin first emerged as the ancient dialect of Latium, the region surrounding Rome, Italy. As the Roman empire spread, it was introduced to other areas by soldiers and settlers who spoke the language. In some places (especially in the West), Latin replaced local dialects as the people's first language; in others, it was used alongside other languages (such as Greek, Egyptian, and Aramaic). Latin was the administrative language of Roman soldiers and lawyers, and (along with Greek) of other imperial functionaries. The Romans also produced a literature to rival that of the Greeks.

As a literary language, Latin became increasingly standardized. Scholars and teachers determined which words, grammatical constructions, and spellings were "correct." The result was that while spoken Latin evolved into the modern "Romance" languages, written Latin remained in a more or less stable form. This stability assured the cultural unity of Western Europe, despite constant shifts in its political and religious boundaries. Latin continued to serve as an international language, especially in the arts, sciences, and religion, well into the modern period—and in some venues continues to do so today.

WHY LEARN LATIN?

If you are reading these words, you probably have a good answer to this question already. You may be interested to know, however, some of the most common reasons that bring people to study the language of the Romans.

For many people, Latin is a means to an end. Perhaps something they wish to know about was originally communicated in Latin, and they want to understand the *ipsíssima verba,* "the very words" that were used. In this way, Latin is relevant to all sorts of interests: history, literature, science, philosophy, and religion. Specialists in fields as diverse as botany and mathematics profit from knowing some Latin.

Many others just find the language itself appealing. Perhaps these people want to know something about the common basis of modern Romance languages, such as French and Spanish. Others are curious about the Latin origins of many English words. Then there are those who are simply fascinated by language in general, and want to become familiar with one of the great languages of history.

Finally, many people are drawn to Latin because it has the status of a "classical tongue," which it shares with such languages as Greek, Hebrew, Sanskrit, Chinese, and Arabic. Classical languages are important because they are not limited to particular places and times. Although Latin began as the local dialect of ancient Rome, it was eventually used to bring people from opposite ends of the globe—and from different centuries—into contact with each other. Classical languages tend to absorb what is most profound and universal in human thought and culture.

The object of this book, then, is twofold: to acquaint you with the structure of the Latin language, and to give you an idea of the variety of things to which you will have access as you continue your study. At the beginning of a new millennium, when all our talk is about "globalization," it is still easy to be imprisoned in the here and now. Latin opens the door to a larger world.

How to Use This Book

One of the challenges of learning any language is to get used to a different way of saying things. Learning new vocabulary is only half the battle.

The hour-long lessons in this book concentrate on the forms and sentence patterns that are the basic building blocks of a Latin sentence. Each lesson is introduced by a short reading adapted from a real Latin text. Read these in conjunction with the English translation given immediately afterward. Note especially the words in bold; these are examples of the new grammatical information that appears in each hour.

After the reading, you will learn basic rules of Latin grammar. Latin is a highly inflected language. Changes in the ending of a word often convey the same information that prepositions, helping verbs, and word order do in English. Thus, it will be a good idea for you to memorize the tables that are given in each chapter. Note that certain basic tables are gradually built up over several lessons. Furthermore, as each new grammatical rule is introduced, you will have a chance to apply it in a series of short tasks. Check the answer key to see how you are doing.

At the end of the grammar section in each hour, you will find two vocabulary lists. One contains "essential" vocabulary. Here you will find roughly two dozen of the most frequently used words in Latin. These words should also be memorized because they will occur frequently in the reading exercises of this book, and in any Latin text you want to read. The second list contains "recognition" vocabulary. These are less common terms that closely resemble English words; thus, they can be learned without any special effort at memorization. Read through this section a couple of times, and then move on.

Next, you will find a reading exercise based on an ancient, medieval, or modern Latin text. The text has been adapted to suit your level of knowledge at each stage, but it will have the flavor of authentic Latin. You may find it helpful—especially in the later chapters—to go to the answer key and *read the English translation of this passage first.* Then work through the Latin as best you can, using the reading vocabulary given after the reading.

At the end of each hour are one or more review exercises. These will help you put things together, or give you a second look at the grammar and vocabulary of the reading exercise.

Finally, I have one other suggestion: As you work through the tables and exercises, it will help if you *read the Latin parts out loud.* When we learn a language, our memories grasp what we hear as much as what we see. To do this, however, you will need to know how to pronounce Latin.

SIMPLE RULES FOR PRONOUNCING LATIN

The following rules are somewhat simpler than those often found in textbooks of Classical Latin. If you follow them you will be perfectly intelligible to Latin "speakers" world-wide.

VOWELS

If you have already learned to speak a little Spanish, German, or virtually any other European language, you should have no trouble with Latin vowels. Pure vowels are the sounds represented by the letters **a, e, i, o,** and **u.**

In Latin, the pure vowels have the following basic sounds.

Sound	As in ...	Example	Pronunciation
a	*Father*	**pater**	[PAH-tehr]
e	*they*	**deus**	[DEH-oos]
i	*machine*	**hi**	[HEE]
o	*potato*	**dono**	[DOH-noh]
u	*rule*	**diu**	[DEE-oo]

(Some words, borrowed from Greek, also contain the letter **y,** pronounced like **i**.)

Sometimes Latin vowels are pronounced with a less "open" sound: the **a** in *America,* the **e** in *bet,* the **i** in *sit,* the **o** in *boss,* the **u** in *wuss*. The simplest rule of thumb, however, is to *use the open sound*.

For practice, pronounce the musical scale, which also follows the rules for Latin vowels: **do, re, mi, fa, so, la, ti, do.** (Since **u** is not on the scale, try this one for practice: **bu hu.**)

DIPHTHONGS

A "diphthong" is a combination of two vowels. In English, for example, the **ou** in "house" is a diphthong. The following are the most common diphthongs in Latin.

Diphthong	Like ...	Example	Pronunciation
ae	*ai* in *aisle*	**caeli**	[KAI-lee]
au	*ow* in *wow*	**autem**	[OW-tehm]
ei	*ei* in *beige*	**eia**	[EH-ah]
eu	*eh-oo*	**Europa**	[Eh-oo-ROH-pah]
oe	*oi* in *oil*	**poena**	[POY-nah]

For practice, pronounce the following words: **tau, hei, heu, evoe, hae.**

CONSONANTS

Consonants are the sounds that are made by forcing air between the tongue, lips, teeth, palate, and larynx—in other words, all the other letters of the alphabet. Most Latin consonants have the same sound in Latin as in English. The following are the exceptions:

- **c** is always "hard," as in *can:* **cena** [KAY-nah].
- **ch** is like a hard **c: Christi** [KREES-tee].
- **g** is always "hard," as in *gun:* **genua** [GEH-noo-ah].
- **i** as a consonant has the sound of the English **y: iusta** [YOOS-tah]
- **v** pronounced as a **w** (but see below): **vis** [wees].

Note that if **v** is pronounced as a "w," Julius Caesar's famous motto **Veni, vidi, vici** (*I came, I saw, I conquered*) is pronounced as follows: [way-nee, wee-dee, wee-kee]. Shortly after Caesar, though, the Latin **v** began to sound more like the "v" sound of English. You may use this sound if you prefer.

For practice, read the alphabet as it was pronounced by the ancient Romans:

a, be, ce, de, e, ef, ge, ha, i, ka, el, em, en, o, pe, qu (=cu), er, es, te, u, ix, ypsilon, zeta.

ACCENTUATION

Words can be divided into units called *"syllables."* A syllable is a group of sounds centered around a vowel or diphthong:

Gal-li-a est om-nis di-vi-sa in par-tes tres.

All Gaul is divided into three parts.

In words of two or more syllables, one syllable takes the accent, or *"stress"*: That is, one syllable is pronounced with a little more "oomph." Stress is evident in a few words pronounced differently by American and British speakers of English. For example, *controversy* is pronounced [KON-troh-ver-see] by Americans, but [kon-TROV-er-see] by the British. A similar variant is found in the name *Augustine:* Some people say [AW-gu-steen], whereas others say [a-GU-stin].

In Latin, the rules for stress are fairly simple.

1. If a word has two syllables, the stress falls on the first syllable:

   fata [FAH-tah], **debes** [DEH-behs], **Caesar** [KAI-sahr]

2. If the word has more than two syllables, unless otherwise marked, the stress will fall on the next-to-last syllable:

   videre [vee-DEH-reh], **amici** [ah-MEE-kee], **amata** [ah-MAH-tah]

3. Sometimes the stress falls on the "next-to-the-next-to-last" syllable. In this book, such words will have a stress mark:

   "fílio [FEE-lee-oh], **cápite** [KAH-pee-teh], **hábeo** [HAH-beh-oh]

For practice, read aloud the following passage from the *Gallic War* of Julius Caesar:

Gállia est omnis divisa in partes tres, quarum unam "íncolunt Belgae, áliam Aquitánii, tértiam qui ipsorum lingua Celtae, nostra Gállii appellantur.

All Gaul is divided into three parts, of which one is inhabited by the Belgae, another by the Aquitanii, and the third by people who in their own language are called "Celts," in ours, "Gauls."

Congratulations! You are now ready to begin learning Latin.

Finally, this book has a lot of miscellaneous cross-references, tips, shortcuts, and warning sidebar boxes. Here's how they stack up:

A MINUTE

Just a Minute sidebars offer advice or teach an easier way to do something.

SAVER

Time Saver sidebars give you a faster way to do something.

EED WITH CAUTION

Proceed with Caution notes are warnings. They warn you about potential problems and help you steer clear of trouble.

These sidebars contain quick, betcha didn't know bits of information.

About the Author

Dr. Stephen M. Beall is an Assistant Professor of Classics at Marquette University in Milwaukee, Wisconsin. He has taught college-level Latin courses since 1983. He has also published articles on Latin literature and translation theory, and his own translations of Latin texts.

Acknowledgments

The author wishes to thank Susan Zingraf, Alana Morgan, JoAnna Kremer, and Michael Sanders at Macmillan for their assistance. He also wishes to thank Jennifer Ganley for drafting the answer key and the overview of Latin forms, and Bryan Mount for reading and correcting the manuscript. Finally, he is thankful, as always, to Judith Beall for her support and encouragement.

Basic Grammatical Terms; Singular and Plural; Agreement

LESSON PLAN:

In this hour you will learn about …

- Some key grammatical terms, such as *"part of speech," "number,"* and *"gender"*
- The forms of plural nouns and adjectives
- The agreement of nouns, verbs, and adjectives

For hundreds of years, students have learned Latin through the "metalanguage" of formal grammar (*ars grammática*). The terms and rules first developed by ancient grammarians still provide a quick and convenient way of talking about the way Latin (or any other language) is put together.

THE STAGES OF THE LATIN LANGUAGE

Before we get into the rules, though, let's get our feet wet with a snippet of Latin adapted from the seventh-century bishop and scholar, Isidore of Seville.

INTRODUCTORY READING

> *"Latinae" linguae quattuor sunt: prisca, latina, romana, et mixta. Lingua prisca est qua vetustíssimi Itali dicebant. "Latina" est lingua, qua locuti sunt quando Latinus et Tusci reges erant. "Romana" lingua est, quam Naévius, Plautus, Énnius, Virgílius poetae, et oratores Gracchus et Cato et Cícero et céteri effuderunt.*

> There are four "Latin" languages: the original, the Latin, the Roman, and the mixed. The "original" language is that which the ancient Italians spoke. "Latin" is the language that they spoke when Latinus and Tuscus were kings. The "Roman" language is that which the poets Naevius, Plautus, Ennius, and Vergil, and the orators Gracchus, Cato, Cicero, and the others used.

As you read through this passage, you undoubtedly noticed a couple of features that make Latin sound "strange" to speakers of English. Let's tackle these first.

A AND *THE*

One of the first things that occurs to beginning students is that Latin has no words for *the* and *a/an.* Thus, *lingua* can mean "the language" or "a language," depending on the context.

- *Latina est **lingua** antiqua:* Latin is **an** ancient language.
- *Latina est **lingua,** qua Romani locuti sunt:* Latin is **the** language that the Romans spoke.

In fact, many languages—such as modern Russian—get along without the words *a/an* and *the,* which are called *articles.* That is why Boris and Natasha, the villains of the *Rocky and Bullwinkle* cartoon series, are always in pursuit of "moose and squirrel."

TASK 1: USING ARTICLES

The following could be a literal translation of a Latin paragraph. Insert *the* and *a/an* into the reading as necessary.

> Latin was widely spoken language. It was spoken throughout territory of Roman empire. It gradually evolved into romance languages. Example is Spanish, which is primary language of Spain and Central and South America. Latin is considered important part of liberal education. To paraphrase Spanish philosopher: "Gentleman or lady is someone who has forgotten Latin and Greek."

LATIN WORD ORDER

Another surprise is that the order of Latin words is often different from English, but there are no hard and fast rules. Thus we have *lingua prisca* for "the original language," but one can also say *vetustíssimi Itali* for "the most ancient Italians." In another sentence, we have *Latinae linguae quattuor sunt,* literally, "Latin languages four are" for "There are four Latin languages."

The basic rule of thumb is that Latin words can be mixed up at will, although there are certain recurring patterns. You will learn these as you go along.

Task 2: Working with Word Order

The following is a word-for-word translation of Isidore's essay on the sounds of various foreign languages. See whether you can turn it into acceptable English.

All however Eastern peoples in the throat sounds make, such as the Hebrews and the Syrians. All Mediterranean peoples on the palate words form, such as the Greeks and the Asians. All Western people words on the teeth make, such as Italians and Spaniards. Syrian or Chaldean close to Hebrew is in speech and the sound of the letters. Some people however think that the Hebrew language the same as Chaldean is because Abraham from Chaldea was. But if this is accepted, how in the Book of Daniel the Hebrew boys a language which they do not know to be taught are ordered?

The Parts of Speech

Our first task, then, will be to learn how to make words fit together in simple sentences. When talking about language, however, it is helpful to have a set of terms for the different kinds of words. Ancient grammarians divided all words into categories called the *parts of speech* (*partes orationis*). The basic parts of speech are: nouns, pronouns, verbs, adjectives, adverbs, prepositions, and conjunctions. Here is an overview:

- A **noun** (Latin *nomen*) is a word that names a person, place, or thing: **Rome** is a **city. Caesar** is a **man.**
- A **pronoun** (*pronomen*) is a word that "stands in" for a noun: The Romans once spoke Latin; now **they** speak Italian.
- A **verb** (*verbum*) indicates an action or state: Latin **is** a language; the Romans **spoke** it.
- An **adjective** (*adiectivum*) "modifies" (that is, tells us something about) a noun or a pronoun: Rome is a **beautiful** city.
- An **adverb** (*advérbium*) is a word that modifies a verb, adjective, or adverb: Caesar conquered **very** many countries **rather quickly.**
- A **preposition** (*praepositio*) is a "little" word that introduces a *prepositional phrase*. The latter indicates some sort or relationship in time, space, cause, and so on: Caesar was assassinated **after** breakfast **in** Rome.
- A **conjunction** (*coniúnctio*) is another kind of "little" word that is used to link other words, groups of words, or even whole sentences: Caesar **and** Antony fought a civil war **because** each of them wished to rule the empire.

The following sentence exemplifies all the basic parts of speech:

Adjective	Great
Noun	Caesar
Conjunction	and
Pronoun	I
Adverb	quickly
Verb	conquered
Adjective	fierce tribes
Preposition	in Gaul.

In this lesson, we will be working with nouns, adjectives, and verbs.

TASK 3: IDENTIFYING PARTS OF SPEECH

In the following sentences, identify the part of speech exemplified by each of the words in bold.

The "Latin" **people** came to Italy **from** the East, and settled in the vicinity of Rome. **Neighboring** tribes **spoke** other dialects. **When** the Romans conquered Italy, however, **they** settled throughout the peninsula. **Soon all** Italians spoke Latin. The language then spread **to** all of **Western** Europe. **In** the East, Greek remained the **language** of trade and culture, **but** those who **joined** the army had to learn Latin.

SINGULAR AND PLURAL OF NOUNS; DECLENSION

As we have seen, a noun is a word that names a person, place, or thing. However, it often happens that we are speaking of more than one item. In English, we indicate this by adding –*s:*

- They speak their own **language.** They speak several **languages.**

This distinction is called *number.* If the form of the noun points to only one item, it is called *singular;* if there is more than one, the form is *plural.*

In Latin, there are several ways of changing singular nouns to plural. The plural form depends on the "family" or group of nouns to which it belongs. These families are traditionally called *declensions*. In Latin, there are five declensions, which can be recognized by the singular ending. Study the following chart.

The Five Declensions

	I	II	III
	girl	master	king
Singular	puell-a	dómin-us	rex
Plural	puell-ae	dómin-i	reg-es

	IV	V
	chariot	thing
Singular	curr-us	r-es
Plural	curr-us	r-es

Note that words of the third declension have no standard ending in the singular. The plural is built on a stem, which may be different from the singular form:

- *rex* (king) becomes *reg-es* (kings)
- *urbs* (city) becomes *urb-es* (cities)

This stem will be given in your vocabulary lists: for example, *homo, homin–*.

The singular ending for the second and fourth declensions is the same: *–us*. Fourth declension nouns, however, are few in number. They will be identified as such in your vocabulary lists: for example, *manus* (IV).

Note also that the plural ending of fourth and fifth declension nouns is spelled the same as the singular. However, you can usually guess the number of these nouns from the context:

- *una res* (one thing) becomes *multae res* (many things)

JUST A MINUTE

Like English, plural nouns of the third, fourth, and fifth declensions end in *–s*. To remember the endings of the first two declensions, it may help to think of the English loanword *alumnus,* for which the plural is *alumni*. A female *alumnus* is called an *alumna;* the plural is *alumnae.*

TASK 4: NOUNS AND THEIR PLURALS

Give the plural form for each of the following nouns.

1. *servus* (slave)
2. *manus* (IV) (hand)

3. *fémina* (woman)

4. *casa* (house)

5. *lingua* (language)

6. *dies* (day)

7. *hortus* (garden)

8. *spes* (hope)

9. *múlier* (*mulíer–*) (woman)

10. *colonus* (farmer)

11. *urbs* (*urb–*) (city)

12. *homo* (*hómin–*) (human being)

GRAMMATICAL GENDER

Like Spanish, French, German, and many other languages, Latin has a feature known as grammatical gender. In the case of people and animals, gender is often identical to sex:

- *dóminus* (master) is a masculine noun
- *dómina* (mistress) is a feminine noun

However, nouns referring to things that have no sexual differentiation are also classified by gender:

- *hortus* (garden) is a masculine noun
- *casa* (house) is a feminine noun

In such cases, the gender is determined by the form of the noun. Study the following chart.

Determining Gender with Nouns

Nouns Ending in	In Declension	Are Usually
–*a*	I	feminine
–*us*	II	masculine
—	III	masculine or feminine
–*us*	IV	masculine
–*es*	V	feminine

FYI A noun of the third declension is as likely to be masculine as feminine. Thus, the gender of each of these nouns must be learned as you go along. It will be given in the vocabulary lists.

PROCEED WITH CAUTION

 There are a few exceptions to the rules given previously. Some first declension nouns ending in *–a* are masculine, if they refer to male persons, such as *propheta* (prophet), *poeta* (poet), and *nauta* (sailor). The fourth declension noun *manus* (hand) is feminine; the fifth declension noun *dies* (day) is masculine. You will learn these exceptions as you go along.

TASK 5: WORKING WITH NOUNS AND GENDER

Guess the gender (masculine or feminine) of the following nouns.

1. *via* (road)
2. *exércitus* (IV) (army)
3. *spécies* (kind)
4. *modus* (way, mode)
5. *spes* (hope)
6. *casa* (house)
7. *fides* (faith)
8. *hortus* (garden)

NEUTER NOUNS

Many Latin nouns are neither masculine nor feminine; these are called *neuter* (neither). Neuter nouns are found in the second, third, and fourth declensions.

Neuter Nouns in the Second, Third, and Fourth Declensions

	II	III	IV
	word	*name*	*horn*
Singular	*verb-um*	*nomen*	*corn-u*
Plural	*verb-a*	*nómin-a*	*córn-ua*

 FYI All neuter nouns have a plural form ending in *–a*.

A handful of neuter nouns in the third declension are called *i-stems* because they have the plural ending, *–ia:*

- *mare* becomes *már-ia*
- *ánimal* becomes *animál-ia*

PROCEED WITH CAUTION

 The plural ending of neuter nouns (such as *sax-a*) can be confused with the singular ending of first declension nouns (such as *puell-a*). When looking up a new word, be careful to note which declension it belongs to.

TASK 6: NOUNS AND THEIR PLURALS

Give the plural of the following nouns.

1. *perículum* (danger)
2. *genu* (knee)
3. *genus* (*géner–*) (type)
4. *verbum* (word)
5. *litus* (*lítor–*) (beach)
6. *spátium* (space)
7. *saxum* (stone)
8. *opus* (*óper–*) (work)

SINGULAR AND PLURAL IN VERBS

As we have seen, nouns have singular and plural forms. Many languages also change the form of the verb to match a plural noun.

- Caesar **is** a man. The Romans **are** people.
- Caesar **speaks.** The Romans **speak.**

This phenomenon is called *agreement*. The verb changes its form to "agree" with the number of the *subject*—that is, the word or words indicating the "do-er" of the verb.

TASK 7: SUBJECT-VERB AGREEMENT

Change the verb in the first sentence so that it agrees with the subject of the second sentence.

1. Caesar **invades** Gaul once a week. The Romans ….
2. The Carthaginians **live** in Africa. Hannibal ….
3. Marc Antony **is** a heavy drinker. Roman soldiers ….

SUBJECT-VERB AGREEMENT IN LATIN

In Latin, the form of a verb is always matched to the number of its subject:

- *Caesar **appare-t:*** Caesar **appears.**
- *Romani **appare-nt:*** The Romans **appear.**

The singular ending is *–t;* the plural ending is *–nt.* The same endings are seen in the irregular Latin forms for the English *is* and *are:*

- *Caesar homo **es-t.*** Caesar **is** a man.
- *Romani hómines **su-nt.*** The Romans **are** men.

Here are a few common verbs and their plural forms:

ámbula-t (walks)	*ámbula-nt* (walk)
doce-t (teaches)	*doce-nt* (teach)
vivi-t (lives)	*vivu-nt* (live)
éveni-t (comes out)	*evéniu-nt* (come out)

Differences in the stem-vowel (as in *doc-E-t* vs. *viv-I-t*) will be explained in Hour 4.

TASK 8: WORKING WITH VERB FORMS

Choose the form of the verb that best completes the sentence, and translate.

1. *Dómini vivit/vivunt.*
2. *Féminae docet/docent.*
3. *Verba évenit/evéniunt.*
4. *Puella ámbulat/ámbulant.*

NOUN-ADJECTIVE AGREEMENT

Before we look at complete sentences, one further thing must be learned. In many languages, adjectives must resemble the nouns they describe by having the same markers for *number* and *gender*. If you know a little Spanish, you have already encountered variations such as these:

- *El hombre está **loco:*** The man is crazy.
- *La mujer está **loca:*** The woman is crazy.
- *Los hombres están **locos:*** The men are crazy.

In Latin, adjectives have variable endings, depending on the number and gender of the noun they are paired with.

- *Vir insan-**us** est:* The man is crazy.
- *Fémina insan-**a** est:* The woman is crazy.
- *Viri insan-**i** sunt:* The men are crazy.

These endings are "borrowed" from nouns in the first two declensions. Look at this chart for the adjective *bonus* (good).

The Adjective *Bonus*

	Masculine	Feminine	Neuter
Singular	bon-us	bon-a	bon-um
Plural	bon-i	bon-ae	bon-a

To match the English adjective *good* with a singular masculine noun such as *dóminus* (master), use the form *bonus;* to match it with a feminine noun such as *casa* (house), switch to *bona.* A neuter noun such as *verbum* (word) pairs with *bonum.* For a plural noun such as *casae,* you must choose the form in the feminine, plural column: *bonae.*

Other common adjectives of this type are: *magnus* (big) and *novus* (new). You have already seen the adjectives *latinus* and *romanus.*

JUST A MINUTE

In this hour, adjectives are used in two ways. They may be used as the *complement* of a sentence (as in *Puella est **bona**,* "The girl is **good**"), or simply as attributes of a noun (as in *puella **bona**,* "a good girl"). When an adjective is used attributively, it usually (but not always) comes after the noun.

Nouns and their adjectives will sometimes have identical endings, but not always. Notice the following pairs:

- *puer bonus:* a good boy
- *homo bonus:* a good man
- *dies bonus:* a good day

All three nouns are masculine and singular; thus, they all are paired with the form *bonus.*

TASK 9: NOUN-ADJECTIVE AGREEMENT I

In the following pairings, make the form of the adjective agree with the noun.

1. the Latin language: *lingua* (*Latinus*)
2. many masters: *dómini* (*multus*)
3. Latin words: *verba* (*Latinus*)
4. a good thing: *res* (*bonus*)
5. new chariots: *currus* (*novus*)
6. a Roman woman: *múlier* (*Romanus*)
7. Latin poets: *poetae* (masculine) (*Latinus*)
8. good girls: *puellae* (*bonus*)
9. other things: *res* (*alius*)

LINKING SENTENCES

In this hour, we have seen a number of linking sentences. Here are some examples:

- *Caesar est homo:* Caesar is a man.
- *Caesar est Romanus:* Caesar is Roman.
- *Itali sunt vetustíssimi:* The Italians are very ancient.

These sentences consist of three elements: a subject, a verb (usually a form of "to be" or a similar verb), and a third element, which is called a *complement*. The complement may be either a noun or an adjective. If it is an adjective, it must agree in gender and number with the subject:

- *Lingua latina est **pulchra**:* The Latin language is **beautiful.**
- *Multae linguae sunt **pulchrae**:* Many languages are **beautiful.**

PROCEED WITH CAUTION

The verb *est* (in the plural, *sunt*) is often postponed to the end of the sentence. Thus: *Viri boni sunt* means "The men are good," *not* "The good men are."

SUMMARY

In this hour, you have learned some basic concepts of Latin grammar: the parts of speech, number, gender, and agreement. You have also learned how to form the plural of nouns, adjectives, and verbs, and how to make them agree in a sentence. You are now ready to do some Latin reading. Note that several new words are glossed in the section entitled "Reading Vocabulary," following the text. You do not have to memorize these words.

ESSENTIAL VOCABULARY

The following are some of the most common words in the Latin language. These should be learned by heart. Luckily, memory-work in Latin is sometimes made easier by the fact that so many English words have derived from Latin. You can use the words in the third column to help you memorize the basic meanings of some of these words.

Essential Vocabulary

Latin	Meaning	Related Word
Nouns		
dóminus	lord, master	dominate
lingua	language	linguistics
puella	girl	
res	thing	reality
Verbs		
ámbulat/ámbulant	walks/walk	ambulatory
dicit/dicunt	says/say	diction
est/sunt	is/are	
erat/erant	was/were	
Adjectives		
bonus, –a, –um	good	bon-bons
latinus, –a, –um	Latin	
multus, –a, –um	much, many	multitude
nonnullus, –a, –um	some	
romanus, –a, –um	Roman	
Adverbs		
autem	however, moreover, now	
enim	for	
nam	for	
Conjunctions		
aut	either, or	
et	and	et cetera

READING EXERCISE

Isidore was bishop of the southern Spanish city of Seville in the first part of the seventh century, A.D. The Roman empire had unravelled in western Europe, and Spain was under the control of a Germanic people known as the Visigoths. While the "Dark Ages" were not as dark as we sometimes imagine, it was important to preserve Latin as a link to the culture of ancient Rome and the early Church.

Isidore wrote a book titled *Etymológiae,* which functioned as a kind of encyclopedic dictionary of Latin terms. The ninth book is devoted to listing the major languages and peoples of the known world. (Adapted)

THE WORLD'S LANGUAGES

Erant diversae linguae post dilúvium, cum turris Babylónica erat exstructa. Nam in princípio erat una lingua, hebraea, qua patriarchae et prophetae dicebant. Inítio autem erant tot linguae, quot gentes; deinde plures gentes quam linguae, quia ex una lingua multae gentes evéniunt.

Tres sunt linguae sacrae: hebraea, graeca, et latina, quae in toto orbe máxime excellunt. In his linguis causa Dómini erat scripta super crucem eius. Unde, et quia Sanctae Scripturae obscurae sunt, hae linguae multum prosunt.

Reading Vocabulary

Babylónicus, –a, –um	Babylonian
causa	charge, accusation
crucem	cross
cum	when
deinde	then, next
dicebant	spoke
dilúvium	flood
diversus, –a, –um	different, various
Dómini	of the Lord
eius	his
evéniunt	come
ex	from
excellunt	excel, stand out

continues

Reading Vocabulary   (continued)

exstructus, –a, –um	built
gens, gent– (feminine)	race, nation, people
graecus, –a, –um	Greek
hae, his	these
hebraeus, –a, –um	Hebrew
in	in
inítio	in the beginning
linguis	languages
máxime	in particular, most of all, very much
multum	much, a lot
obscurus, –a, –um	obscure
orbe	world
patriarcha (masculine)	patriarch
plures	many, more
post	after
princípio	in the beginning
propheta (masculine)	prophet
prosunt	are useful
qua, quam	which, that
quia	because
quot ... tot ...	as many ... as ...
sacer, sacra, sacrum	sacred
sanctus, –a, –um	holy
scriptus, –a, –um	written
scriptura	writing
super	over
toto	all the ...
tres	three
turris, turr– (feminine)	tower
una	one
unde	thus, hence

Third Declension Adjectives; Substantival Adjectives; Verbs with an Implied Subject

LESSON PLAN:

In this hour you will learn about ...

- How to form adjectives that take their endings from the third declension
- How to use adjectives as nouns
- How to translate verbs with an implied subject

In the last hour, you learned that Latin depends on the endings of nouns, verbs, and adjectives to pull sentences together. You also learned that nouns and adjectives share the same endings and must be "matched" in number and case. This allows Latin to have a much more flexible word order than English.

THIRD DECLENSION ADJECTIVES

Most adjectives in Latin resemble *bonus* and take their endings from the first two declensions. A number of adjectives, however, have endings from the third declension. These adjectives have the same forms for the masculine and feminine genders. Study the following chart, which shows the adjective *omnis* (every, all).

Third Declension Adjectives

	Masculine/Feminine	Neuter
Singular	omn-*is*	omn-**e**
Plural	omn-*es*	ómn-**ia**

Remember that an adjective must agree with the noun it modifies in number and gender, even if the noun and adjective have different endings:

- *fémina **omnis*** (every woman); *féminae **omnes*** (all women)

- *verbum **omne*** (every word); *verba **ómnia*** (all words)

Other common adjectives of this type are *fortis,* (brave) *fácilis,* (easy) and *diffícilis,* (difficult).

TASK 1: NOUN AND ADJECTIVE AGREEMENT

In the following pairs, make the form of the adjective agree with the noun.

1. all languages: *linguae (omnis)*
2. all names: *nómina (omnis)*
3. easy things: *res (fácilis)*
4. a difficult language: *lingua (diffícilis)*
5. brave kings: *reges (fortis)*

RECOGNIZING ADJECTIVE TYPES

How do you know whether an adjective belongs to the *bonus* type or to the *omnis* type? Latin dictionaries usually give the singular forms of an adjective at the beginning of the entry. For example, *bonus* is entered as *bonus, –a, –um. Omnis* is listed as *omnis, –e.*

Thus, the endings *–us, –a, –um* (or more rarely, *–er, –a, –um*) indicate an adjective of the *bonus* type. The endings *–is, –e* are typical of third declension adjectives.

TASK 2: IDENTIFYING ADJECTIVE TYPES

To which type (first and second declension, like *bonus,* or third declension, like *omnis*) do the following adjectives belong?

1. *útilis, –e* (useful)
2. *térritus, –a, –um* (terrified)
3. *grácilis, –e* (elegant)
4. *honestus, –a, –um* (honorable)

TASK 3: NOUN AND ADJECTIVE AGREEMENT II

In each pair, make the adjective agree with the noun.

1. useful words: *verba (útilis, –e)*
2. an honorable name: *nomen (honestus, –a, –um)*
3. terrified kings: *reges (térritus, –a, –um)*

4. elegant women: *féminae (grácilis, –e)*

5. an honorable poet: *poeta (honestus, –a, –um)*

6. useful things: *res (útilis, –e)*

SUBSTANTIVAL ADJECTIVES

Sometimes adjectives can be used by themselves as noun substitutes. These are called *substantival* adjectives. Study the following sentences:

- *Romani invadunt:* The Romans invade.
- *Graeci resistunt:* The Greeks resist.
- *Omnes pugnant:* All (the people) fight.

In these sentences, the masculine plural form *Romani* means "Roman people." In the same way, *omnes* can mean "all the people." The neuter form refers to a class of things:

- *Ómnia sunt bona:* All things are good.

 FYI When a group consists of men and women together, *masculine* plural forms are used.

TASK 4: TRANSLATING SUBSTANTIVAL ADJECTIVES

Translate the expressions in bold into Latin.

1. The **good,** the **bad,** and the **ugly** (*bonus, malus, deformis;* use masc. plural)

2. In life there are **good** things and **bad.** (*bonus, malus*)

3. The **beautiful** and the **damned** (*formosus, damnatus;* use feminine plural)

4. **Difficult** things must be overcome. (*diffícilis*)

TRANSLATING VERBS WITHOUT A NOUN SUBJECT

We have seen that Latin did not have words for *a* and *the*. It could be terse in other ways, too—no doubt because the Romans were too busy conquering foreign tribes to do a lot of talking.

For example, the verb form *ámbulat* can appear by itself to mean "he walks," "she walks," or "it walks." The context will tell you what the implied subject is. *Ámbulant* by itself means "they walk."

TASK 5: TRANSLATING FROM CONTEXT

Translate the verb in bold on the basis of the context. Example: *Puella in lecto manet. Numquam **ámbulat:*** The girl stays in bed; **she** never walks.

1. *Rex sanus est. Bis in diem **ámbulat:*** The king is healthy. … twice a day.

2. *Romani cauti sunt; cápite erecto **ámbulant:*** The Romans are cautious; … with their heads up.

3. *Puella cauta est; cápite erecto **ámbulat:*** The girl is cautious; … with her head up.

4. *Monstrum immane bacchatur; per vias urbis **ámbulat:*** A giant monster is on the rampage; … through the streets of the city.

PROCEED WITH CAUTION

A further wrinkle is that the verb *est* by itself can mean "there is," and *sunt* can mean "there are":

- *Minister! **Est** musca in iure meo!:* Waiter! There is a fly in my soup!
- ***Sunt** nonnulli qui Latine dicant:* There are some people who speak Latin.
- *Latinae linguae quattuor **sunt:*** There are four Latin languages.

ESSENTIAL VOCABULARY

The following common words should be memorized.

Essential Vocabulary

Latin	Meaning	Related Word
Nouns		
poeta (masculine)	poet	
rex, reg– (masculine)	king	regal
verbum	word	verbal
Verbs		
docet/docent	teach	docent, doctor
vivit/vivunt	live	vivid

Latin	Meaning	Related Word
Adjectives		
álius, –a, –ud	other, else	alien
fortis, –e	brave	fortitude
omnis, –e	every/all	omniscient
Adverb		
enim	for	

RECOGNITION VOCABULARY

The following words occur in the passage that you will read shortly. Although they are less common than the words listed in the Essential Vocabulary, they can also be learned easily because of their close resemblance to English. Go through this list once or twice, and then look for these words in the reading exercise.

Recognition Vocabulary

Latin	Meaning	Related Word
ánimal, plural *–ia*	animal	
brutus, –a, –um	unspeaking	brute
communis, –e	common	community
corruptus, –a, –um	corrupt	
diffícilis, –e	difficult	
impérium	empire	imperial
mixtus, –a, –um	mixed	
primus, –a, –um	first	prime
quartus, –a, –um	fourth	quarter
quintus, –a, –um	fifth	quintuplets
secundus, –a, –um	second	
tértius, –a, –um	third	tertiary
varíetas, –tat	variety	

FYI Many English abbreviations come from Latin expressions. Here are a few of the most common: **i.e.** (*id est*), "that is"; **e.g.** (*exempli grátia*), "for the sake of an example"; **etc.** (*et cétera*), "and the rest"; and **v.** (*vide*) "see."

SUMMARY

In this hour you have learned how to form the singular and plural of third declension adjectives, and how to use adjectives as nouns. You have also learned how to translate sentences that have implied subjects. Now you are ready to continue reading about the world's major languages, as understood in the seventh century.

READING EXERCISE

In the following passage, Isidore reflects the ancient Romans' admiration of Greek as the "most elegant" of the world's languages. He also anticipates the idea, still encountered in schools today, that Latin literature went downhill after Cicero and Vergil. (Adapted)

ISIDORE OF SEVILLE ON THE WORLD'S MAJOR LANGUAGES (CONTINUED)

Graeca autem lingua clárior quam céterae est habita. Est enim sonántior quam Latina et omnes linguae. Haec lingua in quinque varietates divisa est. Prima est coene, id est, mixta sive communis, quam omnes usurpant. Secunda Áttica, vidélicet Atheniensis, qua omnes auctores graeci scribunt. Tértia Dórica, quam habent Egýptii et Syri. Quarta Iónica, et quinta Aeólica est.

Latinae autem linguae sunt quattuor: prisca, latina, romana, et mixta. Prisca est lingua, qua vetustíssimi Itali sub Iano et Saturno dicebant. Latina dicebant quando Latinus et Tusci reges erant. Romana est lingua quam Naévius, Plautus, Énnius, Vergílius poetae, et oratores Gracchus et Cícero et céteri effuderunt. Mixta lingua dicebant, postquam impérium látius promotum erat, et erat corrupta.

Omnis autem lingua, sive graeca, sive latina, sive ália, aut discíbilis est audiendo, aut quia praeceptor docet. Quamquam nemo est, cui omnes linguae notae sunt, nemo tamen tam desidiosus est, ut nésciat linguam suae gentis. Nam quid áliud est putandus, nisi detérior quam bruta animália?

Reading Vocabulary

Aeólicus, −a, −um	Aeolic (associated with certain Greek islands)
Atheniensis, −e	Athenian
Átticus, −a, −um	Attic (associated with Athens)

auctor, auctor–	author
audiendo	by hearing
céteri, –ae, –a	the rest
Cícero	Cicero, a Roman statesman
clárior	more illustrious
coene	*koine,* the Greek word for "common"
cui	to whom
desidiosus, –a, –um	lazy, useless
detérior	worse
discíbilis	learnable, able to be learned
divisus, –a, –um	divided
docet	teaches
Dóricus, –a, –um	Doric (associated with southern Greece and Southern Italy)
effuderunt	spoke
Egýptius	Egyptian
eius	his
Énnius	Ennius, a Roman poet
ex	from
excellunt	stand out, excel
exstructa	built
gens, gent–	people, country
gentis suae	of his country
Gracchus	Gracchus, a Roman statesman
Graecus, –a, –um	Greek
habebant	had
hábita	considered
hae, his	these
haec	this
Iano	Janus, a Roman god and the mythical ruler of Italy
in	in, on
inter	between
Iónicus, –a, –um	Ionic

continues

Reading Vocabulary   **(continued)**

Italus, –a, –um	Italian
Latinus	Latinus, mythical first king of the Latins
látius	more widely
linguarum	of languages
Naévius	Naevius, a Roman poet
nemo	no one
nésciat	knows
notus, –a, –um	known
obscurus, –a, –um	obscure
orator, orator– (masculine)	orator
patriarcha (masculine)	patriarch
Plautus	Plautus, writer of Roman comedies
post	after
praeceptor, –tor (masculine)	teacher
priscus, –a, –um	original
promotus, –a, –um	extended
putandus, –a, –um	to be considered
nisi	unless, except
qua, quae, quam	which, that
quam	than
quamquam	although
quando	when
quattuor	four
quia	because, since
quid	what
quinque	five
sacer, –ra, –rum	sacred
sanctus, –a, –um	holy
Saturno	Saturn, a god and mythical ruler of Italy
scribunt	write
sive ... sive	whether ... or
sonántior	more sonorous, better-sounding
sub	under
super	over

suus, –a, –um	one's own
Syrus	Syrian
tam	so
tamen	nevertheless
Tuscus	Etruscan
unus, –a, –um	one
usurpant	use
ut	as, that
Vergílius	Vergil, a Roman poet
vetustíssimus, –a, –um	very old, oldest
vidélicet	that is

Quiz

From the list of words given below, complete the sentences and translate.

corrupta, corruptus, docet, docent, est, erat, multae, multi, omnis, omnes, sunt

1. *Latina "mixta" est ().*
2. *Ex una lingua () gentes evéniunt.*
3. *Tres () linguae sacrae: Latina, Graeca, Hebraea.*
4. *Graeca est sonántior quam Latina et () linguae.*
5. *() lingua discíbilis est audiendo, aut quia praeceptor docet.*
6. *Nemo (), cui omnes linguae notae sunt.*

HOUR 3

The Nominative and Accusative Cases; Prepositions with the Accusative; the Infinitive Mood; Negation

So far, you have learned how to translate linking sentences and how to distinguish singular from plural. Now you are ready to work with other sentence types.

INTRODUCTORY READING

Let's begin this time with a look at a medieval account of the adventures of Alexander the Great in India. Alexander is the narrator. (The text has been adapted.)

ALEXANDER VS. THE MAN-EATING HIPPOPOTAMI

Tunc ego mitto in flúvium ducentos mílites Macédones, lévia arma habentes. Súbito novus terror apparet. De profunda aqua véniunt hippopótami, fortiores quam sunt elephanti. Hippopótami dicti sunt, quia médii sunt hómines, médii caballi. Dum nos clamamus, hippopótami devorare incípiunt illos viros, qui in flúvium missi sunt.

Translation:

Then I send into the river two hundred Macedonian soldiers, having light arms. Suddenly a new terror appears. From the deep water come hippopotami, stronger than elephants (are). They are called hippopotami because they are half men, half horses. While we shout, the hippopotami begin to devour those men who were sent into the river.

CHAPTER SUMMARY

LESSON PLAN:

In this hour you will learn about …

- A few more important terms, such as case and mood
- Using the nominative and accusative cases to form transitive sentences
- Using the accusative case in prepositional phrases
- Making negative statements

In this passage, we see sentences that have both a subject (the "doer" of an action) and an object (the "doee," or the person or thing that the action is done to):

- *Hippopótami* *dévorant* *illos viros:* The hippos devour those men.

Here, the *hippopotami*, as the "devour-ers," are the subject; the men, as "devourees," are the object.

Sentences of this sort are called *transitive* because the action "passes" (Latin *transit*) from one noun to another. To form these sentences, however, we must deal with another distinction in Latin grammar called *case.*

NOMINATIVE AND ACCUSATIVE CASES

Latin nouns change their form to indicate whether they function as the subject or the object of a transitive sentence. In the language of Roman grammarians, they "fall" (Latin *cadunt*) into these forms, which are called cases (*casus*).

The case of the subject (and, in linking sentences, of the complement) is called the *nominative* or "naming" case (Latin *casus nominativus*):

- *Romani* *véniunt:* The Romans arrive.
- *Illi viri sunt* *Romani:* Those men are Romans.

The case of the object is called the *accusative* or "attacking" case (*casus accusativus*):

- *Hippopótami* *Romanos* *dévorant:* The hippopotami devour the Romans.

Note that the form *Romani* changes to *Romanos* as we switch from the nominative to the accusative case.

TASK 1: NOMINATIVE OR ACCUSATIVE

Indicate whether the word in bold would be in the nominative or the accusative case in Latin.

Next, a **beast** of amazing size attacked the **Macedonians.** The **Indians** call the beast a "toothy tyrant" (*odontotyrannus*). It is a large **animal** and has three **horns.** After it drank some **water,** it charged the soldiers. But **Alexander** ran back and forth, comforting his **men.**

FORMS OF THE ACCUSATIVE CASE: MASCULINE AND FEMININE NOUNS

Nouns in the accusative case have distinctive forms in both the singular and the plural. You can compare them to the nominative case forms, which you have already learned, in the following chart:

Forms of the Accusative Case

	I	*II*	*III*
	girl	*master*	*king*
Singular			
Nominative	*puell-a*	*dómin-us*	*rex*
Accusative	*puell-am*	*dómin-um*	*reg-em*
Plural			
Nominative	*puell-ae*	*dómin-i*	*reg-es*
Accusative	*puell-as*	*dómin-os*	*reg-es*

	IV	*V*
	chariot	*thing*
Singular		
Nominative	*curr-us*	*r-es*
Accusative	*curr-um*	*r-em*
Plural		
Nominative	*curr-us*	*r-es*
Accusative	*curr-us*	*r-es*

PROCEED WITH CAUTION

In the third, fourth, and fifth declensions, plural nouns have the same form in both the nominative and accusative cases. Thus, you will sometimes have to guess which case fits the context. Consider, for example, this sentence:

- *Reges currus habent:* The **kings** have **chariots**.

Here, *reges* and *currus* could be either nominative or accusative forms. Common sense tells you, however, that the kings own the chariots.

TASK 2: CONVERSION OF NOMINATIVE TO ACCUSATIVE

Convert the following nouns from the nominative case to the accusative.

1. *regina*
2. *dómini*
3. *pater (patr–)*
4. *manus* (singular)
5. *dies* (singular)
6. *spes* (plural)
7. *linguae*
8. *miles (mílit–)*

TASK 3: NOUN FORMS

Give the form of the noun in parentheses that best fits the sentence.

1. *Mílites (hippopótamus) timent:* The soldiers fear the hippos.
2. *Hippopótami (miles, mílit–) dévorant:* The hippos eat the soldiers.
3. *Poeta (puella) laudat:* The poet praises the girl.
4. *Rex (res) bene éxplicat:* The king explains the matter well.
5. *Mílites (manus) tollunt et clamant:* The soldiers raise their hands and shout.

ACCUSATIVE CASE: NEUTER NOUNS

As we saw in the last lesson, some nouns in the second, third, and fourth declensions are neither masculine nor feminine: They are *neuter*. A peculiar feature of all neuter nouns is that they have the same form in the nominative and accusative cases.

Neuter Nouns

	II	III	III (i-stem)	IV
	word	name	sea	horn
Singular				
Nominative	*verb-um*	*nomen*	*mare*	*corn-u*
Accusative	*verb-um*	*nomen*	*mare*	*corn-u*

	II	III	III (i-stem)	IV
	word	*name*	*sea*	*horn*
Plural				
Nominative	*verb-a*	*nómin-a*	*már-ia*	*córn-ua*
Accusative	*verb-a*	*nómin-a*	*már-ia*	*córn-ua*

Here again, you may have to use common sense to figure out whether a form such as *verba* is the subject or the object of the sentence:

- ***Verba** numquam mihi nocebunt:* Words will never hurt me.
- ***Verba** terrífica audiunt:* They hear terrifying words.

ADJECTIVES IN THE ACCUSATIVE CASE

We saw in the last chapter that adjectives must agree with the nouns or pronouns they describe in gender and number:

- ***Omnis** lingua est **pulchra** eis, qui eam norunt:* Every language is beautiful to those, who know it.
- ***Omnes** linguae sunt **pulchrae:*** All languages are beautiful.

The rule of agreement also applies to case. For example, an adjective that modifies a noun in the accusative case must also have an accusative form:

- *Hippopótami **Macédones térritos** devorant:* The hippos devour the terrified Macedonians.

Here the adjective *térritus, –a, –um* (terrified) takes the form *térritos* to agree with *Macédones,* in the accusative case, plural.

Luckily, the accusative endings for adjectives are borrowed from the noun endings you have just learned. Remember that there are two kinds of adjectives in Latin. One type has endings taken from the first and second declensions, as follows.

First and Second Declension Adjectives

	Masculine	Feminine	Neuter
Singular			
Nominative	*magn-us*	*magn-a*	*magn-um*
Accusative	*magn-um*	*magn-am*	*magn-um*

continues

First and Second Declension Adjectives   (continued)

	Masculine	Feminine	Neuter
Plural			
Nominative	*magn-i*	*magn-ae*	*magn-a*
Accusative	*magn-os*	*magn-as*	*magn-a*

The other type of adjective has endings similar to those of third declension nouns.

Third Declension Adjectives

	Masculine/Feminine	Neuter
Singular		
Nominative	*omn-is*	*omn-e*
Accusative	*omn-em*	*omn-e*
Plural		
Nominative	*omn-es*	*ómn-ia*
Accusative	*omn-es*	*ómn-ia*

 FYI Like neuter nouns, neuter adjectives have the same form in the nominative and accusative cases.

TASK 4: NOUN-ADJECTIVE PAIRS

Complete the following noun-adjective pairs. Remember that the adjective must agree with the noun in gender, number, and case.

1. *féminas (fortis)*
2. *rex (magnus)*
3. *rem (omnis)*
4. *cornu (magnus)*
5. *spes (bonus)*
6. *dómini (fortis)*
7. *linguam (fácilis)*
8. *mílites (bonus)*
9. *nómina (magnus)*

The Accusative Case After Prepositions

As we saw in Hour 1, a preposition is a little word that indicates some relationship to a noun or pronoun:

- *Macédones festinant **in** flúvium:* The Macedonians hasten into the river.

In this example, the preposition *in* combines with the noun *flúvium* to form a prepositional phrase ("into the river"). *Flúvium* is called the *object* of the preposition. Here are some other examples of prepositional phrases:

- ***Ad** flúvium currunt:* They run **to** the river.
- ***Trans** flúvium natant:* They swim **across** the river.

Notice that in all these examples, the accusative case of the noun *flúvius* is used. Several prepositions require an accusative object. Here is a partial list:

- *ad* (to, at)
- *in* (into)
- *per* (through)
- *trans* (across)
- *circum* (around)
- *propter* (because of)

 FYI In Latin, prepositional phrases often come before the verb: *Mílites **in flúvium** festinant:* The soldiers hurry into the river.

Task 5: Working with Prepositions

Complete the following sentences, and translate.

1. *Macédones trans (fluvius) natant:* The Macedonians swim ... river.
2. *Rex circum (urbs, urb–) ámbulat:* The king walks ... city.
3. *Mílites propter (terror, terror–) clamant:* The soldiers shout ... fear.
4. *Aves ad (terra) cadunt:* The birds fall ... earth.
5. *Puella in (casa) currit:* The girl runs ... house.
6. *Pulla trans (via) ambulat:* The chicken walks ... road.

THE INFINITIVE MOOD

In the introductory reading, we saw this sentence:

- *Dum nos plangimus, hippopótami* **devorare** *incípiunt illos viros:* While we shout, the hippos begin **to devour** those men.

The form *devorare* (to devour) is called *infinitive* (Latin *infinitivus*) because it does not have a "limiting" subject of its own. It is used instead to complete the idea started by the verb *incípiunt* (they begin) Here are some other examples:

- *Ille homo non potest* **natare:** That man is not able to swim.
- *Alexander iubet eos per flúvium* **natare:** Alexander orders them to swim through the river.

The term *infinitive,* by the way, comes under the category of *mood.* This term has nothing to do with emotional states; it comes from the Latin word *modus,* referring to a "mode" or "way" of looking at a verb. Other verbs we have seen, such as *habet* and *est,* are in the indicative mood (*modus indicativus*) because they "indicate" a specific action or state.

The regular infinitive ending is *–re.* Here are some other infinitive forms:

- *habe-re* (to have)
- *clama-re* (to shout)
- *ambula-re* (to walk)
- *díce-re* (to say)
- *doce-re* (to teach)
- *víve-re* (to live)

A few verbs in Latin have unusual infinitive forms. Two of the most common are these:

- *esse* (to be; compare English "essence")
- *posse* (to be able; compare English "posse")

TASK 6: WORKING WITH INFINITIVES

Complete the translation of the following sentences.

1. *Miles* **dícere** *non potest:* The soldier is not able ….
2. *Hippopótami* **clamare** *incípiunt:* The hippos begin ….
3. *Rex iubet hómines* **ambulare:** The king orders the people ….

4. *Alexander non vult **esse** fortis:* Alexander is not willing ... brave.

5. *Velit **posse docere** Latinam:* He would like ... Latin.

NEGATION

Forming negative sentences in Latin is very simple. All you have to do is put the adverb *non* before the verb:

- *Hippopótami natare possunt:* The hippos are able to swim.

- *Macédones natare **non** possunt:* The Macedonians are not able to swim.

 English negative sentences often require "helping" verbs, such as *do* and *does*. These are not necessary in Latin:

- *Hippopótami hómines **non** dévorant:* Hippos do not eat human beings.

TASK 7: NEGATION

Negate the following sentences, and retranslate.

1. *Alexander hippopótamos timet:* Alexander fears the hippos.

2. *Hómines hippopótamos comedunt:* People eat hippos.

3. *Mílites ignes accendunt:* The soldiers light fires.

4. *Álexander mílites confortat:* Alexander comforts the soldiers.

ESSENTIAL VOCABULARY

The following common words should be memorized.

Essential Vocabulary

Latin	Meaning	Related Word
Nouns		
ánimus	mind	animate
corpus, –or (neuter)	body	corporate
exércitus (IV)	army	
flúvius	river	
homo, hómin–	(common) man, person	hominid
dies (masculine)	day	diurnal
lux, luc– (feminine)	light	lucid
miles, mílit– (masculine)	soldier	military

continues

Essential Vocabulary   (continued)

Latin	Meaning	Related Word
Nouns		
servus	slave	servile
terra	earth	terrestrial
Verbs		
facit/fáciunt, facere	do	fact
habet/habent, habere	have	
incipit/–iunt, incípere	begin	inception
iubet/iubent, iubere	order	
potest/possunt, posse	be able	possible
venit/véniunt, venire	come	intervene
Adjectives		
magnus, –a, –um	big	magnate
tantus, –a, –um	so great	
totus, –a, –um	the whole	total
unus, –a, –um	one	unity
Adverb		
deinde	then	
Prepositions		
ad	to, at	
circa, circum	around	circumference
contra	against	
in	into, in	
per	through	
post	after	P.M. (*post meridiem*) means "after noon"
propter	because of	
Conjunctions		
ac	and	
sed	but	
cum	when	
–que	and	

FYI *Homo* has "common" gender because it can refer to either a masculine or a feminine human being. When no particular gender is intended, the masculine is used.

RECOGNITION VOCABULARY

Again, these are some less-common words that you can pick up without much effort because they resemble English words. Read through this list two or three times, and look for these words in the reading.

Recognition Vocabulary

Latin	Meaning	Related Word
arma	arm (weapon)	
color, color– (masculine)	color	
confortare	strengthen	comfort
dens, dent– (masculine)	tooth	dental
erectus, –a, –um	erect	
facies	face	facial
humanus, –a, –um	human	
hora	hour	
luna	moon	lunar
mortalis, –e	mortal	
mórtuus, –a, –um	dead	mortuary
pes, ped– (masculine)	foot	pedestrian
scórpio, –ion (masculine)	scorpion	
serpens, –nt (common)	snake	
spatiosus, –a, –um	spacious	
simíliter	similarly, like	
victória	victory	
vultur, vúltur (masculine)	vulture	

JUST A MINUTE

You now have seen three ways of saying "and": *et, ac,* and *–que.* The last word is not really a word at all, but a suffix (technically called an *enclitic*). It attaches itself to the last element in a pair or series, as in *Latina Graeca-que,* "Latin and Greek."

SUMMARY

In this hour, you have learned how to form transitive sentences and preposi-tional phrases with the help of the accusative, and how to use the infinitive mood. You are now ready to tackle another reading passage, adapted from a medieval historical romance.

READING EXERCISE

For the Romans and their medieval successors, Alexander the Great was the conqueror *par excellence.* His expedition (in the 320s B.C.) to the heart of the Persian empire and beyond remained unequalled in boldness. Small wonder, then, that his adventures became the stuff of legend, not to say fantasy. The most spectacular events were associated with his excursion into India. The following is adapted from a fourteenth-century account, entitled *Historia de proeliis Alexandri.*

ALEXANDER THE GREAT IN INDIA

Girantes flúvium, circa horam undécimam véniunt ad stagnum mellífluum ac dulce, et castra ponunt. Deinde Alexander iubet mílites incídere silvam quae est circum stagnum. Et est spatiosus stagnus ad unum miliárium. Tunc Alexander iubet eos accéndere focos plúrimos. Cumque luna lucere íncipit, súbito véniunt scorpiones ad bibendum ad ipsum stagnum. Deinde incípiunt venire serpentes et dracones magni et diversicolores, et tota terra résonat propter síbilos eorum. Ipsi namque dracones habent cristas et péctora erecta, ora aperta; flatus eorum est mortalis, et per oculos scintillat venenum. Videntes eos, mílites pertérriti exístimant quod omnes sunt morituri. Tunc Alexander íncipit confortare eos, dicens, "O commili-tiones fortíssimi, non turbetur ánimus vester, sed sicut me videtis fácere, ita fácite." Et haec dicens statim apprehendit venábulum et scutum et íncipit pugnare contra dracones et serpentes qui super illos véniunt. Videntes autem hoc, mílites confortati sunt valde, et apprehendentes armas incípiunt et illi simíliter pugnare contra eos. Álios occidunt ad armas, álios vero ad ignem; et péreunt viginti mílites propter dracones, et triginta servi. Plúrimas angústias perfert Alexander et omnis exércitus, statim que iubet mílites accéndere focos plúrimos extra ipsum exércitum.

Deinde éxeunt ex arundineto mures maiores sicut vulpes et cómedunt córpora mórtua. Volant et ibi vespertiliones maiores sicut columbae, habentes dentes ut dentes humanos, feriuntque in fácies eorum et plagant eos: ad álios tollunt nares, et ad álios aures. Ut lux appropinquat, véniunt aves magnae ut vúltures; colorem habent rubicundum, pedes et rostra habent nigros; et non nocent eos, sed implent totam ripam et incípiunt exinde tráhere pisces et anguillas et cómedunt eos.

Deinde dimittunt loca periculosa et véniunt in loca Bactriana, quae habent aurum et álias divítias, et benigne recípiunt eum hómines ibi, et stant dies viginti. Et invéniunt ibi gentes quae nominatae sunt Seres. Suntque ibi árbores quae mittunt fólia velut lana, quae ispa gens cólligit et vestimenta exinde facit. Mílites enim incípiunt habere fortem ánimum propter victórias et próspera quae habent post tanta adversa. (376)

Reading Vocabulary

accéndere	to light
adversa	misfortunes
anguilla	eel
angústia	difficulty
apertus, –a, –um	open
apprehendentes	seizing
apprehendit	seizes
appropinquat	approaches
arbor, abor– (feminine)	tree
arundinetum	thicket of reeds
auris, aur– (feminine)	ear
aurum	gold
avis, av– (feminine)	bird
Bactrianus, –a, –um	Bactrian
benigne	benignly
bibendum	to drink
castra (neuter, plural)	camp

continues

Reading Vocabulary   (continued)

cólligit	collects
columba	dove
comedunt	eat
commilitiones	fellow soldiers
confortatus, –a, –um	comforted
crista	crest
dicens	saying
dimittunt	dismiss; leave
diversícolor (adjective)	variously colored
divítiae	riches
draco, dracon– (masculine)	dragon
dulcis, –e	sweet
eorum	their
eos	them
eum	him, it
ex	from
éxeunt	go out
exinde	from there, thereupon, from then
exístimant	think
extra	beyond
fácere	to do
fácite	Do! (command)
fériunt	strike
flatus	breath
focus	fire, campfire
fólium	leaf
fortíssimus, –a, –um	very brave
gens, gent–	tribe, people
girantes	circling
habentes	having
haec, hoc	this
ibi	there
ignis, ign– (masculine)	fire

illi, illos	they, them; those
implent	fill
incidere	to cut down
invéniunt,	find
ipse, –a, –um, –i	the same, he, she, it, they
ita	so
iubet	orders
lana	wool
loca (neuter, plural)	lands, territory
lucere	to shine
maior, maior–	bigger
me	me
mellífluus, –a, –um	sweet, like honey
miliárium	mile
mittunt	drop, send
moriturus, –a, –um	about to die
mus, mur– (common)	mouse, rat
namque	for
naris, nar– (feminine)	nostril
niger, –ra, –rum	black
nocent	harm
nominatus, –a, –um	called, named
O	O!
occidunt	kill
óculus	eye
os, or– (neuter)	mouth
pectus, pector– (neuter)	breast
perferre	to endure
periculosus, –a, –um	dangerous
perit, péreunt	perish
pertérritus, –a, –um	terrified
piscis, pisc– (masculine)	fish

continues

Reading Vocabulary   (continued)

plagant	hit
plúrimi, –ae, –a	many
ponunt	put, pitch
praécipit	commands
próspera	prosperous circumstances
pugnare	to fight
qui, quae, quod	which
recípiunt	receive
resonat	resounds
ripa	bank
rostrum	beak
rubicundus, –a, –um	red
scintillat	shines
scutum	shield
Seres (plural)	Chinese
síbilus	hissing
sicut	just as
silva	forest, wood
stagnum	lake, pool
stant	stand
statim	immediately
súbito	suddenly
super	above, over
tollunt	rip off
tráhere	to drag
triginta	thirty
tunc	then
turbetur	let … be troubled
undécimus, –a, –um	eleventh
ut	like, as
valde	very
velut	just like
venábulum	spear
venenum	venom
vero	but

vespertilio, –on– (masculine)	bat
vester, –ra, –rum	your
vestimentum	vestment
videntes	seeing
videtis	you see
viginti	twenty
volat, volant	fly
vulpes, vulp– (feminine)	wolf

QUIZ

A

In the following table, each noun is paired with an adjective that agrees with it. Complete the table by filling in the blanks.

	brave girl	good king	great name
Singular			
Nominative	_____ *fortis*	*rex* _____	*nomen magnum*
Accusative	*puellam* _____	_____ *bonum*	_____ _____
Plural			
Nominative	*puellae fortes*	_____ *boni*	_____
Accusative	_____ *fortes*	*reges* _____	*nómina magna*

B

Choose the form that best completes the sentence, and translate.

1. *Alexander iubet (miles/mílites) incídere silvam.*
2. *Stagnus est (spatiosus/spatiosum) ad unum miliárium.*
3. *Tota terra resonat propter (síbili/síbilos) eorum.*
4. *Mílites pertérriti exístimant quod (ómnes/ómnia) sunt morituri.*
5. *Tunc Alexander íncipit (confortare/confortat) eos.*
6. *Et statim apprehendit scutum et (incípiunt/íncipit) pugnare contra dracones.*

QUIZ

7. *Ut lux appropinquat, véniunt aves (magna/magnae) ut vúltures.*

8. *Deinde invéniunt (gentem/gentes) quae nominatae sunt Seres.*

9. *(Est/sunt) ibi árbores quae mittunt ipsa fólia velut lana.*

10. *Mílites (habent/habere) fortem ánimum propter victórias.*

HOUR 4

Conjugation of Verbs; the Imperative Mood; Duration of Time

CHAPTER SUMMARY

LESSON PLAN:
In this hour you will learn about ...

- How to conjugate verbs fully in the present tense
- How to issue commands
- How to express duration of time

So far, you have learned how to form linking and transitive sentences in which the subject is a noun or third person pronoun (*he, she,* or *they*).

INTRODUCTORY READING

To get ready, have a look at this tale, which is adapted from a medieval collection entitled *The Deeds of the Romans:*

ADVICE FROM A TALKING NIGHTINGALE

*Tria mandata **hábeo,** et, si diligéntius ea **observas,** magnam inde utilitatem obtinere potes. **Audi** me! Noli rem, quam apprehéndere non potes, apprehéndere temptare! Ob rem perditam et irrecupíbilem **noli dolere!** Verbum incredíbile noli credere! Haec tria custodi, et bene tibi est.*

Translation:

I have three rules, and, if **you follow** them carefully, you can gain a great advantage. **Hear** me! Don't try to seize a thing that you cannot seize! **Don't sorrow** over something lost and irrecoverable! Don't believe an impossible word! Keep these three things, and it is well for you.

Apart from the useful advice it contains, the passage shows you some new Latin forms. For example, you now know how to say "I have" (*hábeo*), as opposed to "he has" (*habet*), and "you keep" (*conservas*), as opposed to "he keeps" (*conservat*). It also contains commands, such as "Listen!" (*audi*) and "Don't sorrow!" (*noli dolere*).

CONJUGATION OF VERBS

We have already seen that verbs change their endings to indicate whether the subject is singular or plural.

- *Caesar ámbula-t:* Caesar walks.
- *Romani ámbula-nt:* The Romans walk.

Other endings can be used to show that the subject has some role in the conversation, such as the "I" of the speaker or the "you" of the addressee. Here we are working with a distinction called person. Verbs belong to one of three persons, as follows:

- The **first** person includes the speaker (I, we).
- The **second** person includes the addressee (you).
- The **third** person refers to someone else (he, she, it, they, Caesar, the Romans).

The categories of person and number can be combined to create a conjugation table, which gives an overview of verb forms.

Conjugation Table

	Singular	*Plural*
First person	**I** walk	**we** walk
Second person	**you** walk	**you** walk
Third person	**he** walks	**they** walk

JUST A MINUTE

Note that standard English no longer distinguishes between singular and plural in the second person; both are indicated by "you." In Elizabethan English, however, it was easier to tell them apart:

- Singular: thou walkest
- Plural: ye walk

American colloquial and regional speech also retains special forms for the second person plural pronoun: "y'all," "youse," "yins," "you guys." You may find it helpful to borrow one of these nonstandard forms when translating Latin.

TASK 1: IDENTIFYING PERSON AND NUMBER

Identify the following English verb forms for person and number. (For example, "I walk" is first person singular.)

1. they walk
2. y'all walk
3. we walk
4. I walk
5. she walks
6. you walk (thou walkest)

CONJUGATING LATIN VERBS

In English, we rely mainly on pronouns to identify the first and second persons. In other words, the form "walk" alone would not be sufficient to indicate the subject; we must add "I" or "you" to be clear. In Latin, however, the ending on the verb is usually enough to tell you the person and the number of a verb.

Indicating Person and Number

Singular	Plural
ámbul-o (I walk)	*ambula-**mus*** (we walk)
ámbula-s (you walk)	*ambula-**tis*** (y'all walk)
ámbula-t (he walks)	*ámbula-**nt*** (they walk)

In other words, if you want to say "I walk" in Latin, all you need is the one word, *ámbulo.*

TASK 2: CONJUGATING IN LATIN I

How would you say the following in Latin?

1. they walk
2. y'all walk
3. we walk
4. I walk
5. she walks
6. you (singular) walk

PROCEED WITH CAUTION

Remember that a form such as *ámbulat* can mean "he/she/it walks," or simply "walks," if it agrees with some noun in the sentence:

- *In casam ámbulat:* He walks into the house.
- *Caesar ámbulat:* Caesar walks.

TASK 3: TRANSLATING VERB FORMS I

Translate the following forms of the verbs *rogo, rogare* (ask) and *ausculto, auscultare* (listen):

1. *rogant*
2. *auscultat*
3. *rogamus*
4. *auscultant*
5. *rogas*
6. *ausculto*
7. *rogatis*
8. *auscultatis*

THE FOUR LATIN CONJUGATIONS

We have seen that Latin nouns are grouped into families called declensions and that the grouping is based on the stem vowel of the noun (the vowel that usually figures in the ending).

A similar grouping was devised for Latin verbs. These verb families are called *conjugations* (from the Latin *coniugátio*). There are four conjugations. They are distinguished by the vowel that occurs before the infinitive ending.

Conjugations

I	II	III	IV
to walk	to teach	to send	to hear
ambula-re	*doce-re*	*mítte-re*	*audi-re*

Thus, all verbs that have an infinitive ending in *–are* belong to the first conjugation; infinitives in *–ire* belong to the fourth conjugation.

FYI The second and third conjugations both have an *e* in the stem, but there is an audible difference. The *e* of *doce-re* takes the stress; the *e* in *mítte-re* does not. An unstressed *–ere* always signals a third conjugation verb.

TASK 4: IDENTIFYING CONJUGATIONS

To which conjugation (I, II, III, or IV) do the following verbs belong?

1. *iubere*
2. *cantare*
3. *scríbere*
4. *custodire*
5. *interfícere*
6. *salire*
7. *monere*

PERSONAL ENDINGS IN THE FOUR CONJUGATIONS

Once you know the conjugation to which a verb belongs, you can predict all its forms in the present tense (that is, if the action takes place at the present time). Here are conjugation tables for the four verbs given previously.

I	II	III	IV
walk	teach	send	hear
Singular			
ámbul-o	*dóce-o*	*mitt-o*	*aúdi-o*
ámbula-s	*doce-s*	*mitti-s*	*audi-s*
ámbula-t	*doce-t*	*mitti-t*	*audi-t*
Plural			
ambula-mus	*doce-mus*	*mítti-mus*	*audi-mus*
ambula-tis	*doce-tis*	*mítti-tis*	*audi-tis*
ámbula-nt	*doce-nt*	*mittu-nt*	*aúdiu-nt*

Other verbs in the same conjugation are similarly formed.

I	II	III	IV
love	order	lead	come
Singular			
am-o	*iúbe-o*	*duc-o*	*véni-o*
ama-s	*iube-s*	*duci-s*	*veni-s*
ama-t	*iube-t*	*duci-t*	*veni-t*

TASK 5: CONJUGATION

Form complete conjugation tables for the following verbs.

I	II	III	IV
ask	warn	say	find
Singular			
rog-o	*móne-o*	*dic-o*	*invéni-o*

TIME SAVER

Be sure to commit to memory the following personal endings: *–o, –s, –t, –mus, –tis, –nt.*

TASK 6: CONJUGATING IN LATIN II

Using the verbs in the previous drill, how would you say the following?

1. we ask
2. they ask
3. he warns
4. I warn
5. they say
6. y'all say
7. you find
8. she finds

Task 7: Translating Verb Forms II

Translate the following forms.

1. *rogat*
2. *rogo*
3. *rogamus*
4. *monemus*
5. *monent*
6. *monet*
7. *dicis*
8. *dicit*
9. *dicunt*
10. *invéniunt*
11. *invenitis*
12. *ínvenis*

Third Conjugation –io Verbs

A number of verbs in the third conjugation acquired a barely audible *y* sound between the stem and the endings, a process known as *palatalization*. When this sound was clearly audible, the Romans wrote it as an *i*. This produced the following variations in the usual conjugation table.

III	III –io
send	do
Singular	
mitt-o	*fáci-o*
mitti-s	*faci-s*
mitti-t	*faci-t*
Plural	
mítti-mus	*fáci-mus*
mítti-tis	*fáci-tis*
mittu-nt	*fáci-unt*

These are called *–io* verbs because of the ending in the first person singular.

TASK 8: CONJUGATING *–IO* VERBS

Fully conjugate the following *–io* verbs:

- *cápio:* catch
- *interfício:* kill

DICTIONARY FORM OF VERBS

When you learn a new verb or look it up in the dictionary, you will find it listed under the first person singular form (*amo:* I love) and the infinitive form (*amare:* to love). The latter will tell you the conjugation to which a verb belongs. The first person singular form helps you to distinguish *–io* verbs from regular verbs in the third conjugation. It also helps you to distinguish second conjugation verbs (*–eo*) from third conjugation verbs (*–o*) at a glance.

Here are the dictionary entries for verbs you have already encountered.

ámbulo, ambulare	walk
dico, dícere	say
dóceo, docere	teach
fácio, fácere	do, make
incípio, incípere	begin
invénio, invenire	find
vénio, venire	come
vivo, vívere	live

TASK 9: IDENTIFYING CONJUGATIONS

To which conjugation do each of the preceding verbs belong? (In the case of third conjugation verbs, point out those of the *–io* type.)

THE IMPERATIVE MOOD

In the last chapter, we encountered the idea of mood (*modus*), referring to particular ways of presenting the verb:

- *ámbulat* is in the *indicative* mood because it refers to a fact or event: "he walks"

- *ambulare* is in the *infinitive* mood because it refers to an action in the abstract: "to walk"

In this chapter's readings, we encounter a third way of presenting the verb: as a command. This is called the *imperative* or "commanding" mood (*modus imperativus*).

- ***Ausculta,** fili!:* **Listen,** son!
- ***Noli** transilire!:* **Don't** jump!

TASK 10: IDENTIFYING THE MOOD

In the following story, what is the mood of the verbs in bold type?

Once there was a tyrant, who tried to **deprive** all his noble subjects of their inheritances. These in turn **went** to Constantine, king of Britain, and were honorably received by him. They urged him to **raise** an army against the tyrant, saying, "Why do you delay, Constantine? **Help** us! For you **belong** to our generation!" Moved by this appeal, Constantine raised an army and drove out the tyrant.

JUST A MINUTE

Standard English no longer distinguishes between commands given to one person (singular) and commands given to more than one person (plural). This distinction is observed, however, in some regional expressions:

- **Come** back now, hear? (singular)
- **Y'all come** back now, hear? (plural)

THE IMPERATIVE MOOD IN LATIN

In Latin, the imperative mood is clearly marked by special endings in each of the four conjugations:

I	II	III	III –io	IV
walk	teach	send	catch	hear
Singular				
ámbula	*doce*	*mitte*	*cape*	*audi*
Plural				
ambula-te	*doce-te*	*mítti-te*	*cápi-te*	*audi-te*

Notice that Latin has a special form for the plural imperative:

- *Ámbula:* Walk!
- *Ambulate:* Y'all walk!

 The imperative singular is usually just the stem; that is, the infinitive minus the *–re* ending. The plural is formed by adding *–te*.

TASK 11: IMPERATIVE FORMS

Give the imperative forms (singular and plural) of the following verbs.

1. *rogo, rogare*
2. *incípio, incípere*
3. *móneo, monere*
4. *invénio, invenire*
5. *vivo, vívere*

 A few verbs in the third conjugation have a shortened imperative singular, which drops the final *–e: Fac!* (Do!); *Dic!* (Say!); *Duc!* (Lead!).

TASK 12: TRANSLATION

Translate the following forms.

1. *Íncipe!*
2. *Vive!*
3. *Monete!*
4. *Ínveni!*
5. *Duc!*
6. *Roga!*
7. *Fácite!*
8. *Dícite!*

NEGATIVE COMMANDS

So far, we have learned how to issue commands such as "Listen!" or "Walk!" But suppose we say, "Don't listen!" This is called a negative command. In Latin, negative commands are formed this way:

- *Noli ambulare!:* Don't walk!
- *Nolite ambulare!:* (Y'all) don't walk!

Noli and *nolite* are imperative forms of the verb *nolo* (I don't want to). They are combined with the infinitive form *ambulare* (to walk). Thus, *noli ambulare* literally means "Don't want to walk!"

TASK 13: WORKING WITH NEGATION

Convert the following commands to negative commands, and translate.

1. *roga!*
2. *incípite!*
3. *mone!*
4. *invenite!*
5. *vive!*

ANOTHER USE OF THE ACCUSATIVE CASE: DURATION OF TIME

In the last lesson, you learned that the accusative case is used to mark the direct object of a sentence and also serves as object after certain prepositions:

- *Alexander illos mílites **in flúvium** mittit:* Alexander sends those soldiers into the river.

The accusative can also be used without a preposition to indicate length or duration of time:

- *Aristóteles Alexandrum **multos annos** docet:* Aristotle teaches Alexander for many years.
- *Empórium **totam noctem** patet:* The market is open all night (for the whole night).

 FYI To express length of time, English often resorts to prepositions such as "for" or "during." These do not occur in Latin.

PROCEED WITH CAUTION

Because duration is expressed without the use of prepositions in Latin, you will have to be careful not to confuse an expression of time with a direct object. *Hippopótami **mílites** multas **horas** dévorant* means "The hippos devour soldiers for many hours."

TASK 14: TRANSLATING THE ACCUSATIVE

Complete the translation of the following sentences.

1. *Empórium patet **XXIV horas:*** The supermarket is open ….

2. ***Multos dies** laboramus:* We work ….

3. ***Totum diem** manemus:* We wait ….

4. ***Tres (III) horas** ludunt:* They play ….

5. ***Multos annos** Troiam óbsident:* They besiege Troy ….

FORMS OF THE VERB *TO BE*

The Latin verb *sum, esse* (to be) does not quite fit the standard conjugation tables. Thus, it is called an *irregular* verb. You should commit the following table to memory.

The Verb *Sum*

Singular	Plural
sum (I am)	*sumus* (we are)
es (you are)	*estis* (y'all are)
est (he is)	*sunt* (they are)

TASK 15: WORKING WITH THE VERB *SUM*

How would you say the following?

1. we are
2. I am
3. it is
4. y'all are
5. they are
6. he is
7. you are

COMPOUND VERBS BUILT ON *SUM*

A handful of verbs in Latin are composed of the verb *sum* with a prefix. Two of the most common are *possum, posse* (be able) and *prosum, prodesse* (be useful). These verbs have the following forms:

The Verbs *Possum* and *Prosum*

Singular

possum	*prosum*
potes	*prodes*
potest	*prodest*

Plural

póssumus	*prósumus*
potestis	*prodestis*
possunt	*prosunt*

The verb *pro-sum* literally means "I am for." Before a vowel, a *d* is inserted after the prefix (as in *pro-d-est*). *Possum* is built on the adjective *potis* (able), shortened to *pot–*. This stem is retained before vowels (as in *pot-es*), but for the sake of a smoother sound, it changes to *pos–* before another *s* (*pos-sum*).

TASK 16: WORKING WITH COMPOUNDS OF *SUM*

How would you say the following?

1. y'all are able
2. we are able
3. I am useful
4. it is useful
5. he is able
6. they are useful
7. you are able
8. y'all are useful

TASK 17: TRANSLATING IRREGULAR VERBS

Translate the following forms.

1. *est*

2. *prodestis*

3. *potes*

4. *potest*

5. *sunt*

6. *estis*

7. *prodest*

8. *possunt*

9. *prosum*

10. *prosunt*

11. *sum*

12. *es*

ESSENTIAL VOCABULARY

These words should be memorized. Note that verbs are now listed in the first person singular (I) form, followed by the infinitive (to) form.

Essential Vocabulary

Latin	Meaning	Related Word
Nouns		
consílium	plan, idea	counsel
mare	sea	marine
mundus	world	mundane
Verbs		
ago, ágere	do, act	agenda
aúdio, audire	hear	audio
cápio, cápere	catch	capture
credo, crédere	believe, trust	credible
cúpio, cúpere	want, wish	Cupid
débeo, debere	ought, should	debt
hábeo, habere	have	
noli (plural, *nolite*)	Don't …	

Latin	Meaning	Related Word
Verbs		
perdo, pérdere	lose	perdition
possum, posse	can, be able	possible
prosum, prodesse	be useful	
scio, scire	know	science
vénio, venire	come	venture
voco, vocare	call	vocation
Adjectives		
grandis, –e	big	grand
malus, –a, –um	bad	malicious
meus, –a, –um	my	
multus, –a, –um	much; many	multitude
nullus, –a, –um	no, none	null
parvus, –a, –um	small	
tuus, –a, –um	your	
Adverbs		
bene	well	benefit
diu	for a long time	
hodie	today	
non	not	
primum	first	prime
semper	always	*Semper Fi!* (Marine Corps motto, "Always Faithful")
statim	immediately	
tam	so	
tandem	finally	
valde	very much	
Preposition		
iuxta	according to	
Conjunctions		
cum	when	
nam	for	

Tandem is the Latin word for "finally, at last, at length." It is also the English name for a two-seater bicycle because the latter is a bicycle drawn out "at length."

RECOGNITION VOCABULARY

The following words closely resemble English words. Go through this list once or twice, and look for them in the Reading Exercise.

Recognition Vocabulary

Latin	Meaning	Related Word
apprehendo, –ere	seize, get	apprehend
dimitto, –ere	let (go)	dismiss
expando, –ere	stretch out	expand
incredíbilis, –e	incredible	
mandatum	command	mandate
observo, observare	keep	observe
obtíneo, obtinere	get	obtain
promíssio, –ion– (feminine)	promise	
promitto, promíttere	promise	
respóndeo, –ere	answer	respond
tempto, temptare	try	attempt
útilis, –e	useful	utility
utílitas, utilitat– (feminine)	advantage	utility
voluntas, voluntat– (feminine)	will, wish	voluntary

SUMMARY

In this hour, you have learned how to conjugate verbs and make commands in Latin, and how to use the accusative case to express duration of time. Now it is time to cut your teeth on some medieval "wisdom" literature.

READING EXERCISE

Every preacher knows that a good sermon is built around one or two good stories. Consequently, the literature of the Middle Ages includes collections of anecdotes that can be used to teach a lesson. One of the most popular was the *Gesta Romanorum,* or "Deeds of the Romans." The title comes from the fact that many of the stories are (anachronistically) set in the reigns of Roman emperors. The collection was probably compiled in the thirteenth or fourteenth century, and was subsequently mined by writers such as Chaucer, Boccacio, and Shakespeare. (Adapted)

THE BOWMAN AND THE NIGHTINGALE

Sagittárius quidam avículam parvam capit, nómine philomelam. Cum cupit eam occídere, philomela íncipit dícere, et ait, "Quid prodest, o homo, si me occidis? Non enim ventrem tuum de me implere potes. Sed si dimíttere me vis, tria mandata hábeo; si diligéntius ea observas, magnam inde utilitatem obtinere potes." Ille vero, ad eius loquelam stupefactus, promittit eam dimíttere, si haec tria mandata utília pronúntiet. At illa, "Audi me! noli rem, quam apprehéndere non potes, apprehéndere temptare! Hoc est primum. Audi secundum! Ob rem pérditam et irrecupíbilem noli dolere! Audi tértium! Verbum incredíbile noli credere! Haec tria custodi, et bene tibi est. Ille autem, iuxta promissionem, eam volare dimíttit. Philomela per aera vólitans dúlciter cantat."

Post cantum dicit: "Vae tibi, homo; malum consílium habes et magnum thesaurum hódie perdis! Est enim in meis viscéribus margarita, quae grándior est quam struthionis ovum." Ille haec aúdiens contristatus est valde. Expandit rete suum et temptat eam deprehéndere, dicens, "Veni in domum meum; ego te páscere volo. Ad voluntatem volare potes." Cui philomela, "Nunc pro certo scio, quod fátuus es. Nam ex his, quae tibi dixi, nullum profecto custodis, quia et de me pérdita sed irrecuperábili doles, et me cápere per rete temptas, etsi non potes me cápere, et ínsuper credis quod margarita tam grandis in meis viscéribus est, etsi ego tota ad modum ovi struthionis non possum attíngere. Stultus es et in stultítia semper permansurus es." Homo dolens ad domum suum revertit.

Reading Vocabulary

aera, aer– (neuter, plural)	air
ait	says
at	but
attingo, attíngere	attain to, equal
aúdiens	hearing
autem	but, and, moreover
avícula	bird
canto, –are	sing
cantus (IV)	song
certo	certain
contristatus, –a, –um	saddened
cui	to which
cum	when; with
custódio, –ire	keep, guard
deprehendo, deprehéndere	catch
dicens	saying
diligéntius	more carefully
dolens	sorrowing
dóleo, dolere	hurt, be sad
domum	home
dúlciter	sweetly
ea	them
eam	her, it
ego	I
eius	his, her, its
ex	from
fátuus, –a, –um	foolish
grándior	bigger
haec	this, these
his	these
hoc	this
ille, illa	he, she, it; that
ímpleo, implere	fill
in	in
inde	from it
ínsuper	moreover
irrecuperábilis, –e	irrecoverable

loquela	speech
margarita	pearl
me	me
meis	my
modus	measure, size
nómine	called, by name
nunc	now
ob	because of
occido, occídere	kill
ovi	of an egg
ovum	an egg
pasco, páscere	feed
pérditus, –a, –um	lost
permansurus, –a, –um	going to remain
philomela	nightingale
pro	for
profecto	indeed, at all
pronúntiet	he should pronounce
quae	which
quam	which; than
quia	because
quid	what
quidam	a certain
quod	that
rete, ret– (neuter)	net
sagittárius	bowman
secundus, –a, –um	second
si	if
struthionis	ostrich's
stultítia	stupidity
stultus, –a, –um	stupid
stupefactus, –a, –um	astounded
suus	his, her, its, their
te	you
tértius, –a, –um	third
thesaurus	treasure
tibi	to you

continues

Reading Vocabulary   (continued)

tria	three
vae	Woe!
venter, ventr– (masculine)	stomach
verbum	word
vero	but
vis	you are willing
viscéribus	stomach, insides
volo, are	fly
volo, velle	wish, be willing
vólitans	flying

QUIZ

A

Convert the following forms from singular to plural, and from plural to singular. Keep the same case.

1. *margarita grandis*
2. *fortunam meliorem*
3. *consília fórtia*
4. *res pérdita*
5. *margaritas grandiores*

B

Complete the following sentences with the correct form of the word in parentheses, and translate.

1. *Sagittárius avículam parvam (capio, capere), nómine philomelam.*
2. *Philomela íncipit (dico, dícere), et ait, "Quid (prosum, prodesse), o homo, si me occidis?"*
3. *Non enim ventrem (tuus, –a, –um) de me implere (possum, posse).*
4. *(Audio, audire) me! (nolo, nolle) rem, quae apprehéndere non potes, apprehéndere temptare!*
5. *Vae tibi, homo, quam (malus, –a, –um) consílium (hábeo, habere)! (Vénio, venire) in domum meum; ego te páscere volo.*
6. *Nunc pro certo scio, quod (fatuus, –a, –um) es.*
7. *Ego (totus, –a, –um) ad (modus) ovi stuthionis non (possum, posse) attíngere.*

HOUR 5
The Ablative Case

CHAPTER SUMMARY

LESSON PLAN:

In this hour you will learn about ...

- A third case, called the *ablative*
- Using the ablative case with certain prepositions
- Using the ablative case to indicate manner, means, place, time, and other relationships without a preposition

So far, we have seen that Latin nouns "fall" into different cases, depending on how they function in the sentence. For example, the doer of the action (the subject) falls into the nominative case, and the one who receives the action (the object) is in the accusative case. Each case has distinctive endings.

INTRODUCTORY READING

Look for this new case in the following extract from a medieval miracle story.

ST. GEORGE AND THE DRAGON

*Forte Sanctus Geórgius est in **illo loco** ubi fília imperatoris draconem expectat. Et dicit: "Múlier, cur ploras?" Et puella **magna voce** clamat, "Dómine, recede hinc cum **equo tuo**; fuge velóciter!" Et Geórgius: "O múlier; noli timere; ego liberabo te e **perículo**."*

Translation:

By chance, St. George is in **the place** where the emperor's daughter waits for the dragon. And he says, "Woman, why do you weep?" And the girl shouts **in a loud voice,** "Sir, withdraw from here with **your horse;** flee quickly!" And George says, "O woman, do not be afraid; I will free you from danger."

The story illustrates three important things about the ablative case:

- It has special endings (for example, *loc-o, voc-e*).

- It is used after certain prepositions, such as *in* and *cum* (*in illo loco,* "in that place"; *cum equo tuo,* "with your horse").

- It can also be used without a preposition (*magna voce,* "with a great voice").

FORMS OF THE ABLATIVE CASE: NOUNS

Nouns in each of the five declensions have special endings for the ablative case. Study the following table.

Nouns in the Ablative Case

	I	*II*	*III*
	girl	*master*	*king*
Singular			
Nominative	*puell-a*	*dómin-us*	*rex*
Accusative	*puell-am*	*dómin-um*	*reg-em*
Ablative	*puell-a*	*dómin-o*	*reg-e*
Plural			
Nominative	*puell-ae*	*dómin-i*	*reg-es*
Accusative	*puell-as*	*dómin-os*	*reg-es*
Ablative	*puell-is*	*dómin-is*	*rég-ibus*

	IV	*V*
	chariot	*thing*
Singular		
Nominative	*curr-us*	*r-es*
Accusative	*curr-um*	*r-em*
Ablative	*curr-u*	*r-e*
Plural		
Nominative	*curr-us*	*r-es*
Accusative	*curr-us*	*r-es*
Ablative	*cúrr-ibus*	*r-ebus*

JUST A MINUTE

The ablative singular ending is usually based on the stem vowel for each declension (as in *puell-a* and *curr-u*); the plural form has the ending *–is* or *–bus*.

In the first declension, the spelling of the ablative form is identical to the nominative (as in *puella*).

NEUTER NOUNS IN THE SECOND AND THIRD DECLENSIONS

Neuter nouns in the second and third declensions usually have the same endings in the ablative case as other nouns. The handful of nouns that we have identified as third declension "i-stems" (see Hour 1), however, have the ending *–i*.

Neuter Nouns in the Second and Third Declensions

	II	III	III i-stem
	word	*name*	*sea*
Singular			
Nominative	*verb-um*	*nomen*	*mare*
Accusative	*verb-um*	*nomen*	*mare*
Ablative	*verb-o*	*nómin-e*	*mar-i*
Plural			
Nominative	*verb-a*	*nómin-a*	*már-ia*
Accusative	*verb-a*	*nómin-a*	*már-ia*
Ablative	*verb-is*	*nomín-ibus*	*már-ibus*

	IV
	horn
Singular	
Nominative	*corn-u*
Accusative	*corn-u*
Ablative	*corn-u*
Plural	
Nominative	*corn-ua*
Accusative	*corn-ua*
Ablative	*corn-ibus*

TASK 1: WORKING WITH THE ABLATIVE CASE

For each of the following nouns, give the ablative singular and plural forms.

1. *fémina*
2. *equus*
3. *perículum*
4. *draco, dracon-* (masculine)
5. *exércitus* (IV)
6. *res*

TASK 2: IDENTIFYING CASES

For each of the following nouns, identify the case (nominative, accusative, or ablative) and the number (singular or plural). Some forms have two or three possible identifications.

1. *equus*
2. *dóminum*
3. *mari*
4. *fémina* (2)
5. *fíliae*
6. *génera* (2)
7. *rege*
8. *draconem*
9. *puella* (2)
10. *currus* (3)
11. *puellas*
12. *máribus*
13. *rem*
14. *re*
15. *nomen* (2)

ADJECTIVES IN THE ABLATIVE CASE

As you have seen, adjectives must *agree* with the nouns or pronouns they describe in gender, number, and case. This means that all adjectives have a special set of endings to match nouns in the ablative case:

- *cum **magno** equo:* with a big horse
- *in **magna** urbe:* in a big city

As usual, the endings for adjectives are borrowed from the noun endings you have just learned. Study the following table.

Adjectives in the Ablative Case

(First/Second Declension Adjectives)

	Masculine	Feminine	Neuter
Singular			
Nominative	magn-us	magn-a	magn-um
Accusative	magn-um	magn-am	magn-um
Ablative	magn-o	magn-a	magn-o
Plural			
Nominative	magn-i	magn-ae	magn-a
Accusative	magn-os	magn-as	magn-a
Ablative	magn-is	magn-is	magn-is

(Third Declension Adjectives)

	Masculine/Feminine		Neuter
Singular			
Nominative	omn-is	omn-e	
Accusative	omn-em	omn-e	
Ablative	omn-i	omn-i	
Plural			
Nominative	omn-es	ómn-ia	
Accusative	omn-es	ómn-ia	
Ablative	ómn-ibus	ómn-ibus	

PROCEED WITH CAUTION

The endings for adjectives in the ablative case are like those of nouns, except that third declension adjectives end in *–i*, whereas nouns (except neuter i-stems) end in *–e*.

Task 3: Noun-Adjective Pairings

Complete the following noun-adjective pairings. Remember that the adjective must agree with the noun in gender, number, and case.

1. *fémina* (ablative) (*tristis*)
2. *rege* (*magnus*)
3. *rebus* (*omnis*)
4. *cúrribus* (*magnus*)
5. *die* (*tristis*)
6. *dóminis* (*fortis*)

Uses of the Ablative Case

Nouns go into the ablative case after certain prepositions. We have already learned several prepositions that govern the accusative case, such as *ad* (to, at) and *per* (through). Here are some common prepositions that take the ablative:

- *a* or *ab:* from, by
- *e* or *ex:* out of
- *de:* down from, about
- *cum:* with
- *in:* in, on
- *sub:* under
- *super:* above
- *pro:* in front of, on behalf of

Most of these prepositions express stationary position or separation (such as "from"). Remember that prepositional phrases often come before the verb:

- *Fémina **e casa** exit:* The woman goes **out of the house.**
- *Feles **sub mensa** dormit:* The cat sleeps **under the table.**

TIME SAVER

The variant forms *ab* and *ex* (for *a* and *e*) are used when the following word begins with a vowel, or in other situations where the longer form sounds better:

- *ab equo:* (away) from the horse
- *ex urbe:* out of the city

TASK 4: TRANSLATING PREPOSITIONAL PHRASES

Translate the following phrases:

1. *cum equo*
2. *sub mari*
3. *in mensa*
4. *in casa*
5. *super terra*
6. *ex urbe*
7. *de móntibus*
8. *e loco*
9. *a curru*
10. *cum rege*
11. *pro urbe*
12. *a mari*

ABLATIVE WITHOUT A PREPOSITION

Occasionally, a noun may appear in the ablative case without a preposition going before it. This commonly occurs when the noun expresses the *means* or the *manner* of an action. It also occurs in expressions of *time* and *place*.

- *Puella **mánibus** laborat:* The girl works **with [her] hands.**
- ***Magna cura** laborat:* She works **with great care.**
- ***Terra** et **mari** pugnamus:* We fight **on land and sea.**
- ***Die Saturni** requiéscimus:* We rest **on Saturday** (Saturn's day).

Notice that when we translate these sentences into English, we often add prepositions, such as "with" and "in." Often you will have to make a guess, based on the rest of the sentence, as to which of these prepositions fits the best.

TIME SAVER

When in doubt, apply the **FWIB** rule. When you see a noun by itself in the ablative case, chances are that it will mean: From, With, In (on), or By. Test these different meanings until you find the one that fits best.

TASK 5: FWIB

Use the FWIB rule to complete the translation of the words or phrases in bold.

1. *Brutus Caésarem* **gládio** *necat:* Brutus kills Caesar … sword.
2. **Roma** *tandem redit:* She finally returns … Rome.
3. **Magna diligéntia** *laboramus:* We work … great diligence.
4. *Troiam* **ferro et igne** *cápiunt:* They capture Troy … fire and the sword.
5. **Illo die,** *draco ad urbem venit:* … that day, a dragon comes to the city.
6. **Magna voce** *clamamus:* We shout … a great [loud] voice.
7. *Faber* **málleo et clávibus** *laborat:* A carpenter works … hammer and nails.
8. **Pátria** *statim fúgiunt:* They flee at once … their country.

ESSENTIAL VOCABULARY

The following common words should be committed to memory.

Essential Vocabulary

Latin	Meaning	Related Word
Nouns		
aqua	water	aquarium
caelum	sky	celestial
Deus	God	deity
fémina	woman	feminine
locus	place	location, local
pópulus	people	popular
vir	man	virile
Verbs		
do, dare	give	data = "given" information
hábito, –are	dwell	habitation
pugno, –are	fight	pugnacious
sédeo, sedere	sit	sedentary
tímeo, timere	fear	timid
vídeo, videre	see	video

Latin	Meaning	Related Word
Adjectives		
médius, –a, –um	middle	medium
Adverbs		
iam	now, already	
nunc	now	
cur	why?	
Prepositions		
a, ab	from	
de	from, down from (+ ablative)	
cum	with (+ ablative)	
in	in (+ ablative); into (+ accusative)	
e, ex	from, out of (+ ablative)	
pro	in front of, on behalf of, for	
sub	under (+ ablative)	
Conjunctions		
ubi	when	

RECOGNITION VOCABULARY

Go through this list once or twice, and then look for these words in the Reading Exercise.

Recognition Vocabulary

Latin	Meaning	Related Word
ámbulo, –are	walk	ambulatory
aúdio, –ire	hear	audio
clamo, –are	shout	exclaim
contra	against	contrary
dévoro, –are	devour	

continues

Recognition Vocabulary   (continued)

Latin	Meaning	Related Word
ego	I	egotist
exclamo, –are	exclaim	
hábito, –are	dwell	inhabit
ínvoco, –are	call upon	invoke
lacus (IV)	lake	
máximus, –a, –um	very great	maximum
miráculum	miracle	
óptimus, –a, –um	best	optimal
péssimus, –a, –um	awful	pessimism
ploro, –are	implore	
repletus, –a, –um	filled	replete
respóndeo, –ere	respond	
sanctus, –a, –um	holy	saint, sanctity
tandem	finally, at length	tandem (bicycle)
unicus, –a, –um	only	unique
velóciter	quickly	velocity
virtus, virtut– (feminine)	strength	virtue
vox, voc– (feminine)	voice	voice, vocal

Summary

In this hour, you have learned how to recognize and translate the ablative case in both nouns and adjectives. Now you can apply this knowledge to some of the religious literature of the Middle Ages, which still echoes in our modern fairy tales.

READING EXERCISE

St. George was a Christian convert who was martyred in the persecution of the emperor Diocletian in the third century, A.D. The legend of his battle with a dragon seems to be based on the ancient Greek myth of Perseus, who liberated the princess Andromeda from a hideous monster. Both heroes were associated with the city of Joppa (modern Jaffa). The following account is adapted from the biography of John of Amalfi (around 1000 A.D.).

Sanctus Geórgius ínvenit puellam sedentem prope lacum et valde ploran-tem. Et dicit ei: "Múlier, cur ploras? Cur sedes tu, fémina tam pulchra, in indigno loco isto?" Et respondet puella, "Dómine mi, ista est cívitas Lísia quae est valde bona et óptima, omnibusque rebus bonis repleta. Sed habet in se unum máximum malum, quod súperat ómnia mala. In aqua hábitat draco péssimus qui cotídie exit de aqua et pugnat contra imperatorem et contra pópulum et dévorat multos. Omnes cives fílios suos iam dederunt; pater meus unicam fíliam suam dat. Ecce habes ómnia. Vade ergo in pace."

Sed sanctus Geórgius élevans óculos suos ad caelum ínvocat Deum, dicens: "Ostende signum nunc per magnam misericórdiam tuam, et mitte hanc malignam béstiam sub pédibus meis." Tunc venit ad eum vox de caelo dicens: "O Georgi, aúdio orationem tuam. Ecce fácio sicut petis."

Post haec audit sanctus Geórgius rúgitum magnum in aqua. Puella excla-mat voce magna: "Dómine, fuge velóciter: ecce malignus draco venit." Sanctus Geórgius festinans ad eum facit signum Sanctae Crucis, dicens, "Dómine Deus, da mihi virtutem contra draconem istum. Auxílio tuo eum superabo." Ubi haec dicit, statim cadit draco ante pedes eius. Dicit puel-lae: "Solve zonam tuam et frenum meum et apporta ad me." Illa solvit traditque zonam et frenum. Sanctus Geórgius dixit, "Apprehende dra-conem et ámbula cum eo per médiam civitatem."

Ut videt pópulus hoc magnum miráculum, vir sanctus exclamat magna voce, "Nolite timere! Crédite in Deum vivum et Iesum Christum fílium eius, et ego draconem occidam." Pópulus clamat, "Crédimus!" Tunc sanctus Geórgius amputat caput draconis.

Reading Vocabulary

ámputo –are	amputate, cut off
appórto, –are	bring
apprehéndo, apprehendere	grab, take hold

continues

Reading Vocabulary (continued)

auxílium	help
béstia (feminine)	beast
cado, cádere	fall
caput, cápit– (neuter)	head
civis, civ– (masculine)	citizen
cívitas, civitat– (feminine)	city
contra	against
cotídie	every day
credo, crédere	believe
dederunt	have given
dicens	saying
Dómine	Sir! Lord!
draconis	of the dragon
ecce	Look!
ei	to her
eius	his, her
élevans	lifting
eo	him, it
ergo	then, therefore
eum	him, it
éxeo, exire	go out
fácio, fácere	do, make
festínans	hastening
fília	daughter
fílius	son
frenum	bridle
haec	these things
hanc, hoc	this
ille, illa, illud	he, she, it, that one
in se	in it(self)
indignus, –a, –um	unworthy, awful
invénio, –ire	find

iste, ista, istum	this, that
Lísia	Lisia
malignus, –a, –um	evil
malum	evil
meus, –a, –um	my
mi	my
mihi	to me
misericórdia	mercy
mitto, míttere	send
múlier, mulíer– (feminine)	woman
occídam	I will kill
óculus	eye
orátio, oration– (feminine)	prayer
osténdo, osténdere	show
pater, patr– (masculine)	father
pax, pac– (feminine)	peace
pes, ped– (masculine)	foot
peto, pétere	ask, seek
plorantem	weeping
post	after
prope	near
pulcher, –ra, –rum	beautiful
qui, quae, quod	who, which
rúgitus (IV)	bellowing
Sanctae Crucis	of the Holy Cross
sedentem	sitting
sicut	just as
signum	sign
solvo, sólvere	undo
statim	immediately
superábo	I will overcome
súpero, –are	overcome

continues

Reading Vocabulary   (continued)

suus, −a, −um	his, her, its, their
tam	so, such
trado, trádere	hand over
tu	you
tunc	then
tuus, −a, −um	your
ut	when, as
vado, vádere	Go!
valde	very, a lot
velóciter	quickly
vivus, −a, −um	living
zona	belt

Quiz

A

Translate the following verbs into English.

1. *videmus*
2. *dicunt*
3. *datis*
4. *hábeo*
5. *sedes*
6. *timet*
7. *véniunt*
8. *es*
9. *potestis*
10. *it*

B

Review the prepositions in Hours 3 and 5, and translate the following phrases with *casa* (house).

1. *pro casa*

2. *ad casam*

3. *per casam*

4. *super casa*

5. *in casa*

6. *a casa*

7. *de casa*

8. *e casa*

9. *sub casa*

C

Complete the following sentences with the correct form of the word in parentheses, and translate.

1. *Sanctus Geórgius ínvenit (puella) sedentem prope lacum.*

2. *"Múlier, cur (ploro, –are)?"*

3. *"Cur sedes in (indignus, –a, –um) loco?"*

4. *Lísia est cívitas óptima, (omnis, –e) bonis repleta.*

5. *In (aqua) hábitat draco péssimus, qui cotídie dévorat cives (multus, –a, –um).*

6. *Sanctus Geórgius élevat óculos ad caelum et (Deus) ínvocat.*

7. *"(Ostendo, –ere) signum nunc, et mitte hanc béstiam sub (pes, ped–, masculine) meis."*

8. *Puella exclamat (vox, voc–, feminine) (magnus, –a, –um) "Dómine, fuge velóciter."*

9. *"Dómine, da mihi (virtus, virtut–, feminine) contra draconem istum."*

10. *"(Auxílium) tuo eum superabo."*

11. *Puella ámbulat cum eo per médiam (cívitas, civitat–, feminine).*

12. *Omnes viri, ubi hoc magnum miráculum (vídeo, –ere), exclamant, "Crédimus!"*

Questions; Complex Sentences; Relative Clauses

CHAPTER SUMMARY

LESSON PLAN:

In this hour you will learn about ...

- How to ask and answer questions
- How to analyze complex sentences
- How to form relative clauses

So far, you have learned how to make certain kinds of statements and commands in the form of simple sentences.

INTRODUCTORY READING

First, let's eavesdrop on a fictional conversation between an ignorant abbot (Antronius) and a learned woman (Magdala), composed by Erasmus of Rotterdam (Adapted).

A LEARNED DIALOGUE

Antronius: *Quam hic suppellectilem vídeo?*

Magdala: *Nonne elegantem?*

Antronius: *Néscio an elegantem; certe parum decoram matronae.*

Magdala: *Quam ob rem?*

Antronius: *Quia libris plena sunt ómnia.*

Magdala: *Nonne matronae est, administrare rem domesticam, erudire líberos?*

Antronius: *Est.*

Magdala: *An rem tantam exístimas administrari posse sine sapiéntia?*

Translation:

Antronius: What furniture do I see here?

Magdala: Isn't it elegant?

Antronius: I don't know whether it is elegant; it is certainly hardly suited to a woman.

Magdala: Why?

Antronius: Because everything is filled with books.

Magdala: Isn't it the matron's job to administer the house and raise the children?

Antronius: Yes.

Magdala: Do you suppose such a matter can be managed without wisdom?

In this conversation, you notice a number of questions. Sometimes these are indicated by questioning words, such as "what?" (*quam?*) and "why?" (*cur?*). Others are set up by little words, such as *nonne,* that function essentially as question marks. These words may give a hint of the kind of answer that is expected.

QUESTIONS FOR INFORMATION: INTERROGATIVE PRONOUNS

In any language, there are different types of questions. Sometimes the questioner is looking for a simple answer of "yes" or "no." More often than not, however, the questioner is seeking a particular kind of information.

If the answer can be expressed as a noun or pronoun, the question may include a questioning or interrogative pronoun (*pronomen interrogativum*):

- *Quid sub mensa est?:* **What** is under the table?:
- *Quis prope te stat?:* **Who** is standing near you?:

 FYI Latin words beginning with the letters *qu* often correspond to English words beginning with "wh" (as in *quid,* "what," and *quem,* "whom").

Interrogative pronouns in both languages are marked for case:

- *Quem quaeris?:* **Whom** are you seeking?
- *Quo laboras?:* With **what** are you working?

Here is a declension table for the interrogative pronouns *quis* (who) and *quid* (what).

Quis and Quid

Nominative	*quis* (who?)	*quid* (what?)
Accusative	*quem* (whom?)	*quid* (what?)
Ablative	*quo* (FWIB whom?)	*quo* (FWIB what?)

TASK 1: TRANSLATION OF INTERROGATIVE PRONOUNS

Translate the pronoun in bold, and identify its case (nominative, accusative, or ablative).

1. ***Quis*** *avículam parvam capit?:* … captures a small bird?
2. ***Quem*** *Sanctus Geórgius prope flúvium ínvenit?:* … does St. George find near the river?
3. ***Quid*** *dicit philomela?:* … does the nightingale say?
4. *De* ***quo*** *dolet sagittárius?:* … is the bowman sorry?
5. ***Quid*** *est in mensa?:* … is on the table?

INTERROGATIVE ADJECTIVES: *WHAT …?*, *WHICH …?*

Sometimes the questioner has a general idea of the answer, but is looking for some specifying information:

- ***Quam*** *suppellectilem video?:* **What** furniture do I see?
- ***Quibus*** *instrumentis laboras?:* With **which** tools are you working?

In these sentences, the questioning word is an adjective, which agrees with a noun in gender, number, and case. Here is the entire declension table for the adjective *qui* (what, which).

The Interrogative Adjective *Qui*

	Masculine	Feminine	Neuter
Singular			
Nominative	qui	quae	quod
Accusative	quem	quam	quod
Ablative	quo	qua	quo
Plural			
Nominative	qui	quae	quae
Accusative	quos	quas	quae
Ablative	quibus	quibus	quibus

JUST A MINUTE

The interrogative adjective has endings in common with adjectives of the *bonus* type (*quam, quo, quae, quos,* and *quae*) and the *omnis* type (*quem* and *quibus*). Other forms, however, are irregular.

TASK 2: WORKING WITH INTERROGATIVE ADJECTIVES

Supply the form of the interrogative adjective *qui* that best completes the Latin sentence. Then translate.

1. *(Qui) homo avículam capit? Sagittárius.*
2. *(Qui) avículam sagittárius capit? Philomelam.*
3. *(Qui) puella draconem expectat? Imperatoris* (the emperor's) *fília.*
4. *(Qui) monstrum* (neuter) *Sactus Geórgius occidit? Draconem.*
5. *(Qui) ob … rem dolet sagittárius? Ob magaritam pérditam.*
6. *In (qui) urbe* (feminine) *hábitat puella? Lísia.*

OTHER INTERROGATIVE ADJECTIVES: *QUALIS, QUANTUS, QUOT*

Some questions fish for information that describes, rather than identifies, some noun or pronoun. These may be indicated by the interrogative adjectives *qualis, –e* (what kind of?); *quantus, –a, –um* (how much?, how big?); and *quot* (how many?).

- *Qualem suppellectilem vídeo?:* What kind of furniture do I see?
- *Quantam suppellectilem habes?:* How much furniture do you have?
- *Quot hómines vides?:* How many men do you see?

Qualis declines in the same way as *omnis; quantus* follows the *bonus* type. *Quot,* however, is indeclinable: It never changes its form.

TASK 3: TRANSLATING INTERROGATIVE ADJECTIVES

Translate the words in bold.

1. *Quot mílites hippopótami dévorant?:* … soldiers do the hippos devour?
2. *In quanto perículo sumus?:* In … danger are we?
3. *Quales libros legis?:* … books do you read?
4. *Quot monstra Geórgius superavit?:* … monsters has St. George overcome?
5. *Cum quálibus viris habitamus?:* With … men do we live?

TASK 4: *QUALIS* AND *QUALE*

From the following list, choose the form of *qualis, quale* that best completes the sentence, and translate.

qualis, quale, qualem, quali, quales, qualia, quálibus

1. *... avícula est philomela?*
2. *In ... casa hábitas?*
3. *... librum in manu habes?*
4. *... féminae latine discunt?*
5. *... verba dicit pópulus?*
6. *... monstrum terret civitatem?*
7. *De ... libris sapiéntiam díscimus?*

INTERROGATIVE ADVERBS

A third type of informational question has to do with the action of the verb:

- *Cur haec suppellex tibi dísplicet?:* **Why** does this furniture displease you?
- *Ubi poeta hábitat?:* **Where** does the poet live?
- *Quómodo laborat?:* **How** does he work?
- *Quando draco venit?:* **When** does the dragon arrive?

These are interrogative adverbs; their form never changes.

TIME SAVER

Students of rhetoric once had to memorize the *adiuncta* (circumstances) of any action for use in forensic oratory. The following verse was devised as a mnemonic aid:

Quis? Quid? Ubi? Quo instrumento? Cur? Quómodo? Quando? (Who? What? Where? By what means/instrument? Why? How? When?)

TASK 5: INTERROGATIVE PRONOUNS AND ADVERBS

In view of the answer, supply the interrogative pronoun or adverb that best completes the question.

1. *... Magdala in manu tenet? Librum latinum:* ... does Magdala have in her hand? A Latin book.

2. *... Magdala libros legit? Sápiens esse cupit:* ... does Magdala read books? She wants to be wise.

3. *... draco Lísiam terret? Cotídie:* ... does the dragon terrify Lisia? Every day.

4. *... imperatoris fíliam servat? Geórgius:* ... saves the emperor's daughter? George.

5. *... latinam díscimus? Celériter:* ... do we learn Latin? Quickly.

6. *... hanc lectionem complemus? Mox:* ... do we finish this lesson? Soon.

7. *... Geórgius caput draconis ámputat? Gládio:* ... does George cut off the dragon's head? With a sword.

YES/NO QUESTIONS

The other basic type of question does not seek any information, but only a simple answer of "yes" or "no":

- *Est**ne** haec suppellex élegans?:* **Is** this furniture elegant?
- *Vides**ne** libros?:* **Do** you **see** the books?

Notice that in English, a "yes/no" question is set up by putting the verb (or a helping verb, such as "does" or "do") at the beginning of the sentence. In Latin, too, the verb is usually put first, and the suffix *–ne* is added to it.

TASK 6: FORMING QUESTIONS

Turn the Latin sentences into questions, and retranslate.

1. *Hippopótami mílites terrent:* The hippos terrify the soldiers.

2. *Féminae sapiunt:* Women are wise.

3. *Draco ante Sanctum Geórgium cadit:* The dragon falls before St. George.

4. *Sagittárius dolet:* The bowman is sad.

5. *Velóciter díscimus:* We learn Latin quickly.

TASK 7: TRANSLATING QUESTIONS

Translate the following Latin sentences.

1. *Pugnatne Sanctus Geórgius cum dracone?*

2. *Estne Lísia cívitas optima* (very good)*?*

   3. *Sedetne puella prope aquam?*

   4. *Timetne pópulus draconem?*

   5. *Suntne dracones magni?*

LOADED QUESTIONS

The questions we have just studied leave the door open to an affirmative or negative answer. At times, however, the questioner has definite expectations about the answer:

- **Isn't** this furniture elegant?
- This furniture **is** elegant, **isn't** it?
- This furniture **isn't** elegant, **is** it?

In the first two examples, the questioner expects the answer "yes"; in the third, the anticipated answer is "no." The structure of the question hints at the expected reply.

TASK 8: FORMING LOADED QUESTIONS

Turn the following English sentences into loaded questions expecting an affirmative answer. Then reword the questions to anticipate a negative reply.

   1. Does the abbot drink wine?

   2. Do hippos eat people?

   3. Is St. George afraid?

   4. Do the people believe in God?

   5. Are hippos friendly?

NONNE AND NUM

In Latin, as we have seen, neutral questions of the "yes/no" type add the suffix *–ne* to the first word of the question. Loaded questions are indicated by special interrogative adverbs: *nonne* and *num*.

- *Nonne matrona domum administrat?:* **Doesn't** the matron manage the household?
- *Num haec suppellex tibi dísplicet?:* This furniture **doesn't** displease you, **does** it?

The following should help you keep track of the various ways of posing a "yes/no" question.

- *–ne* expects a **yes** or **no** answer
- *nonne* expects a **yes** answer
- *num* expects a **no** answer

TASK 9: TRANSLATING YES/NO QUESTIONS

Translate the questions as rephrased.

1. *Terrentne hippopótami mílites?:* Do the hippos scare the soldiers? **Num** *hippopótami mílites terrent?:* …?

2. *Sapiuntne féminae?:* Are women wise? **Nonne** *féminae sápiunt?:* …?

3. *Discimusne Latine celériter?:* Do we learn Latin quickly? **Num** *díscimus Latine celériter?:* …?

4. *Doletne sagittárius?:* Is the bowman sad? **Nonne** *dolet sagittárius?:* …?

ANSWERING YES/NO QUESTIONS

In classical Latin, the usual way of answering a question in the affirmative is to repeat the verb:

Magdala: *Nonne matronae **est**, administrare rem domesticam, erudire liberos?* (Isn't it the matron's job to administer the house and raise the children?)

Antronius: ***Est.** (Yes. It is.)*

To reply in the negative, repeat the verb with *non:*

- *Terretne draco Geórgium? **Non terret:*** Does the dragon frighten George? **No.**

In colloquial Latin, however, there were also other ways of saying "yes" or "no." Two of the most common were *sic* (thus) for "yes" and *non* for "no." Other ways included these.

Saying Yes or No

Yes	No
étiam (even so)	*mínime* (not at all)
máxime (most of all)	*immo* (nay, rather)
sane (indeed)	
ita (thus, so)	
ita vero (so truly)	

TASK 10: TRANSLATION

Translate the responses to the following questions.

1. *Sapitne sagittárius?:* Is the bowman wise? *Non sapit:* ….
2. *Nonne timet Geórgius?:* Isn't George afraid? *Immo draco timet:* ….
3. *Devoratne draco puellam?:* Does the dragon devour the girl? *Mínime!:* ….
4. *Estne Latina diffícilis?:* Is Latin difficult? *Ita vero! (Est!):* ….

MAIN AND SUBORDINATE CLAUSES

A clause is a group of words containing a subject and a verb. Some sentences consist of one clause:

- *In aqua habitat draco péssimus:* An evil dragon lives in the water.

These are called simple sentences. Two or more of these can be strung together with the help of conjunctions, such as *et:*

- *Sanctus Geórgius orat **et** draco cadit sub pédibus eius:* St. George prays **and** the dragon falls beneath his feet.

Such sentences are called *compound* sentences. It often happens, however, that one clause supplies information about another:

- ***Quia** Sanctus Geórgius orat, draco cadit sub pédibus eius:* **Because** St. George prays, the dragon falls beneath his feet.

In this example, the clause *quia Sanctus Geórgius orat* gives the reason *why* the dragon falls at his feet. To put it another way, the dragon's action is in the "foreground," and St. George's prayer provides the "background." Clauses in the foreground are called *main* clauses; those that supply background information are called *subordinate* or *dependent* clauses. They are usually marked by subordinating conjunctions and pronouns. Here are some of the most common:

- *ubi:* when, where
- *cum:* when
- *etsi:* although
- *quia, quod:* because
- *si:* if
- *qui, quae, quod:* who, which, that

TASK 11: IDENTIFYING SUBORDINATE CLAUSES

In the following English story, identify all subordinate clauses.

Once upon a time two clerics were walking outside the city at nightfall. Soon they came to a place where ruffians were known to meet. One cleric said, "Let us go another way. As the philosopher says, 'Do not pass through an unjust nation.'" The other said, "It won't hurt to pass through." Then they heard a sweet song that came from a nearby inn. One of the clerics went his way, but the other, because he was pleased by the song, entered and sat down. Suddenly, the sheriff entered the house and arrested all those present, because the inn was a notorious den of thieves. Although he protested, the cleric was led with the rest to execution.

TASK 12: WORKING WITH CONJUNCTIONS

Supply the missing Latin conjunction.

1. *Pópulus timet, … draco dévorat multos:* The people are afraid, **because** the dragon devours many.

2. *… Geórgius haec dicit, cadit draco ante pedes eius:* **When** George says these things, the dragon fall before his feet.

3. *… créditis in Deum, nolite timere draconem!:* **If** you believe in God, don't fear the dragon!

4. *Puella manet prope flúvium, … draco hábitat:* The girl waits near the river, **where** the dragon lives.

RELATIVE CLAUSES

A common type of subordinate clause identifies or describes a noun in the main clause:

- *Ecce Geórgius, **qui** dracones domat:* Here is George, **who** tames dragons.
- *Hic hábitat monstrum, **quod** civitatem terret:* Here lives a monster, **which** terrifies the city.

In each of these sentences, the subordinate clause provides information about a noun in the main clause (*Geórgius, monstrum*). This noun is called the antecedent. The antecedent is linked by a pronoun (*qui, quod,* "who," "which," "that") that stands in for the pronoun in the main clause.

TASK 13: IDENTIFYING ANTECEDENTS

For each of the following English sentences, identify the antecedent of the relative pronoun in bold.

1. St. George sees a girl **who** is sitting by the road, weeping.
2. The horse, **which** George was riding, feared the dragon.
3. The people to **whom** George showed the dragon believed in God.

RELATIVE CLAUSES IN ENGLISH

In English, relative clauses begin with the words *who, which,* or *that. Who* always refers to persons; *which* and *that* refer to things. Note also that in standard English, *who* changes to *whom* when it is the object of a verb or preposition:

- Here is St. George, **whom** the dragons fear.
- The abbot, with **whom** Magdala is speaking, does not like books.

TASK 14: RELATIVE CLAUSES

Supply the form (who, whom, which) that best fits the sentence.

1. The girl, … St. George once rescued, is sitting by the river.
2. George sees a girl, … is weeping.

3. St. George, to … God gave the power to slay dragons, walked into Lisia.

4. The soldiers, … are swimming in the river, are afraid of the hippos.

5. Alexander, about … we have heard many wonderful things, spoke Greek.

RELATIVE CLAUSES IN LATIN

Like English, Latin marks relative clauses with pronouns that clearly refer to a noun in the main clause. One difference, though, is that Latin-speakers do not worry about the distinction between persons and things:

- *Ecce Geórgius,* **qui** *dracones domat:* Here is George, **who** tames dragons.

- *Ecce liber meus,* **qui** *fábulam narrat:* Here my book, **which** tells the story.

Note that the Latin pronoun *qui* can mean either "who" or "which." On the other hand, Latin-speakers make sure that the pronoun agrees with the antecedent in gender and number:

- *Ecce puella,* **quae** *Geórgium monuit:* Here is the girl **who** warned George.

In this example, the form *quae* is used for "who" because the antecedent is a feminine singular noun (*puella*). This is not to say, however, that the pronoun and its antecedent will always be in the same case:

- *Ibi stat puella,* **quam** *Geórgius olim servavit:* There stands the girl **whom** George once saved.

Just as the English sentence contains the object form "whom," the Latin sentence uses *quam.* This shows that in the relative clause, the girl is the object of the verb *servavit; Geórgius* is the subject. Similarly, relative pronouns that come after prepositions must be in the appropriate case:

- *Flúvium videmus, in* **quo** *hippopótami natant:* We see the river, in which the hippos swim.

Thus, the Latin relative pronoun must be marked for gender and number (to agree with the antecedent) and also case (to indicate its role in the relative clause). The whole range of possibilities can be set out as follows.

The Relative Pronoun

	Masculine	Feminine	Neuter
Singular			
Nominative	qui	quae	quod
Accusative	quem	quam	quod
Ablative	quo	qua	quo
Plural			
Nominative	qui	quae	quae
Accusative	quos	quas	quae
Ablative	quibus	quibus	quibus

These forms are identical to those you learned as interrogative adjectives.

TASK 15: WORKING WITH RELATIVE PRONOUNS

For each of the following sentences, choose the appropriate form of the relative pronoun.

1. *Ista cívitas est Lísia, ... est valde bona:* This city is Lisia, which is very good.

2. *Lísia habet unum máximum malum, ... súperat ómnia mala:* Lisia has one great evil, which tops all evils.

3. *Hic hábitat draco péssimus, ... dévorat multos:* Here lives an evil dragon, which devours many.

4. *Draco, ... vides, omnes cives terret:* The dragon that you see terrifies all the citizens.

5. *Cives, cum ... habitamus, draconem timent:* The citizens, with whom we live, fear the dragon.

6. *Puella, ... Geórgius videt, prope flúvium sedet:* The girl, whom George sees, sits near the river.

7. *Féminae, ... latine sciunt, omnes sápiunt:* Women who know Latin are all wise.

8. *Libri, ... vídeo, non mihi placent:* The books that I see do not please me.

PROCEED WITH CAUTION

Remember that any form of the relative pronoun, if its antecedent is a thing, will have to be translated into English as "which" or "that."

ESSENTIAL VOCABULARY

These common words should be memorized.

Essential Vocabulary

Latin	Meaning	Related Word
Nouns		
liber, libr– (masculine)	book	library
múlier, mulier– (feminine)	woman	
perículum	danger	peril
Pronouns		
qui, quae, quod	who, which, what	
quis, quid	who, what	
Verbs		
amo, amare	love	amatory
constítuo, constitúere	put, establish	constitution
curro, cúrrere	run	current
móneo, monere	warn, advise	admonish
puto, –are	think, believe	putative
reddo, réddere	give back, repeat	render
Adjectives		
quantus, –a, –um	how much	quantity
qui, quae, quod	what ...? which ...?	

Latin	Meaning	Related Word
Adjectives		
qualis, quale	what kind of …?	quality
quot	how many?	
tot	so many	
Adverbs		
cur	why?	
igitur	then, therefore	
nisi	unless	
nonne	expects a "yes" answer, as in, "Doesn't it …?"	
num	expects a "no" answer, as in, "It doesn't … does it?"	
quamobrem	why?	
quando	when?	
quapropter	Why?	
quidem	indeed	
quómodo	how?	
ubi	where?	
vix	scarcely, hardly	
Prepositions		
a, ab	from	
inter	between	
Conjunctions		
at	at, but	
etsi	although	
neque	nor	
quia	because	
quod	that, because	
sed	but	
si	if	

RECOGNITION VOCABULARY

Go through this list once or twice, and look for these words in the Reading
Exercise.

Recognition Vocabulary

Latin Word	Meaning	Related Word
auctor, auctor– (masculine)	author	
avis, avis (feminine)	bird	aviation
canis, can– (common)	dog	canine
cerebrum	brain	cerebral, cerebellum
certe	certainly	certain
collóquium	conversation	colloquial
contendo, conténdere	contend	
dissimilis, –e	unlike	dissimilar
ego	I	ego-maniac
erudítio, –ion (feminine)	learning	erudition
eruditus, –a, –um	learned	erudite
frequenter	frequently	
Latine	in Latin	
Maria	Mary	
nóbilis, –e	noble	
Paula	Paula	
potens, potent–	powerful	potent
punctum	point	punctual
quintus, –a, –um	fifth	quintuplets
rarus, –a, –um	rare	
sacer, sacra, sacrum	sacred	
satis	rather, enough	satisfy
schola	class	school
séntio, –ire	think, feel	sentient, sense
stúdium	study, pursuit	
templum	church	temple
theológicus, –a, –um	theological	
virgo, vírgin– (feminine)	virgin	

SUMMARY

In this hour, you have learned how to ask and answer questions, and how to form various dependent clauses, including relative clauses. Now you are ready to resume the dialogue on women's education, with which the hour began.

READING EXERCISE

Early in his career, the Dutch humanist Erasmus composed a number of dialogs (*Collóquia*) as examples of "good" Latin to be imitated by his pupils. He also found in the dialog format an opportunity to exercise his wit and to comment on the issues of the day. In a dialog titled *Abbas et Erudita*, Erasmus indicates both his endorsement of women's education and his desire for a more learned and vigorous clergy.

AN ABBOT AND A LEARNED WOMAN

Antronius: *Fero libros, non fero Latinos.*

Magdala: *Quapropter?*

Antronius: *Quia non cónvenit ea lingua féminis.*

Magdala: *Nonne decorum est, si fémina in Germánia nata discit Gállice?*

Antronius: *Máxime.*

Magdala: *Quamobrem?*

Antronius: *Collóquium habere potest cum homínibus, qui sciunt Gállice.*

Magdala: *Et putas quod indecorum est, si disco Latine, et cotídie collóquium hábeo cum tot auctóribus, tam facundis, tam eruditis, tam sapiéntibus, tam fidis consultóribus?*

Antronius: *Libri adimunt multum cérebri a féminis.*

Magdala: *Quantum cérebri habes, néscio; certe ego, quantulumcumque hábeo, malim in bonis stúdiis consúmere, quam in pernóctibus convíviis, in exhauriendis capácibus páteris.*

Antronius: *Ego sane nolo uxorem doctam.*

Magdala: *At ego gaúdeo, quia hábeo maritum tui dissímilem. Nam, quia erudita sum, magis me amat ille, quem ego quoque amo propter eruditionem.*

Antronius: *Frequenter aúdio dictum, quod fémina sápiens bis stulta est.*

Magdala: *Istuc quidem dicunt homines, qui stulti sunt. Fémina quae vere sapit, non putat se sapientem. Contra illa, quae putat se sapientem, et non sapit, ea demum bis stulta est. Quid sentis de Maria Vírgine? De Paula et Eustóchio? Nonne legebant sacros libros?*

Antronius: *Verum istum nunc rarum est.*

Magdala: *Sic olim rara avis fuit abbas indoctus; nunc nihil est vulgátius. Olim príncipes et Caésares non minus eruditi quam potentes erant. Neque adeo rara est fémina docta, ut tu putas; sunt non paucae mulíeres adprime nóbiles, quae cum quovis viro possunt conténdere. Cavete ígitur! praesidébimus in scholis theologicis; orábimus in templis!*

Reading Vocabulary

abbas, abbat– (masculine)	abbot
adeo	so
adimo, adímere	take away
adprime	thoroughly
advenio, –ire	arrive
bis	twice
Caesar, Caésar– (masculine)	Caesar
capax, capác– (adjective)	large, capacious
cáveo, cavere	beware
consultor, –tor (masculine)	adviser
consumo, consúmere	consume
contra (adverb)	on the other hand
convénio, –ire	suit
convívium	party
quotídie	every day
cum	with
de	concerning, about
decorus, –a, –um	appropriate
demum	finally
dictus, –a, –um	said
disco, –ere	learn
doctus, –a, –um	learned
Eustóchium	Eustochium
exhauriendus, –a, –um	drinking
facundus, –a, –um	eloquent

Reading Vocabulary

fero, ferre	endure, put up with
fidus, −a, −um	faithful
Gállice	French; in French
gaúdeo, gaudere	rejoice
homo, homin− (masculine)	man, person
ia, ea, id	this, that
ille	he
indecorus, −a, −um	inappropriate
indoctus, −a, −um	ignorant
istuc	that
istum	that
legebant	did read
magis	more
malim	I would like
manus (feminine) (IV)	hand
maritus	husband
máxime	quite, yes
me	me
minus	less
mórica	more
multum	a lot
natus, −a, −um	born
néscio, −ire	not know
nihil	nothing
nolo, nolle	not wish
non	not
olim	once, formerly
orábimus	we will preach
pátera	cup
pauci, −ae, −a	few
pernox, −noct− (adjective)	nocturnal
praesídeo, praesidere	preside
princeps, princip− (masculine)	prince
quam	than
quantulumcumque	the little that …

continues

Reading Vocabulary   (continued)

quoque	also
quovis	any
sane	indeed
sápiens, sapient– (adjective)	wise
sápio, –ere	be wise
se	himself
sic	thus
stultus, –a, –um	stupid
tu	you
tui	you
ut	that, in order that; as
uxor, uxor– (feminine)	wife
vere	truly
verum	but
vester, –ra, –rum	your
vulgátius	more common

QUIZ

Choose the form in parentheses that best completes the sentence, and translate.

1. *Fero libros, non fero (Latinum/Latinos).*

2. *Quapropter? (Quid/quia) non cónvenit féminis.*

3. *(Nonne, num) decorum est, si fémina discit Gállice?*

4. *Ego nolo uxorem (doctum/doctam).*

5. *Fémina (quam/quae) vere sapit, non putat se sapientem.*

6. *Neque adeo rara est fémina docta, ut tu (putas/putat).*

7. *Sunt in Itália non (paucae/pauca) mulíeres adprime nóbiles, quae cum quovis viro (possum/possunt) conténdere.*

HOUR 7

The Future and Imperfect Tenses

So far, you have learned how to use verbs describing action in the present time.

INTRODUCTORY READING

For the sake of illustration, look at the following snippet adapted from the *Gesta Romanorum* (see Hour 3).

A DIFFICULT CHOICE

*Imperator ait: "Caríssima fília, antequam fílium meum habúeris in maritum, te **probabo** per unum actum." Intérea **producebat** tres cóphinos. Primus **erat** de auro puríssimo et lapídibus pretiosis. Et erat talis superscríptio super cóphinum: "Qui me apériet, in me **invéniet** quod méruit." Et totus cóphinus erat plenus óssibus mortuorum.*

Translation:

The emperor said, "Dear daughter, before you have my son as (your) husband, **I will test** you through one action." Meanwhile, he **brought out** three caskets. The first **was** of the purest gold and precious stones. And such was the inscription over the jar: "Whoever **will open** me, will find in me what he deserves." And the whole jar was full of the bones of the dead.

In the story, you notice that some verbs indicate what will happen in the future (such as *probabo,* "I will test"; *invéniet,* "he will find"). The basic narrative, however, refers to actions in the past (such as *producebat,* "he brought out"; *erat*, "was"). Thus, Latin verbs are marked not only for person and number, to tell us who performs the action, but also for *tense*, to give us a time frame.

TENSE

The grammatical term *tense* comes from the Latin word *tempus* (time). In fact, however, tense involves more than the time of a verb. We can see this by comparing the following sentences:

- I **walked** to school.
- I **was walking** to school.
- I **used to walk** to school.

In all three sentences, the time of the action "walked" is past. However, there is a difference in the way we look at the action.

- In the first sentence, we are looking at it simply as something that *happened* in the past.
- In the second, we are looking at the action more specifically as *on-going* or *progressing* in the past.
- In the third example, we are looking at the action as *repeated* or *habitual* in the past.

These three different ways of looking at the verb are called *aspects*. Thus, tense is a combination of time and aspect. English grammarians describe the previous forms as follows.

Past Tense

	Tense =	
	Time +	*Aspect*
I walked	past	simple
I was walking	past	progressive
I used to walk	past	habitual

Differences of aspect can also be seen in verbs relating to present and future time.

Present and Future Tenses

	Tense =	
	Time +	*Aspect*
I walk	present	simple
I am walking	present	progressive
I will walk	future	simple
I will be walking	future	progressive

TASK 1: IDENTIFYING TIME AND ASPECT

In the following story, identify the time (present, past, or future) and aspect (simple, progressive, or habitual) of each of the verbs.

THE BATTLE OF THE HORATII AND THE CURII

In ancient times, the Romans **used to fight** with the neighboring Albans. They **made** a pact, as follows: "Two teams of three brothers will fight for each side. The winners **will decide** the outcome of the war." At the signal, the Roman brothers (named Horatii) joined battle with the Alban champions (the Curatii). The Curatii **killed** two of the Horatii and received wounds themselves. The remaining Roman brother, however, survived unharmed. When he saw that the Curatii **were coming** to kill him, he fled. For he thought, "My enemies **are running** slowly, because they are tired. If I keep running, they **will** soon **be falling** over with exhaustion." And so he kept running, while they followed. Soon they grew tired. The surviving Horatius **turned** and killed them, one by one.

LATIN TENSES

Ordinarily, languages do not strictly separate every possible combination of time and aspect. English, for example, regularly uses the simple form to talk about habitual action in the present:

- I **walk** around the block every day.

The Romans also worked with a somewhat simplified tense system. In this lesson, you will encounter three Latin tenses. Each of them can be translated in more than one way:

Three Latin Tenses: Present, Imperfect, and Future

Tense	Present	Imperfect	Future
Form	*ámbulo*	*ambulabam*	*ambulabo*
Time	present	past	future
Aspect	simple	progressive	simple
	I walk	I was walking	I will walk
	progressive	habitual	progressive
	I am walking	I used to walk	I will be walking.

The key thing to know is that, depending on the context, *ámbulo* can mean either "I walk" or "I am walking." Likewise, *ambulabam* can mean either "I was walking" or "I used to walk."

JUST A MINUTE

English often uses the simple past (I walked) when referring to progressive or habitual actions. These ordinarily will be in the imperfect tense in Latin. For example, "**I walked** to school every day" is equivalent to *Cotídie ad scholam ambulabam* (literally, "I used to walk to school every day").

FORMS OF THE IMPERFECT TENSE

As we have seen, Latin-speakers use the imperfect tense (Latin *tempus imperfectum*) to refer to progressive or habitual action in the past. Thus, the word *ambulabam* means "I was walking," "I used to walk," or simply "I walked" in a habitual sense. The Latin form is marked by an inserted syllable (technically called an *infix*), *ba*, which appears between the stem and the person/number endings:

The Imperfect Tense

Singular	Plural
ambula-ba-m	*ambula-ba-mus*
ambula-ba-s	*ambula-ba-tis*
ambula-ba-t	*ambula-ba-nt*

FYI The first person singular ending *–o* changes to *–m* after the *ba* infix.

Task 2: Using the Imperfect

Using the previous table, how would you say the following?

1. he was walking
2. y'all walked
3. I walked
4. we were walking
5. they used to walk
6. you used to walk

Task 3: Translating the Imperfect

Translate the following forms.

1. *ambulabatis*
2. *ambulabam*
3. *ambulabamus*
4. *ambulabat*
5. *ambulabant*
6. *ambulabas*

The Imperfect Tense Throughout the Conjugations

Ámbulo is a verb of the first conjugation, so the *ba* infix is added to a stem ending in the vowel *a*. The other conjugations build the imperfect tense on an *–e* stem, as the following table shows:

The Imperfect Tense in the Four Conjugations

I	II	III	IV
walk	*teach*	*send*	*hear*
Singular			
ambula-bam	*doce-bam*	*mitte-bam*	*audie-bam*
ambula-bas	*doce-bas*	*mitte-bas*	*audie-bas*
ambula-bat	*doce-bat*	*mitte-bat*	*audie-bat*

continues

The Imperfect Tense in the Four Conjugations (continued)

I	II	III	IV
walk	teach	send	hear
Plural			
ambula-bamus	doce-bamus	mitte-bamus	audie-bamus
ambula-batis	doce-batis	mitte-batis	audie-batis
ambula-bant	doce-bant	mitte-bant	audie-bant

Third-conjugation –io verbs have the same stem as the fourth conjugation: *capie-bam, capie-bas,* and so on.

TIME SAVER

The quickest way to familiarize yourself with the imperfect tense is to memorize the infix and endings together, as follows: *bam, bas, bat, bamus, batis, bant.*

TASK 4: USING THE IMPERFECT II

Using the previous tables, how would you say the following?

1. I was teaching
2. we taught
3. y'all used to teach
4. you sent
5. she was sending
6. they kept sending
7. they were hearing
8. I heard
9. we used to hear

TASK 5: TRANSLATING THE IMPERFECT II

Translate the following verbs.

1. *docebamus*
2. *docebas*
3. *docebant*
4. *mittebam*
5. *mittebatis*

6. *mittebat*

7. *audiebas*

8. *audiebat*

9. *audiebatis*

FORMS OF THE FUTURE TENSE

In Latin, future action that is viewed as simple or habitual (I will walk) or progressive (I will be walking) is conjugated in the future tense (*tempus futurum*).

As it happens, Latin inherited two different ways of forming this tense. One way is employed for verbs in the first and second conjugations; the other is used for third- and fourth-conjugation verbs.

THE FUTURE TENSE: FIRST AND SECOND CONJUGATIONS

Verbs from these conjugations use an infix, similar to that of the imperfect tense:

The Future Tense in the First Two Conjugations

I	II
walk	**teach**
Singular	
ambula-b-o	*doce-b-o*
ambula-bi-s	*doce-bi-s*
ambula-bi-t	*doce-bi-t*
Plural	
ambulá-bi-mus	*docé-bi-mus*
ambulá-bi-tis	*docé-bi-tis*
ambula-b-unt	*doce-b-unt*

FYI The infix for the future tense is *bi*. The *i* drops out before the ending –o and changes to a *u* before the ending –nt.

PROCEED WITH CAUTION

Be careful not to confuse future forms having the infix *bi* with imperfect forms, which end in *ba*. To avoid confusion, it will help to memorize the future infix with its endings, as you did the imperfect: *bo, bis, bit, bimus, bitis, bunt*.

TASK 6: WORKING WITH THE FUTURE

How would you say the following?

1. I will walk
2. you will walk
3. they will walk
4. she will teach
5. we will teach
6. y'all will teach

THE FUTURE TENSE: THIRD AND FOURTH CONJUGATIONS

These conjugations form the future tense by inserting the vowel *e* between stem and endings. (In the first person singular, however, the inserted vowel is *a*.)

The Future Tense in the Third and Fourth Conjugations

III	*III –io*	*IV*
send	*do*	*hear*
Singular		
mitt-a-m	*faci-a-m*	*aúdi-a-m*
mitt-e-s	*faci-e-s*	*aúdi-e-s*
mitt-e-t	*faci-e-t*	*aúdi-e-t*
Plural		
mitt-e-mus	*faci-e-mus*	*audi-e-mus*
mitt-e-tis	*faci-e-tis*	*audi-e-tis*
mitt-e-nt	*faci-e-nt*	*aúdi-e-nt*

TIME SAVER

The infix of *a/e* is added directly to the root of regular third conjugation verbs, which, strictly speaking, have no stem vowel. In the case of third –*io* and fourth-conjugation verbs, it is added to the *i* stem.

TASK 7: WORKING WITH THE FUTURE II

How would you say the following?

1. I will send
2. we will send

3. they will send

4. y'all will send

5. he will hear

6. you will hear

7. I will hear

8. they will hear

PROCEED WITH CAUTION

It is easy to confuse the future tense of third conjugation verbs with the present tense of second conjugation verbs because both have an –e on the stem: *iubet* (he/she orders), *mittet* (he/she will send).

TASK 8: CONVERTING TENSES

Turn the following present-tense forms into the future tense. Remember that the form you choose will depend on the conjugation of the verb in question.

1. *ámbulat*

2. *aúdio*

3. *amo*

4. *mittit*

5. *ducunt*

6. *iubetis*

7. *facit*

8. *cápimus*

9. *véniunt*

10. *docet*

11. *iubes*

12. *capis*

IRREGULAR VERBS IN THE IMPERFECT AND FUTURE TENSES

The verb *sum* and its derivatives have irregular forms in the imperfect and future tenses.

The Irregular Verb Sum in the Imperfect and Future Tenses

Imperfect	Future
Singular	
eram (I was)	*ero* (I will be)
eras	*eris*
erat	*erit*
Plural	
eramus	*érimus*
eratis	*éritis*
erant	*erunt*

Note that both tenses are built on the root *er–,* which is related to the *es–* in *es, est,* and *estis.* In the imperfect, the stem vowel is *a* (analagous to *ba*); in the future, the endings are added to an *i* stem (analogous to *bi*). The *i* drops out before *o* and changes to *u* before *nt.*

Task 9: Converting Tenses II

Convert the following forms into the imperfect and future tenses, and translate the new forms.

1. *est*
2. *estis*
3. *sunt*
4. *sum*
5. *sumus*
6. *es*

The same forms appear in verbs derived from *sum,* as in *póteram* (I was able) and *próderam* (I was useful).

Task 10: Translation

Translate the following forms:

1. *potestis*
2. *proderatis*

3. *póteras*

4. *pródero*

5. *potérimus*

6. *próderunt*

7. *possunt*

8. *prosum*

ESSENTIAL VOCABULARY

The following common words should be committed to memory.

Essential Vocabulary

Latin	Meaning	Related Word
Nouns		
bellum	war	belligerent
fília	daughter	filial
fílius	son	
navis, nav– (feminine)	ship	naval
pars, part– (feminine)	part	
vita	life	vital
vox, voc– (feminine)	voice	vocal
Verbs		
apério, –ire	open	aperture
clamo, –are	shout	clamorous
cógito, –are	think	excogitate
do, dare	give	data
probo, –are	test	probation
Adjectives		
altus, –a, –um	high, deep	altitude
iustus, –a, –um	just	
talis, –e	like this, such	
totus, –a, –um	whole	total

continues

Essential Vocabulary (continued)

Latin	Meaning	Related Word
Adverbs		
hic	here	
ídeo	thus, so	
numquam	never	
satis	enough	satisfy
tamen	nevertheless	
tantum	only	
tunc	then	
Prepositions		
contra (+ accusative)	against	contradict
de (+ ablative)	(down) from, made of	
super (+ accusative or ablative)	over	superman
Conjunction		
ántequam	before	

RECOGNITION VOCABULARY

Go through this list once or twice, and then look for these words in the Reading Exercise.

Recognition Vocabulary

Latin	Meaning	Related Word
adversárius	adversary	
cópulo, –are	join	copulate
devasto, –are	devastate	
fama	reputation	fame
gemma	gem	
ignoro, –are	not know	ignorant
maritus	husband	marital
matrimónium	marriage	matrimony

Latin	Meaning	Related Word
natura	nature	
pax, pac– (feminine)	peace	pacify
perpétuus, –a, –um	lasting	perpetual
pretiosus, –a, –um	precious	
produco, –ere	bring out	produce
regno, –are	reign	
secundus, –a, –um	second	
primus	first	prime
signum	sign	
scriptura	writing	Scripture
prudenter	prudently	
terra	earth, land	terrestrial
unicus, –a, –um	only, one	unique

SUMMARY

In this hour, you have learned how to form the imperfect and future tenses. Now you are ready to read a story illustrating how love, if combined with wisdom, *vincit omnia*.

READING EXERCISE

The following story is taken from the *Gesta Romanorum*, a medieval collection of stories, which you learned about in Hour 3.

THE THREE CASKETS

> *Honórius regnabat, dives valde, qui unicum fílium habebat quem multum diligebat. Fama imperatoris per mundum volabat, quod in ómnibus probus erat et iustus. Tamen contra unum regem bellum gerebat et eum devastabat. Rex tandem cogitabat: "Tantum unicam fíliam hábeo et adversárius meus unicum fílium. Si áliquo modo fíliam meam pótero cum fílio eius in matrimónium copulare, pacem perpétuam obtinebo." Misit fíliam suam ad imperatorem in nave cum thesauro et milítibus quinque, cum ancillis.*

Imperator, cum eam vidit, ait: "Caríssima fília, ántequam fílium meum habebis in maritum, te probabo per unum actum." Dum haec dicebat, producebat tres cóphinos. Primus erat de auro puríssimo et lapídibus pretiosis. Et erat talis superscríptio super cóphinum: "Qui me apériet, in me invéniet quod méruit." Et totus cóphinus erat plenus óssibus mortuorum. Secundus erat de argento puríssimo, et de gemmis ex omni parte, qui talem superscríptionem habebat: "Qui me éliget, in me invéniet quod natura dat." Iste cóphinus terra plenus erat. Tértius cóphinus erat de plumbo habens superscriptionem talem: "Pótius éligo hic esse et requiéscere quam in thesauris regis permanere." In cóphino isto erant tres ánuli pretiosi.

Tunc ait imperator: "Caríssima, hic sunt tres cóphini; élige quemcumque vis; et si bene éliges, fílium meum in maritum obtinebis." Illa vero tres cophinos íntime inspexit et ait in corde suo: "Deus, qui ómnia vides, da mihi grátiam sic eligendi ut non defíciam illum, pro quo multum laboravi." Quae primum cóphinum tétigit et scripturam legit: "Qui me ...." Illa cogitabat: "Cóphinus extérius est pretiosus, sed quid intérius láteat, pénitus ignoro, ídeo eum elígere nolo." Deinde secundum legit. Quae ait: "Numquam natura dat quod fília patris mei débeat núbere fílio imperatoris. Et ídeo ...." Tértium cóphinum legit dicens, "Mélius est mihi cum fílio regis requiéscere quam in thesauris patris mei." Et alta voce clamabat: "Istum cóphinum tértium éligo." Imperator ait: "O bona puella, satis prudenter éligis. In isto cóphino sunt tres ánuli mei pretiosi; unus pro me, unus pro fílio, tértius pro te in signum desponsationis." Statim núptias celebravit, et trádidit ei fílium suum, et sic in pace vitam finierunt.

Reading Vocabulary

actum	act, action
ait	said
aliquo	some
ancilla	handmaiden
ánulus	ring
argentum	silver
aurum	gold
caríssimus, –a, –um	dearest
celebravit	celebrated
cóphinus	casket

cor, cord (neuter)	heart
de	from, of
débeat	ought, must
defício, defícere	fail
desponsationis	of engagement
det	may (God) grant
dicens	saying
díligo, dilígere	love
dives, dívit[s] (adjective)	rich
ei	to him, to her
eius	his, her, its
eligendi	of choosing
éligo, elígere	choose
eum	him, it
extérius	outside
finierunt	finished
gero, gérere	wage (a war)
grátia	grace, favor
habens	having
Honórius	Honorius
illa	she
illum	him, the man
imperator, imperator– (masculine)	emperor
imperatoris	emperor's
inspexit	inspected
intérius	inside
íntime	closely
iste, ista, istud	this
laboravi	I have labored
lapis, lápid– (masculine)	stone
láteat	lies hidden
legit	read (past tense)

continues

Reading Vocabulary   (continued)

me	me
mei	my
mélius	better
méruit	deserves
mihi	(to, for) me
misit	sent
modo	(in) … way
mórtuus, –a, –um	dead
multum	a lot
nolo, nolle	not want
nubo, núbere	marry
núptiae	wedding
obtíneo, obtinere	obtain
os, oss– (neuter)	bone
patris	of father
pénitus	completely, at all
permáneo, permanere	remain
plenus, –a, –um	filled
plumbum	lead (the metal)
pótius	rather
probus, –a, –um	upright
puríssimus, –a, –um	purest
quemcumque	whichever
quinque	five
regis	of the king
requiesco, requiéscere	rest
sic	so, thus
statim	immediately
superscríptio, –ionis (feminine)	inscription
suus, –a, –um	his, her
te	you
tértius, –a, –um	third

tétigit	touched
thesaurus	treasure
trádidit	handed over
tres	three
ut	that, so that
vero	then, however
volo, volare	spread, fly

Quiz

A

Identify the Latin tense (present, imperfect, or future) of the following verbs and translate.

1. *clamabant*
2. *habent*
3. *áperis*
4. *póterat*
5. *probabit*
6. *dicet*
7. *cógitant*
8. *veniemus*

B

Choose the form in parentheses that best completes the sentence, and translate.

1. *Honórius unicum fílium (habebat/habebit).*
2. *Fama imperatoris per (mundus/mundum) volabat, quod in ómnibus probus (est/erat/erit) et iustus.*
3. *Misit fíliam suam ad imperatorem in (navem/nave) cum (thesaurum/thesauro).*
4. *Primus cóphinus erat de auro puríssimo et lapídibus (pretiosos/ pretiosis).*

QUIZ

5. *"(Qui/Quem) me apériet, in me invéniet quod méruit."*

6. *Secundus habebat (talis/talem) superscriptionem.*

7. *Pótius éligo hic esse quam in thesauris regis (permáneo/permanere).*

8. *In (cóphinum/cóphino) sunt tres (ánulus/ánuli).*

HOUR 8
The Genitive Case

CHAPTER SUMMARY

LESSON PLAN:

In this hour you will learn about ...

- Another case, called the *genitive* case
- The genitive and how it covers various relationships expressed in English by the preposition "of"

So far, you have learned how to recognize the function of a noun or pronoun by its case. The subject or complement of a clause or sentence, for example, falls in the nominative case; the direct object is in the accusative case; nouns that come after stated or implied prepositions fall into either the accusative or the ablative case.

INTRODUCTORY READING

Look for the genitive case in this famous hymn to the Virgin Mary:

HAIL, STAR OF THE SEA

> Ave **maris** stella,
> **Dei** mater alma,
> Atque semper virgo
> Felix **caeli** porta.

> Sumens illud "ave"
> **Gabrielis** ore,
> funda nos in pace,
> mutans **Evae** nomen.

Hail star **of the sea,**
Kindly mother **of God,**
And always a virgin,
The joyful gate **of heaven.**

Receiving that "Hail"
From the mouth **of Gabriel,**
Establish us in peace,
Changing **Eve's** name.

The second stanza refers to a medieval pun, whereby the name *Eva* spelled backwards is the *Ave* in *Ave Maria* (Hail Mary).

Notice that in several places, a single word in Latin is translated "of …," or occasionally "…'s." Examples are *maris*, "of the sea"; *caeli*, "of heaven"; and *Evae*, "Eve's." These words are all in the genitive case.

FORMS OF THE GENITIVE CASE

The genitive case is traditionally given in the second position of declension tables. Study the following.

The Genitive and Other Cases Through the Five Declensions

	I	*II*	*III*
	girl	*master*	*king*
Singular			
Nominative	*puell-a*	*dómin-us*	*rex*
Genitive	***puell-ae***	***dómin-i***	***reg-is***
Accusative	*puell-am*	*dómin-um*	*reg-em*
Ablative	*puell-a*	*dómin-o*	*reg-e*
Plural			
Nominative	*puell-ae*	*dómin-i*	*reg-es*
Genitive	***puell-arum***	***domin-orum***	***reg-um***
Accusative	*puell-as*	*dómin-os*	*reg-es*
Ablative	*puell-is*	*dómin-is*	*rég-ibus*

	IV	*V*
	chariot	*thing*
Singular		
Nominative	*curr-us*	*r-es*
Genitive	***curr-us***	***r-ei***
Accusative	*curr-um*	*r-em*
Ablative	*curr-u*	*r-e*

	IV	V
	chariot	*thing*
Plural		
Nominative	*curr-us*	*r-es*
Genitive	***cúrr-uum***	***r-erum***
Accusative	*curr-us*	*r-es*
Ablative	*cúrr-ibus*	*r-ebus*

Note that the genitive plural always ends in *–um*. In the first, second, and fifth declensions, an *r* is added: *–arum*, *–orum*, *–erum*. The genitive singular is a trickier business. It may help, though, to remember two things:

- For masculine and feminine nouns of the first, second, and fourth declensions, the genitive singular is identical to the nominative plural.
- In the third and fourth declension, the endings *–is* and *–us* are reminiscent of the *'s* ending on English possessive forms.

Neuter nouns in the second, third and fourth declensions usually have the same genitive endings as masculine nouns.

Neuter Nouns in the Second and Third Declension

	II	III	IV
	stone	*name*	*horn*
Singular			
Nominative	*sax-um*	*nomen*	*corn-u*
Genitive	***sax-i***	***nómin-is***	***corn-us***
Accusative	*sax-um*	*nomen*	*corn-u*
Ablative	*sax-o*	*nómin-e*	*corn-u*
Plural			
Nominative	*sax-a*	*nómin-a*	*córn-ua*
Genitive	***sax-orum***	***nómin-um***	***córn-uum***
Accusative	*sax-a*	*nómin-a*	*córn-ua*
Ablative	*sax-is*	*nomín-ibus*	*córn-ibus*

TASK 1: WORKING WITH THE GENITIVE CASE

Give the genitive singular and plural of the following nouns.

1. *fémina*

2. *equus*

3. *perículum*

4. *draco, dracon–* (masculine)

5. *manus* (IV)

6. *spes*

7. *genus, gener–* (neuter)

8. *miles, mílit–*

"I-STEM" NOUNS: ALL GENDERS

Third declension i-stem nouns in all genders present a special case. In the genitive plural, the usual ending *–um* becomes *–ium*.

I-Stem Nouns

	Masculine/Feminine	*Neuter*
	city	*sea*
Singular		
Nominative	*urbs*	*mare*
Genitive	**urb-is**	**mar-is**
Accusative	*urb-em*	*mare*
Ablative	*urb-e*	*mar-i*
Plural		
Nominative	*urb-es*	*már-ia*
Genitive	**úrb-ium**	**már-ium**
Accusative	*urb-es*	*már-ia*
Ablative	*úrb-ibus*	*már-ibus*

TASK 2: WORKING WITH I-STEM NOUNS IN THE GENITIVE

The following are i-stem nouns. Give the genitive singular and plural of each.

1. *finis, fin–*

2. *ánimal, animal–*

3. *civis, civ–*

PROCEED WITH CAUTION

The forms of the genitive case often overlap other forms. The context of the sentence will usually eliminate any confusion. Consider the following sentence:

- **Puellae** *libros in mensa pono:* I put the **girl's** books on the table.

While *puellae* by itself could be identified either as genitive singular or nominative plural, you know at once that it cannot be the nominative subject of *pono* (I put).

TASK 3: IDENTIFYING CASE AND NUMBER

Cover up the previous charts, and for each of the following nouns, identify the case and number. Ambiguous forms are marked with the number of possible identifications (2).

1. *equi* (2)

2. *rei*

3. *puellas*

4. *puellarum*

5. *dóminum*

6. *re*

7. *márium*

8. *regis*

9. *fília* (2)

10. *maris*

11. *genus* (2)

12. *manus* (4)

13. *draconem*

14. *génera* (2)

THE GENITIVE CASE IN INTERROGATIVE AND RELATIVE PRONOUNS AND ADJECTIVES

The genitive case forms of the pronoun/adjective *qui* can be seen on the following table.

The Interrogative Adjective *Qui*

	Masculine	Feminine	Neuter
Singular			
Nominative	*qui*	*quae*	*quod*
Genitive	***cuius***	***cuius***	***cuius***
Accusative	*quem*	*quam*	*quod*
Ablative	*quo*	*qua*	*quo*
Plural			
Nominative	*qui*	*quae*	*quae*
Genitive	***quorum***	***quarum***	***quorum***
Accusative	*quos*	*quas*	*quae*
Ablative	*quibus*	*quibus*	*quibus*

Cuius is also the genitive singular of the interrogative pronouns *quis* and *quid.*

Notice that the form *cuius* relates back to antecedents of all genders, but that the plural forms of *quorum, quarum,* and *quorum* indicate that the antecedent is masculine, feminine, or neuter:

- *Rex adducebat tres cóphinos,* **quorum** *inscriptiones tales erant:* The king brought out three caskets, **whose** inscriptions were as follows.
- *Rex tres fílias habebat,* **quarum** *forma pulchra erat:* The king had three daughters, **whose** appearance was beautiful.

JUST A MINUTE

Note that the form *cuius* resembles its English cognate, "whose." The parliamentary term "quorum" comes from an old formula for appointment to a commission: *quorum te unum esse vélimus* (of whom we wish you to be one). When a sufficient number of appointees were present, the commission had a "quorum."

ADJECTIVES IN THE GENITIVE CASE

Remember that adjectives must agree with the nouns or pronouns they describe in gender, number, and case. This means that all adjectives have a special set of endings to match nouns in the genitive case:

- *laeti regis:* of a happy king
- *tristis puellae:* of a sad girl

The endings for adjectives are taken, as usual, from the noun tables that you have already learned.

Adjectives in the Genitive Case

(First/Second Declension Adjectives)

	Masculine	Feminine	Neuter
Singular			
Nominative	magn-us	magn-a	magn-um
Genitive	**magn-i**	**magn-ae**	**magn-i**
Accusative	magn-um	magn-am	magn-um
Ablative	magn-o	magn-a	magn-o
Plural			
Nominative	magn-i	magn-ae	magn-a
Genitive	**magn-orum**	**magn-arum**	**magn-orum**
Accusative	magn-os	magn-as	magn-a
Ablative	magn-is	magn-is	magn-is

(Third Declension Adjectives)

	Masculine/Feminine	Neuter
Singular		
Nominative	omn-is	omn-e
Genitive	**omn-is**	**omn-is**
Accusative	omn-em	omn-e
Ablative	omn-i	omn-i
Plural		
Nominative	omn-es	ómn-ia
Genitive	**ómn-ium**	**ómn-ium**
Accusative	omn-es	ómn-ia
Ablative	ómn-ibus	ómn-ibus

TIME SAVER

Third declension adjectives follow the table for "i-stems." Thus, the genitive plural form for all genders –ium.

TASK 4: NOUN-ADJECTIVE PAIRINGS

Complete the following noun-adjective pairings in the genitive case. Remember that there must be agreement also in gender and number.

1. *féminae (omnis)*

2. *regis (magnus)*

3. *rerum (omnis)*

4. *cúrruum (magnus)*

5. *diei (omnis)*

6. *dominorum (fortis)*

USES OF THE GENITIVE CASE

The genitive case is often used to indicate *possession:*

- *nomen **Evae*** (Eve's name, the name of Eve)
- ***Gabrielis** ore* (Gabriel's mouth, the mouth of Gabriel)

Note that in English, possession can be indicated either by attaching *'s* (or in the plural, *s'*) to a noun, or by putting it in a prepositional phrase after "of."

TASK 5: TRANSLATING THE GENITIVE CASE

Translate the following phrases using both English constructions for possession.

1. *equus Geórgii*

2. *fília regis*

3. *mílites Alexandri*

4. *libri féminae*

5. *lingua Romanorum*

6. *dentes hippopotamorum* (*dentes* means "teeth")

GENITIVES IN OTHER RELATIONSHIPS

The genitive also covers some other relationships, which can be expressed only with the preposition "of." Consider the following:

- *nonnulli Romanorum:* some of the Romans
- *timor Romanorum:* fear of the Romans
- *vir magnae humanitatis:* a man of great kindness

These phrases show that the genitive is used to express:

1. Part/whole relationships ("some **of** the Romans")
2. Situations where one noun is the object of another ("fear **of** the Romans")
3. Qualities that attach to another noun ("a man of …")

TIME SAVER

You will never go far wrong if you think of the genitive simply as the "of" case.

Task 6: More Fun with the Genitive

Change the words in parentheses into the genitive case; then translate.

1. *multi (mílites)*
2. *timor (hippopótami)*
3. *fémina (magna sapiéntia)* (*sapiéntia* means wisdom)

Dictionary Entry for Nouns

Ancient grammarians determined that the genitive singular form of every noun provides two important pieces of information:

- The declension to which the noun belongs
- The stem to which most case endings are added

For this reason, it is still customary in Latin dictionaries to list each noun as follows.

Dictionary Entries for Nouns

Entry	Meaning
puella, puellae (feminine)	girl
dóminus, dómini (masculine)	lord
rex, regis (masculine)	king
currus, currus (masculine)	chariot
res, rei (feminine)	thing

The fact that *puella,* for example, has the genitive singular form *puellae* identifies it as a first-declension noun. In fact, each of the five declensions has a unique genitive singular form, according to the following table.

The Genitive Singular Through the Five Declensions

I	II	III	IV	V
–ae	–i	–is	–us	–ei

For each noun, you can also discover the stem for most cases by dropping the genitive singular ending. Thus, the stem of *rex* is *reg–,* derived from *regis.* Likewise, the entry *miles, militis* indicates that the stem is *milit–.*

If the stem of a noun is easily guessed from the nominative case form, dictionaries will sometimes save ink by printing only the ending of the genitive form:

- *puella, –ae,* (feminine): the full form is *puell-ae*
- *dóminus, –i,* (masculine): the full form is *domin-i*

For each of these words, the stem can be guessed by dropping the nominative singular ending (*puell-a, domin-us*).

From now on, your vocabulary lists will present nouns in the traditional manner.

Task 7: Working with Dictionary Entries

For each noun given here, identify the declension to which it belongs and its stem.

1. *aquila, –ae* (feminine): eagle
2. *celéritas, celeritatis* (feminine): speed
3. *cibus, –i* (masculine): food
4. *scelus, scéleris* (neuter): crime
5. *fácies, facíei* (feminine): face
6. *latratus, –us* (masculine): barking

More on Third Declension Adjectives: One-Termination Forms

We have seen that some Latin adjectives have endings in common with i-stem nouns of the third declension. They usually appear in dictionaries as follows:

- *omnis, omne:* every, all
- *fortis, forte:* brave

The dictionary lists the nominative singular form in the masculine and feminine genders (*omnis*) and the neuter gender (*omne*). These are called "two-termination" adjectives because they are entered under these two forms.

A few adjectives, however, have only one termination; in other words, they have the same nominative singular form in all three genders. An example is *ingens* (huge). Study the following table.

One-Termination Adjectives: *Ingens*

	Masculine/Feminine	Neuter
Singular		
Nominative	*ingens*	*ingens*
Genitive	*ingent-is*	*ingent-is*
Accusative	*ingent-em*	*ingens*
Ablative	*ingent-i*	*ingent-i*
Plural		
Nominative	*ingént-es*	*ingént-ia*
Genitive	*ingént-ium*	*ingént-ium*
Accusative	*ingent-es*	*ingént-ia*
Ablative	*ingént-ibus*	*ingént-ibus*

TIME SAVER

Apart from the form *ingens*, the table follows the analogy of two-termination adjectives such as *omnis*.

Because these adjectives have an unchanging and unpredictable nominative singular form, the stem used in forming the cases is not evident. For this reason, dictionaries usually list these adjectives in the same way as nouns, with the genitive singular form given after the nominative:

- *ingens, ingentis* (adjective): huge
- *audax, audacis* (adjective): bold

Just drop the *–is* of the genitive singular, and you have the stem.

TASK 8: WORKING WITH ONE-TERMINATION ADJECTIVES

On the basis of the dictionary entries given previously, match the adjectives with the nouns given. (Recall that *monstrum* is a neuter noun of the second declension.)

1. *fémina (audax)*
2. *monstrum (ingens)*
3. *feminarum (audax)*
4. *monstris (ingens)*
5. *féminae (audax)*
6. *monstrorum (ingens)*

MORE ON THIRD DECLENSION ADJECTIVES: CONSONANT STEM ADJECTIVES

Another variation on the theme of third declension adjectives is that a few of them do not have i-stem endings. In other words, they have endings identical to those of nouns, such as *rex* and *genus*. An example is *pauper* (poor).

Third Declension Adjectives Without an I-Stem

	Masculine/Feminine	*Neuter*
Singular		
Nominative	*pauper*	*pauper*
Genitive	*paúper-is*	*paúper-is*
Accusative	*paúper-em*	*pauper*
Ablative	*paúper-e*	*paúper-e*
Plural		
Nominative	*paúper-es*	*paúper-a*
Genitive	*paúper-um*	*paúper-um*
Accusative	*paúper-es*	*paúper-a*
Ablative	*paupér-ibus*	*paupér-ibus*

Dictionaries list these adjectives as they do other one-termination adjectives. They will be specially marked in this book.

Task 9: Agreement

Give the form of *pauper* that agrees with the following forms:

1. *puellas*
2. *puellarum*
3. *úrbium*
4. *dómino*
5. *regis*
6. *res* (2)
7. *féminae* (2)
8. *dómini* (2)

Essential Vocabulary

The following common words should be committed to memory.

Essential Vocabulary

Latin	Meaning	Related Word
Nouns		
amicus, –i (masculine)	friend	amicable
caput, cápitis (neuter)	head	capital
domus, –us (feminine)	house	domicile
nox, noctis (feminine)	night	nocturnal
stúdium, –i (neuter)	zeal, study application	study
urbs, urbis (feminine) (genitive plural *úrbium*)	city	urban
Verbs		
accípio, accípere	receive	accept
ait	says, said	
desum, deesse	be lacking	
laudo, –are	praise	laudatory
ostendo, osténdere	show	ostensible
vinco, víncere	conquer	invincible

continues

Essential Vocabulary   (continued)

Latin	Meaning	Related Word
Adjectives		
audax, audacis (adjective)	bold	audacious
ingens, ingentis (adjective)	huge, big	
pauper, paúperis (adjective, consonant stem)	poor	pauper
vetus, véteris (adjective, consonant stem)	old	inveterate
Adverbs		
celériter	quickly	
ibi	there	
inde	then, from there	
ita	thus, in this way	
ítaque	and so	
saepe	often	
tum	then	
Conjunctions		
atque	and	
dum	while	

RECOGNITION VOCABULARY

Recognition Vocabulary

Latin	Meaning	Related Word
asséntio, –ire	agree	assent
ávide	eagerly	avidly
ávidus, –a, –um	eager	avid
canis, canis (common)	dog	canine
clamor, clamoris (masculine)	noise, din	clamor
contínuo, –are	continue	
demens, dementis (adjective)	crazy	demented
dens, dentis (masculine)	tooth	dental
designatus, –a, –um	agreed upon	designated

Latin	Meaning	Related Word
destinatus, –a, –um	destined, intended	destination
elegántia, –ae (feminine)	elegance	
emitto, –ere	let go from	emit
motus, –us (masculine)	motion	
mus, muris (common)	mouse	
óffero, offerre	offer	
prior, prior– (adjective)	first	prior
rústicus, –a, –um	country–, of the country	rustic
spátium, –i (neuter)	space	spatial
suavis, –e	pleasant	suave
trépido, –are	be scared	trepidation
victor, –oris (masculine)	victor	victorious

SUMMARY

In this hour, you have learned how to form and recognize the genitive case and some variations on the declension of third declension adjectives. Now you are ready to work with another very ancient type of story: the fable.

READING EXERCISE

A fable is an allegorical tale that teaches a moral. The genre became popular in Greece with the fables of Aesop (sixth century B.C.), which were translated into Latin verse by the poet Phaedrus (first century A.D.). They played an important part in ancient and modern rhetorical training because they appealed to young people and could easily be expanded into a speech. The following are adapted from an eighteenth-century rhetoric textbook.

THREE FABLES

CORVUS ET VULPES

Corvus raptum de fenestra cáseum comedebat, celsa residens árbore. Hunc videns Vulpes, laudare íncipit pennarum nitorem et decorem cápitis, totiusque córporis elegántiam. "Una," ait, "res deest, nempe vox sonora. Quam si haberet, omnes álites fácile superaret." At corvus demens, cupiebat osténdere quod vocem habebat canoram quidem ac suavem. Ítaque dum se ad canendum cómparat, cáseum emittit rostro, quem celériter dolosa Vulpes ávidis árripit déntibus.

Epimýthium: Qui laudatores libenter audit, fabellam hanc audire debet.

TESTUDO ET ÁQUILA

Testudo certamen conficiendi cuiusdam spátii cum áquila súscipit. Locum proponit et ait, "uter prior ad hunc locum pervéniet die tértio, erit victor." Áquila, contemnens tarditatem testúdinis, provolare íncipit, et saepe desidere, et álias res ágere, denique totam noctem acquiéscere, neque valde mane evolare. At testudo nihil remittit in itínere, dies atque noctes procedit, rectaque contendit ad destinatum locum. Ítaque sedulitate sua ad locum designatum prior ádvenit, et áquilam vincit.

Epimýthium: stúdii et ánimi motus est ad celeritatem efficaciores, quam córporis.

MURES URBANUS ET RUSTICUS

Olim rústicus mus urbanum murem in paúpere áccipit cavo. Ille tamen non vult cibum tenuem, quem offert hospes, cíceres scílicet et avenas. "Cur," inquit, "ita vivis? Nonne vis mecum ad urbem venire, ubi mélius nos habébimus?" Rústicus mus assentit. Inde ambo ad urbem média nocte pergunt, donec ad domum locupletem advéniunt. Multa ibi fércula de magna cena supersunt, in magnis canistris pósita. Ibi urbanus mus amicum locat et dapem continuatum apponit. Ille ávide comedens de mutata sorte gaudet. Súbito tamen ingens clamor éxcutit utrumque: exánimes trépidant et pávidi per totam domum currunt. Pérsonat domus alta latratu canum Molossiorum.

Tum rústicus:

"Haud mihi vita est opus hac," ait "et váleas; me silva, cavusque tutus ab insídiis tenui solábitur ervo."

("I hardly need this kind of life," he said. "Farewell; the forest and my cave, safe from attack, will console me with their meager seeds.")

Reading Vocabulary

acquiesco, acquiéscere	rest
ad	to, for
adhuc	still
advénio, –ire	arrive
ales, álitis (masculine)	bird
ambo	both
ánimus, ánimi (masculine)	mind, spirit
appono, appónere	set
áquila, –ae (feminine)	eagle
arbor, árboris (feminine)	tree
arrípio, arrípere	seize
avena, –ae (feminine)	oat
canendum	singing
canistrum, –i (neuter)	basket
canorus, –a, –um	pleasant
cáseus, –i (masculine)	cheese
cavus, –i (masculine)	cave
celéritas, –tatis (feminine)	speed
celsus, –a, –um	high
cena, –ae (feminine)	dinner
certamen, certáminis (neuter)	contest
cibus, –i (masculine)	food
cicer, cíceris (masculine)	chickpea
cómedo, –esse	eat
cómedens	eating
cómparo, –are	get ready
conficiendi	covering
contemnens, contemnentis (adjective)	holding in contempt
contendo, conténdere	go, march
corvus, corvi (masculine)	crow
cuiusdam	a certain
daps, dapis (feminine)	food, banquet

continues

Reading Vocabulary   (continued)

decor, decoris (masculine)	beauty
dénique	finally
desídeo, desidere	sit, rest
dolosus, –a, –um	sneaky
donec	until
efficácior, –oris (adjective)	more efficacious
epimythium, –i (neuter)	moral
évolo, evolare	fly off
exánimis, –e	out of one's wits
excútio, –ere	shake
fenestra, –ae (feminine)	window
facile	easily
férculum, –i (neuter)	leftover
gaúdeo, gaudere	rejoice
haberet	(if) he had
hospes, hóspitis (masculine)	host
hunc	him; this
ille	he, the other one
inquit	he says
iter, itíneris (neuter)	journey
latratus, –us (masculine)	barking
laudator, laudatoris (masculine)	flatterer
libenter	gladly, willingly
loco, –are	place, seat
locuples, –pletis (adjective)	rich
mane	in the morning, early
mecum	with me
mélius	better
mélius nos habébimus	we will be better off
Molóssius, –a, –um	Molossian
mutatus, –a, –um	changed
nempe	namely
neque	nor
nihil	nothing, not at all
nitor, nitoris (masculine)	shine
nos	us, ourselves
olim	once upon a time

pávidus, –a, –um	scared
penna, pennae (feminine)	wing
pergo, pérgere	continue
persono, –are	echo, ring
pervénio, –ire	arrive, get
pósitus, –a, –um	placed
propono, propónere	propose
propósitus, –a, –um	proposed
próvolo, –are	fly ahead
quam	than
–que	and
raptus, –a, –um	snatched
recta (adverb)	straight
remitto, remíttere	let up
resídeo, residere	sit down again
rostrum, rostri (neuter)	beak
scílicet	namely
se	himself
sedúlitas, –tatis (feminine)	diligence
sonorus, –a, –um	beautiful
sors, sortis (feminine)	fortune
superaret	he would outdo
suus, –a, –um	his
súbito	suddenly
supersum, superesse	be left
suscípio, suscípere	take up
tárditas, tarditatis (feminine)	slowness
ténuis, –e	slight
tértius, –a, –um	third
testudo, testúdinis (masculine)	tortoise
tótius	of the whole …
ubi	where
urbanus, –a, –um	city, of the city
uter	whichever
utrumque	both
vis	you want
vulpes, vulpis (masculine)	wolf
vult	wishes

Quiz

A

Convert the plural forms to the singular, and the singular forms to the plural.

1. *amici véteris*
2. *domus alta*
3. *reges audaces*
4. *fíliae tristes*
5. *nóctibus longis*
6. *mílites bonos*
7. *córpora ingéntia*
8. *urbis óptimae*
9. *die bono*

B

Choose the form that best completes the sentence, and translate.

1. *Corvus raptum de (fenestrae/fenestra) cáseum comedebat.*
2. *Vulpes laudare íncipit (pennarum/pennis) nitorem.*
3. *At corvus demens, cupiebat (ostendit/osténdere) quod vocem (habebat/habebant) canoram.*
4. *Dum se ad canendum cómparat, cáseum emittit (rostrum/rostro).*
5. *Testudo ait, "uter prior ad hunc locum pervéniet die (tértia/tértio), victor (erat/erit)."*
6. *Ítaque (sedulitatis/sedulitate) sua ad locum designatum prior ádvenit.*
7. *Mus (urbanus/urbanum) "Cur," inquit, "ita (vivis/vívitis)? Nonne vis mecum ad (urbem/urbe) venire?"*
8. *Multa ibi fércula de magna cena (superest/supersunt), in magnis canistris pósita.*
9. *(Exánimis/Exánimes) trépidant et (pávidae/pávidi) per (totum/totam) domum currunt.*
10. *Pérsonat domus alta latratu (canem/canum) Molossiorum.*

The Perfect Tense; Adverbs

So far, you have learned to recognize verbs in the present, imperfect, and future tenses. You have also learned that the imperfect tense covers only some aspects of the past—namely, actions or states that are progressive or habitual.

INTRODUCTORY READING

To get started, let's look at a bit of Middle Eastern "wisdom literature," as translated for a Western audience:

A LONG JOURNEY

*Arabs fílium suum **castigavit**, dicens, "Séquere calles, etsi sunt longiores quam sémitae." Ad haec fílius: "Verum est quod **dixisti**. Nam quodam die, dum vesperascebat, ego et sócii mei pergebamus ad urbem, et **vídimus** sémitam quae secundum visum promittebat compéndium. Quam insistentes, ad dexteram et ad sinistram, quanta **fuit** nox, **deerrávimus**, nec ad civitatem **pervénimus**."*

An Arab **scolded** his son, saying: "Follow the highways, even if they are longer than the byways." To this the son (said): "What you **have said** is true. For one day, when it was getting onto evening, my companions and I were going to a city, and we **saw** a path, which, according to its appearance, promised a short trip. But travelling along it, we **wandered** to the left and to the right, as long as the night **lasted,** and we didn't **get** to the city."

In the story, you noticed several verbs that are rendered in English with the *simple* past (*vídimus,* "we saw"; *deerrávimus,* "we wandered"). One verb, however, was rendered in what is called the *present perfect* (*dixisti,* "you have said"). Both of these English tenses are covered by the Latin *perfect* tense.

FORMS OF THE PERFECT TENSE

In many Indo-European languages, simple past forms are recognizable not only by distinctive endings, but also by a change in the verb stem. Consider, for example, the following forms.

Simple English Past Forms

Simple Present	Simple Past
we walk	we walked
we see	we saw

In English, many verbs go into the past tense by adding the suffix *–ed*. Others, however, undergo a change in the vowel of the stem (see, saw).

In Latin, the perfect tense (Latin *tempus perfectum*) is formed by combining a special form of the stem with a set of distinctive endings. For this reason, most perfect forms are easy to pick out. Here, for example, are the perfect tense forms of *ámbulo* (walk).

Latin Perfect Tense Forms

Singular	Plural
ambulav-i	ambuláv-imus
ambulav-isti	ambulav-istis
ambulav-it	ambulav-erunt

Notice that each form of the verb is built on the stem *ambulav–;* to this are added the endings *–i, –isti, –it, –imus, –istis, –erunt.*

TASK 1: WORKING WITH THE PERFECT TENSE

How would you say the following?

1. we walked
2. they walked

3. she walked

4. I walked

5. you walked

6. y'all walked

FORMATION OF THE PERFECT STEM

Most verbs in the first and fourth conjugations follow *ambulo* by adding a *v* to the stem of the present tense.

Forming the Perfect Stem: First and Fourth Conjugations

Present	Perfect
laudat	lauda-v-it
amat	ama-v-it
audit	audi-v-it

Similarly, most second conjugation verbs have a stem ending in *–u.*

Forming the Perfect Stem, Second Conjugation

Present	Perfect
habet	hábu-it
monet	mónu-it

However, there are exceptions.

Forming the Perfect Stem, Exceptions to the Rule

Present	Perfect
dat	ded-it
manet	mans-it
pérvenit	perven-it

Notice the change of accent in *pervenit*. You have now seen the whole range of possible formations of the perfect stem. They are summarized in the following table (present tense forms are given in parentheses).

Possible Formations of the Perfect Stem

Perfect Stem Type	Examples
v/u stem	*amavit (amat), habuit (habet)*
s/x stem	*misit (mittit), dixit (dicit)*
vowel change	*cepit (capit), fecit (facit)*
vowel "lengthening"	*venit (venit), vidit (videt)* (see the following note)
reduplication	*dedit (dat), dídicit (discit)*
no change	*contendit (contendit)*

FYI The phenomenon of vowel lengthening is not indicated in writing, but it was distinctly audible in Classical Latin pronunciation. "Long vowels" were pronounced for an instant longer than "short" ones:

- *pérvenit:* she arrives
- *pervenit:* (originally pronounced *perve-e-nit*): she arrived

In post-Classical pronunciation, vowel length gradually disappeared, but it continued to affect the stress.

Third conjugation verbs are the most unpredictable; they can be found to exemplify all six varieties of the perfect stem.

Forming the Perfect Stem, Third Conjugation Verbs

Present	Perfect
cupit	*cupivit*
dicit	*dixit*
facit	*fecit*
emit (sells)	*emit*
tangit (touches)	*tétigit*
ostendit (shows)	*ostendit*

TASK 2: CONVERTING PRESENT TO PERFECT

Convert the following verbs to the perfect tense, keeping the same person and number. The perfect stem is given in parentheses.

1. *áperit (apéru–)*
2. *áccipis (accep–)*

3. *das (ded–)*

4. *iubemus (iuss–)*

5. *víncitis (vic–)*

6. *díscimus (didíc–)*

7. *dicunt (dix–)*

8. *curro (cucurr–)*

9. *capit (cep–)*

Dictionary Entry for Verbs

Because the perfect stem is so unpredictable, it is usually given at the begin-ning of the dictionary entry for a Latin verb, as follows:

- *fácio, fácere, **feci***
- *tango, tángere, **tétigi***

The third form, also called the "third principal part," is the first person, sin-gular, perfect tense form (*tetigi*, "I touched"). Occasionally, the principal parts are given in shorthand:

- *amo, **–are, –avi:*** the full forms are *amo, amare, amavi*

PROCEED WITH CAUTION

 It often happens that a perfect form can be recognized by its ending alone. Such is the case, for example, with the forms *fec-isti* and *fec-erunt*. However, the endings *–it* and *–imus* are also found in the present tense of many verbs. Consider, for example, the forms *facit/fecit* and *fácimus/fécimus*. Hence, know-ing the perfect stem of the verb is important.

Here are the three principal parts of all verbs learned so far in the survival vocabulary lists. Read through this list two or three times, paying special attention to perfect stems that seem either unusual or very similar to the pres-ent stem.

V-type

- *ámbulo, –are, –avi* (walk)
- *amo, amare, amavi* (love)
- *aúdio, audire, audivi* (hear)
- *clamo, –are, –avi* (shout)
- *cógito, –are, –avi* (think)

- *cúpio, cúpere, cupivi* (want, wish)
- *hábito, –áre, –avi* (dwell)
- *laudo, –are, –avi* (praise)
- *pugno, –áre, –avi* (fight)
- *puto, –are, –avi* (think, believe)
- *voco, –are, –avi* (call)
- *probo, –are, –avi* (test)
- *scio, scire, scivi (scii)* (know)

U-type:

- *apério, aperire, apérui* (open)
- *débeo, debere, débui* (ought, should)
- *dóceo, docere, dócui* (teach)
- *hábeo, habere, hábui* (have)
- *móneo, monere, mónui* (warn, advise)
- *tímeo, timere, tímui* (fear)

X-type:

- *iúbeo, iubere, iussi* (order)
- *dico, dícere, dixi* (say)

Vowel change:

- *accípio, accípere, accepi* (receive)
- *ago, ágere, egi* (do, act)
- *cápio, cápere, cepi* (catch)
- *fácio, fácere, feci* (do)
- *incípio, incípere, incepi* (begin)

Vowel lengthening:

- *vídeo, –ére, vidi* (see)
- *vinco, –ere, vici* (conquer)
- *vénio, venire, veni* (come)
- *sédeo, sedere, sedi* (sit)

Reduplication:

- *credo, crédere, crédidi* (believe, trust)
- *curro, cúrrere, cucurri* (run)

- *do, dare, dedi* (give)
- *reddo, –ere, réddidi* (give back, render, recite)
- *perdo, pérdere, pérdidi* (lose)

No change:

- *constítuo, constitúere, constítui* (put, establish)
- *ostendo, osténdere, ostendi* (show)

Task 3: Distinguishing the Present and Perfect Tenses

After studying the previous list (and referring back to it, as necessary), indicate whether each of the following verbs is in the present or perfect tense:

1. *cuccurrit*

2. *dicit*

3. *réddidit*

4. *vincit*

5. *dixit*

6. *videt*

7. *hábuit*

8. *fecit*

9. *habet*

10. *amat*

11. *dedit*

12. *vidit*

Perfect of the Verb *esse*

The verb *esse* is conjugated in the perfect tense as a regular verb (like *ambulavi*). The perfect stem is *fu*.

Perfect Conjugation of the Verb *esse*

Singular	Plural
fu-i	*fu-imus*
fu-isti	*fu-istis*
fu-it	*fu-erunt*

Here are the principal parts of other verbs related to *sum*. They all have regular perfect forms.

- *desum, deesse, défui* (be lacking)
- *possum, posse, pótui* (can)
- *prosum, prodesse, prófui* (be useful)

MEANING OF THE PERFECT TENSE

We have seen that the Latin tense system is somewhat simpler than that of English. For example, where English distinguishes between present simple (I walk) and present progressive (I am walking), Latin expresses either idea with the form *ámbulo.*

In the same way, the Latin perfect tense has two possible meanings. Most commonly, it functions as a simple past tense:

- *ambulavi:* I walked
- *dixi:* I said

In some contexts, however, it is used to indicate an action that is viewed as recently completed:

- **Dixi;** *nunc responsum tuum expecto:* **I have** (just) **spoken;** now I am waiting for your answer.

In English grammar, this is described as the present perfective tense. The term *perfective* is related to the Latin *perfectum,* meaning "completed."

TASK 4: TRANSLATING THE PERFECT TENSE

Choose the translation in parentheses that best fits the context.

1. *Olim, Arabs fílium* **vocavit:** Once upon a time, a father (summoned/has summoned) his son.
2. *"Nunc vere* **dixisti,** *pater":* "Now you (spoke/have spoken) truly, Father."
3. *Tum amici* **dixerunt,** *"Totam noctem iam* **deerrávimus."** Then my friends (said/have said), "We already (wandered/have wandered) the entire night."
4. *Deinde domum* **redíimus:** Then we (returned/have returned) home.

FORMING ADVERBS FROM ADJECTIVES

You have already learned a number of Latin adverbs (*bene, diu, numquam, saepe*). A great many more are simply converted adjectives, to which special adverb endings are added. This kind of word-building also occurs in English.

Forming Adverbs from Adjectives

Adjective	Adverb
avid	avidly
happy	happily
brave	bravely
unanimous	unanimously

In these examples, the suffix *–ly* changes a word from an adjective to an adverb. In the same way, Latin uses the suffix *–e* for most adjectives of the first/second declension type:

- *ávidus, –a, –um* becomes *avide,* which means "avidly"
- *laetus, –a, –um* becomes *laete,* which means "happily"

Adjectives of the third declension type are usually converted with the suffix *–(i)ter*:

- *fortis, –e* becomes *fórtiter* (bravely)
- *unánimis, –e* becomes *unanímiter* (unanimously)

Of course, every language has a number of irregular adverbs, which do not quite follow the set pattern:

- "good" becomes "well"
- *bonus, –a, –um* becomes **bene**

These must be learned as you go along.

TASK 5: CONVERTING ADJECTIVES TO ADVERBS

The following adjectives are converted to adverbs in the regular way. Make the conversion, and translate.

1. *iustus, –a, –um* (just)
2. *nóbilis, –e* (noble)
3. *certus, –a, –um* (certain)

4. *aequus, –a, –um* (equal)

5. *rationalis, –e* (rational)

6. *gravis, –e* (grave)

TWO IRREGULAR VERBS

The verbs *eo* (go) and *fero* (carry) are irregular; like *sum,* they do not belong to any of the four conjugations. They are conjugated as follows.

Conjugating *Eo* and *Fero*

Singular	Plural	Singular	Plural
Present			
eo	imus	fero	férimus
is	itis	fers	fertis
it	eunt	fert	ferunt
Imperative			
i!	ite!	fer!	ferte!
Imperfect			
ibam	ibamus	ferebam	ferebamus
ibas	ibatis	ferebas	ferebatis
ibat	ibant	ferebat	ferebant
Future			
ibo	íbimus	feram	feremus
ibis	íbitis	feres	feretis
ibit	ibunt	feret	ferent
Perfect			
ii	íimus	tuli	túlimus
iisti	iistis	tulisti	tulistis
iit	ierunt	tulit	tulerunt

The root of the verb *eo* is *i*. *Fero* has regular endings, but the stem vowel drops out of most forms.

TASK 6: TRANSLATING IRREGULAR VERBS

Translate the following forms.

1. *ibam*

2. *ite!*

3. *ferunt*

4. *iisti*

5. *tulerunt*

6. *feram*

7. *ferent*

8. *eo*

9. *ibis*

10. *tulit*

ESSENTIAL VOCABULARY

These common words should be committed to memory.

Essential Vocabulary

Latin	Meaning	Related Word
Nouns		
família, –ae (feminine)	family	
pater, patris (masculine)	father	paternal
poena, poenae (feminine)	penalty	
uxor, uxoris (feminine)	wife	uxorious
Pronoun		
nemo, néminis	no one	Captain Nemo

continues

Essential Vocabulary   (continued)

Latin	Meaning	Related Word
Verbs		
adiuvo, –are, adiuvi	help	
cognósco, –ere, cognovi	learn	cognition
defício, –ere, defeci	fail	defect
eo, ire, ii	go	
narro, –are, –avi	tell	narrate
respóndeo, –ere, respondi	answer	respond
rédeo, redire, rédii	return	
rogo, –are, –avi	ask	interrogate
Adverbs		
ergo	therefore, and so	
forte	by chance	fortuitous
sic	thus, in this way	
vix	scarcely	

RECOGNITION VOCABULARY

Go through this list once or twice, and then look for these words in the Reading Exercise.

Recognition Vocabulary

Latin	Meaning	Related Word
acquiro, –ere, acquisivi	obtain	acquire
Arabs, Árabis (masculine)	Arab	
mórtuus, –a, –um	dead	mortuary
necessitas, –tatis (feminine)	necessity	

Latin	Meaning	Related Word
philósophus, –i (masculine)	philosopher	
perfectus, –a, –um	complete	perfect
responsum, –i (neuter)	answer	response
saccum, –i (neuter)	sack	
secretum, –i (neuter)	secret	
suspectus, –a, –um	suspected, under suspicion	

SUMMARY

In this hour, you have learned how to form the perfect tense and how to create regular adverbs. Now you are ready for another pearl of wisdom, brought to medieval Europe from the Middle East.

READING EXERCISE

The culture that formed Latin literature did not come exclusively from ancient Greece and Rome. In the Middle Ages, the flourishing culture of Islam, as well as that of the Renascent Jewish diaspora, also made its way to the West in Latin translations. A popular source of Eastern lore was the *Disciplina clericalis* of Petrus Alfonsi, a Sephardic Jew who converted to Christianity in 1106. Many of its stories are introduced by a dialogue between a wise Arab and his son (slightly adapted).

THE HALF-FRIEND

Arabs moriturus vocavit fílium suum et dixit: "Dic, fili: quot, dum vixi, acquisivisti amicos?" Respondens fílius dixit, "Centum, ut puto, acquisivi amicos." Dixit pater: "Philósophus dicit: 'Noli laudare amicum, donec probáveris eum.' Ego quidem senex sum et dimídium amicum vix acquisivi. Tu ergo centum quómodo acquisivisti? Vade igitur et proba omnes, et cognosces si ullus perfectus erit amicus!" Dixit fílius, "Quómodo probabo eos?" Dixit pater, "Vítulum intérfice et frustatim comminutum in saccum repone, et saccus forínsecus sánguine infectus erit." Et cum ad amicum vénies, dic: "Hóminem, care mi, forte interfeci; rogo te, sepeli eum; nemo enim te suspectum habebit, sicque me salvare póteris." Fecit fílius sicut pater imperavit. Primus autem amicus ad quem venit dixit, "Fer tecum mórtuum super collum tuum! Sicut fecisti malum, poenam da! In domum meam non intrabis." Ut autem per síngulos sic fecit, eodem responso omnes responderunt. Ad patrem ergo rédiens nuntiavit quae fecit. Dixit pater, "Cóntigit tibi quod dixit philósophus: 'Multi sunt in prósperis amici, sed in necessitate pauci.' Vade ad dimídium amicum quem hábeo et vide, quid dicat!" Venit et, sicut áliis dixit, huic ait. Qui dixit, "Intra domum! Non debemus hoc secretum propalare!" Emisit ergo uxorem cum omni família sua et sepulturam fodit. Cum autem ille ómnia parata vidit, rem, prout erat, disséruit, grátiam agens. Deinde ad patrem rédiit et ómnia narravit. Pater vero ait, "Pro tali amico dicit philósophus, 'Hic est vere amicus qui te ádiuvat, cum saéculum déficit.'"

Reading Vocabulary

agens	giving
áliis	to the others
care	dear
centum	one hundred
collum, –i (neuter)	neck
comminutus, –a, –um	cut up
contingo, –ere, cóntigit	happen
dicat	says
dimídius, –a, –um	half
díssero, –ere, dissérui	explain
donec	until
ego	I
emitto, emíttere, emisi	send out
eodem	the same
eos	them
eum	him, it
fili	son
fódio, fódere, fodi	dig
forínsecus	outside
frustatim	in pieces
grátiam	thanks
hic	this one
hoc	this
huic	to him, to this one
ille	he

ímpero, –are, –avi	command
infectus	died, soaked
interfício, ére, interfeci	kill
intro, –are, –avi	enter
malum, –i (neuter)	evil
me	me
mi	my
moriturus, –a, –um	about to die
numerantur	they are counted
núntio, –are, –avi	announce
paratus, –a, –um	prepared
pauci, –ae, –a	few
poenam da!	Pay the penalty!
primus, –a, –um	first
probáveris	you (will) have tested
própalo, –are, –avi	spread abroad
próspera, –orum (neuter plural)	good times
prout	just as
rédiens	returning
repono, repónere, repósui	put back
respondens	answering
saéculum, –i (neuter)	world
salvo, –are, –avi	save
sanguis, sánguinis (masculine)	blood
senex, senis (masculine)	old man
sepélio, –ire, sepelivi	bury
sepultura, –ae (feminine)	burial
sicut	just as
sínguli, –ae, –a	single, one by one
suus, –a, –um	his
te	you
tecum	with you
ullus	any
tu	you
ut	so that, as, when

continues

Reading Vocabulary (continued)

vado, vádere	go
vere	truly
vero	then, however
vítulum, –i (neuter)	veal, calf

QUIZ

A

Supply the required form of the words in parentheses, and translate the sentences.

1. *Vade ígitur et* (*probo, –are, –avi:* imperative) *omnes amicos.*

2. *Quómodo* (*probo, –are, –avi:* future) *eos?*

3. *Fecit fílius sicut pater* (*ímpero, –are, –avi:* perfect).

4. *Sicut tu* (*fácio, facere, feci:* perfect) *malum, poenam da! In domum meam non* (*intro, –are, –avi:* future).

5. *Ad patrem rédiit et ómnia* (*narro, –are, –avi:* perfect).

6. *Vade ad amicum quam ego* (*hábeo, habere, habui:* present tense) *dimídium.*

7. *Fílius ad patrem* (*rédeo, redire, redii:* perfect) *et ómnia narravit.*

B

Answer in Latin the following questions about the reading passage.

1. *Quot amicos fílius Árabis acquisivit?*

2. *Quid dixit philósophus de laudandis* (praising) *amicis?*

3. *Qualem amicum Árabs habet?*

4. *Quid intérfecit fílius?*

5. *Acceperuntne amici fílium?*

6. *Secundum philósophum, quot amici sunt in necessitate?*

7. *Quis est verus amicus?*

The Dative Case

LESSON PLAN:
In this hour you will learn about …

- Another case, called the dative
- Declining the pronouns *ego* (I), *tu* (you), *nos* (we), and *vos* (y'all).

So far, you have learned how to use nouns in the nominative, genitive, accusative, and ablative cases.

INTRODUCTORY READING

First, let's look at an excerpt from the Latin translation of the Book of Psalms, revised by St. Jerome in the fourth century (adapted):

PSALM 131:1–5

Memento, Dómine, David, et omnis mansuetúdinis eius. Sicut iuravit Dómino, votum vovit Deo Jacob: Non introibo in tabernáculum domus meae, non ascéndam in lectum strati mei, non dabo somnum ócculis meis, et palpebris meis dormitationem, et réquiem tempóribus meis, donec invéniam locum Dómino, tabernáculum Deo Iacob.

O Lord, remember David, and all his meekness. How he swore to the Lord, he vowed a vow to the God of Jacob: I shall not enter into the tabernacle of my house, I shall not go up into the bed wherein I lie, I shall not give sleep to my eyes, nor slumber to my eyelids, nor rest to my temples: until I find out a place for the Lord, a tabernacle for the God of Jacob.

Here you find several places where English phrases beginning with "to" or "for" are rendered in Latin by nouns such as *Dómino* (to the Lord) and *Deo* (to/for God). These words are in the *dative* or "giving" case

(Latin *casus dativus*). It gets its name from situations in which the subject gives something *to* another noun.

FORMS OF THE DATIVE CASE

The dative case is traditionally listed in declension tables after the genitive and before the accusative. Study the following table.

The Dative Case in the Five Declensions

	I	II	III
	girl	*master*	*king*
Singular			
Nominative	*puell-a*	*dómin-us*	*rex*
Genitive	*puell-ae*	*dómin-i*	*reg-is*
Dative	***puell-ae***	***dómin-o***	***reg-i***
Accusative	*puell-am*	*dómin-um*	*reg-em*
Ablative	*puell-a*	*dómin-o*	*reg-e*
Plural			
Nominative	*puell-ae*	*dómin-i*	*reg-es*
Genitive	*puell-arum*	*domin-orum*	*reg-um*
Dative	***puell-is***	***dómin-is***	***rég-ibus***
Accusative	*puell-as*	*dómin-os*	*reg-es*
Ablative	*puell-is*	*dómin-is*	*rég-ibus*

	IV	V
	chariot	*thing*
Singular		
Nominative	*curr-us*	*r-es*
Genitive	*curr-us*	*r-ei*
Dative	***cúrr-ui***	***r-ei***
Accusative	*curr-um*	*r-em*
Ablative	*curr-u*	*r-e*

	IV	V
	chariot	*thing*
Plural		
Nominative	*curr-us*	*r-es*
Genitive	*cúrr-uum*	*r-erum*
Dative	***cúrr-ibus***	***r-ebus***
Accusative	*curr-us*	*r-es*
Ablative	*cúrr-ibus*	*r-ebus*

JUST A MINUTE

In the plural, the dative case is always identical to the ablative. In the singular, the third, fourth, and fifth declensions all show the ending *–i*. This ending was also once found in the first declension (*–ai*), but the spelling was changed to *–ae*.

Task 1: Working with the Dative Case

Give the dative case forms (singular and plural) for the following nouns.

1. *dóminus, –i* (masculine)

2. *exércitus, –us* (masculine)

3. *fémina, –ae* (feminine)

4. *homo, hóminis* (masculine)

5. *manus, –us* (feminine)

6. *lux, lucis* (feminine)

7. *mundus, –i* (masculine)

8. *spécies, –ei* (feminine)

The Dative Case: Neuter and I-stem Nouns

Neuter nouns have the same endings as masculine and feminine nouns in the dative case.

Dative Case of Neuter Nouns

	II	III	IV
	stone	*name*	*horn*
Singular			
Nominative	*sax-um*	*nomen*	*corn-u*
Genitive	*sax-i*	*nómin-is*	*corn-us*
Dative	***sax-o***	***nómin-i***	***corn-u***
Accusative	*sax-um*	*nomen*	*corn-u*
Ablative	*sax-o*	*nómin-e*	*corn-u*
Plural			
Nominative	*sax-a*	*nómin-a*	*córn-ua*
Genitive	*sax-orum*	*nómin-um*	*córn-uum*
Dative	***sax-is***	***nomín-ibus***	***córn-ibus***
Accusative	*sax-a*	*nómin-a*	*córn-ua*
Ablative	*sax-is*	*nomín-ibus*	*córn-ibus*

I-stem nouns also have regular dative endings. Note, however, that in neuter i-stems such as mare, the dative and ablative singular are identical.

Dative Case of I-stem Nouns

	III	
	city	*sea*
Singular		
Nominative	*urbs*	*mare*
Genitive	*urb-is*	*mar-is*
Dative	***urb-i***	***mar-i***
Accusative	*urb-em*	*mare*
Ablative	*urb-e*	*mar-i*
Plural		
Nominative	*urb-es*	*már-ia*
Genitive	*úrb-ium*	*már-ium*
Dative	***úrb-ibus***	***már-ibus***
Accusative	*urb-es*	*már-ia*
Ablative	*úrb-ibus*	*már-ibus*

Task 2: Singular and Plural of Dative Nouns

Give the dative singular and plural of the following nouns.

1. *consílium, –i* (neuter)
2. *corpus, córporis* (neuter)
3. *finis, finis* (masculine)
4. *ánimal, animalis* (neuter i-stem)

PROCEED WITH CAUTION

Needless to say, dative endings overlap with other case forms throughout the five declensions. The context of a noun will often clear up any confusion:

- *Vox puellae pulchra est:* The girl's voice is beautiful.
- *Puellae pulchrae sunt:* The girls are beautiful.
- *Librum puellae dédimus:* We gave the book to the girl.

Task 3: Identifying Case and Number

Referring to the previous tables, give all possible case and number identifications for the following nouns.

1. *féminis*
2. *dómino*
3. *corpóribus*
4. *fíliae*
5. *mari*
6. *rei*

Task 4: Translation

Translate the following sentences.

1. *Pueri cum puellis ámbulant.*
2. *Pueri puellis flores dant.* (*flores* means "flowers")
3. *Puellae flores a pueris accípiunt.*
4. *Pater vocem fíliae audit.*
5. *Pater fíliae responsum dat.* (*responsum* means "an answer")
6. *Fíliae patrem amant.*

THE DATIVE CASE IN INTERROGATIVE AND RELATIVE PRONOUNS AND ADJECTIVES

The dative case forms of the pronoun/adjective *qui* can be seen in the following table.

The Interrogative/Relative Adjective *Qui*

	Masculine	Feminine	Neuter
Singular			
Nominative	*qui*	*quae*	*quod*
Genitive	*cuius*	*cuius*	*cuius*
Dative	***cui***	***cui***	***cui***
Accusative	*quem*	*quam*	*quod*
Ablative	*quo*	*qua*	*quo*
Plural			
Nominative	*qui*	*quae*	*quae*
Genitive	*quorum*	*quarum*	*quorum*
Dative	***quibus***	***quibus***	***quibus***
Accusative	*quos*	*quas*	*quae*
Ablative	*quibus*	*quibus*	*quibus*

These are also the dative forms of the interrogative pronouns *quis* and *quid:*

- *Cui librum dedisti?:* To whom did you give the book?

ADJECTIVES IN THE DATIVE CASE

To match nouns in the dative case, adjectives borrow endings (as usual) from the noun tables given previously. Study the following table.

Adjectives in the Dative Case

(First/Second Declension Adjectives)

	Masculine	Feminine	Neuter
Singular			
Nominative	*magn-us*	*magn-a*	*magn-um*
Genitive	*magn-i*	*magn-ae*	*magn-i*

	Masculine	Feminine	Neuter
Singular			
Dative	***magn-o***	***magn-ae***	***magn-o***
Accusative	*magn-um*	*magn-am*	*magn-um*
Ablative	*magn-o*	*magn-a*	*magn-o*
Plural			
Nominative	*magn-i*	*magn-ae*	*magn-a*
Genitive	*magn-orum*	*magn-arum*	*magn-orum*
Dative	***magn-is***	***magn-is***	***magn-is***
Accusative	*magn-os*	*magn-as*	*magn-a*
Ablative	*magn-is*	*magn-is*	*magn-is*

(Third Declension Adjectives)

	Masculine/Feminine	Neuter
Singular		
Nominative	*omn-is*	*omn-e*
Genitive	*omn-is*	*omn-is*
Dative	***omn-i***	***omn-i***
Accusative	*omn-em*	*omn-e*
Ablative	*omn-i*	*omn-i*
Plural		
Nominative	*omn-es*	*ómn-ia*
Genitive	*ómn-ium*	*ómn-ium*
Dative	***ómn-ibus***	***ómn-ibus***
Accusative	*omn-es*	*ómn-ia*
Ablative	*ómn-ibus*	*ómn-ibus*

The endings seen in *omnis, omne* are also found in one-termination and consonant-stem adjectives.

Task 5: Noun-Adjective Pairings in the Dative Case

Complete the following noun-adjective pairings in the dative case. Remember that there must be agreement also in gender and number.

1. *féminae (omnis)*
2. *cúrrui (magnus)*

3. *consílio (omnis)*

4. *regi (magnus)*

5. *diei (omnis)*

6. *rei (magnus)*

7. *rebus (omnis)*

8. *mari (magnus)*

9. *dóminis (fortis)*

TASK 6: IDENTIFYING CASE AND NUMBER

Identify the case and number of the following noun-adjective pairs.

1. *exércitu omni*

2. *regis magni*

3. *hómini omni*

4. *hómines magni*

5. *animali forti* (2)

USES OF THE DATIVE CASE

The dative case is used to mark the *indirect object* of a verb:

- Latin gives my **students** a headache.
- I send my **mother** a letter.

In each sentence, we find a subject (Latin, I) and a direct object (a headache, a letter). We also find, however, that a third party profits or suffers from the action (students, mother). This third party is the indirect object. Latin avoids all ambiguity by putting it in the dative case:

- *Epístolam **matri** mitto:* I send my **mother** a letter.

English also once had dative case forms, but when these dropped out it often had to rely on the prepositions "to" and "for" as dative substitutes:

- "I will give **you** this" became "I will give this **to you**."
- "I cooked **him** a big dinner" became "I cooked a big dinner **for him**."

Hence, we can think of the dative as the "to/for" case. The dative not only indicates the indirect object, it also indicates other relationships expressed in English by "to" and "for":

- *Tabaccum* **saluti** *nociva est:* Tobacco is harmful to **your health.**
- *Nero* **Calígulae, avúnculo suo,** *simíllimus erat:* Nero was very similar **to Caligula, his uncle.**

Task 7: Translation

Translate the nouns in bold.

1. *Librum* **Caésari** *ostendam:* I will show the book ....
2. *Cenam delectábilem* **matri** *cóquimus:* We cooked a delicious meal ....
3. *Arsénicum* **homínibus** *periculosum est:* Arsenic is dangerous ....
4. *Haec solútio* **ómnibus** *evidentissima est:* This solution is evident ....
5. *Illa pellícula non est* **pueris** *idónea:* That film is not suitable ....

Idiomatic Uses of the Dative Case

The term "idiomatic" describes expressions that, if translated literally into another language, sound strange or nonsensical. For example, there are two ways of saying "Caesar has an army" in Latin:

- *Caesar exércitum habet:* Caesar has an army.
- **Caésari** *exércitus est:* An army is **to/for Caesar.** (Caesar has an army.)

The second construction seems odd to English-speakers, but it is quite common in Latin. The same construction, incidentally, is used to name people. If you want to say, "The girl's name is Mary," you say:

- **Puellae** *nomen est* **Mariae:** The name **to/for the girl** is **Mary.** (The girl's name is Mary.)

Note that both *puellae* and *Mariae* are in the dative case.

There are a few other situations where Latin uses the dative case, even though English would not use "to" and "for." For example, if you want to say that this book is helpful or useful to everyone, you might say:

- *Hic liber* **auxílio** *est* **ómnibus:** This book is **for help to all.** (This book is helpful to all.)
- *Hic liber* **úsui** *est* **ómnibus:** This book is **for use to all.** (This book is useful to all.)

Notice that both nouns are in the dative case; hence, this construction is commonly called the "double dative."

There are also a few verbs in Latin that do not take an object in the accusative case, but rather one in the dative:

- *Caésari páreo:* I obey **Caesar.** (I am obedient to Caesar.)
- *Romae sérvio:* I serve **Rome.**
- *Latinae stúdeo:* I study **Latin.**
- *Tabaccum **saluti** nocet:* Tobacco harms **your health.**
- *Suppelectile **abbati** placet:* The furniture pleases **the abbot.**
- *Alexander **hippopótamis** occurrit:* Alexander meets **the hippos.**

Notice that in English these verbs take a direct object, but in Latin the object must be in the dative case. Verbs that fall into this category will be indicated in your vocabulary.

TASK 8: TRANSLATION

Translate the following sentences.

1. *Iusto dómino servimus.*
2. *Lingua latina úsui fuit Romanis.*
3. *Flores, quos dedi, puellae non placent.*
4. *Multis rebus in schola studemus.*
5. *Fílii pátribus semper parére debent.*
6. *Brutus Caésari in urbe occurrebat.*

REVIEW OF THE CASES

You have now learned all the cases that appear in ordinary statements. You have also noticed that many of the endings you have learned indicate more than one combination of case, number, and (for adjectives) gender.

TASK 9: CASE AND NUMBER

Using the tables contained in this lesson for reference, identify the case and number of the following nouns and adjective pairs.

1. *linguae omnes*
2. *regum bonorum*
3. *perícula grándia*

4. *draco péssimus*

5. *naves multas*

6. *urbi magnae*

7. *manus una*

8. *manus déxtrae* (right)

9. *res pública*

10. *dómini fortis*

11. *féminae omni*

12. *viro paúpere*

THE PRONOUNS *EGO, TU, NOS,* AND *VOS*

You will recall that a pronoun is a "little" word (such as "I," "you," "he," "who") that stands in for a noun. The noun that is replaced is called the *antecedent* of the pronoun. In your readings, you occasionally have seen the Latin pronouns *ego* (I), *tu* (you), *nos* (we), and *vos* ("you," referring to more than one person: "y'all"). They are declined as follows.

Declension of Pronouns

Nominative	*ego*	*tu*	*nos*	*vos*
Genitive	*mei*	*tui*	*nostri*	*vestri*
			nostrum	*vestrum*
Dative	*mihi*	*tibi*	*nobis*	*vobis*
Accusative	*me*	*te*	*nos*	*vos*
Ablative	*me*	*te*	*nobis*	*vobis*

JUST A MINUTE

There are two forms for the genitive of *nos* and *vos*:

- The form ending in *–i* is used when a verb/object relationship is involved: *timor nostri* means "fear of us," that is, "someone fears us"

- The *–um* form is used for part/whole relationships: *nonnulli nostrum* means "some of us"

The genitive case of these pronouns is never used to indicate possession (my, your, our). Instead, adjective forms are used: *meus, –a, –um* for "my, mine"; *tuus, –a, –um* for "your, yours"; *noster, nostra, nostrum* for "our, ours"; and *vester, vestra, vestrum* for "your, yours, y'all's."

TASK 10: PRONOUN FORMS

Insert the form of the pronoun in parentheses that best translates the word(s) in bold.

1. *Non (nos), sed nómini tuo da glóriam!:* Not **to us,** but to your name give the glory! (Ps. 115:1)

2. *Vídeo (tu); potesne (ego) videre?:* I see **you;** can you see **me?**

3. *Timor (vos) non movet (ego), sed amor:* Fear **of you** does not compel **me,** but rather love.

4. *Numquam (ego) flores das exinde:* You never give **me** flowers anymore.

5. *Grátias ágimus (tu), quia (nos) adiuvisti:* We give thanks **to you,** because you have helped **us.**

6. *Magna pars (ego) cupit hoc exercítium pérgere:* A big part **of me** wants this exercise to continue.

TIME SAVER

The forms *nos* and *vos* often are confused by beginners. It may help to remember the argument for the natural origin of language advanced by the Roman grammarian, Nigidius Figulus. He thought that we say *vos* (*wohs*) because the lips bend outward to the addressee (you); when we say *nos,* we hold our lips in.

EMPHATIC USE OF SUBJECT PRONOUNS

When you first learned to conjugate verbs, you noticed that the form *ámbulo* by itself means "I walk," that *ámbulas* means "you walk," and so on. Ordinarily, the subject forms *ego, tu, nos,* and *vos* are not needed in a Latin sentence. Sometimes, though, they are added for emphasis:

- *Ego Latinae studeo; tu, Bulgaricae:* **I** am studying Latin; **you,** Bulgarian.
- *Ego tibi flores do; tu mihi nihil das:* **I** give you flowers; **you** give me nothing.
- *Et tu, Brute?:* **You,** too, Brutus?

ESSENTIAL VOCABULARY

The following common words should be committed to memory.

Essential Vocabulary

Latin	Meaning	Related Word
Nouns		
annus, –i (masculine)	year	annual
frater, –ris (masculine)	brother	fraternal
genus, géneris (neuter)	type, family	generic
impérium, –i (neuter)	empire	imperial
mater, matris (feminine)	mother	maternal
óppidum, –i (neuter)	town	
poena, –ae (feminine)	penalty	
Roma, –ae (feminine)	Rome	
saxum, –i (neuter)	stone	
soror, sororis (feminine)	sister	sorority
uxor, uxoris (feminine)	wife	uxorious
Pronoun		
nihil	nothing	nihilism
Verbs		
interfício, –ere, interfeci	kill	
iúdico, –are, –avi	judge	judicial
mitto, –ere, misi	send	missive
óbeo, obire, óbii	die	obituary
fúgio, fúgere, fugi	flee	fugitive
quaero, –ere, quaesivi	seek	quest
sustollo, –ere, sústuli	take away	
compono, –ere, compósui	make, put an end to	compose
Adverbs		
ante	formerly	antebellum
olim	once	
omnino	completely	
paene	almost	penultimate
simul	at the same time, together	simultaneous
Conjunctions		
postquam	after	
atque	and	

RECOGNITION VOCABULARY

Go through this list once or twice, and look for these words in the Reading Exercise.

Recognition Vocabulary

Latin	Meaning	Related Word
canto, –are, –avi	sing	chant
committo, –ere, commisi	commit	
deformo, –are, –avi	deform	
infinitus, –a, –um	infinite	
légio, legionis (feminine)	legion	
luxúria, –ae (feminine)	luxury	
militaris, –e	military	
prostítuo, –ere, –ui	prostitute	
públicus, –a, –um	public	
scaena, –ae (feminine)	stage	scenic
senatus, –us (masculine)	senate	
spectáculum, –i (neuter)	spectacle	
trágicus, –a, –um	tragic	
villa, –ae (feminine)	villa	

SUMMARY

In this hour, you have learned how to recognize and use the dative case and also some common pronouns. Now you are ready to read a Roman's view of one of the darker episodes in his nation's history.

READING EXERCISE

Nero was a disastrous ruler, even by ancient standards. Ominous rumors circulated that he had killed his own mother and other family members, that he had caused the great fire in Rome of 64 A.D., and that he had even "fiddled" while the city burned! The following is adapted from the fourth-century epitome of Roman history by Eutropius.

THE EMPEROR NERO

Successit Claúdio Nero, Calígulae, avúnculo suo, simíllimus: qui Romanum impérium et deformavit et mínuit, homo inusitatae luxúriae sumptuumque. Infinitam senatus partem interfecit; bonis ómnibus hostis fuit. Ad postremum se multo dedécore prostítuit; nam saltabat et cantabat in scaena citharoédico vel trágico hábitu. Parricídia multa commisit, fratrem, uxorem, sororem, matrem interfíciens. Urbem Romam incendit, quia tale spectáculum cérnere cupiebat, quali olim Troia capta arsit. In re militari nihil omnino ausus, Brittániam paene amisit. Nam sub eo hostes duo nobilíssima óppida ceperunt et everterunt. Arméniam Parthi sustulerunt legionesque Romanas sub iugum miserunt.

Per haec Romano orbi exsecrábilem omnes eum simul destiterunt et senatus eum hostem iudicavit; cum quaerebant eum ad poenam, quae poena erat talis: nudum eum per públicum ductum et furcam portantem virgis caédere et e saxo praecipitare. Ille ergo e Palátio fugit et in suburbana villa liberti sui interfecit se. Is aedificavit Romae thermas, quas ante "Neronianas," nunc "Alexandrinas" appellamus. Óbiit tricésimo et áltero aetatis anno, impérii quarto décimo, atque in eo omnis Augusti família périit. (147)

Reading Vocabulary

aedífico, –are, –avi	build
aetas, –tatis (feminine)	age
Alexandrinus, –a, –um	Alexandrian
alter, –a, –um	second
amitto, –míttere, amisi	lose
appello, –are, –avi	call
árdeo, ardere, arsi	burn
Arménia, –ae (feminine)	Armenia
Augustus, –i (masculine)	Augustus
ausus, –a, –um	having dared
avúnculus, –i (masculine)	uncle
boni, –orum (masculine)	"good people," nobles
Brittánia, –ae (feminine)	Britain
caedo, caédere, cécidi	beat, flog
Calígula, –ae (masculine)	Caligula, a Roman emperor
captus, –a, –um	captured

continues

Reading Vocabulary   (continued)

cerno, –ere, cérnui	see
citharoedicus, –a, –um	of the lyre
Claúdius, –i (masculine)	Claudius, a Roman emperor
décimus, –a, –um	tenth
dédecus, dedécoris (neuter)	disgrace
desisto, –ere, déstiti	desert
ductus, –a, –um	(having been) led
duo	two
eo	him
eum	him
everto, –ere, everti	overturn
exsecrábilis, –e	detestable
furca, –ae (feminine)	fork, cross
hábitus, –us (masculine)	clothing
haec	these things
hostis, hostis (common)	enemy
huic	him
ille	he
incendo, –ere, incendi	burn
interfíciens, interficientis (adjective)	killing
inusitatus, –a, –um	unaccustomed, unusual
is	he
iugum, –i (neuter)	yoke (*sub iugum* means "into slavery")
libertus, –a, –um	freedman, ex-slave
mínuo, minúere, mínui	lessen
multo	much
Nero, –onis (masculine)	Nero
Neronianus, –a, –um	Neronian
nobilíssimus, –a, –um	very noble
nudus, –a, –um	naked
orbis, orbis (masculine)	world
Palátium, –i (neuter)	Palatine villa
parricídia, –ae (feminine)	parricide, murder of a relative
Parthus, –i (masculine)	Parthian
per	through, on account of

péreo, –ire, périi	die, perish
portans, portantis (adjective)	carrying
postremum, –i (neuter)	the end
praecipito, –are, –avi	precipitate
qualis, –e	such as
quartus, –a, –um	fourth
Romae	at Rome
salto, –are, –avi	dance
se	himself
simíllimus, –a, –um	very similar
suburbanus, –a, –um	suburban
succedo, –ere, successi	succeed
sumptus, –us (masculine)	extravagance
suus, –a, –um	his, her, its, their
talis, –e	such (with *qualis,* it means "such … as")
thermae, –arum (feminine)	bath
tricésimus, –a, –um	thirtieth
Troia, –ae (feminine)	Troy
vel	or
virga, –ae (feminine)	switch, whip

Quiz

A

Complete the following noun paradigms by filling in the blanks.

	I	*II*	*III*	*IV*	*V*
	girl	**master**	**king**	**chariot**	**thing**
Singular					
Nominative	puell-a	domin-us	rex	curr-us	r-es
Genitive	puell-ae	domin-i	_____	curr-us	r-ei
Dative	_____	domin-o	reg-i	curr-ui	_____
Accusative	puell-am	domin-um	reg-em	curr-um	r-em
Ablative	puell-a	_____	reg-e	_____	r-e

	I	II	III	IV	V
	girl	**master**	**king**	**chariot**	**thing**
Plural					
Nominative	_____	domin-i	reg-es	_____	r-es
Genitive	puell-arum	_____	reg-um	curr-uum	r-erum
Dative	puell-is	domin-is	reg-ibus	curr-ibus	_____
Accusative	puell-as	domin-os	_____	curr-us	r-es
Ablative	puell-is	domin-is	reg-ibus	curr-ibus	_____

B

Choose the form that best completes the sentence, and translate.

1. *Successit Nero, (Calígula/Calígulae) simíllimus.*

2. *(Infinitum/Infinitam) senatus partem interfecit; bonis ómnibus hostis fuit.*

3. *Nam saltabat et cantabat in (scaenam/scaena).*

4. *Parricídia multa (commisit, commiserunt), fratrem, uxorem, sororem, matrem interfíciens.*

5. *Urbem Romam incendit, quia spectáculum (cernit, cérnere) cupiebat.*

6. *In Brittánia (hostis/hostes) duo óppida ceperunt.*

7. *Nero e (Palátium/Palátio) fugit.*

QUIZ

HOUR 11

The Pluperfect and Future Perfect Tenses; More Pronouns

LESSON PLAN:

In this hour you will learn about …

- Two new tenses: the pluperfect and the future perfect
- The pronouns/adjectives *is* and *ille* (he, she, it; this, that)

So far, you have learned how to conjugate verbs in the present, future, imperfect, and perfect tenses. You have also learned how to decline the pronouns *ego, tu, nos,* and *vos.*

First, let's have a look at two snippets of medieval Latin poetry.

A Swan on the Dinner Table

> *Olim lacus colúeram*
> *olim pulcher exstíteram,*
> *dum cygnus ego fúeram.*
> *Miser! Miser! Modo niger et ustus fórtiter!*

Translation:

> Once I had lived on a lake,
> Once I had been beautiful,
> while I had been a swan.
> O poor me! Now I'm black and roasted well!

A Repentant Poet

> *Electe Colónie, parce penitenti,*
> *fac misericórdiam veniam petenti,*
> *et da poeniténtiam culpam confitenti:*
> *feram quicquid iússeris ánimo libenti.*

Translation:

> (Bishop) Elect of Cologne, spare a penitent,
> have mercy on one seeking pardon,

and grant repentance to one who confesses his fault.

I will bear whatever you (will have) command(ed) with a willing spirit.

In these passages you see new verb forms, such as *fú-eram* and *iúss-eris,* which are built on the perfect stem (the third principal part, minus the ending *–i*). This stem indicates an emphasis on the fact that verb is "completed" (Latin *perfectus*).

If an action is viewed as already completed in the past, it is conjugated in the *pluperfect* tense (from Latin *plus quam perfectum,* "more than perfect"). If it is viewed as completed in the future, it is conjugated in the *future perfect.*

FORMS OF THE PLUPERFECT TENSE

The pluperfect tense is easy to recognize. It is based on the perfect stem. Study the following table.

The Pluperfect Tense

Singular	Plural
ambuláv-eram (I had walked)	*ambulav-eramus*
ambuláv-eras	*ambulav-eratis*
ambuláv-erat	*ambuláv-erant*

Similarly, one uses the third principle part to create the forms *habúeram* (I had had), *míseram* (I had sent), *fúeram* (I had been), and so on.

JUST A MINUTE

The pluperfect endings are identical with the imperfect forms of the verb *sum* (*eram, eras, erat,* and so on), as if to say, "I **was** in a state of **having** walked."

TASK 1: WORKING WITH THE PLUPERFECT TENSE

Convert the following verbs from the present tense to the pluperfect tense, keeping the same person and number. The perfect stem is given in parentheses.

1. *áperit (aperu–)*
2. *iubemus (iuss–)*
3. *dicunt (dix–)*
4. *áccipis (accep–)*
5. *víncitis (vic–)*
6. *curro (cucurr–)*

FORMS OF THE FUTURE PERFECT TENSE

The future perfect tense is also based on the perfect stem. Study the following table.

The Future Perfect Tense

Singular	Plural
ambuláv-ero (I will have walked)	*ambulav-érimus*
ambuláv-eris	*ambulav-éritis*
ambuláv-erit	*ambuláv-erint*

By analogy, we create the forms *habúero* (I will have had), *mísero* (I will have sent), *fúero* (I will have been), and so on.

JUST A MINUTE

On the analogy of the pluperfect, the future perfect endings are almost identical with the future of *sum* (ero and so on); the exception is –*erint* (compare *erunt*).

TASK 2: WORKING WITH THE FUTURE PERFECT TENSE

Convert the following verbs from the present to the future perfect tense, keeping the same person and number. The perfect stem is given in parentheses.

1. *das* (*ded–*)
2. *díscimus* (*didic–*)
3. *capit* (*cep–*)
4. *óbeo* (*obi–*)
5. *potestis* (*potu–*)
6. *sunt* (*fu–*)

PROCEED WITH CAUTION

The pluperfect and the future perfect are easily confused. Remember to look for the *a* that distinguishes the pluperfect (as in *ambuláveram*).

USING THE PLUPERFECT AND THE FUTURE PERFECT TENSES

As you saw in the Introductory Readings, the pluperfect and future perfect tenses refer to different times, but they both emphasize the "completedness" of the verb, usually in relationship to some other verb. For example, the following sentence has two verbs in past time:

- *In Itália multos annos* **habitáveram;** *tum in Graéciam emigravi:* I **had lived** in Italy for many years; then I moved to Greece.

The pluperfect *habitáveram* makes it clear that I was "finished" with living in Italy when I moved to Greece. The same relationship can exist between two verbs referring to the future:

- *Si hoc féceris, dolebis:* If you will have done this, you will be sorry.

It is clear from this sentence that the "doing" must be completed before the sorrow begins.

 FYI Conditions ("if" clauses) in English often have the present tense where Latin has the future perfect: *Si Latinae* **studúeris,** *beatus eris* means "If you **study** Latin, you will be happy."

TASK 3: TRANSLATING THE PLUPERFECT AND FUTURE PERFECT TENSES

Translate the verbs in bold.

1. *Puer fáciet sicut pater* **iússerit:** The boy will do just as his father ....
2. *Cum regem* **interféceras,** *ex urbe fugisti:* When ... the king, you fled the city.
3. *Patri narravit ómnia, quae* **fécerat:** He told his father everything that ....
4. *Cum Caesar hostes* **vícerat,** *insoléntius egit:* When Caesar ... his enemies, he acted insolently.
5. *Mus urbanus ait, "Si mecum* **véneris,** *bene manducabis":* The city mouse said, "If you ... with me, you will eat well."

THE PRONOUN *Is*

You have often encountered words such as *eum, eam,* and *eos,* meaning "him," "her," "them," and so on. These are derived from the pronoun *is,* the most basic third person pronoun. Study the following tables:

The Pronoun *Is*

Singular	Masculine	Feminine	Neuter
Nominative	is	ea	id
Genitive	eius	eius	eius
Dative	ei	ei	ei
Accusative	eum	eam	id
Ablative	eo	ea	eo

Plural	Masculine	Feminine	Neuter
Nominative	ei	eae	ea
Genitive	eorum	earum	eorum
Dative	eis	eis	eis
Accusative	eos	eas	ea
Ablative	eis	eis	eis

JUST A MINUTE

The plural forms are built on the stem e–, and follow the table for first and second declension adjectives. In the singular, note the –*ius* ending (unique to pronouns) in the genitive and the –*i* ending of the dative (compare the third, fourth, and fifth declensions). The form *id,* though irregular, will remind you of Freudian psychoanalysis and the "it" that lurks in our subconscious.

TASK 4: WORKING WITH THE PRONOUN *IS*

Translate the following English pronouns into Latin, using *is*.

1. she
2. to her
3. of them (masculine)
4. it (neuter)
5. its
6. him
7. to them
8. with it
9. he
10. to him
11. his
12. them (feminine)

USING THE PRONOUN *Is*

Is has two functions in Latin: it is a personal pronoun (he, she, it, they) and a demonstrative pronoun/adjective (this, that, these, those).

When it is used as a personal pronoun, it agrees in gender and number with its antecedent (compare the rules for *qui* in Hour 5):

- *Marcum vídeo; **eum** vocabo:* I see Marcus; I will call **him.**
- *Reginam vídeo; **eam** vocabo:* I see the queen; I will call **her.**

Note, however, that when the antecedent is a thing, its grammatical gender determines the form of the pronoun:

- *Librum vídeo; **eum** legam:* I see the book; I will read **it.**
- *Urbem vídeo; **eam** intrabo:* I see the city; I will enter **it.**
- *Monstrum vídeo; **id** déstruam:* I see the monster; I will destroy **it.**

When *is* has a demonstrative sense, it may occur by itself as a pronoun or as an adjective paired with a noun:

- ***Ea** est silva primaeva:* **This** is the forest primeval.
- ***Eo** die, coniurati Caésarem interfecerunt:* **That** day, the conspirators killed Caesar.

 FYI The English abbreviation "i.e." comes from *id est,* meaning "that is."

Finally, *is* is often combined with the relative pronoun *qui* to mean "he who," "that which," "those who," and so on:

- *Non confido eis, qui Caésarem interfecerunt:* I do not trust those (the men) who killed Caesar.
- *Iudith manducavit ea, quae ancilla paráverat:* Judith ate the things that her slave girl had prepared.

TASK 5: TRANSLATING THE PRONOUN *Is*

Complete the translation of the following sentences.

1. *Honórius contra unum regem bellum habebat et **eum** devastabat:* Honorius waged war against a king and was clobbering ….

2. *Geórgius dixit, "Deus, da mihi virtutem contra draconem. Auxílio tuo **eum** superabo":* George said, "God, grant me power against the dragon. With your help, I will overcome …."

3. *Rex cogitabat: "Unam fíliam hábeo. Si fílio Honórii **eam** copulávero, pacem habebo":* The king thought, "I have one daughter. If I marry ... to Honorius' son, I will have peace."

4. *Casa mea ardet! Ad **eam** festinabo:* My house is burning! I will hasten to ....

5. *Ad **eam** urbem festinamus, in qua draco hábitat:* We are hastening to ... city, in which the dragon lives.

6. ***Eos** qui Latine sciunt omnes laudamus:* We all praise ... who know Latin.

THE PRONOUN *ILLE*

Latin also has another personal pronoun, which (especially in later Latin) is virtually interchangeable with *is*. Study the following table.

The Pronoun *Ille*

Singular	Masculine	Feminine	Neuter
Nominative	*ille*	*illa*	*illud*
Genitive	*illius*	*illius*	*illius*
Dative	*illi*	*illi*	*illi*
Accusative	*illum*	*illam*	*illud*
Ablative	*illo*	*illa*	*illo*
Plural	Masculine	Feminine	Neuter
Nominative	*illi*	*illae*	*illa*
Genitive	*illorum*	*illarum*	*illorum*
Dative	*illis*	*illis*	*illis*
Accusative	*illos*	*illas*	*illa*
Ablative	*illis*	*illis*	*illis*

JUST A MINUTE

The forms of *ille* closely parallel those of *is*. Note, for example, the genitive singular ending *–ius,* and the *–d* ending in the neuter singular nominative and accusative forms.

USES OF *ILLE*

As a personal pronoun, *ille* has the same meaning as *is*. However, it is often used to indicate a change of subject:

- *Rodan Godzillam oppugnat. **Ille** clamat fórtiter:* Rodan attacks Godzilla. He (Godzilla) bellows fiercely.
- *Caesar Ptolemaeum vicit. **Ille** in Aegyptum fugit:* Caesar defeated Ptolemy. He (Ptolemy) fled to Egypt.

Like *is, ille* can also be used as a demonstrative. However, it has the specific meaning "that."

- ***Illo** tempore, Nero regnabat:* At **that** time, Nero ruled.

TASK 6: TRANSLATING *ILLE*

Translate the following sentences.

1. *Abbas Magdalam vocat; illa ei respondet.*
2. *Ille liber mihi non placet.*
3. *Illo témpore, Nero contra senatum pugnavit; ille eum denuntiavit (denounced).*
4. *Geórgius ad draconem festinavit; ille clamavit fórtiter.*
5. *Illi hómines hippopótamos non timent; illi autem hómines dévorant.*

ESSENTIAL VOCABULARY

The following common words should be committed to memory.

Essential Vocabulary

Latin Word	Meaning	Related Word
Nouns		
ánima, –ae (feminine)	soul	animal, animate
cívitas, civitatis (feminine)	city	
cor, cordis (neuter)	heart	cordial

Latin Word	Meaning	Related Word
manus, –us (feminine)	hand	manual
opus, óperis (neuter)	work	operate
vestimentum, –i (neuter)	clothing	vestment
vinum, –i (neuter)	wine	vineyard

Verbs

ábeo, –ire, ábii	go away	
apprehendo, –ere, apprehendi	seize	apprehend
bibo, bíbere, bibi	drink	bibulous
festino, –are, –avi	hasten	
paro, –are, –avi	prepare	
pláceo, –ere, plácui (+ dative)	please	placate
sto, –are, steti	stand	static
suádeo, –ere, suasi	persuade	
surgo, súrgere, surrexi	rise	surge
vado, vádere, vasi	go	

Adjective

solus, –a, –um	alone	solitary

Adverbs

multum	much, a lot	
nimis	excessively, very much	
porro	further	

Prepositions

ante	before	
coram (+ ablative)	before	

RECOGNITION VOCABULARY

Go through this list once or twice, and then look for these words in the
Reading Exercise.

Recognition Vocabulary

Latin	Meaning	Related Word
ardens	burning	ardent
Assyrius, –a, –um	Assyrian	
columna, –ae (feminine)	column	
concupiscéntia, –ae (feminine)	concupiscence	
concussus, –a, –um	stricken	concussion
confirmo, –are, –avi	strengthen	confirm
contradico, –ere, –dixi	contradict	
eunuchus, -i (masculine)	eunuch	
fácies, –ei (feminine)	face	
Hebraea, –ae (feminine)	Hebrew woman	
immunis, –e	immune, unscathed	
motus, –us (masculine)	motion	
promitto, promíttere, promisi	promise	
siléntium, –i (neuter)	silence	

SUMMARY

In this hour, you have learned how to form the pluperfect and future perfect
tenses, and how to employ third person pronouns. Now you are ready to
encounter one of the more formidable heroines of the Latin Bible.

READING EXERCISE

The Bible was first translated into Latin, in various editions, around the second century A.D. In the fourth century, St. Jerome (*Didymus Hieronymus*) was
given the task of revising the sacred books for the church in Rome. He was

clearly the man for the job: Not only was he an excellent Latinist and well-versed in Greek, he was the first Latin translator to make a serious study of Hebrew. Jerome's revision eventually acquired the status of *Vulgata edítio:* the "Common Version" (slightly adapted).

JUDITH AND HOLOFERNES

In quarto die Holofernes fecit cenam servis suis, et dixit ad Vágao, eunuchum suum: "Vade, et suade Hebraeam illam sponte habitare mecum. Foedum est enim apud Assýrios si fémina irridet virum et immunis ab eo transit."

Tunc introivit Vágao ad Iudith, et dixit: "Noli timere, bona puella, introire ad dóminum meum; honorificabit te et manducabis cum eo, et bibes vinum in iucunditate." Cui Iudith respondit, "Num contradicam dómino meo? Omne quod erit ante óculos eius bonum et óptimum fáciam; quidquid autem illi placúerit, hoc mihi erit óptimum ómnibus diebus vitae meae." Et surrexit, et ornavit se vestimento suo; et ingressa stetit ante fáciem eius. Cor autem Holofernis concussum est, erat enim ardens in concupiscéntia eius. Et dixit ad eam Holofernes, "Bibe nunc, et accumbe in iucunditate, quóniam invenisti grátiam coram me." Et dixit Iudith, "Bibam, dómine, quóniam magnificata est ánima mea hódie prae ómnibus diebus meis." Et accepit, et manducavit, et bibit coram ipso, ea quae paráverat illi ancilla eius. Et iucundus factus Holofernes ad eam, bibit vinum multum nimis, quantum numquam bíberat in vita sua.

Ut autem sero erat, festinaverunt servi illius ad hospítia sua; et conclusit Vágao óstia cubículi, et ábiit. Erant autem omnes fatigati a vino; eratque Iudith sola in cubículo. Porro Holofernes iacebat in lecto, nímia ebrietate sopitus. Stetitque Iudith ante lectum, orans cum lácrimis, et labiorum motu in siléntio, dicens, "Confirma me, Dómine, Deus Israel, et réspice in hac hora ad ópera mánuum mearum, et sicut promisisti, Ierúsalem, civitatem tuam, érige, et hoc quod per te posse fieri cogitavi, perfíciam." Et cum haec dixerat, accessit ad columnam quae erat ad caput léctuli eius et pugionem eius, quia in ea legatus pendebat, exsolvit. Cumque evaginaverat illum, apprehendit comam cápitis eius, et ait, "Confirma me, Domine Deus, in hac hora." Et percussit bis in cervicem eius, et ábscidit caput eius, et ábstulit conopaeum eius a columnis, et evolvit corpus eius truncum.

Reading Vocabulary

abscido, –ere, –idi	cut off
áufero, –auferre	take away
accedo, –ere, accessi	go to
accumbo, –ere, accúbui	recline
ancilla, –ae (feminine)	handmaiden
apud	among
bis	twice
cena, –ae (feminine)	dinner
cervix, cervicis (masculine)	neck
coma, –ae (feminine)	hair
concludo, –ere, conclusi	close
conopaeum, –i (neuter)	canopy, mosquito net
credens	believing
cubículum, –i (neuter)	bedroom
dicens	saying
ebríetas, –tatis (feminine)	drunkenness
érigo, –ere, erexi	raise up
evágino, –are, –avi	draw (a sword)
evolvo, –ere, evolvi	roll away
factus	having become
fatigatus, –a, –um	tired
fíeri	be done
foedus, –a, –um	foul, unseemly
grátia, –ae (feminine)	favor
hac, haec, hoc	this
Holofernes, –is (masculine)	Holofernes
honorifico, –are, –avi	honor
hora, –ae (feminine)	hour
hospítium, –i (neuter)	lodging
iáceo, –ere, iácui	lie, recline
Ierúsalem (neuter)	Jerusalem
ingressus, –a, –um	having entered
intróeo, –ire, –ii	go in
ipso	him
irrideo, –ere, irrisi	mock

Israel (masculine)	Israel
iucunditas, –tatis (feminine)	enjoyment
iucundus, –a, –um	delighted
Iudith (feminine)	Judith
lábium, –i (neuter)	lip
lácrima, –ae (feminine)	tear
léctulum, –i (neuter)	bed
lectum, –i (neuter)	bed
legatus, –a, –um	tied up
magnificatus, –a, –um	magnified, elated
manduco, –are, –avi	eat
mecum = cum me	with me
nímius, –a, –um	excessive
óptimus, –a, –um	very good
orans	praying
orno, –are, –avi	dress
óstium, –i (neuter)	door
pendeo, –ere, pependi	hang
percutio, –ere, pecussi	strike
perfício, –ere, perfeci	accomplish
prae (+ ablative)	before, more than
púgio, pugionis (masculine)	dagger, short sword
quantum	as much as
quartus, –a, –um	fourth
quicquid	whatever
quóniam	because
respi–cio, –ere, respexi	look upon
se	herself
sero	late
sicut	just as
sopítus, –a, –um	drunk
sponte	voluntarily
suus, –a, –um	his, her, their
tránseo, –ire, –ii	pass across
truncus, –a, –um	headless
ut	as, when
Vágao (masculine)	Vagao

QUIZ

A

Complete the following verb synopses. Keep the same person and number throughout the six tenses.

Verb Synopsis Table

Present	_____	*míttimus*
Imperfect	_____	_____
Future	*amabunt*	_____
Perfect	_____	_____
Pluperfect	*amáverant*	_____
Future Perfect	_____	*misérimus*
Present	_____	_____
Imperfect	*capiebam*	*erat*
Future	_____	_____
Perfect	*cepi*	_____
Pluperfect	_____	*fúerat*
Future Perfect	_____	_____

B

Choose the form in parentheses that best completes the sentence, and translate.

1. *In (quarto/quarta) die Holofernes fecit cenam (servis/servos).*
2. *Dixit Vágao ad Iudith: "(Noli/Nolite) timere, bona puella."*
3. *Honorificabit (tibi/te) et manducabis cum (ei/eo).*
4. *Quicquid Domino meo (placúerat/placúerit), hoc (mei/mihi) erit óptimum.*
5. *Holofernes (erat/erit) ardens in concupiscéntia (ea/eius).*
6. *Et dixit ad eam "Bibe nunc, quóniam (invenisti/invenistis) grátiam coram me."*

HOUR 12

Present Participles; Gerunds

CHAPTER SUMMARY

LESSON PLAN:
In this hour you will learn about ...

- How to turn verbs into verbal adjectives, called *participles*
- How to turn verbs into verbal nouns, called *gerunds*

So far, you have learned how to distinguish nouns, verbs, and adjectives.

INTRODUCTORY READING

Look for the new forms in this seventeenth-century treatise on the "occupational hazards" of the intellectual life.

HEALTH PROBLEMS OF THE WELL-EDUCATED

*Litterati hómines omnes fere vitae sedentáriae incómmoda súbeunt. Nihil nótius (est) quam quod homo **sedendo** sápiens fit; tota ergo die ac nocte **sedentes,** inter litterarum oblectamenta, córporis damna non séntiunt, donec morborum causae sensim obrepentes eos lectis affíxerint.*

Translation:

Practically all literate people undergo the problems of a sedentary life. Nothing is more obvious than (the fact) that a person becomes wise **by sitting;** and so, **sitting** day and night amidst the pleasures of letters, they do not notice injuries of the body, until the causes of diseases, gradually creeping up on them, confine them to their beds ....

Note that two words in the passage mean "sitting": *sedendo* and *sedentes*. The forms are different in Latin because they are, in fact, functioning differently in the grammar of the sentence:

- *Sedendo* is a noun, showing us **by what** people become wise.
- *Sedentes* is an adjective, agreeing with the subject of *séntiunt* (they, literate people).

A verbal noun like *sedendo* is called a *gerund;* a verbal adjective like *sedentes* is called a *participle.*

FORMS OF THE PRESENT PARTICIPLE (*–ING*)

The participle (Latin *particípium*) gets its name from the verb *partícipo* (I share), because it "shares" the properties of both verbs and adjectives. English participles ending in *–ing* are called *present participles* because they refer to actions occurring at the same time as the main verb.

There are two parts to every participle: the stem, which comes from the verb, and the ending, which turns the verb into an adjective.

The stem for the present participle is similar to the stem for the imperfect tense. Study the following table.

Participle Stems

I	*II*	*III*
ámbula-ns	*habe-ns*	*mitte-ns*
walking	having	sending

III –io	*IV*
cápie-ns	*aúdie-ns*
catching	hearing

In the same way, we construct the forms *amans, iubens, ducens, interfíciens, véniens,* and so on. The ending *–ns* (which becomes *–nt* before other case endings) is equivalent to the English form *–ing*.

The following are participle forms for some irregular verbs you have learned:

- *sum, esse* becomes *ens*
- *possum, posse* becomes *potens*
- *eo, ire* becomes *eunt*

TASK 1: WORKING WITH PARTICIPLES

Using the Participle Stems table as a model, convert the following verbs into participles:

1. *accípio, accípere*

2. *paro, parare*

3. *ostendo, osténdere*

4. *pláceo, placere*

5. *scio, scire*

6. *puto, putare*

DECLINING THE PRESENT PARTICIPLE

Because the present participle functions as an adjective, it must vary its forms to agree with nouns in gender, number, and case. Study the following table.

Declining the Present Participle

Singular	Masculine/Feminine	Neuter
Nominative	*ámbulans*	*ámbulans*
Genitive	*ambulant-is*	*ambulant-is*
Dative	*ambulant-i*	*ambulant-i*
Accusative	*ambulant-em*	*ámbulans*
Ablative	*ambulant-e* or *ambulant-i*	*ambulant-e* or *ambulant-i*

Plural	Masculine/Feminine	Neuter
Nominative	*ambulant-es*	*ambulánt-ia*
Genitive	*ambulánt-ium*	*ambulánt-ium*
Dative	*ambulánt-ibus*	*ambulánt-ibus*
Accusative	*ambulant-es*	*ambulánt-ia*
Ablative	*ambulánt-ibus*	*ambulánt-ibus*

JUST A MINUTE

The ablative singular ending may be *–i* or *–e*. The *–e* is standard in the ablative absolute construction, which is discussed later.

Task 2: Declension of Participles

Decline ámbulans to match each noun (after ambiguous forms, the number of possible matches is given).

1. *puellas*
2. *puellae* (3)
3. *puella* (2)
4. *virum*
5. *viro* (2)
6. *viri* (2)
7. *mánui*
8. *mánuum*
9. *manus* (3)

Using Participles

As in English, participles can turn a whole clause into a tidy noun phrase:

- *In theatro sedent, patienter expectantes:* They sit in the theatre, waiting patiently. (They sit in the theatre and they wait patiently; they sit in the theatre while they wait patiently.)

Because the Romans had a taste for brevity, Latin writers of all periods used participles more than English writers would:

- *Mílites exspirantes corruerunt:* The soldiers, dying, fell. (The soldiers fell and died.)
- *Omnes circumstantes convocavit:* He called together all the around-standing ones (all the people who were standing around).
- *Romani ovantes Caésarem redeuntem salutaverunt:* The Romans, cheering, greeted Caesar, returning. (When Caesar returned, the Romans greeted him with cheers.)

Notice that Latin participles often occur where English would coordinate two clauses or where we would find a dependent clause beginning with "who," "when," or a similar word.

TIME SAVER

First, translate all present participles literally, with *–ing*. If this sounds awkward, turn the participle into a clause with "who/which," "when/as," "if," "because," or "although."

TASK 3: TRANSLATING PARTICIPLES

Translate the participles in bold in two ways: literally and as a clause that fits the context.

1. *Geórgius, ad urbem festinans, puellam vidit:* George, … to the city, saw the girl.

2. *Puellae lacrimanti ait, "Noli timere"* (*lácrimo* means "weep"): To the girl …, he said "Don't be afraid."

3. *Draconem ignem exhalantem non tímuit* (*exhalo* means "exhale"): He did not fear the dragon … fire.

4. *"Credentes vos Deus salvabit"* (*credo* means "believe"): "God will save you …."

5. *Geórgium draconem ducentem pópulus laudavit:* The people praised George … the dragon.

THE ABLATIVE ABSOLUTE

One very common type of participial phrase is the ablative absolute. In this construction, a noun or pronoun is paired with a participle in the ablative case to mean "with (noun) (verb) -ing."

- *Honório regnante, cives in pace vivebant:* With Honorius ruling, the citizens lived in peace. (While Honorius was ruling ….)

- *Deo volente, Latinam linguam discemus:* With God willing, we will learn Latin. (If God wills ….)

- *Adiuvántibus nobis, Caesar Gallos vicit:* With us helping, Caesar conquered the Gauls. (Since we helped ….)

Like other participial phrases, the ablative absolute is used as a substitute for dependent clauses meaning "when …," "if …," "since …," and "although …."

JUST A MINUTE

The participle *ens* (*being*) is not used in ablative absolute phrases. In certain phrases, it must be supplied:

- *Cicerone Hortensioque consúlibus:* With Cicero and Hortensius (being) consuls (When Cicero and Hortensius were consuls …)

The ablative noun or pronoun in an ablative absolute phrase is always understood as the *subject* of the participle: *adiuvántibus nobis* means "with us helping," not "helping us."

Task 4: Translating the Ablative Absolute

Translate the ablative absolute phrases literally, and then as dependent clauses according to the context.

1. *Cleopatra urgente, Marcus Antónius bellum civile movit (úrgeo* means urge): …, Marc Antony started a civil war.

2. *Pópulo rogante, Geórgius draconem occidit:* …, George killed the dragon.

3. *Philomela cantante, sagittárius arcum tetendit: …, the bowman stretched his bow.*

4. *Hippopótamis Macédones devorántibus, Alexander dolebat:* …, Alexander was sad.

5. *Holoferne dormiente, Iudith gládium evaginavit (dórmio* means sleep): …, Judith drew her sword.

The Gerund

At the beginning of this hour, you saw another Latin word for "sitting": *sedendo.* This form, however, talks about "sitting" as a *thing,* instead of portraying it as an action with a subject:

- *Legendo multa díscimus:* **By reading,** we learn many things.
- *Novum modum vivendi optamus:* We want a new way of living.

"Reading" is here regarded as the *means* by which we learn many things. *Vivendi,* "living," is added, like any genitive noun, to explain *modum.* Roman grammarians called these forms *gerunds* (from Latin *gerúndium*).

Like participles, gerunds consist of two elements: a stem and endings. The gerund stem is similar to that of the present participle, except that the infix is always *–nd.*

The Gerund Stem

I	II	III
amand-o	habend-o	mittend-o
by loving	by having	by sending

IV	V
capiend-o	audiend-o
by catching	by hearing

To the stem are added endings borrowed from the second declension:

Gerund Endings

Case	Gerund	Meaning
Nominative	—	—
Genitive	*amand-i*	of loving
Dative	*amand-o*	to/for loving
Accusative	*amand-um*	loving
Ablative	*amand-o*	FWIB loving

Notice that the gerund table does not have a nominative form. To talk about "loving" as the subject or complement of a sentence, we use the infinitive form, *amare*.

- *Cognóscere eum est amare:* To know him is to love him. (Knowing him is loving him.)

- *Errare humanum est; ignóscere, divinum:* To err is human; to forgive, divine. (Erring is human; forgiving, divine.)

 Both the infinitive and the gerund are regarded as neuter nouns.

SPECIAL USES OF THE GERUND

In general, as you have seen, gerunds function in the same ways as nouns and pronouns. However, you should take note of two special constructions in which the gerund is used to express purpose:

- *Vivo ad edendum:* I live to eat (for eating).
- *Vivo edendi causa:* I live to eat (for the sake of eating).

Causa (for the sake ...) is in the ablative case.

TASK 5: TRANSLATING GERUNDS

Translate the gerunds in bold.

1. ***Bibendo** Holofernes vitam amisit:* ... Holofernes lost his life.

2. *Sanctus Georgius ecclesiam intravit ad **orandum** (**orandi** causa):* St. George entered the church ....

3. *Nunc operam damus **cogitando**:* Now we give some time ....

4. *Omnes scelesti modum **operandi** habent* (*óperor* means "operate"): All criminals have a mode ....

5. *Multi hómines non edunt ad **vivendum,** sed vivunt ad **edendum:*** Many people do not eat ..., but live ....

ESSENTIAL VOCABULARY

The following common words should be committed to memory.

Essential Vocabulary

Latin	Meaning	Related Word
Nouns		
cibus, –i (masculine)	food	ciborium
copia, –ae (feminine)	supply, amount	copious
mens, mentis (feminine)	mind	mental
Res Pública	Commonwealth, state	Republic
usus, –us (masculine)	use	
Verbs		
duco, –ere, duxi	lead	induce
laboro, –are, –avi	suffer, labor	labor
libet	it pleases	
servo, –are, –avi	save, preserve	conserve
sóleo, –ere	be accustomed	
Adjectives		
aequus, –a, –um	right, fitting	equity
albus, –a, –um	white	album
céteri, –ae, –a	other(s), the rest	et cetera
dulcis, –e	sweet	
sápiens, –nt	wise	homo sapiens
tutus, –a, –um	safe	tutor
várius, –a, –um	varied	

Latin	Meaning	Related Word
Adverbs		
ádeo	so, as	
fere	practically	
hinc	hence, from this (come)	
male	badly	

RECOGNITION VOCABULARY

Go through this list once or twice, and look for these words in the Reading Exercise.

Recognition Vocabulary

Latin	Meaning	Related Word
acíditas, –tatis (feminine)	acidity	
aer, aeris (masculine)	air	aerial
bilis, bilis (feminine)	bile	
cerebrum, –i (neuter)	brain	cerebral
cónsequens, –ntis (neuter)	consequence	
defraudatus, –a, –um	deprived of	
imbecíllitas, –tatis (feminine)	weakness	
infesto, –are	infest	
ingeniosus, –a, –um	intelligent	ingenious
ingestus, –a, –um	ingested	
languor, –oris (masculine)	languor	
mácies, –ei (feminine)	leanness	emaciated
moderatus, –a, –um	moderate	
morosus, –a, –um	morose	
oráculum, –i (neuter)	oracle	

continues

Recognition Vocabulary   (continued)

Latin	Meaning	Related Word
pótio, –ionis (feminine)	drink	potion
praeferendus, –a, –um	preferable	
professor, –oris (masculine)	professor	
primórdia, –iorum (neuter)	beginnings	primordial
purus, –a, –um	pure	
régimen, regíminis (neuter)	regimen	
sánitas, sanitatis (feminine)	health	sanity
sedentárius, –a, –um	sedentary	
serenus, –a, –um	serene	
síleo, –ere, sílui	be silent	
solitárius, –a, –um	solitary	
temperamentum, –i (neuter)	temperament	
terrestris, –e	earthly	terrestrial
victus, –us (masculine)	food	victuals, "vittles"

SUMMARY

In this chapter, you have learned how to form and translate present participles and gerunds. You are now ready to read some more medical advice from the seventeenth century.

READING EXERCISE

Most people come to study Latin for its connection to the liberal arts, but it is also indispensable for the historian of science. As late as the nineteenth century, dissertations in such subjects as astronomy, biology, botany, and medicine were still written in Latin. The following is adapted from a treatise by the Italian doctor Bernadino Ramazzini (1633–1714), who specialized in "preventive" medicine for the various professions. His advice to scholars (and, indeed, to all office workers) still holds true today.

DISEASES OF LEARNING

Litterati hómines, qui, ut ait Ficinus, "quantum mente et cérebro negotiosi sunt, tantum córpore sunt otiosi," omnes fere vitae sedentáriae incómmoda subeunt ....

In universum litterati omni stómachi imbecillitate laborare solent. Nam fere omnes qui sério litterarum stúdio dant óperam, stómachi languore laborant; dum enim cérebrum cóncoquit ea, quae sciendi libido et litterarum orexis íngerit, nónnisi male potest concóquere ea, quae fuerunt ingesta alimenta .... Hinc ergo cruditates, flátuum ingens cópia, córporis totius pallor et mácies, partes geniali succo defraudatae: summatim ómnia damna, quae cacochýliae sunt consequéntia, ortum ducunt. Sic studiosi paulatim, licet Ioviali temperamento praéditi, saturnini ac melanchólici fiunt; sic dícere solemus, quod melanchólici sunt ingeniosi; at forte áptius, ingeniosi fiunt melanchólici, quia spirituósior sánguinis pars circa mentis ópera absumpta est, dum pars magis terrestris intus relicta est .... Melanchólicis ergo passiónibus plúrimum obnóxii sunt Litterarum professores, eoque magis si a primórdiis tale temperamentum habúerint: sic hábitu gráciles, luridi, plúmbei, morosi ac solitáriae vitae cúpidi esse solent.

Verum, quia pro bono Rei públicae tanti ínterest sapiéntium valetudo, aequum est, quantum fíeri potest, eam servare et resitúere eam. Illi ergo aura liberiore gaudere debent, ac várium vitae genus adhibere .... Quod victum spectat, debent Hippócratis dictum pro oráculo habere: "Sanitatis stúdium est non repletus esse cibis" .... Quoad potum, vinum céteris potiónibus est praeferendum; merácum laudamus, sed módicum. Scio quod multi e litteratis, suorum medicorum consílio, vina alba, tenúia in usu habere, ítaque putant quod bíbere possunt quantum libet. Sed hoc non est adeo tutum, ut putant. Nam vina haec tenúia, aestate praecípue, aciditatem quandam adsciscunt .... Quoad ceterarum rerum régimen ... moderata córporis exercitatione cotídie debent uti, si tamen aer purus ac serenus est, et venti silent .... Lavacrum quoque aquae dulcis, aestate praesertim, ubi atra bilis litteratos infestat, valde salutare est.

Reading Vocabulary

absumptus, –a, –um	used up
adhíbeo, –ere, adhíbui	use, adopt
adscisco, –ere, adscivi	acquire
aestas, aestatis (feminine)	age
alimentum, –i (neuter)	food, nourishment
áptius	more appropriately
ater, –ra, –rum	black
aura, –ae (feminine)	air
cacochylia, –ae (feminine)	"bad humor," an imbalance of the humors
cóncoquo, –ere, concoxi	cook
cotídie	every day
crúditas, –tatis (feminine)	indigestion
cúpidus, –a, –um	desirous (of)
damnum, –i (neuter)	injury, damage
dictum, –i (neuter)	saying
eoque	all the (more)
exercitátio, –onis (feminine)	exercise
Ficinus, –i (masculine)	Ficino, a philosopher
fio, fíeri (irregular verb)	become
flatus, –us (masculine)	flatulence
gaúdeo, –ere (+ ablative)	enjoy
genialis, –e	reproductive
grácilis, –e	slender
hábitus, –us (masculine)	stature
haec, hoc	this, these
Hippócrates, –is (masculine)	Hippocrates
incómmodum, –i (neuter)	problems, afflictions
íngero, –ere, –gessi	bring in, cause
ínterest (+ genitive)	it is in the interest of …
intus	within, inside
Iovialis, –e	like Jupiter, "jovial"
lavacrum, –i (neuter)	bath, wash
libérior, –is (adjective)	freer
libido, libídinis (feminine)	lust
licet	although

lítterae, –arum (feminine)	literature
litteratus, –a, –um	literate, intellectual
lúridus, –a, –um	sallow
magis	more
médicus, –i (masculine)	physician
melanchólicus, –a, –um	melancholic, depressed
meracum, –i (neuter)	unmixed, undiluted wine
módicus, –a, –um	a little
negotiosus, –a, –um	busy, occupied
nónnisi	only ("not unless")
obnóxius, –a, –um	subject to
ópera, –ae (feminine)	attention
orexis, –is (feminine)	appetite
ortus, –us (masculine)	origin (with *duco:* take its origin …)
otiosus, –a, –um	at ease, unoccupied
pallor, palloris (masculine)	pallor
pássio, passionis (feminine)	passion
paulatim	little by little
plúmbeus, –a, –um	leaden
plúrimum	especially
potus, –us (masculine)	drink
praecípue	especially
praéditus, –a, –um	endowed
praesertim	especially
quandam	a certain
quantum	as much as
quoad	as far as … is concerned, as for …
quoque	also
relictus, –a, –um	left
repletus, –a, –um	filled, replete
restítuo, –ere, restítui	restore
salutaris, –e	healthy
sanguis, sánguinis (masculine)	blood
saturninus, –a, –um	"Saturnine," morose
sério	seriously

continues

Reading Vocabulary (continued)

spectat	(as far as) is concerned
spirituósior, –ioris	more spiritual (adjective)
studiosus, –a, –um	studious
súbeo, –ire, súbii	undergo
succus, –i (masculine)	juice, sap
summatim	summarily
suus, –a, –um	his, her, its, their
tanti (+ interest)	it is so much in the interest of
ténuis, –e	light
universum	(in) general
ut	as
uti	(to) use
valetudo, –túdinis (feminine)	health
ventus, –i (masculine)	wind
verum	but

QUIZ

A

Complete the following table.

Verb Review

Present	Infinitive	Participle	Gerund	Perfect
amo	*amare*	*amans*	*amandi*	*amavi*
laudo	_____	_____	_____	_____
hábeo	_____	_____	_____	_____
dico	_____	_____	_____	_____
cápio	_____	_____	_____	_____
aúdio	_____	_____	_____	_____

B

The following words have deceptively similar forms. How should they be translated?

1. *mílitis*
2. *mittis*
3. *reges*
4. *vides*
5. *amas*
6. *puellas*
7. *videndo*
8. *ostendo*
9. *córnui*
10. *timui*

C

Answer in Latin the following questions about the reading passage:

1. *Cur litterati hómines stómachi imbecillitate laborant?*
2. *Quibus passionibus sunt litterarum professores obnóxii?*
3. *Debentne litterati hómines multum edere?*
4. *Quale vinum praeferendum est?*
5. *Nonne vinum album tutum est? Quidni?* (Why not?)
6. *Quando praecípue debent exercitatione uti?*
7. *Quo témpore lavacra praecípue salutária sunt? Cur?*

The Passive Voice: Present, Imperfect, and Future Tenses; Passive Imperative and Infinitive

CHAPTER SUMMARY

LESSON PLAN:

In this hour you will learn about ...

- Forming sentences in which the subject is acted upon by an agent
- Distinguishing verbs in the *passive* voice from those in the *active* voice
- Expressing the agent with a passive verb

So far, you have learned how to form transitive sentences, in which the subject acts upon an object.

INTRODUCTORY READING

Let's start by looking at a brief passage describing the customs of the Chinese, as reported by missionaries of the sixteenth century.

MARRIAGE IN OLD CHINA

Deprehensum adultérium aeque viri ac féminae, cápite **lúitur.** *Ad núptias, dotem non viro fémina, sed vir féminae defert. Síngulae uxores in matris famílias* **numerantur** *loco; péllices procul a conspectu váriis locis* **aluntur.**

Manifest adultery, whether on the part of a man or a woman, **is punished** by death. At a wedding, a woman does not give a dowry to a man, but a man to a woman. Wives (of which a man has only one) **are counted** as matrons; concubines **are kept** in various places, far out of sight.

Notice that in some of these sentences, the subject (for example, *uxores*, "wives") does not *do* the action, but plays a passive role. This is indicated in English by verb forms such as "are counted." In Latin, the corresponding marker is a special ending (*–tur*). Such verbs are said to be in the *passive* voice.

ACTIVE AND PASSIVE VOICE

We have already seen that verbs are marked for person (first, second, third), number (singular, plural), and tense (present, imperfect, and so on). Another important distinction is traditionally called voice (Latin *vox*). The difference can be seen in the following sentences:

- Man **bites** dog: "bites" is a verb in the *active voice*
- Man **is bitten** by dog: "is bitten" is a verb in the *passive voice*

In terms of meaning, a verb is called active if the subject is doing the action, and passive if the subject is receiving the action. Passive verbs are often accompanied by an expression of agent (for example, "by dog"), to indicate the doer of the action.

FORMS OF THE PASSIVE VOICE: PRESENT TENSE

In English, the passive voice is formed by combining a form of the verb "to be" with the passive participle, which often has the ending *–ed:*

- In China, mistresses **are** not **counted** as wives.
- Alexander's men **are warned** about the hippos.

In Latin, however, the present, imperfect, and future tenses are "pacified" by using a special set of endings. Here is the present tense of the verb *amo, amare, amavi* (love).

The Passive Voice, Present Tense

Singular

am-or	(I am loved; I am being loved)
ama-ris	(you are loved; you are being loved)
*ama-**tur***	(he, she, or it is loved; … is being loved)

Plural

ama-mur	(we are loved; we are being loved)
amá-mini	(y'all are loved; y'all are being loved)
*ama-**ntur***	(they are loved; they are being loved)

TIME SAVER

Remember that the basic sign of the passive voice in the present, imperfect, and future tenses is *–r*. It shows up in all forms except *–mini*. You should memorize these endings: *–(o)r, –ris, –tur, –mur, –mini, –ntur.*

Task 1: Matching Forms

On the analogy of *amo* (given previously), give the form of *laudo, –are, –avi* that matches each of the following:

1. I am praised
2. they are praised
3. y'all are praised
4. she is praised
5. we are praised
6. you are praised

The Present Passive Throughout the Conjugations

The endings you have just learned are added to the present stem of each conjugation, as follows.

Present Passive, All Conjugations

I	II	III
love	**teach**	**send**
Singular		
am-or	*dóce-or*	*mitt-or*
ama-ris	*doce-ris*	*mítte-ris*
ama-tur	*doce-tur*	*mítti-tur*
Plural		
ama-mur	*doce-mur*	*mítti-mur*
amá-mini	*docé-mini*	*mittí-mini*
ama-ntur	*doce-ntur*	*mittu-ntur*

III –io	IV	
catch	**hear**	
Singular		
cápi-ior	*aúdi-ior*	
cápe-ris	*audi-ris*	
cápi-tur	*audi-tur*	
Plural		
cápi-mur	*audi-mur*	
capí-mini	*audí-mini*	
capiu-ntur	*audiu-ntur*	

JUST A MINUTE

The stem vowel of the third conjugation changes, depending on what sounds best (to ancient Romans, at least). It is usually –*i*, but it changes to –*e* before –*ris*, and –*u* before –*ntur*. In fact, the Romans liked the sound of –*untur* so much that they also tacked it onto the stem of the fourth conjugation (as in *audi–untur*).

TASK 2: TRANSLATING VERB FORMS

Translate each of the following verb forms.

1. *doceris*
2. *docetur*
3. *míttitur*
4. *mittímini*
5. *audimur*
6. *audiuntur*
7. *cáperis*
8. *cápior*

FORMS OF THE PASSIVE VOICE: IMPERFECT TENSE

The passive endings you learned for the present tense are also adapted to the stem of the imperfect tense, –*ba*. Here are the imperfect forms of the verb *amo:*

The Passive Voice, Imperfect Tense

Singular	
*ama-**ba-r***	(I was loved; I was being loved)
*ama-**ba-ris***	(you were loved; …)
*ama-**ba-tur***	(he, she, or it was loved; …)

Plural	
*ama-**ba-mur***	(we were loved; …)
*ama-**bá-mini***	(y'all were loved; …)
*ama-**ba-ntur***	(they were loved; …)

The other conjugations form the imperfect passive on the same stem as the imperfect active.

Imperfect Passive, All Conjugations (First Person Singular)

I	II	III	IV
love	teach	send	hear
ama-ba-r	*doce-ba-r*	*mitte-ba-r*	*audie-ba-r*

Third conjugation *–io* verbs have the same imperfect stem as fourth conjugation verbs. For example, the imperfect passive of *cápio* is *capie-ba-r*, etc.

TASK 3: TRANSLATING VERBS

Translate the following verbs.

1. *docebantur*
2. *ducebamur*
3. *audiebámini*
4. *laudabar*
5. *monebatur*
6. *interficiebantur*
7. *inveniebaris*
8. *parabatur*

THE FUTURE PASSIVE: THE FIRST AND SECOND CONJUGATIONS

You recall that the future tense is formed in two ways: The first and second conjugations add the personal endings to a *bi* infix, while the third and fourth conjugations add them to the future stem vowels *e* and *a*. These same stems can be combined with the passive endings you have just learned. Here is an overview of the first two conjugations in the future tense, passive voice.

Future Passive, First and Second Conjugations

I	II
love	*teach*
Singular	
*ama-**b-or*** (I will be loved)	*doce-**b-or*** (I will be taught)
*amá-**be-ris***	*docé-**be-ris***
*amá-**bi-tur***	*docé-**bi-tur***

continues

Future Passive, First and Second Conjugations   (continued)

I	II
love	teach
Plural	
amá-**bi-mur**	docé-**bi-mur**
ama-**bí-mini**	doce-**bí-mini**
ama-**bu-ntur**	doce-**bu-ntur**

JUST A MINUTE

The *–bi* infix changes to *–b* before the ending *–or,* to *–be* before the ending *–ris* (compare *mitte-ris* in the present tense), and to *–bu* before the ending *–ntur.*

TASK 4: WORKING WITH THE FUTURE PASSIVE

Using the verbs *laudo, –are, –avi* (praise), and *móneo, monere, mónui* (warn), tell how you would say the following:

1. they will be praised
2. I will be warned
3. he will be praised
4. we will be warned
5. y'all will be praised
6. you will be warned

THE FUTURE PASSIVE: THIRD AND FOURTH CONJUGATIONS

In the third and fourth conjugations, the future stem is combined with passive endings, as follows.

Future Passive, Third and Fourth Conjugations

III	III –io	IV
send	catch	hear
Singular		
mitt-**a-r**	cápi-**a-r**	aúdi-**a-r**
mitt-**e-ris**	capi-**e-ris**	audi-**e-ris**
mitt-**e-tur**	capi-**e-tur**	audi-**e-tur**

III	*III –io*	*IV*
send	*catch*	*hear*
Plural		
*mitt-e-**mur***	*capi-e-**mur***	*audi-e-**mur***
*mitt-é-**mini***	*capi-é-**mini***	*audi-é-**mini***
*mitt-e-**ntur***	*capi-e-**ntur***	*audi-e-**ntur***

PROCEED WITH CAUTION

As in the active voice, the future forms of the third and fourth conjugations are easily confused with various present-tense forms. For example, the present stem of the second conjugation and the future stem of the third and fourth conjugations both end in –e:

- *docetur:* he **is** taught
- *mittetur:* he **will be** sent

It is also easy to confuse the present and the future in the second person singular form of the third conjugation, although the accentuation is different:

- *mítteris:* you **are** sent
- *mitteris:* you **will be** sent

TASK 5: TRANSLATING VERBS

Translate the following verbs.

1. *míttitur*
2. *mittetur*
3. *mittentur*
4. *aúdior*
5. *aúdiar*
6. *audieris*
7. *cáperis*
8. *capieris*
9. *capiémini*

REVIEW OF VERB FORMS

When you translate a Latin verb form, you are essentially reading backwards.

Translating Verbs

Root	Infix/stem	Ending
ama	*bi*	*t* (active)
love	will	he
ama	*bi*	*tur*
love	will	he be (passive)

This can be a difficult skill for English-speakers, who are used to analyzing verbs from left to right. Practice, however, makes perfect. Look carefully at the components of each verb you encounter, and soon understanding Latin forms will be second nature.

TASK 6: VERB FORMS

Match the verb forms with the correct translation from the list at the bottom.

1. *amabor*
2. *docebamur*
3. *míttimur*
4. *capientur*
5. *amabatur*
6. *docéberis*
7. *mítteris*
8. *cápiar*
9. *amabar*
10. *docémini*

we are sent; you will be taught; I was being loved; y'all are taught; they will be caught; I will be loved; he was loved; I will be caught; you are sent; we were being taught

THE PASSIVE INFINITIVE

The active infinitive (as in *amare*, "to love") can also be converted into the passive voice by changing to the ending *–re* to *–(r)i*. Study the following table.

The Passive Infinitive

I	II	III
*ama-**ri***	*doce-**ri***	*mitt-**i***
to be loved	to be taught	to be sent

IIIio	IV
cap-**i**	audi-**ri**
to be caught	to be heard

Note that in all third-conjugation verbs, the −*r* element drops out of the passive infinitive.

Task 7: Converting Active to Passive

Convert the following active infinitive forms into the passive, and translate.

1. *laudare*

2. *monere*

3. *dícere*

4. *interfícere*

5. *sentire* (to feel)

The Passive Imperative

Finally, the active imperative (as in *ama! amate!* "Love!") can also be converted into the passive voice as follows.

The Passive Imperative

	I	II	III
Singular	*amare!*	*docere!*	*míttere!*
Plural	*amámini!*	*docémini!*	*mittímini!*
	Be loved!	Be taught!	Be sent!

	III −io	IV
Singular	*capere!*	*audire!*
Plural	*capímini!*	*audímini!*
	Be caught!	Be heard!

Note that the singular form of the passive imperative is identical to the active infinitive (as in *amare*, "to love"); the plural passive imperative form is identical to the second person plural, present passive form (as in *amámini*, "you are loved").

Task 8: Converting Active to Passive II

Convert the following active imperative forms into the passive, and translate.

1. *lauda!*

2. *monete!*

3. *áccipe!* (*accípio, –ere,* means "accept")

4. *audite!*

Agency

At the beginning of the hour, we saw that in sentences with passive verbs, the subject receives the action. If we want to know the agent, or doer, of the action, we must add another phrase:

• Dog is bitten **by man.**

In this example, *dog* is the subject and *man* is the agent. The sign of agency is the preposition *by*. In Latin, we say:

• *Canis **ab hómine** mordetur.*

The preposition *a/ab* (from) doubles as a sign of agency (by); it is always followed by a noun in the ablative case.

PROCEED WITH CAUTION

In English, we use "by" to indicate not only agency (by *someone*), but also instrument or means (by *something*):

• Caesar is killed **by Brutus.** (agent)
• Caesar is killed **by a dagger.** (instrument)

In Latin, *a/ab* is used only for agency; instrument is marked by a noun in the ablative case, without a preposition:

• *Caesar a **Bruto** necatur.* (agent)
• *Caesar **pugione** necatur.* (instrument)

Task 9: Working with Agency and Instrument

Translate the words in bold.

1. *Holofernes **a fémina Hebraea** interfícitur:* Holofernes is killed ….

2. *Viri litterati **morbis** stómachi saepe affliguntur.* Educated men are often afflicted … (*morbus, –i* [masculine] means "disease").

3. *Nos **a viris litteratis** docemur:* We are taught ….

4. *Nos **lingua Latina** torquemur:* We are tormented ….

ABLATIVE OF DESCRIPTION

While we are on the subject of the ablative case, the Reading Exercise will show you another way of using it without a preposition. This is the ablative of description. It occurs in noun/adjective pairs, such as the following:

- *Caesar est vir **magna diligéntia:*** Caesar is a man **of great diligence.**

- *Sinarum gens est **summa urbanitate:*** The Chinese are a people **of the highest sophistication.**

JUST A MINUTE

The ablative of description is equivalent in meaning to a use of the genitive case discussed earlier:

- *Caesar est vir **magna diligentia:*** Caesar is a man **of great diligence.**

- *Caesar est vir **magnae diligéntiae:*** Caesar is a man **of great diligence.**

Note that English always uses the preposition "of" for this construction.

ESSENTIAL VOCABULARY

The following common words should be committed to memory.

Essential Vocabulary

Latin	Meaning	Related Word
Nouns		
cura, –ae (feminine)	care	
honor, honoris (masculine)	honor	honor, honorable
laus, laudis (feminine)	praise	laudatory
ordo, órdinis (masculine)	order	ordinal
pes, pedis (masculine)	foot	pedal
rátio, rationis (feminine)		reason, rational account, calculation

continues

Essential Vocabulary (continued)

Latin	Meaning	Related Word
Verbs		
addo, áddere, áddidi	add	
confício, –ere, confeci	make, put together	confection
constítuo, –ere, constítui	make, establish	constitution
tego, –ere, texi	cover	protection
Adjectives		
longus, –a, –um	long	
nóbilis, –e	noble	
privatus, –a, –um	private	
públicus, –a, –um	public	
síngulus, –a, –um	single, individual	
summus, –a, –um	highest, top	summit
Adverbs		
deinde	and then	
magis	more	
minus	less	diminish
Preposition		
apud	at, by, with, among	
Conjunctions		
quoque	also	
vel	and	

RECOGNITION VOCABULARY

Go over this list once or twice, and then look for these words in the Reading Exercise.

Recognition Vocabulary

Latin	Meaning	Related Word
áctio, actionis	action (feminine)	
brévitas, brevitatis (feminine)	shortness	brevity
caelebs, caélibis (adjective)	unmarried	celibate
célebro, –are, –avi	celebrate	
color, colóris (masculine)		color
comoédia, –ae (feminine)	comedy	
dígitus, –i (masculine)	finger	digit
díligens, diligentis (adjective)	diligent	
discrímino, –are, –avi	separate	discriminate
distinctus, –a, –um	distinct	
distínguo, –ere, –ui	distinguish	
exhíbeo, –ere, exhíbui	exhibit	
forma, –ae (feminine)	form, beauty	
gemma, –ae (feminine)	gem	
história, –ae (feminine)	history	
infántia, –ae (feminine)	infancy	
invito, –are, –avi	invite	
hiláritas, –tatis, –tati (feminine)	cheer	hilarity
lunaris, –e	lunar	
milítia, –ae (feminine)	militia	military service
maritus, –a, –um	married man	marital
matrona, –ae (feminine)	married woman	matron
nota, –ae (feminine)	mark	note
observo, –are, –avi	observe	
ornatus, –us (masculine)	ornament	ornate
períoda, –ae (feminine)		period
principium, –i (neuter)	beginning	principal

continues

Recognition Vocabulary (continued)

Latin	Meaning	Related Word
raro	rarely	
rustícitas, –tatis (feminine)	boorishness	rusticity
sumptuosus, –a, –um	rich	sumptuous

SUMMARY

In this hour, you have learned how to form the passive voice in three tenses—the present, the imperfect, and the future—and also how to form the infinitive and imperative in the passive voice. You have learned how to express the agent of a passive verb and how to distinguish this from other uses of the ablative case.

Now, test your new skills on a bit of ethnographic lore assembled by one of the great missionary efforts of early modern times.

READING EXERCISE

Ancient and medieval Europeans had a vague idea of Eastern peoples, but it was not until the Renaissance that they had frequent and direct contact with Asian civilizations. After the spectacular missionary successes of St. Francis Xavier (who died in 1552), the Jesuits in particular turned their attention to the Far East. Here is the account of Jesuit Father Petro Maffei (1536–1603) of the sophisticated culture of China. (Adapted)

A DESCRIPTION OF OLD CHINA

Sunt autem Sinarum pópuli magis aut minus aéneo colore, vel cándido: simis náribus, exíguis admodum ocellis, rara barba, longis crínibus, quos accurate comunt. Neque tamen est una rátio capillamenti ómnibus: quippe caélibes comam a fronte discríminant; mariti (comam) confundunt; atque ea praecípue nota órdinem utrumque distínguit. Primárii ac dívites, quique milítiam exercent, versicolore sérico córpora tegunt; plebeii ac paúperes (córpora tegunt) lino seu gossípio.

Mulíeres circa curam cápitis diligentes sunt. Crines diu pexos concinnatosque in summo circúmligant vitta gemmis auroque distincta. Réliqui córporis ornatus est mínime lascivus. Praecípuam decoris ac formae laudem in pedum brevitate et exilitate constítuunt: ideoque pedes tenelli ab infántia fásciis constringuntur. Magnum apud nóbiles matronas honorem habet pudicítia. Raro visuntur: nec in públicum pródeunt nisi in gestatória sella, quae velis tégitur.

Annum e lunáribus períodis duódecim (XII) confíciunt, et tértio quoque anno ad duódecim unam addunt. Princípium anni in Mártii mensis novilúnio celebratur. Eum diem pública hilaritate (célebrant); natalem quisque suum privata gratulatione observat. Múnera et spórtulas ínvicem mittunt; apparatíssimas deinde épulas habent, in quibus exquisimitíssimi interponuntur ludi. Comoediae ac tragoediae exhibentur sumptuosae, vel fábulae praesertim a poetis confictae, vel actiones e vétere história repetitae .... Conviviorum autem rátio est talis. Invitantur multi: síngulis convivis mensa própria appónitur ex ligno adinstar ébeni splendidíssimo .... Cibos dígitis attrectare, notam rusticitatis putant.

Reading Vocabulary

accurate	carefully
adinstar	like (+ genitive)
ádmodum	rather, very
aéneus, –a, –um	bronze-colored
apparatíssimus, –a, –um	elaborate
appono, –ere, appósui	serve, put before
attrecto, –are, –avi	handle
aurum, –i (neuter)	gold
barba, –ae (feminine)	beard
cándidus, –a, –um	white
capillamentum, –i (neuter)	hairstyling
cibi, –orum (masculine plural)	dishes, kinds of food
circúmligo, –are, –avi	bind up, tie around
coma, –ae (feminine)	hair
como, cómere, compsi	comb, style
concinnatus, –a, –um	arranged
confictus, –a, –um	made up, composed
confundo, –ere, –fudi	mix up, comb together
constringo, –ere, –nxi	bind up, constrict
convívium, –ii (neuter)	party
crines, crínium (masculine plural)	hair

continues

Reading Vocabulary (continued)

decor, decoris (masculine)	beauty
dives, dívitis (masculine)	rich man
duódecim	twelve
e, ex	(made) of, from
ébenus, –i (masculine)	ebony
épulae, –arum (feminine plural)	banquet
exérceo, –ere, excércui	be engaged in, practice
exíguus, –a, –um	small
exílitas, exilitatis (feminine)	slenderness
exquisitíssimus, –a, –um	most exquisite
fábula, –ae (feminine)	play
fáscia, –ae (feminine)	cord
frons, frontis (feminine)	forehead
gestatórius, –a, –um	hand-carried
gossípium, –i (neuter)	cotton
gratulátio, –ionis (feminine)	festivity
interpono, –ere, interpósui	interpose, insert
ínvicem	each other
lascivus, –a, –um	alluring, playful
lignum, –i (neuter)	wood
linum, –i (neuter)	linen, flax
ludus, –i (masculine)	game
Mártius, –a, –um	of March
mensa, –ae (feminine)	table
mensis, –is (masculine)	month
mínime	very little, minimally
munus, múneris (neuter)	gift
nares, nárium (feminine plural)	nostrils
natalis, –e	natal
natalis dies	birthday
nec	nor, not (= *neque*)
nisi	except
novilúnium, –ii (neuter)	new moon
ocellus, –i (masculine)	eye
pexus, –a, –um	combed

plebéius, –a, –um	common, lower class
praecípuus, –a, –um	principal, special
praecípue	especially
primárius, –a, –um	primary
pródeo, –ire, pródii	go forth
próprius, –a, –um	(their) own, proper
públicus, –a, –um	public
pudicítia, –ae (feminine)	modesty
quippe	for
quisque	each one
rarus, –a, –um	sparse
réliquus, –a, –um	remaining
repetitus, –a, –um	taken (from)
sella, –ae (feminine)	chair, litter
séricus, –a, –um	silk
seu	or
sím(i)us, –a, –um	simian, like an ape's
Sinae, –arum (masculine plural)	Chinese people
splendidíssimus, –a, –um	most splendid
spórtula, –ae (feminine)	basket
suus, –a, –um	his/her own
tenellus, –a, –um	delicate
tértius, –a, –um	third
tragoédia, –ae (feminine)	tragedy
utrumque	both
velum, –i (neuter)	veil
versícolor, –coloris (adjective)	multicolored
viso, vísere, visi	see
vitta, –ae (feminine)	headband

Quiz

A

Convert the following verbs from active to passive, or from passive to active, and translate.

1. *docet*
2. *capiuntur*
3. *amabamus*
4. *audietur*
5. *monébitis*
6. *mittet*
7. *audis*
8. *laudor*
9. *dicebam*
10. *interfíceris*

B

Choose the form that best completes the sentence, and translate.

1. *Mulíeres circa curam cápitis (diligens/diligentes) sunt.*
2. *(Réliqui/réliquae) córporis ornatus est mínime lascivus.*
3. *Pedes tenelli fásciis (constringitur/ constringuntur).*
4. *(Magnum/magnam) apud (nobilis/nobiles) matronas honorem habet pudicítia.*
5. *Non in públicum pródeunt nisi in gestatória sella, (qui/quae) velis tégitur.*
6. *Múnera et spórtulas ínvicem (mittunt/mittent).*
7. *Comoédiae ac tragoédiae (exhibent/exhibentur) sumptuosae.*
8. *Conviviorum autem rátio est (talis/tale).*
9. *Invitantur (multi/multa).*
10. *Cibos (dígitos/dígitis) attrectare, notam rusticitatis putant.*

HOUR 14

The Passive Participle; the Perfect, Pluperfect, and Future Perfect Passive

CHAPTER SUMMARY

LESSON PLAN:

In this hour you will learn about …

- The *perfect passive* participle (corresponding to English forms ending in *–ed*)
- The participle used in the construction called the "ablative absolute"
- Forming the passive voice of the perfect, pluperfect, and future perfect tenses

So far, you have learned how to use the passive voice in the "non-perfective" tenses (present, imperfect, future), and also how to use the present active participle (corresponding to English *–ing*).

INTRODUCTORY READING

Look for the passive participle in the following extract adapted from the *Aeneid* of Vergil (first century A.D.), which covers events during and after the fall of Troy.

THE BUILDING OF THE TROJAN HORSE

> ***Fracti*** *bello fatisque* ***repulsi,*** *ductores dánaum, tot iam labéntibus annis, instar montis equum divina Pálladis arte aedíficant,* ***sectaque*** *intexunt* ***abíete*** *costas; votum pro réditu símulant; ea fama vagatur.*

> **Broken** by war and **repelled** by the fates, while so many years already slip by, the leaders of the Danaans build, with the art of Pallas, a horse as big as a mountain, and **when the oak has been cut**, they join the ribs together. They simulate a prayer for their return; this rumor is spread abroad.

Notice that the subject of the first sentence (*ductores,* meaning "leaders") is described by verbal adjectives referring to things that have already happened to them (*fracti,* meaning "broken"; *repulsi,* meaning "repelled"). These are examples of the *perfect passive participle.* We also see this participle used "absolutely" in the expression *secta abíete* ("with the oak having been cut," meaning "when the oak has been cut").

The Perfect Passive Participle

"Broken" and "cut" are typical forms of the passive participle. It is called "passive" because the noun it modifies is the recipient of some action:

- "the **broken** leaders" means "the leaders **who have been broken**"

Latin grammarians also describe this form as "perfect" because it shows that the action has been completed:

- "the **spoken** word" means "the word **that has** (already) **been spoken**"

These two features distinguish the perfect passive participle from the present active participle (*–ing*, which you learned about in Hour 12).

- "a **talking** horse" means "a horse **that is** (now) **talking**"

Task 1: Identifying Participles

In each of the following sentences, state whether the participle in bold is present active or perfect passive.

1. Caesar, **fearing** disaster, wanted to stay home that day.
2. **Convinced** by Brutus, he changed his mind.
3. **Looking** at Brutus, Caesar said, "You, too?"
4. **Doomed** to a season of frustration, the Cubs settled for fourth place.

Forms of the Perfect Passive Participle

English passive participles most commonly end in *–ed;* some, however, end in *–en* or undergo a change of vowel.

Passive Participles in English

Basic Form	Passive Participle
call	called
see	seen
fight	fought

In Latin, the perfect passive participle usually contains the element *t* (related to the English *–ed*).

Perfect Passive Participles in Latin

Basic Forms	Perfect Passive Participle
amo, –are, –avi (love)	*ama-tus, –a, –um*
laudo, –are, –avi (praise)	*lauda-tus, –a, –um*
móneo, –ere, mónui (warn)	*móni-tus, –a, –um*
hábeo, –ere, hábui (have)	*hábi-tus, –a, –um*
dico, dícere, dixi (say)	*dic-tus, –a, –um*
fácio, facere, feci (do, make)	*fac-tus, –a, –um*
credo, crédere crédidi (believe)	*creditus, –a, –um*
aúdio, audire, audivi (hear)	*audi-tus, –a, –um*

Note that the *e* stem of the second conjugation mutates to an unstressed *i*. In the third conjugation, the *t* infix is sometimes added directly to the consonant stem (as in *captus*), and sometimes to an unstressed *i* (as in *créditus*).

Task 2: Translating Participles

Translate the following participles, taken from the previous table, into English.

1. *laudatus*
2. *mónitus*
3. *dictus*
4. *factus*
5. *auditus*

 FYI The perfect passive participle is always declined as a first/second declension adjective.

Other Ways of Forming the Perfect Passive Participle

Some verbs, however, form the perfect passive participle without the *t* element. Often this is replaced by an *s*.

Perfect Passive Participles in *S*

Basic Forms	Perfect Passive Participle
mitto, míttere, misi (send)	*missus, –a, –um*
iúbeo, iubere, iussi (order)	*iussus, –a, –um*
vídeo, videre, vidi (see)	*visus, –a, –um*

Moreover, some participles may change or add a letter (such as *p*) for ease of pronunciation.

Perfect Passive Participles: Altered Spellings

Basic Forms	Perfect Passive Participle
emo, émere, emi (buy)	*emptus, –a, –um*
scribo, –ere, scripsi (write)	*scriptus, –a, –um*

Finally, a few verbs derive the perfect passive participle from another "root" or basic form.

Perfect Passive Participles: Different Root

Basic Forms	Perfect Passive Participle
fero, ferre, tuli (carry)	*latus, –a, –um*
tollo, –ere, sústuli (lift)	*sublatus, –a, –um*

Because the form of the perfect passive participle is not always predictable, it is commonly listed in dictionaries as the fourth (and last) principal part, as follows:

- *amo, amare, amavi,* **amatus** (love)
- *vídeo, videre, vidi,* **visus** (see)

JUST A MINUTE

It often happens that English words are based on the fourth principal part of a Latin verb.

- *pono, pónere, pósui,* **pósitus** (put) becomes *posit,* "position"
- *incípio, incípere, incepi,* **inceptus** (begin) becomes "inception."

From now on, your vocabulary lists will also follow this format. Here are the full entries for some verbs you have already learned, for which the fourth principal part is not predictable.

Principal Parts of Previously Learned Verbs

Latin	English	Related word
accípio, –ere, accepi, acceptus	take	accept
addo, áddere, áddidi, ádditus	add	addition
adiuvo, –are, adiuvi, adiutus	help	
ago, ágere, egi, actus	do, act	act, action
apério, –ire, apérui, apertus	open	aperture
apprehendo, –ere, –hendi, –hensus	seize	apprehend
cognosco, –ere, cognovi, cognotus	learn	cognition
compono, –ere, compósui, compósitus	compose	composition
confício, –ere, confeci, –fectus	make	confection
do, dare, dedi, datus	give	data
incípio, –ere, –cepi, –ceptus	begin	inception
invénio, –ire, –inveni, inventus	find	invention
ostendo, osténdere, ostendi, ostensus	show	ostensible
quaero, –ere, quaesivi, quaesitus	seek	inquisition
reddo, –ere, –réddidi, rédditus	give back	
respóndeo, –ere, respondi, responsus	answer	response
suádeo, –ere, suasi, suasus	persuade	persuasion
tego, –ere, texi, tectus	cover	protect

TASK 3: PRINCIPAL PARTS AND PARTICIPLES

Cover up the previous table, and for each of the participles given, state the first principal part (for example, *amo*) and translate the participle.

1. *ádditus*
2. *suasus*
3. *actus*
4. *rédditus*
5. *quaesitus*
6. *inventus*
7. *tectus*

MEANING OF THE PERFECT PASSIVE PARTICIPLE

Depending on the context, the perfect passive participle can be translated as follows:

1. As an English passive participle (as in "loved" and "warned")
2. As a participial phrase with "having been" (as in "having been loved")
3. As a clause (as in "who was loved" and "when he was loved")

Some writers, especially historians, use participles to make their style more concise:

*Hunc **infammatum** a plerisque tres gravíssimi histórici summis laúdibus extulerunt.*

This man (Alcibiades), **condemned** by most, three eminent historians extolled with the highest praise. (Although this man has been condemned by most historians, three of the most eminent have praised him to the skies).

Needless to say, this can be a little confusing to beginners. Your best strategy is the following:

1. Translate the participle literally, matching it to the noun with which it agrees (as in *hunc infammatum,* meaning "this one having been condemned").
2. If this sounds too awkward, change the participial phrase to a subordinate clause after "who," "which," "that," "when," "if," "because," or "although."

   - *Geórgius draconem **súbditum** per vias ducebat:* George led the dragon having-been-tamed through the streets. (George led the dragon that he had tamed through the streets.)
   - *Holofernum ita **deceptum** Iudith fácile interfecit:* Judith easily killed Holofernes having-been-deceived in this way.

(After/Because she had deceived him in this way, Judith easily killed Holofernes.)

Once in a while, a participle may come out more smoothly in English as a second "main" verb:

- *Geórgius draconem in urbem **ductum** interfecit:* George killed the dragon having-been-led into the city. (George led the dragon into the city and killed it.)

TIME SAVER

 If you do an idiomatic translation of a participial phrase, always make sure that it means the same thing as your literal translation.

TASK 4: WORKING WITH PARTICIPLES

In each of the following sentences, translate the participle (in bold) literally, and then choose a smoother alternative translation.

1. *Brutus Caésarem **interfectum** in theatro reliquit:* Brutus left Caesar … in the theatre.
2. *Brutus, a senatóribus **laudatus**, Roma tamen discessit:* Brutus … by the senators, left Rome nonetheless.
3. *Vir uxorem ad novam domum **ductam** super limen sústulit:* The husband carried his wife, … to their new home, over the threshold.
4. *Mílites in flúvium **missos** hippopótami devoraverunt:* The hippos devoured the soldiers … into the river.
5. *Regis fília, cóphinum elígere **iussa**, tértium elegit:* The king's daughter, … to choose a casket, chose the third.

THE ABLATIVE ABSOLUTE REVISITED

We saw in Hour 12 that the present active participle can be paired with a noun in the ablative case as a clause substitute:

- ***Deo volente,** Latinam linguam discemus:* With God willing, we will learn Latin. (If God wills ….)

The same construction occurs with still greater frequency using the perfect passive participle:

- ***Gallis victis,** Caesar Romam rédiit:* **With the Gauls having been conquered,** Caesar returned to Rome. (After the Gauls had been conquered ….)

- *Caésare interfecto, Brutus e theatro festinavit:* **With Caesar having been killed,** Brutus hastened from the theatre. (When Caesar had been killed ….)

Your default translation for this construction will be "with (noun) having been (verb)-ed." Depending on the context, though, the phrase may be retranslated as a subordinate clause with the conjunctions "when," "if," "because," or "although":

- *Gallis victis, Caesar tamen dolebat:* With the Gauls having been conquered, Caesar nevertheless was sad. (**Although** the Gauls had been conquered ….)

- *Caésare interfecto, omnes cives gaudebunt:* With Caesar having been killed, all the citizens will rejoice. (**When** Caesar has been killed ….)

TASK 5: TRANSLATING THE ABLATIVE ABSOLUTE

In the following sentences, translate the ablative absolute phrase literally; then retranslate using a subordinate clause.

1. *Dracone interfecto, Geórgius ab urbe discessit:* …, George left the city.
2. *Fíliis meis laudatis, gaúdeo:* …, I rejoice.
3. *Exércitu convocato, Caesar mílites confirmavit:* …, Caesar cheered up his soldiers. (*convoco* means "call together")
4. *Fília visa, rex gaudebat:* …, the king rejoiced.
5. *Cibo parato, omnes ad mensam consédimus:* …, we all sat down to the table.

PASSIVE VOICE: PERFECT, PLUPERFECT, AND FUTURE PERFECT

We saw in the last hour that the passive voice in the present, imperfect, and future tenses is formed by taking the active form and substituting passive endings (*–r, –ris, –tur, –mur, –mini, –ntur*):

- *amo* ("I love") becomes *amo-r* ("I am loved")
- *ama-s* ("you love") becomes *ama-ris* ("you are loved")

The other three tenses, however, form the passive voice in a different way. Passive forms in the "perfective" tenses (perfect, pluperfect, and future perfect) consist of two elements: the perfect passive participle and a form of the verb *sum*. In combination, they identify the person, number, and tense of a passive verb. Study the following table.

Perfect Passive of *Amo*

Singular

amatus, –a, –um sum (I was loved, I have been loved)

amatus, –a, –um es

amatus, –a, –um est

Plural

amati, –ae, –a sumus

amati, –ae, –a estis

amati, –ae, –a sunt

The perfect passive is formed by combining the participle with the present tense of the verb *sum*. In the pluperfect passive, *sum* goes into the *imperfect* tense.

Pluperfect Passive of *Amo*

Singular

amatus, –a, –um eram (I had been loved)

amatus, –a, –um eras

amatus, –a, –um erat

Plural

amati, –ae, –a eramus

amati, –ae, –a eratis

amati, –ae, –a erant

To form the future perfect passive, use *future* forms of *sum*.

Future Perfect Passive of *Amo*

Singular

amatus, –a, –um ero (I will have been loved)

amatus, –a, –um eris

amatus, –a, –um erit

Plural

amati, –ae, –a érimus

amati, –ae, –a éritis

amati, –ae, –a erunt

Note that *amatus sum* means "I was loved," not "I am loved." The reason for this is that, to the Roman way of thinking, *amatus sum* is tantamount to saying, "I *am* in a state of *having been* loved." This is semantically equivalent to "I *was* loved" and "I *have been* loved." The same goes for the other two perfective tenses: *amatus eram*, "I *was* in a state of *having been* loved," is equivalent to "I *had been* loved"; *amatus ero*, "I *will be* in a state of *having been* loved," is equivalent to "I *will have been* loved."

PROCEED WITH CAUTION

If you speak a modern Romance language, you may be confused by the fact that the Latin construction for the perfective tenses is used in modern languages for the **non**-perfective tenses (present, imperfect, future):

- *io **sono** amato:* I **am** loved
- *j'**étais** aimé:* I **was** loved

In Latin, though, *amatus **sum*** is the usual way of saying "I **was** loved."

TASK 6: TRANSLATING PASSIVE FORMS

Translate the following forms of the verb *amo, amare, amavi, amatus.*

1. *amatus ero*
2. *amati erant*
3. *amatus est*
4. *amati eramus*
5. *amati éritis*
6. *amatus sum*

SUBJECT-VERB AGREEMENT IN THE PASSIVE VOICE

You have already learned that a verb must agree in number with its subject.

- ***Romani invadunt:*** The Romans invade.

When the verb consists of a participle and a verb, however, the participle must also agree in gender, number, and case with the subject:

- *Galli **victi** sunt:* The Gauls were conquered.
- *Regina **vocata** erat:* The queen had been called.
- *Monstrum **visum** erit:* The monster will have been seen.

TASK 7: WORKING WITH AGREEMENT IN PASSIVE FORMS

In each of the following sentences, make the participle (in parentheses) agree with the subject.

1. *Mílites ab Alexandro (confirmatus) sunt:* The soldiers were encouraged by Alexander.

2. *Roma a Nerone (accensus) est:* Rome was burned down by Nero.

3. *Illud consílium a Caésare (reiectus) erat:* That plan had been rejected by Caesar.

4. *Sagittárius a philomela (reprobatus) erit:* The bowman will have been reproached by the nightingale.

5. *Illa verba numquam (auditus) sunt:* Those words have never been heard.

IMPERSONAL VERBS AND IMPERSONAL PASSIVES

In English, we have a number of expressions with no real subject. These usually begin with the pronoun "it":

- It is allowed (forbidden) to smoke here.
- It is fun to learn Latin.

These verbs are called *impersonals*. Latin has a number of such verbs, which do not always correspond to English impersonals. Here are some of the most common:

- *licet:* it is permitted (one can …)
- *libet:* it is pleasing (one may well …)
- *liquet:* it is clear
- *decet:* it is fitting
- *oportet:* it is necessary

Note that the foregoing examples are all in the third person, singular (it), and the active voice. The present tense form can be converted to other tenses (as in *lícuit, líbuit, décuit, oppórtuit*).

Two of these verbs, however, can switch to the passive (without change of meaning) in the perfect, pluperfect, and future perfect tenses:

- *libitum est:* it was pleasing
- *licitum est:* it was permitted

Moreover, the passive voice is sometimes used for verbs that normally would be active, but the focus is entirely on the action itself. For example, we might say, "There was a fight yesterday," or "People fought about it." In Latin, this would be expressed as follows:

- *Heri* **pugnatum est (pugnabatur):** **It was fought** yesterday. (There was a fight yesterday).

Note that the indefinite "subject" is neuter; this explains the *–um* ending on *pugnatum*. Impersonal passives are always singular.

Here are some other common uses of the impersonal passive:

- *itur:* it is gone, one goes, people go
- *pervenitur:* it is arrived at, one arrives at, people get to
- *agitur:* it is done, discussed; people talk about
- *vivitur:* it is lived, one lives, people live

TASK 8: TRANSLATING IMPERSONAL VERBS

Translate the words in bold.

1. *In hoc aedifício fumare* **non licet:** In this building … to smoke.
2. *Diligenter studere* **oportebat:** … to study hard.
3. *Non uno itínere ad tam grande secretum* **pervenitur:** Not by one road … to so great a secret.
4. *De bello Gállico in senatu* **actum est:** … in the senate about the Gallic war.
5. *In iuventute lúdere* **lícitum est:** In (my) youth, … to play.

ESSENTIAL VOCABULARY

The following common words should be committed to memory.

Essential Vocabulary

Latin	Meaning	Related Word
Nouns		
arma, –orum (neuter plural)	arms	
civis, –is (masculine)	citizen	civil
gládius, –i (masculine)	sword	
iudícium, –ii (neuter)	judgment, judicial decision	

Latin	Meaning	Related Word
Nouns		
iúvenis, –is (masculine)	young man	
negótium, –ii (neuter)	business, undertaking	negotiate
númerus, –i (masculine)	number	numeral
signum, –i (neuter)	sign	signal
Verbs		
iáceo, –ere, iacui	lie, recline	adjacent
licet, –ere, –uit (or *lícitum est*)	it is permitted	licit
oportet, –ere, –uit	it is necessary	
peto, –ere, petivi	chase, seek, ask	petition
relinquo, –ere, –liqui, –lictus	leave	relinquish
suscípio, –ere, –cepi, –ceptus	take up	susceptible
Adjective		
diffícilis, –e	difficult	
Adverbs		
certe	certainly, surely	
haud	not, hardly	
sicut	just as	
Preposition		
sine	without	sinecure
Conjunctions		
an	or	
quam	than	
vero	but	

RECOGNITION VOCABULARY

Go through this list once or twice, and then look for these words in the Reading Exercise.

Recognition Vocabulary

Latin	Meaning	Related Word
diversus, –a, –um	different	diverse
exspiro, –are, –avi, –atus	die	expire
exulto, –are, –avi, –atus	exult	
facílitas, facilitatis (feminine)	easiness	facility
grávitas, gravitatis (feminine)	seriousness, gravity	
inértia, –ae (feminine)	inertia	
intentus, –a, –um	intent	
secundus, –a, –um	second	
spátium, –i (noun)	space	spatial
promitto, –ere, –misi, –missus	promise	
respública, reipublicae (feminine)	republic, state	
tólero, –are, –avi, –atus	endure, tolerate	

SUMMARY

In this lesson, you have learned how to use the perfect passive participle and how it is combined with *sum* to form the perfective tenses of the passive voice. This information will come in very handy if you want to study Roman history in the original language, as the following passage shows.

READING EXERCISE

Rome's early history was a series of battles with neighboring cities and tribes. In these first tests, the Romans showed the valor, cleverness, and ruthlessness that were to make them masters of the Western world. The following story is liberally adapted from the encyclopedic history of Titus Livius (Livy).

THE BATTLE OF THE HORATII AND CURATII

Foédere icto, trigémini, sicut convénerat, arma cápiunt. Statim in médium inter duas ácies procedunt. Consederunt utrimque pro castris duo exérci-tus, in hoc spectáculum totis animis intenti. Datur signum, infestisque armis terni iúvenes concurrunt. Cum aliquámdiu inter se aequis víribus pugnáverant, duo Romani, super álium álius, vulneratis tribus Albanis, exspirantes corruerunt. Illi supérstitem Romanum circumsistunt. Forte is ínteger fuit. Capessit ergo fugam, ita cógitans: "Illi me certe petent, etsi vulnerati sunt." Iam aliquantum spátii ex eo loco, ubi pugnáverant, aufúgerat, cum respíciens videt eos magnis intervallis sequentes. Unus haud procul ab sese áberat; in eum ítaque magno ímpetu redit, eumque intérficit. Mox próperat ad secundum, eumque páriter neci dat. Iam, aequato Marte, duo supérerant, número pares, sed longe víribus diversi. Romanus exultans; "Duos," inquit, "fratrum Mánibus dedi, tértium nunc dabo." Tum gládium superne illius iúgulo defigit, iacentem spóliat. Romani ovantes ac gratulantes Horátium accípiunt. Inde ex utraque parte suos sepéliunt.

Reading Vocabulary

ácies, –ei (feminine)	battle line
aequatus, –a, –um	equaled
Albanus, –a, –um	Alban
aliquámdiu	for a while
aliquantum, –i (masculine)	a little
álius … álius	one … another
aufúgio, –ere, –fugi	flee
capesso, –ere	seize, take to
castra, –orum (neuter plural)	camp
circumsisto, –ere, –steti	stand around
concurro, –ere, concurri	run together
consedeo, –ere, –sedi	sit down
cónvenit, convenit	it is agreed
córruo, –ere, córrui	fall

continues

Reading Vocabulary   (continued)

defingo, –ere, –figi, –fixus	drive in
duo, duae, duo	two
foedus, foederis (neuter)	treaty
fuga, –ae (feminine)	flight
grátulans, –antis (adjective)	congratulating
hoc	this
Horátius, –i (masculine)	Horatius
ictus, –a, –um	having been struck
ímpetus, –us (masculine)	attack, charge
infestus, –a, –um	hostile
inquit	he says
ínteger, –ra, –rum	not wounded, intact
intervallum, –i (neuter)	interval
iúgulum, –i (neuter)	neck
longe	by far
Mánes, –ium (masculine plural)	the spirits of the dead; hell
Mars, Martis (masculine)	Mars; battle
mox	soon
nex, necis (feminine)	death
ovans, –ovantis (adjective)	cheering
par, paris (adjective)	equal
páriter	likewise
procedo, –ere, –cessi	step forward
procul	far
própero, –are, –avi, –atus	hasten
respício, –ere, –spexi, –spectus	look back on
se	themselves
sepélio, –ire, sepélii	bury
sequens, –entis (adjective)	following
sese	him
spectáculum, –i (masculine)	spectacle
spólio, –are, –avi, –atus	despoil
superne	from above

supérstes, –stitis (adjective)	alive, surviving
supersum, –esse, –fui	survive
suus, –a, –um	their
ternus, –a, –um	in group(s) of three
tértius, –a, –um	third
tres, tria	three
trigémini, –orum (masculine)	three brothers
unus, –a, –um	one
utraque	each
utrimque	on both sides
víres, –ium (feminine plural)	strength, success
vulnero, –are, –avi, –atus	wound

Quiz

A

Convert the following active verbs to their passive equivalents, and translate both forms. (For example, *amavit* [he loved] becomes *amatus est* [he was loved]).

1. *amáverant*
2. *monúeris*
3. *reliqui*
4. *petíveram*
5. *dixerunt*
6. *audivisti*
7. *laudavérimus*
8. *céperint*
9. *monueratis*
10. *dedit*

B

Quiz

Choose the form in parentheses that best completes the sentence, and translate.

1. *(Datur/Dat) signum, infestisque armis terni iúvenes concurrunt.*
2. *(Vulneratos/Vulneratis) tribus Albanis, duo Romani exspirantes corruerunt.*
3. *"Illi me certe petent, etsi (vulneratus/vulnerati) sunt."*
4. *Romanus exultans, "Duos," inquit, "fratrum Mánibus dedi, tértium nunc (dabam/dabo)."*

HOUR 15

Deponent Verbs; Future Participles; Periphrastic Constructions; *Hic* and *Iste*

So far, you have learned how to recognize the active and passive voices, how to use the present and perfect participles, and also how to use the personal/demonstrative pronouns *is* and *ille*.

INTRODUCTORY READING

Let's get started this time with a passage from a great spiritual classic, *The Imitation of Christ*.

GROUND RULES FOR THE SPIRITUAL LIFE

*Si **conamur** quantum póssumus, adhuc léviter defi-ciemus in multis. Semper tamen áliquid certi propo-nendum est, et contra illa praecípue quae ámplius nos impédiunt. **Exteriora** nostra et interiora páriter **nobis scrutanda sunt** et ordinanda, quia utraque expédiunt ad profectum.*

If **we try** as much as we can, we shall still often fail a little in many things. Nevertheless, we must always propose some definite (exercise), especially against the things that particularly hinder us. **We must examine** and set in order our interior and **exterior (habits)**, since both help us to progress.

In this passage, you notice that the verb *conamur* means "we try," even though it has the passive ending *–mur*. This is an example of a class of verbs called *deponent*; these verbs have passive forms but active meanings.

CHAPTER SUMMARY

LESSON PLAN:
In this hour you will learn about …

- A class of verbs called *deponent verbs,* which have passive forms but active meanings
- The future participles, active and passive
- The participles used in *periphrastic* constructions with the verb *sum*
- Two new pronouns: *hic* (this one) and *iste* (this/that one of yours)

You also notice examples of a construction that expresses obligation, as in *Exteriora nostra … nobis scrutanda sunt*. This literally means "Our exterior (habits) are to be examined by us"; it is an ordinary way of saying "We must examine our exterior habits." The construction is called the *passive periphrastic,* one of two "periphrastic" constructions considered in this lesson.

DEPONENT VERBS

Deponent verbs have passive forms but active meanings. There are not very many of them, but they include some very common verbs, such as the following:

- *Grammáticam Latinam díscere conabor:* **I will try** to learn Latin grammar.
- *Gládio numquam utor:* **I** never **use** a sword.
- *Romani Latine loquebantur:* The Romans **spoke** Latin.

Deponent verbs have no active forms, except the present participle (as in *conans,* which means "trying") and the future participle, which will be learned later. They are listed in dictionaries with three principal parts, all in the passive voice. Study the following table of common deponent verbs.

Common Deponent Verbs

Latin	Meaning	Related Word
árbitror, arbitrari, arbitratus sum	judge, think	arbitration
confíteor, confiteri, confessus sum	confess	
conor, conari, conatus sum	try	conative
expérior, experiri, expertus sum	experience, test	expert
hortor, hortari, hortatus sum	encourage	exhortation
loquor, loqui, locutus sum	speak	loquacious
mórior, mori, mórtuus sum	die	mortuary
utor, uti, usus sum (+ ablative)	use	utility, use

You can tell the conjugation of a deponent verb by looking at the second principal part.

I	II	III	IV
Con–ari	confit–eri	loqu–i	exper–iri
to try	to confess	to speak	to experience

Third conjugation *–io* verbs (such as *mórior* in the table above) have an infinitive in *–i;* the first principle part ends in *–ior.*

PROCEED WITH CAUTION

Be careful not to translate a deponent verb as a passive verb:

- *hortor* means "I encourage" (not "I am encouraged")
- *utor* means "I use" (not "I am used")

TASK 1: TRANSLATING DEPONENT VERBS

Translate the verbs in bold. Remember that they have the same forms as passive verbs, but have an active meaning.

1. *Alexander mílites térritos **hortatus est:*** Alexander … his terrified soldiers.
2. *Etsi deficiemus, íterum **conábimur:*** Even if we fail, … again.
3. *Lingua "Romana" est, qua scriptores óptimi **loquebantur:*** The "Roman" dialect is the one that the best writers ….
4. *Caesar et suasione et vi **utetur:*** Caesar … both persuasion and force.
5. *Nonne Sinarum cibos **expertus es?:*** Haven't … Chinese food?

SEMIDEPONENT VERBS

A few verbs in Latin have active forms in the present, imperfect, and future tenses, but become deponent in the "perfective" tenses:

- *Amici **fiunt:*** They **become** friends.
- *Amici **facti sunt:*** They **became** friends.

Such verbs are called *semideponent.* They are listed in the dictionary under three principal parts. The third principal part is a passive form:

- *fio, fíeri, **factus sum*** (become, be done)
- *gaúdeo, gaudere, **gavisus sum*** (rejoice, enjoy)

FUTURE PARTICIPLES

So far, you have seen participles in the present tense, active voice (*amans,* meaning "loving") and the perfect tense, passive voice (*amatus,* meaning "[having been] loved"). Latin also has participles in the future tense, in both the active and passive voices.

THE FUTURE ACTIVE PARTICIPLE

The future active participle (about to ..., going to ...) is formed by adding the suffix *–urus, –ura, –urum* to the stem of the perfect passive participle, as follows:

- *amat-us, –a, –um* becomes *amat-urus, –ura, –urum* (about to love)
- *dict-us, –a, –um* becomes *dict-urus, –ura, –urum* (about to say)

The future active participle is declined as a first/second declension adjective, like *magnus.*

Notice that although this form is derived from the perfect passive participle, it has an active meaning. The noun with which it agrees is the understood *subject* of the action. The participle can also take a direct object:

- *Caésarem **interfecturus**, Brutus pugionem levavit:* (As he was) **about to kill** Caesar, Brutus raised his dagger.
- *Plura **locuturus**, miles tamen obmútuit:* (Although he was) **about to say** more, the soldier nevertheless kept silent.

In the first example, the participle agrees with Brutus and takes Caesarem as its object.

As always, participles can be used as substitutes for relative clauses (marked by "who," "which," or "that") or adverbial clauses (marked by "when," "since," "if," or "although").

TASK 2: WORKING WITH FUTURE PARTICIPLES

Change the form of the participle in parentheses to match the noun, and translate.

1. *Horátius hostes se (interfecturus) fugit:* Horatius fled his enemies ... him.
2. *Geórgius draconem (interfecturus) pópulum oravit:* George, ..., addressed the people.
3. *Pater fílios in perículum (ambulaturus) prohíbuit:* The father stopped his kids, ... into danger.

4. *Nos (moriturus) te salutamus!:* We ... salute you! (*Moriturus* is the future active participle of *mórior, mori, mórtuus,* meaning "die.")

THE FUTURE PASSIVE PARTICIPLE

Latin also has a future passive participle. However, its meaning is somewhat restricted. Your default translation will be "(noun) *to be* (verb)-*ed*."

- *Antónius índicem **senatorum interficiendorum** compósuit:* Antony composed a list of **senators to be killed.**

The future passive participle is built on a stem consisting of the conjugation stem vowel and the infix *nd.* Study the following table.

Future Passive Participle

I	II	III
amand-us	*habend-us*	*mittend-us*
to be loved	to be had	to be sent

III –io	IV	
capiend-us	*audiend-us*	
to be caught	to be heard	

The future passive participle is declined as a first/second declension adjective. Thus *amo* becomes *amandus, –a, –um).*

This form is not a future participle in the true sense. For example, *amandus* never means "about to be loved" or "going to be loved." Instead, it is restricted to situations involving obligation:

- *puella amanda* means "the girl (who ought) to be loved"
- *agenda* means "(things that) ought to be done"

TASK 3: MATCHING PARTICIPLES AND NOUNS

Change the form of the participle in parentheses so that it agrees with its noun, and translate.

1. *Índicem tibi librorum (legendus) dabo:* I will give you a list of books ....

2. *Rationem pecúniae (expendendus) réddidi:* I gave an accounting of money .... (*expendo, –ere, –pendi* means "spend")

3. *Verba memóriae (commitendus) non multa sunt:* The words ... to memory are not many.

PERIPHRASTIC CONSTRUCTIONS

Períphrasis is the Greek word for "talking around" something. The term is used by Latin grammarians to describe synthetic forms created by combining a participle with the verb *sum*.

You have already encountered periphrastic forms in the perfect, pluperfect, and future perfect tenses of the passive voice (such as *amatus sum,* meaning "I was loved"). The future participles are also found in periphrastic constructions.

THE ACTIVE PERIPHRASTIC

Latin sometimes combines the future active participle with *sum* to form the *active periphrastic*. Study the following examples:

- *Caesar Gallos **victurus est:*** Caesar **is about to** (going to) **conquer** the Gauls.
- *Romani Gallos **victuri erant:*** The Romans **were about to conquer** the Gauls.

Note that the verb *sum* is translated according to its Latin tense: *victurus **est*** means "**is** about to conquer."

Note also that the participle always agrees with the subject of the construction (as in *Romani ... victuri sunt*).

TASK 4: TRANSLATING THE ACTIVE PERIPHRASTIC

Translate the periphrastic constructions in bold.

1. *Romani in Gálliam **venturi sunt:*** The Romans ... to Gaul. (*venturus* is the future active participle of *vénio*)
2. *Magister omnes pueros **laudaturus est:*** The teacher ... all the boys.
3. *Caésare imperante, respublica **moritura erat:*** When Caesar was in command, the Republic ....
4. *Calpúrnia Caésarem **moritura erat,** cum Brutus advenit:* Calpurnia ... Caesar, when Brutus arrived.

THE PASSIVE PERIPHRASTIC; DATIVE OF AGENT

The *passive periphrastic* is formed with the future passive participle and *sum*. Such sentences always imply obligation or necessity.

- *Illi libri **legendi sunt:*** Those books **are to be read.** (Those books must be read.)

- *Karthago **delenda erat:*** Carthage **was to be destroyed.** (Carthage had to be destroyed.)

As before, the participle agrees with the subject in gender, number, and case (as in *Karthago **delenda** est*).

The subject of the passive periphrastic is the recipient of the action. To identify the agent, or doer of the action, Latin uses the *dative* case:

- *Illi libri **nobis** legendi sunt:* Those books are to read **by us.** (We must read those books.)

- *Karthago **Romanis** delenda erat:* Carthage had to be destroyed **by the Romans.**

PROCEED WITH CAUTION

Remember that agent is normally expressed by the ablative case after *a/ab*:

- *Karthago **a Romanis** deleta est:* Carthage was destroyed **by the Romans.**

The dative of agent is normally confined to the passive periphrastic, although it sometimes pops up in other constructions.

TASK 5: TRANSLATING THE PASSIVE PERIPHRASTIC

Translate the following sentences.

1. *Lingua latina nobis discenda est.* (*disco, –ere* means "learn")

2. *Hippopótami milítibus non timendi sunt.*

3. *Hoc negótium tibi suscipiendum erat.*

4. *Satis laborávimus! Nunc vinum nobis est bibendum!*

JUST A MINUTE

The verbal adjective terminating in *–ndus* also functions as the *gerundive,* which has a meaning quite different from the participle you have just learned. It will be discussed later.

TWO NEW PRONOUNS: *HIC* AND *ISTE*

We have already seen the pronouns *is* and *ille,* which can be used as personal pronouns (he, she, it), or as demonstrative pronouns or adjectives (this, that):

- *Is est liber quem lego:* **This/that** (one) is the book that I am reading.
- *Is liber mihi placet:* **This** book pleases me.
- *Ille liber non mihi placet:* **That** book does not please me.

As the examples indicate, *is* refers vaguely to a previously mentioned noun (this one, that one), while *ille* has the specific meaning "that."

THE PRONOUN/ADJECTIVE *HIC*

Latin has another pronoun/adjective with the specific meaning "this." Study the following chart.

The Pronoun/Adjective *Hic*

	Masculine	Feminine	Neuter
Singular			
Nominative	*hic*	*haec*	*hoc*
Genitive	*huius*	*huius*	*huius*
Dative	*huic*	*huic*	*huic*
Accusative	*hunc*	*hanc*	*hoc*
Ablative	*hoc*	*hac*	*hoc*
Plural			
Nominative	*hi*	*hae*	*haec*
Genitive	*horum*	*harum*	*horum*
Dative	*his*	*his*	*his*
Accusative	*hos*	*has*	*haec*
Ablative	*his*	*his*	*his*

Like *is* and *ille*, *hic* can be used as a pronoun (this one) or as an adjective (this …):

- *Hoc est enim corpus meum:* For this is my body.
- *Haec verba me terrent:* These words terrify me.

TASK 6: TRANSLATING THE PRONOUN *HIC*

Choose the form of *hic* that fits the context, and translate.

1. *Exercítia in (hic) libro non sunt difficília:* The exercises in … book are not difficult.

2. *(Hic) rem non fácile explanare póssumus:* We cannot easily explain ... thing.

3. *(Hic) sunt nonnulla eorum, quae máxime mihi placent:* ... are some of my favorite things. (Use neuter plural!)

4. *Animália (hic) géneris extra Índiam rara sunt:* Animals of ... type are rare outside India.

5. *(Hic) féminae libros non legunt:* ... women do not read books.

THE PRONOUN/ADJECTIVE *ISTE*

Another pronoun/adjective in Latin has the distinctive meaning "this/that of yours." Study the following table.

The Pronoun/Adjective *Iste*

	Masculine	Feminine	Neuter
Singular			
Nominative	iste	ista	istud
Genitive	istius	istius	istius
Dative	isti	isti	isti
Accusative	istum	istam	istud
Ablative	isto	ista	isto
Plural			
Nominative	isti	istae	ista
Genitive	istorum	istarum	istorum
Dative	istis	istis	istis
Accusative	istos	istas	ista
Ablative	istis	ista	istis

In earlier Latin, *iste* was regularly used, for example, when the speaker wished to point out something belonging to the addressee:

- *Unde **istud** pállium obtinuisti?:* Where did you get **that** coat (that you are wearing)?

Eventually however, *iste* acquired the connotations of "disowning," and a generally pejorative sense:

- ***Iste** fílius autocinetum íterum ábstulit:* **That** (no good) son **of yours** has stolen the car again.

- *Iste homo repúblicam perditurus est:* **That** (disreputable) man is going to ruin the state.

TASK 7: TRANSLATING *ISTE*

Choose the form of *iste* that fits the context, and translate.

1. *(Iste) catus vasum pretiosum meum fregit!:* … cat just broke my precious vase!
2. *(Iste) hómines iuste vituperávimus:* We justly cursed … men.
3. *(Iste) exercítia me ad insániam ádagunt:* … exercises are driving me nuts.

ESSENTIAL VOCABULARY

The following common words should be committed to memory.

Essential Vocabulary

Latin	Meaning	Related Word
Nouns		
amicítia, –ae (feminine)	friendship	
causa, –ae (feminine)	cause, occasion	
culpa, –ae (feminine)	fault	culpable
véritas, veritatis (feminine)	truth, truthfulness	veritable
Pronouns		
hic, haec, hoc	this	
iste, ista, istud	this/that (of yours)	
Verbs		
adsum, adesse, ádfui	be present	
fio, fíeri, factus sum	be done, happen	
náscor, nasci, natus sum	be born, arise	native
pário, –ere, péperi, partus	give birth to, cause	

Latin	Meaning	Related Word
Verbs		
sino, –ere, sivi, situs	allow	
subeo, subire, súbii	undergo	
utor, uti, usus sum	use	utility, use
vídeor, videri, visus sum	seem	
Adjectives		
dignus, –a, –um (+ ablative)	worthy	dignified
líber, líbera, líberum	free	liberate
verus, –a, –um	true	veritable
Conjunction		
quóniam	since	

RECOGNITION VOCABULARY

Go through this list once or twice, and then look for these words in the Reading Exercise.

Recognition Vocabulary

Latin	Meaning	Related Word
ango, –ere, anxi	grieve	anguish
correctio, –ionis (feminine)	correction	
diligéntia, –ae (feminine)	care	diligence
evito, –are, –avi, –atus	avoid	inevitable
familiaris, familiaris (masculine)	friend	familiar
fraus, fraudis (feminine)	deceit	fraud

continues

Recognition Vocabulary (continued)

Latin	Meaning	Related Word
monítio, monitionis (feminine)	warning	admonition
múltiplex, multíplicis (adjective)	multiple	
offénsio, –ionis (feminine)	offense	
ódium, –ii (neuter)	hatred, ill will	odious
retíneo, –ere, retínui, –tentus	retain	retain
tyrannus, –i (masculine)	tyrant	
utílitas, utilitatis (feminine)	utility	
venenum, –i (neuter)	poison	venom
vítium, –ii (neuter)	vice	vicious

SUMMARY

In this chapter, you have learned how to work with deponent verbs, future participles, and a pair of new pronouns. Now that you have become familiar with some of the quirkier features of Latin idiom, you are ready to tackle Latin (almost) as it was written by native speakers of the language. The style of Cicero, featured in this lesson's Reading Exercise, is a good place to start.

READING EXERCISE

Marcus Tullius Cicero (106–43 B.C.) was one of the great statesman of ancient Rome, and also one of its most imitated writers. Throughout antiquity, and again after the Renaissance, he was held up as the primary model of prose-writing in Latin. Among his works are a number of pleasant dialogues on philosophical topics. The following is taken (with slight adaptations) from his short work *On Friendship*. Cicero argues that friends should correct each other, but gently.

CICERO ON FRIENDSHIP

Est várius et múltiplex usus amicítiae, multaeque causae suspicionum offensionumque dantur, quas tum evitare, tum elevare, tum ferre sapientis est. Una illa subeunda offénsio est, si utílitas in amicítia et fides est retinenda; nam et monendi amici saepe sunt et obiurgandi; et haec accipienda amice cum benévole fiunt. Sed néscio quómodo verum est, quod in Ándria familiaris meus dicit:

Obséquium amicos, véritas ódium parit.

Molesta est véritas, si quidem ex ea náscitur ódium, quod est venenum amicítiae; sed obséquium multo moléstius, quod peccatis indulgens praecípitem amicum ire sinit; máxima autem culpa est in eo qui et veritatem aspernatur et in fraudem obséquio impéllitur.

Omni ígitur hac in re habenda rátio et diligéntia est. Primum, si monítio acerbitate, deinde si obiurgátio contumélia carebit. In obséquio autem, quóniam Terentiano verbo lubenter útimur, cómitas adesse debet; sed assentátio, vitiorum adiutrix, procul amovenda est, quae non modo non amico, sed ne líbero quidem digna est. Áliter enim cum tyranno, áliter cum amico vívitur. Scitum est enim illud Catonis, ut multa: "mélius de quibusdam acerbi inimici merentur quam ei qui amici dulces videntur; illi enim verum saepe dicunt, hi numquam." Atque absurdum est, quod ei, qui monentur, eam moléstiam non cápiunt quam debent cápere, et eam cápiunt, qua debent vacare. Non enim anguntur, quod peccaverunt, sed quod obiurgantur, moleste ferunt; nam contra opportebat delicto dolere, correctione gaudere.

Reading Vocabulary

absurdus, –a, –um	absurd
acerbus, –a, –um	bitter
acérbitas, –tatis (feminine)	bitterness
adiutrix, –cis (adjective)	helper, helping
áliter … áliter	in one way … in another way
amice	in a friendly way
amóveo, –ere, amovi, amotus	remove
Ándria, –ae (feminine)	*Andria*, a play by the poet Terence
aspernor, –ari, –atus sum	reject, scorn
assentátio, –ionis (feminine)	flattery, servility
benévole	benevolently, with good will
cápio, –ere, cepi, captus	get, take, obtain

continues

Reading Vocabulary   (continued)

cáreo, –ere, cárui	is without, lacks
Cato, Catonis (masculine)	Cato
cómitas, comitatis (feminine)	courtesy
contra	on the other hand, on the contrary
contumélia, –ae (feminine)	invective, insulting language
delictum, –i (neuter)	sin, misdeed
dóleo, –ere, dólui (+ ablative)	be sorry about
dulcis, –e	pleasant, agreeable
élevo, –are, –avi, –atus	lighten
fero, ferre, tuli, latus	bear (*fero moleste* means "take badly")
fides, –ei (feminine)	good faith
gaúdeo, –ere gavisus sum (+ ablative)	rejoice in
impéllo, –ere, –puli, –pulsus	impel
indúlgeo, –ere, indulsi	forgive
inimicus, –i (masculine)	enemy
lubenter	gladly
máximus, –a, –um	greatest
mélius	better
méreor, mereri, meritus sum	deserve
méreor mélius de (+ ablative)	render better service to
modo	only
moleste	ill, badly
moléstia, –ae (feminine)	annoyance, vexation
moléstius	more harmful
molestus, –a, –um	troublesome, annoying, harmful
multo (adverb)	much
ne … quidem	not even
néscio	some …
néscio quómodo	somehow

obiurgandum –i (neuter)	reproving, scolding
obiurgo, –are, –avi, –atus	reproach
obiurgátio, –ionis (feminine)	reproof
obséquium, –ii (neuter)	complaisance, obsequiousness
peccatum, –i (neuter)	sins
pecco, –are, –avi, –atus	sin
praeceps, praecípitis (adjective)	headlong, down the tubes
primum	first
procul	far away
quibusdam	some people
sápiens, sapientis (masculine)	wise man
scitus, –a, –um	knowing, clever, shrewd
síquidem	since
suspício, –ionis (feminine)	suspicion
Terentianus, –a, –um	of Terence
Tum … tum	sometimes … sometimes
vaco, –are, –avi, –atus	do without, not have

QUIZ

Convert the following sentences from the active voice to the passive, and translate as follows:

- *Calpúrnia Caésarem mónuit:* Calpurnia warned Caesar.
- *Caesar a Calpúrnia mónitus est:* Caesar was warned by Calpurnia.

1. *Nero impérium romanum deformavit:* Nero damaged the Roman empire. (*Nero, Neronis* [masculine]; *deformo, –are, –avi, –atus*)
2. *Parthi mílites Romanos vicerunt:* The Parthians conquered the Roman soldiers. (*vinco, –ere, vici, victus*)
3. *Sinae princípium anni célebrant.* The Chinese celebrate the beginning of the year. (*célebro, –are, –avi, –atus*)
4. *Illi múnera ínvicem mittunt:* They send gifts to each other. (*mitto, míttere, misi, missus*)
5. *Romani ovantes Horátium acceperunt:* Cheering, the Romans greeted Horatius. (*accípio, –ere, accepi, acceptus*)
6. *Amici amicos monere debent: Friends ought to warn friends.* (Use passive periphrastic!) (*móneo, –ere, mónui, mónitus*)

HOUR 16

Perfect and Future Infinitives; Accusative and Infinitive in Indirect Statements; Vocative and Locative Cases

CHAPTER SUMMARY

LESSON PLAN:

In this hour you will learn about ...

- Infinitive forms, both active and passive, in the perfect and future tenses
- A way of using the infinitive as a substitute for a *quod* clause in indirect statement

So far, you have learned to recognize the infinitive mood in the active and passive voices. For example, *amare* means "to love" and *amari* means "to be loved." You have also seen clauses beginning with *quod* (that) after verbs of speaking, hearing, and similar actions. Such clauses are called *indirect statements*.

INTRODUCTORY READING

Examples of this hour's grammar can be found in the opening lines of the great Latin epic, the *Aeneid* of Vergil. In the following extract, the poet explains why the goddess Juno was hostile to the hero, Aeneas, and his fellow Trojans.

THE WRATH OF JUNO

> *Urbs antiqua fuit, Týrii tenuere coloni,*
>
> *Carthago, Itáliam contra, Tiberinaque longe Óstia; dives opum, studiisque aspérrima belli.*
>
> *Quam Iuno fertur terris magis ómnibus unam Post hábita coluisse Samo ....*
>
> ***Progéniem*** *sed enim Troiano a sánquine **duci** Audíerat, Tyrias olim quae vérteret arces. Hinc populum late regem belloque superbum.*
>
> ***Venturum*** *excídio Libyae: sic **vólvere** Parcas.*

There was an ancient city, (which) colonists from Tyre held, opposite Italy and the distant mouth of the Tiber.

It was rich in resources, and harsh in the pursuits of war; which (city)
Juno is said to have favored alone, more than all others, even Samos ....
But she had heard **that a race was being drawn** from Trojan blood,
which would one day overthrow the Tyrian citadel. From this a people ruling widely and haughty in war **would come** to the destruction of Libya;
thus the Fates **were spinning.**

Toward the end of this passage, we see that *audíerat* (she had heard) governs
an unusual construction: *progéniem* ("progeny," in the accusative case) and
duci (to be drawn) are translated "that a progeny was being drawn." This is
an arrangement popularly known as the "accusative and infinitive" construction in indirect statements.

You can use the infinitive forms you have already learned to talk about action
going on at the *same time* as the main verb (for example, *audíerat ... Parcas
vólvere* means "she had heard ... that the Fates **were** spinning"). To talk
about actions that have already happened or that will happen, other infinitive
forms may be used: for example, *pópulum ... **venturum (esse)*** means "that a
people ... **would come.**"

INFINITIVES

The infinitive, as we have seen, is a basic form of the verb that can be used
as a noun or to complement another verb:

- *Errare humanum est:* **To err** is human.
- *Nólumus **errare:*** We don't want **to err.**

An infinitive can be either active or passive:

- *Amare et **amari** cúpimus:* We want **to love** and **to be loved.**

Infinitives are also marked for tense. The forms you have learned so far are
present infinitives. Here is an overview of present infinitive forms, throughout the four conjugations.

Present Infinitive

	I	*II*	*III*
Active	*amare* to love	*monere* to warn	*míttere* to send
Passive	*amari* to be loved	*moneri* to be warned	*mitti* to be sent

	IV
Active	*audire*
	to hear
Passive	*audiri*
	to be heard

The present infinitive does not always refer to the present time; instead, it is used to talk about actions that occur at the *same time* as the main verb:

- *Amari cúpimus:* We want **to be loved.**

- *Amari cupiebamus:* We wanted **to be loved.**

Occasionally, though, the infinitive will relate to the main verb as something that *has happened* or *will happen.* In that case, other tenses of the infinitive must be used.

THE PERFECT INFINITIVE

The perfect infinitive refers to an action completed before the time of the main verb. It is formed and translated as follows:

Perfect Infinitive

Active	*Passive*
amav-isse (to have loved)	*amatus esse* (to have been loved)
monu-isse (to have warned)	*mónitus esse* (to have been warned)
dux-isse (to have led)	*ductus esse* (to have been led)

The perfect active infinitive is composed of the perfect stem (the third principal part without the final *–i*) and the ending *–isse*.

The passive form is periphrastic, consisting of the perfect passive participle (the fourth principal part) and the present infinitive of *sum*. Literally translated, *amatus esse* means "to be in a state of having been loved."

JUST A MINUTE

The participle element in the perfect passive infinitive will change to agree in gender, number, and case with a noun or pronoun:

- *Regina **amata** esse dícitur:* The queen is said to have been loved.

- *Romani in perículum **ducti** esse videntur:* The Romans seem to have been led into danger.

TASK 1: TRANSLATING INFINITIVES

Translate the infinitives in bold.

1. *Hippopótami trans flumen* **natavisse** *dicuntur:* The hippos are said … across the river.

2. *Caesar a Bruto* **interfectus esse** *videtur:* Caesar seems … by Brutus.

3. *Geórgius draconem* **interfecisse** *putatur:* George is thought … a dragon.

4. *Viri litterati váriis morbis* **afflicti esse** *videntur:* Literate men seem … with various diseases.

THE FUTURE INFINITIVE

The future infinitive is used to talk about actions that are subsequent in time to the main verb. The active form is created and translated as follows:

- *amaturus esse:* to be about to (going to) love
- *moniturus esse:* to be about to (going to) warn
- *ducturus esse:* to be about to (going to) lead

This is also a periphrastic form, consisting of the future active participle (*amaturus*) and the present infinitive of the verb *sum* (*esse*). The participle (which is declined as a first and second declension adjective) agrees with a noun or pronoun:

- *Romani perituri esse videbantur:* **The Romans** seemed **to be about to perish.**

The future passive infinitive is very rare in Latin. It is formed as follows:

- *amatum iri:* to be going to be loved
- *mónitum iri:* to be going to be warned
- *ductum iri:* to be going to be led

The first part of the future passive infinitive (*amatum, monitum, ductum,* and so on) never changes. This form is called the *supine,* which will be discussed later. The supine is identical to the neuter singular nominative form of the perfect passive participle.

The second element (*iri*) is the present passive infinitive of the verb *eo* (to go).

Task 2: Translating Infinitives II

Translate the infinitives in bold.

1. *Mílites in proélio **victuri esse** putantur:* The soldiers are thought ... in battle.

2. *Brutus Caésari **responsurus esse** videbatur:* Brutus seemed ... Caesar.

3. *Multi hómines a Deo **salvatum iri** dicuntur:* Many people are said ... by God.

The Passive Periphrastic in the Infinitive Mood

The passive periphrastic construction can also appear in the infinitive mood. It always retains a sense of obligation or necessity:

- *Haec perícula non **evitanda (esse)** videntur:* These dangers do not seem **to be necessary to avoid.** (It does not seem that these dangers should be avoided.)

Infinitives in Indirect Statements

In classical Latin, indirect statements (that ...) are regularly set up without a conjunction and a finite verb. Instead, the verb occurs in its *infinitive* form, and the subject goes into the *accusative* case. The same construction sometimes occurs in English:

- I believed **him to be** honest. (I thought that he was honest.)

This sentence can be translated directly into Latin:

- *Putavi **eum** honestum **esse.***

We find the same construction in Latin after most verbs of saying, perceiving, and thinking (so-called "head verbs"), such as *dico* (I say), *aúdio* (I hear), *vídeo* (I see), and *puto* (I think, I believe).

When translating the "accusative and infinitive" construction, you may find it easier to work in two steps:

- Translate literally. For example, *Vídeo **Caésarem venire*** can be rendered "I see **Caesar to come.**"

- Convert your translation to a "that" clause: "I see **that Caesar is coming.**"

TASK 3: TRANSLATING INDIRECT STATEMENTS

Translate the following sentences literally, and then with a clause using the conjunction "that."

1. *Puto Alexandrum esse iustum.*
2. *Puto Latinam esse diffícilem.*
3. *Puto mundum esse bonum.*
4. *Dico eum mox venire.*
5. *Aúdio eos ómnia scire.*
6. *Vídeo mílites vinci.*

INFINITIVES AND RELATIVE TIME

Indirect statements can refer to situations that take place at the same time, before or after the "head verb":

- *Puto te **venire:*** I think that you **are coming.**
- *Puto te **venisse:*** I think that you **came** (have come).
- *Puto te **venturum esse:*** I think that you **will come.**

As these examples indicate, different tenses of the infinitive are used to express the time of the indirect statement relative to the main verb. The rule can be set out as follows:

- If the infinitive is in the *present* tense, it refers to action that is at the *same time* as the main verb.
- If the infinitive is in the *perfect* tense, it refers to action that is *prior* to the main verb.
- If the infinitive is in the *future* tense, it refers to action that is *subsequent* to the main verb.

Note that the Latin infinitive expresses *relative* time, not the actual time from the speaker's point of view. This means that, when translating from Latin to English, it will sometimes be necessary to execute a tense shift. Note how the example sentences used previously change when *puto* (I think) is replaced by *putabam* (I thought):

- *Putabam te **venire:*** I thought that you **were coming.**
- *Putabam te **venisse:*** I thought that you **had come.**
- *Putabam te **venturum esse:*** I thought that you **would come.**

The shift (for example, from "are coming" to "were coming") occurs because the main verb has shifted from the present tense (*puto*) to the imperfect (*putabam*). *Venire,* however, remains constant in expressing an action that occurs at the same time as the main verb. Likewise, *venisse* will always refer to action prior to the main verb, and *venturum esse* will always refer to action subsequent to the main verb.

TASK 4: TRANSLATING INDIRECT STATEMENTS II

Translate the following sentences.

1. *Saepe dícimus melanchólicos esse viros litteratos.*

2. *Corvus putabat vocem suam esse canoram* (*corvus* means "crow"; *canorus* means "beautiful").

3. *Putávimus imperatorem fuisse virum iustum.*

4. *Abbas putat féminas non debere Latinam díscere.*

5. *Sagittárius credit margaritam esse in stómacho philomelae* (*margarita* means "pearl"; *philomela* means "nightingale").

6. *Alexander putavit, omnes mílites contra hippopótamos pugnaturos esse.*

OTHER WAYS OF MAKING INDIRECT STATEMENTS

The accusative with infinitive construction is the normal way of making indirect statements in Classical Latin. However, in colloquial speech (and increasingly in writing), it became common to frame indirect statements as subordinate clauses with the conjunctions *quod, quia,* and *quóniam:*

- *Iudith credebat, quod Deus sibi Holofernem traditurus erat:* Judith believed that God would deliver Holofernes to her.

- *Dixit quia pecúniam non habebat:* He said that he did not have money.

PROCEED WITH CAUTION

Quod, quia, and *quóniam* can also mean "because." Moreover, the conjunction *quod* can be confused with neuter singular forms of the relative pronoun (*qui, quae, quod*). Therefore, you will have to pay careful attention to the context:

- *Caesar reiecit consílium,* **quod** *Calpúrnia dedit:* Caesar rejected the advice **that** Calpurnia gave.

- *Propheta dicit,* **quod** *regnum Dei venturum est:* The prophet says **that** the Kingdom of God is about to come.

THE VOCATIVE AND LOCATIVE CASES

You have already learned the five cases that regularly appear in Latin sentences: the nominative, genitive, dative, accusative, and ablative cases. However, Latin contains traces of two other cases—the vocative and locative. Their endings usually overlap with other case forms.

THE VOCATIVE CASE

The vocative or "calling" case (Latin *casus vocativus*) is used when a noun is addressed directly:

- *O Georgi! Fácio quod petis:* O George! I will do what you ask.

The vocative case usually has the same form as the nominative. There are two exceptions:

- Singular second declension nouns and adjectives ending in *–us* usually change to *–e.* Thus, *Dóminus* becomes *Dómine* (Lord!).
- Singular second declension nouns and adjectives ending in *–ius* change to *–i.* Thus, *Antónius* becomes *Ántoni.*

TASK 5: WORKING WITH THE VOCATIVE CASE

Convert the following words from the nominative to the vocative case.

1. *Marcus*
2. *fílius*
3. *puer bonus*
4. *Sílius Itálicus*

THE LOCATIVE CASE

The locative case (*casus locativus*) is used to indicate where the action of the sentence takes place. It is used only with the names of cities and with the nouns *domus* (home) and *rus* (countryside):

- *Romae ista fiunt:* These things are happening at (in) Rome.
- *Nos domi, vos ruri manebatis:* We were staying at home; you were staying in the countryside.

The locative form of city names is identical with other case forms you have learned, depending on the original form of the name:

- Singular names belonging to the first and second declensions use the genitive singular as a locative form. Thus, *Roma* becomes *Romae* (in Rome).

- Singular names belonging to the third, fourth, and fifth declensions use the ablative singular as a locative form. Thus, *Carthago* becomes *Carthágine* (in Carthage).

- Plural names of all declensions use the ablative plural form as a locative. Thus, *Athenae* becomes *Athenis* (in Athens).

Note that many ancient cities had plural names, such as Cumae, Hierosolymae (Jerusalem), and Gades (Cadiz).

TASK 6: WORKING WITH THE LOCATIVE CASE

Convert the following city names from the nominative to the locative case.

1. *Milváukia, Milvaúkiae* (feminine)
2. *Detroitum, Detroiti* (neuter)
3. *Chicago, Chicáginis* (feminine)
4. *Syracusae, Syracusarum* (feminine plural)
5. *Parísii, Parisiorum* (masculine plural)

ESSENTIAL VOCABULARY

The following common words should be committed to memory.

Essential Vocabulary

Latin	Meaning	Related Word
Nouns		
amor, amoris (masculine)	love	amorous
caro, carnis (feminine)	flesh	carnal
dux, ducis (masculine)	leader	
óculus, óculi (masculine)	eye	ocular
régio, regionis (feminine)	region	

continues

Essential Vocabulary   (continued)

Latin	Meaning	Related Word
Verbs		
cresco, créscere, crevi	grow	increase
dúbito, –are, –avi, –atus	hesitate, doubt	
intro, –are, –avi	enter	
manduco, –are, –avi, –atus	eat	
muto, –are, –avi, –atus	change	mutation
nosco, –ere, novi, notus	come to know	
novi, novisse	know	
Adjective		
carus, –a, –um	lovable, dear	
Adverb		
numquid	(a question particle)	
Preposition		
supra	above	
Conjunctions		
nec	and not, nor	
nondum	not yet	
Interjection		
o	O!	

RECOGNITION VOCABULARY

Go through this list once or twice, and then look for these words in the Reading Exercise.

Recognition Vocabulary

Latin	Meaning	Related Word
admóneo, –ere, –ui, –mónitus	admonish	
aetérnitas, aeternitatis (feminine)	eternity	
aeternus, –a, –um	eternal	
assumo, –ere, assumpsi, assumptus	take up	assume
cáritas, –tatis (feminine)	love	charity
conspícuus, –a, –um	visible	conspicuous
finitus, –a, –um	limited, finite	
horror, horroris (masculine)	shuddering	horror
inférior, inferioris (adjective)	lower	inferior
infinitus, –a, –um	unlimited	infinite
infírmitas, –tatis (feminine)	infirmity	
iníquitas, iniquitatis (feminine)	iniquity	
íntimus, –a, –um	inward, intimate	
rádio, –are, –avi, –atus	shine	radiate
revérbero, –are, –avi, –atus	shake	reverberate
spátium, –ii (neuter)	space	
supérior, superioris	superior, higher	
vehementer	mightily, strongly	vehemently
vulgaris, –e	common, ordinary	vulgar

SUMMARY

In this hour, you have learned how to form the perfect and future infinitives, and how to translate the accusative and infinitive in indirect statement. Now you are ready for an extract from one of the great spiritual works of Late Antiquity.

READING EXERCISE

The life of Aurelius Augustinus (354–430 A.D.) was in many ways typical of the later Roman empire. Born in Africa of poor but ambitious parents, he rose to become the imperial professor of rhetoric in Milan. However, the pleasure and esteem of the world were not satisfying to the young Augustine. His quest for truth led him in turn to the sect of the Manicheans, to the philosophical school of Neo-platonism, and finally to the Catholic Church. The following passage, from Augustine's autobiographical *Confessions,* refers to a crucial moment in his spiritual journey. Philosophy has convinced him of the existence of a transcendent God, but he still has some "growing" to do. (Slightly adapted)

SAINT AUGUSTINE THE MYSTIC

Et inde admónitus redire ad memetipsum, intravi in íntima mea, duce te, et pótui, quóniam factus es adiutor meus. Intravi et vidi óculo ánimae meae supra eundem óculum ánimae meae, supra mentem meam, lucem incommutábilem: non hanc vulgarem et conspícuam omni carni, nec (quae) quasi ex eodem génere grándior erat. Non hoc illa erat, sed áliud, áliud valde ab istis ómnibus. Nec ita erat supra mentem meam, sicut óleum super aquam, nec sicut caelum super terram; sed supérior, quia ipsa fecit me, et ego inférior, qui factus sum ab ea. Qui novit veritatem, novit eam, et qui novit eam, novit aeternitatem. Cáritas novit eam. O aeterna véritas et vera cáritas et cara aetérnitas! Tu es deus meus, tibi suspiro die ac nocte. Et cum te primum cognovi, Tu assumpsisti me, et vidi esse áliquid, quod viderem; sed nondum ego póteram videre. Et reverberavisti infirmitatem aspectus mei, rádians in me vehementer, et contrémui amore et horrore: et inveni longe me esse a te in régione dissimilitúdinis. Et putavi me audire vocem tuam de excelso: "Cibus sum grándium: cresce et manducabis me. Nec tu me in te mutabis sicut cibum carnis tuae, sed tu mutáberis in me." Et cognovi te pro iniquitate erudire hóminem. Et tabéscere fecisti sicut aráneam ánimam meam, et dixi: "Numquid nihil est véritas, quóniam neque per finita neque per infinita locorum spátia diffusa est?" Et clamavisti de longinquo: "Ego sum qui sum." Et audivi, sicut auditur in corde, et non erat prorsus causa dubitandi. Faciliusque dubitabam vívere me, quam non esse veritatem, quae per ea, quae facta sunt, conspícitur.

Reading Vocabulary

adiutor, adiutoris (masculine)	helper
aliquid	something
aránea, –ae (feminine)	cobweb
aspectus, –us (masculine)	gaze, view
conspício, –ere, conspexi	see
conspicuus, –a, –um	conspicuous, visible
contremisco, –ere, contrémui	tremble
diffusus, –a, –um	diffused, scattered
dissimilitudo, –inis (feminine)	dissimilarity
eodem, eundem	the same
erúdio, –ire, –ivi, –itus	teach
excelsus, –a, –um	high
facílius	more easily
grándior, grandioris (adjective)	bigger, grown up
incommutábilis, –e	unchangeable
ipse, ipsa, ipsum	he, she, it; himself, herself, itself
longe	by far
longinquus, –a, –um	(from) afar
memet	me, my(self)
óleum, –i (neuter)	oil
prorsus	at all
quasi	as it were
suspiro, –are, –avi	sigh
tabesco, –ere, tábui	melt

QUIZ

A

Complete the following table of infinitive forms.

Review Exercise A: Infinitive Forms

	Active Voice	*Passive Voice*
Present	*amare*	_____
Perfect	_____	_____
Future	_____	_____
Present	*míttere*	_____
Perfect	_____	_____
Future	_____	_____

B

Choose the form in parentheses that best completes the sentence, and translate.

1. *Et inde (admónitus/admonitum) redire ad memetipsum, intravi in íntima mea.*

2. *Pótui, quóniam factus (es/estis) adiutor meus.*

3. *Nec lux illa erat supra (mentem meam/mente mea).*

4. *(Qui/Quam) novit veritatem, novit eam.*

5. *Tu es deus meus, (tu/tibi/te) suspiro die ac nocte.*

6. *Et reverberavisti infirmitatem (aspectus/aspéctui) mei, rádians in me vehementer.*

7. *Et putavi me (audire/audiri) vocem tuam de excelso: "Cibus sum grándium: cresce et (manducabas/manducabis) me."*

8. *"Nec tu me in te mutabis sicut cibum carnis (tui/tuae), sed tu (mutáberis/mutábitur) in me."*

9. *Et cognovi (tu/tui/te) pro iniquitate erudire hóminem.*

10. *Faciliusque dubitabam (vívere/vixisse) me, quam non esse veritatem.*

The Comparative and Superlative Degrees

CHAPTER SUMMARY

LESSON PLAN:

In this hour you will learn about …

- How adjectives and adverbs are formed in the *comparative degree* (as in *mélior,* "better") and the *superlative degree* (as in *óptimus,* "best")

- How to coordinate the words involved in comparisons

So far, you have learned how to use adjectives and adverbs (such as *bonus,* meaning "good," and *bene,* meaning "well").

INTRODUCTORY READING

Look for comparisons in the following two selections. The first is from a collection of popular songs, called the *Carmina Burana;* the second is a hymn to the Virgin Mary.

TWO LOVE SONGS

Veni, veni, vénias,
ne me mori fácias!
Pulchra tibi fácies,
oculorum ácies,
capillorum séries—
o quam clara spécies!
Rosa rubicúndior,
lílio candídior,
ómnibus formósior,
semper in te glórior!

Come, come, come,
Don't make me die!
Beautiful is your face,
the glance of your eyes,
the fall of your hair—
what a gorgeous sight!
Redder than the rose,

whiter than the lily,
shapelier than all the rest,
I [will] always glory in you!

O Sanctíssima,
O piíssima,
Dulcis virgo Maria!
Mater amata,
intermerata,
ora, ora pro nobis!

O most holy one,
O most kindly one,
Sweet Virgin Mary!
Beloved Mother
undefiled,
pray, pray for us!

In the first poem, the poet compares his beloved with roses and lilies. Note that she is *lílio candídior,* "whiter than a lily." The suffix *–ior* corresponds to the *–er* in "whiter." This is called the *comparative degree* of the adjective *cándidus,* "white." Note also that the second element in the comparison, *lílium* (lily), goes into the ablative case to mean "than a lily."

In the second poem, the Virgin Mary is addressed as *sanctíssima* and *piíssima* (most holy, most kindly). These forms, based on the adjectives *sanctus* and *pius,* are in the *superlative degree.*

DEGREE IN ADJECTIVES

Some things have "more" of a certain quality than others. For this reason, grammarians distinguish three *degrees* of an adjective:

- The dictionary form of an adjective is called the *positive degree,* because it merely "posits" something about a noun (as in "a **long** book").
- If a noun possesses "more" of the quality than other nouns, the adjective goes into the *comparative degree* (as in "a **longer** book").
- If it possesses the quality to a supreme degree, the adjective goes into the *superlative degree* (as in "the **longest** book").

The difference can be seen in the following table.

Degree in Adjectives

Positive	Comparative	Superlative
happy	happier	happiest
brave	braver	bravest
difficult	more difficult	most difficult
good	better	best

THE COMPARATIVE DEGREE

As the table shows, the comparative degree is usually indicated in English with the suffix *–er,* or by adding the adverb "more":

- Latin is **harder** than other languages.
- Latin is **more** difficult than other languages.

In Latin, the comparative degree is formed in virtually the same way. Most verbs add the suffix *–ior;* a few simply add the adverb *magis* (more) to the positive form:

- *Latina est **difficílior** quam ceterae linguae:* Latin is **harder** (more difficult) than other languages.
- *Hoc consílium est **magis indóneum** quam illud:* This plan is **more suitable** than that one.

FORMING THE COMPARATIVE STEM

To convert a positive adjective into its comparative form, you usually drop the ending of the genitive singular of the positive degree, and add the suffix *–ior.*

The Comparative Stem

Positive Degree	Comparative Degree
laetus, –a, –um (happy) (Genitive singular [masculine] is *laet-i*)	*laet-ior*
fortis, forte (brave) (Genitive singular is *fort-is*)	*fort-ior*
prudens, prudentis (wise) (Genitive singular is *prudent-is*)	*prudent-ior*

Task 1: Working with the Comparative Degree

Form the comparative degree of the following adjectives.

1. *verus, –a, –um*
2. *brevis, breve*
3. *ingens, ingentis*
4. *longus, –a, –um*
5. *audax, audacis*
6. *carus, –a, –um*

Declining the Comparative Degree

Like all adjectives, comparative adjectives agree with the noun or pronoun they modify in case, number, and gender:

- *Latina est **difficílior** quam céterae linguae:* Latin is **more difficult** than other languages.
- *Numquam linguam **difficiliorem** vidi quam Latinam:* I have never seen a **more difficult** language than Latin.

All regular comparative forms are declined as follows.

Declension of Comparative Adjectives

Singular	Masculine/Feminine	Neuter
Nominative	*fórtior*	*fórtius*
Genitive	*fortior-is*	*fortior-is*
Dative	*fortior-i*	*fortior-i*
Accusative	*fortior-em*	*fórtius*
Ablative	*fortior-e, –i*	*fortior-e, –i*

Plural	Masculine/Feminine	Neuter
Nominative	*fortior-es*	*fortior-a*
Genitive	*fortior-um*	*fortior-um*
Dative	*fortiór-ibus*	*fortiór-ibus*
Accusative	*fortior-es*	*fortior-a*
Ablative	*fortiór-ibus*	*fortiór-ibus*

Note that the stem for nearly all forms is *fortior–;* the exception is the neuter nominative and accusative singular form *fórtius*. The endings are all taken from the third declension consonant-stem paradigm.

Note that the ablative singular has two possible forms: *fortiore* and *fortiori*. The latter is usually confined to stock phases such as *a fortiori* (from the stronger [statement]), and *a priori* (from the earlier [statement]).

JUST A MINUTE

All regular comparative adjectives use third declension endings in the comparative degree, even though they may have had first and second declension endings in the positive degree:

- *laetus, –a, –um* becomes *laétior, laétius*
- *fortis, –e* becomes *fórtior, fórtius*

Task 2: Working with the Comparative Degree II

Choose the right form of *fórtior* to agree with the preceding noun. Ambiguous forms are marked by a number in parentheses.

1. *reginam (fórtior)*
2. *reginis*
3. *reginae* (3)
4. *virorum*
5. *viro* (2)
6. *vir*
7. *manu*
8. *mánui*
9. *manus* (3)

Syntax of Comparisons

To do comparisons in Latin, you typically need four things: the item that is compared, the item with which it is compared, a comparative adjective, and some sort of connector between the two items. Study the following examples:

- *Caesar fórtior erat quam Brutus:* Caesar was braver than Brutus.
- *Hippopótami celeriores erant quam mílites:* The hippos were faster than the soldiers.

In the first example, Caesar is compared to Brutus. Accordingly, *fórtior* modifies Caesar, and the two nouns are linked by the conjunction *quam* (than).

When two nouns or pronouns are compared, they should both be in the same case. Study the following examples:

- *Nullum **virum** fortiorem vidi quam **Caésarem:*** I have never seen a braver **man** than **Caesar.**
- *Nulli **viro** fortiori occurri quam **Caésari:*** I have never met a braver **man** than **Caesar.**
- *Néminis mors crudélior erat quam **Caésaris:*** **No one's** death was crueler than **Caesar's.**

TASK 3: WORKING WITH COMPARISONS

Decline the noun in parentheses so that it fits into the sentence, and translate.

1. *Fémina Israelítica fórtior erat quam (rex):* The woman of Israel is stronger than ….
2. *Néminem sanctiorem vidi quam (Geórgius):* I have seen no one holier than ….
3. *Caésaris mílites fortiores sunt quam (Pompeius):* Caesar's soldiers are braver than ….
4. *Nullam viam breviorem vidi quam (illa):* I have seen no road shorter than ….
5. *Quae lingua est facílior quam (latina)?* What language is easier than …?

THE ABLATIVE OF COMPARISON

As an alternative to comparisons with *quam,* Latin sometimes omits *quam* and puts the second item in the ablative case:

- *Hippopótami celeriores sunt **milítibus:*** The hippos are quicker **than the soldiers.**
- *Hic vir fórtior est **illo:*** This man is braver **than that one.**

Notice that in this construction, "than …" is expressed by the ablative case alone; there is no need for *quam.*

TASK 4: WORKING WITH THE ABLATIVE OF COMPARISON

Change the following comparisons with *quam* to constructions using the ablative of comparison, and translate.

1. *Caesar nobílior est **quam Brutus.***

2. *Hippopótami celeriores* (faster) *sunt **quam mílites.***

3. *Nullum hóminem laetiorem vidi **quam Marcum.***

4. *Nulla res difficílior est **quam illa.***

5. *Illa monstra terribiliora sunt **quam haec.***

THE SUPERLATIVE DEGREE OF ADJECTIVES

So far, we have worked with sentences in which one item possesses *more* of some quality than another. If a noun or pronoun has this quality in the highest degree, however, the adjective goes into its *superlative* form.

The usual way of forming the superlative degree is to add the suffix *–issimus, –a, –um* to the stem of the positive adjective (the genitive singular form without the case ending).

The Superlative Stem

Positive Degree	Superlative Degree
laetus, –a, –um (happy) (Genitive singular is *laet-i*)	*laet-íssimus, –a, –um*
fortis, forte (brave) (Genitive singular is *fort-is*)	*fort-íssimus, –a, –um*
prudens, prudentis (wise) (Genitive singular is *prudent-is*)	*prudent-íssimus, –a, –um*

The superlative form is always declined as a first and second declension adjective:

- *Mílites **fortíssimos** habemus:* We have the **bravest** soldiers.
- *Iudith fuit ómnium **prudentíssima:*** Judith was the **most prudent** of all.

In Latin, the superlative degree can also be translated with the adverb "very."

- *Lísia est cívitas **opulentíssima:*** Lisia is a **very wealthy** city.

The context will help you determine which translation is best.

TASK 5: WORKING WITH THE SUPERLATIVE

Form the superlative degree (masculine nominative singular) of the following adjectives.

1. *verus, –a, –um*

2. *brevis, breve*

3. *ingens, ingentis*

4. *longus, –a, –um*

5. *audax, audacis*

6. *carus, –a, –um*

IRREGULAR COMPARATIVE AND SUPERLATIVE FORMS

Latin and English have regular ways of forming the comparative and superlative degrees. However, both languages also show a few exceptions to the rule. These show up in very common words, such as "good."

Irregular Comparative and Superlative Forms

Positive	Comparative	Superlative
bonus	*mélior*	*óptimus, –a, –um*
good	better	best
malus	*peior*	*péssimus, –a, –um*
bad	worse	worst

In English, it would be incorrect to say "gooder" or "goodest"; the comparative and superlative forms are derived from a different root (bet–). The same thing happens with the Latin adjectives *bonus* and *malus*. Here are some other Latin adjectives that have irregular comparative and superlative forms.

More Irregular Comparative and Superlative Forms

Positive	Comparative	Superlative
magnus	*maior* (greater)	*máximus* (the greatest, very great)
multus	*plus, plur–* (more)	*plúrimus* (the most, very much)
parvus	*minor* (smaller)	*mínimus* (the smallest, very little)

Although these forms are built on irregular stems, they are declined in the same way as regular comparative and superlative forms. However, *plus* appears in the singular only as a neuter noun (as in *plus pecuniae*, "more (of) money"). In the plural, it is declined as an ordinary comparative adjective (as in *plures hómines,* "more men").

Irregular forms will become less mysterious if you relate them to English words that are derived from them:

- *mélior* (better) becomes "ameliorated"
- *óptimus* (best) becomes "optimal"
- *peior* (worse) becomes "pejorative"
- *péssimus* (worst) becomes "pessimist"

A few other adjectives have slightly irregular forms in the superlative degree. Adjectives ending in *–er,* and some in *–ilis,* have a shortened superlative form.

Comparative and Superlative Forms of *–er* and *–ilis* Adjectives

Positive	Comparative	Superlative
miser (sad)	*misérior*	*misérrimus*
acer (sharp)	*ácrior*	*acérrimus*
fácilis	*facílior*	*facíllimus*
diffícilis	*difficílior*	*difficíllimus*

Notice that in the superlative forms of these verbs, the suffix *–issimus* is replaced by a doubling of the final *–r* and *–l,* plus the suffix *–imus.*

TASK 6: WORKING WITH IRREGULAR COMPARATIVE AND SUPERLATIVE FORMS

On the analogy of *miser* and *facilis,* give the comparative and superlative forms of the following adjectives.

1. *celer, céleris* (swift)

2. *pulcher, –ra, –rum* (pretty)

3. *húmilis, –e* (humble)

4. *grácilis, –e* (slender)

COMPARATIVE AND SUPERLATIVE ADVERBS

So far you have been working with comparative and superlative adjectives, but you will also find degree in adverbs. Consider the following table.

Regular Comparative and Superlative Forms of Adverbs

Positive	Comparative	Superlative
fórt-iter	*fórt-ius*	*fort-íssime*
bravely	more bravely	most bravely, very bravely
*laet-*e	*laét-ius*	*laet-íssime*
happily	more happily	most happily, very happily

In Latin, the adverb suffix of the positive degree (*–iter, –e*) is replaced in the comparative degree by *–ius* and in the superlative by *–íssime*.

Some adverbs have irregular comparative and superlative forms, analogous to the adjective forms you learned earlier. Here are some common ones.

Irregular Comparative and Superlative Forms of Adverbs

Positive	Comparative	Superlative
mísere (miserably)	*misérius*	*misérrime*
fácile (easily)	*facílius*	*facíllime*
bene (well)	*mélius* (better)	*óptime* (the best, very well)
male (badly)	*peius* (worse)	*péssime* (the worst, very badly)
multum (much)	*plus* (more)	*plúrimum* (the most, very much)
magnópere (much)	*magis* (more)	*máxime* (the most, very much)

Task 7: Working with Comparative and Superlative Adverbs

Form the comparative and superlative of the following adverbs.

1. *vere* (truly)
2. *bréviter* (briefly)
3. *bene* (well)

4. *alte* (highly)

5. *humíliter* (humbly)

6. *celériter* (quickly)

ANOTHER USE OF *QUAM*

When combined with an adjective or adverb in the superlative degree, *quam* means "the most ... possible" or "as ... as possible":

- *Mílites quaesívimus **quam** fortíssimos:* We looked for the bravest possible soldiers (... the bravest soldiers we could find).

- ***Quam** diligentíssime laborávimus:* We worked as diligently as possible.

PROCEED WITH CAUTION

The word *quam* is extremely versatile; it can be translated as "whom/which/that," "than," "how ...!," and "as ... possible":

- *Pecúniam **quam** mérui publicanis trádidi:* I gave the money **that** I earned to the taxmen.

- ***Quam** fortis erat Achilles!:* **How** brave Achilles was!

- *Achilles erat fórtior **quam** Hector:* Achilles was braver **than** Hector.

- *Achilles **quam** celérrime post Hectorem cucurrit:* Achilles **ran as quickly as possible** after Hector.

TASK 8: TRANSLATING *QUAM*

Translate the phrases in bold.

1. *Hippopótami celérius natant **quam mílites**:* The hippos swim faster ....

2. *Hippopótami **quam celérrime** natant:* The hippos swim ....

3. *Rex fíliam, **quam amabat**, ad imperatorem misit:* The king sent the daughter ... to the king.

4. *Rex **pecúniam quam plúrimam** ad imperatorem misit:* The king sent ... to the emperor.

5. *Mágdala litterátior erat **quam abbas**:* Magdala was more literate ....

Essential Vocabulary

The following common words should be committed to memory.

Essential Vocabulary

Latin	Meaning	Related Word
Nouns		
ars, artis (feminine)	art	
labor, laboris (masculine)	labor, effort	
opera, –ae (feminine)	work, effort	operate
pátria, –ae (feminine)	country, fatherland	patriotism
tempus, témporis (neuter)	time	temporary
Verbs		
cólo, –ere, –ui, cultus	cultivate, worship	agriculture, cult
disco, –ere, dídici	learn	discipline
intellego, –ere, –lexi, –lectus	understand	intellect
lego, –ere, legi, lectus	read	lesson
oro, –are, –avi, –atus	speak, pray	oratory
praébeo, –ere, praébui, –bitus	supply, offer	
tempto, –are, –avi, –atus	try	(at)tempt
Adjectives		
pátrius, –a, –um	father's; native	
sanctus, –a, –um	holy, saint	sanctity
qualiscumque, qualecumque	of whatsoever kind, any	
ullus, –a, –um	any	

Latin	Meaning	Related Word
Adverbs		
étiam	also	
mélius	better	ameliorate
plúrimum	a great deal	
raro	rarely	
Preposition		
praeter	beyond, except	preternatural

RECOGNITION VOCABULARY

Go through this list once or twice, and then look for these words in the
Reading Exercise.

Recognition Vocabulary

Latin	Meaning	Related Word
abóminor, –ari, –atus sum	hate	abominate
abstíneo, –ere, –ui	abstain	
antiquus, –a, –um	ancient	antique
adfício, –ere, –feci, –fectus	affect, endow	
astronómia, –ae (feminine)	astronomy	
computo, –are, –avi, –atus	compute, do arithmetic	
contentus, –a, –um	contented	
curiose	curiously, carefully	
dialéctica, –ae (feminine)	dialectic	
disciplina, –ae, (feminine)	(area of) learning	discipline

continues

Recognition Vocabulary   (continued)

Latin	Meaning	Related Word
eloquéntia, –ae (feminine)	eloquence	
exprímo, –ere, expressi, expressus	express	
exúberans, –antis (adjective)	exuberant	
festivitás, –tatis (feminine)	festivity feast	
grammática, –ae (feminine)	grammar	
história, –ae (feminine)	history	
inténtio, –ionis	attention, intention	
liberalis, –e	liberal	
pronúntio, –are, –avi, –atus	pronounce	
rhetórica, –ae (feminine)	rhetoric	
studiose	studiously	
témperans, temperantis (adjective)	temperate	temperance

SUMMARY

In this hour, you have learned how to form the comparative and superlative degrees of adjectives and adverbs and how to coordinate sentences that involve these forms. This knowledge will come in handy when you read Latin historians and biographers (among others), who are seldom content merely to "posit" the qualities of great figures. The following story is a case in point.

READING EXERCISE

When the Frankish king Charles the Great was crowned "Holy Roman Emperor" in 800 A.D., Western Europe enjoyed a political and cultural unity not known since the collapse of the Western empire in the sixth century.

The new face of Europe was in many ways a projection of the emperor himself, as remembered by his biographer, Einhard (who died in 840 A.D.).

THE EMPEROR CHARLEMAGNE

In cibo et potu témperans, sed in potu temperántior, quippe qui ebrietatem in qualicumque hómine, nedum in se ac suis, plúrimum abominabatur. Cibo non ádeo abstinere póterat, et saepe querebatur nóxia córpori suo esse ieiúnia. Convivabatur raríssime, et hoc praecípuis tantum festivitátibus, cum magno hóminum número. Cena cotidiana quaternis tantum férculis praebebatur, praeter assam, quam venatores véribus inferre solebant, qua ille libéntius quam ullo álio cibo vescebatur. Inter cenandum aut aliquod acróama aut lectorem audiebat. Legebantur ei históriae et antiquorum res gestae. Delectabatur et libris Sancti Augustini, praecipueque his qui "De Civitate Dei" praetitulati sunt.

Erat eloquéntia copiosus et exúberans poteratque quicquid volebat apertíssime exprímere. Nec pátrio tantum sermone contentus, étiam peregrinis linguis óperam inpendit. Latinam óptime dídicit et aeque illa ac pátria lingua orabat, Graecam vero mélius intellégere quam pronuntiare póterat. Artes liberales studiosíssime cóluit, earumque doctores magnis adficiebat honóribus. In discenda grammática Petrum Pisanum diaconum senem audivit; in céteris disciplinis Alcoinum, cognomento Albinum, ... virum undecumque doctíssimum, praeceptorem hábuit; apud quem et rhetóricae et dialécticae, praecípue tamen astronómiae plúrimum témporis et laboris impertivit. Discebat artem conputandi, et inténtione sagaci síderum cursum curiosíssime rimabatur. Temptabat et scríbere tabulasque et codicellos in lecto sub cervicálibus circumferre solebat; sed parum successit labor praepósterus ac sero inchoatus.

Reading Vocabulary

acróama	entertainment
aeque ... ac	as well ... as
Albinus, –i (masculine)	Albinus
Alcoinus, –i (masculine)	Alcuin
aliqui, –quae, –quod	some
aperte	openly, clearly
assa, –ae (feminine)	fried meat

continues

Reading Vocabulary   (continued)

Augustinus, –i (masculine)	Augustine
cena, –ae (feminine)	dinner
ceno, –are, –avi	dine, eat
cenandum, cenandi (neuter)	dining, eating
cervicale, –is (neuter)	pillow
circumfero, –ferre, –tuli	carry around
codicellus, –i (masculine)	little book, notebook
cognomentum, –i (neuter)	surname, alias
convivor, –ari, –atus sum	feast, have a banquet
copiosus, –a –um	plentiful
cotidianus, –a, –um	daily
cursus, –us (masculine)	course, movement
delector, –ari, –atus sum	delight (in)
diáconus, –i (masculine)	deacon
doctus, –a, –um	learned, educated
doctor, –oris (masculine)	teacher
ebríetas, ebrietatis (feminine)	drunkenness
férculum, –i (neuter)	dish
gero, –ere, gessi, gestus	do (*res gestae* means deeds)
ieiúnia, –ae (feminine)	fast(ing)
impértio, –ire, –ivi, –itus	devote, spend
incoho, –are, –avi, –atus	begin
infero, inferre, íntuli, illatus	bring in
inpendo, –ere, –pendi, impensus	spend
lectus, –i (masculine)	bed
lector, lectoris (masculine)	reader
libénter	gladly, willingly
nedum	much less, not to speak of
nóxia, –ae (feminine)	harm
parum	too little
peregrinus, –a, –um	foreign

Petrus, –i (masculine)	Peter
Pisanus, –a, –um	of Pisa
potus, –us (masculine)	drink
praeceptor, –oris (masculine)	teacher
praecípue	especially
praecípuus, –a, –um	principal
praepósterus, –a, –um	late, in reverse order
praetitulatus, –a, –um	entitled
quaternus, –a, –um	in fours
queror, queri, questus sum	complain
quisquis, quicquid	whoever, whatever
quippe (qui)	since (he) …
rimor, rimari, rimatus sum	examine, study
sagax, sagacis (adjective)	sharp, perceptive
scríbo, –ere, scripsi, scriptus	write
se	himself
senex, senis (masculine)	old man
sermo, sermonis (masculine)	language, speech
sero	late
sidus, síderis (neuter)	star
succedo, succedere, successi	succeed
suus, –a, –um	his, her, its, their (own)
tabula, –ae (feminine)	writing tablet
undecumque	from all sides, in all subjects
venator, –oris (masculine)	hunter
veru, verus (neuter)	stake
vescor, –i	eat, feed on (with ablative)

Quiz

A

Complete the following table, making the adjective in all three degrees agree with the noun on the left.

Review Exercise A

	Positive	Comparative	Superlative
reginarum (fortis)	_____	_____	_____
amicos (fortis)	_____	_____	_____
rege (laetus)	_____	_____	_____
cúrrui (bonus)	_____	_____	_____
rebus (magnus)	_____	_____	_____

B

Supply the form of the word in parentheses that best completes the sentence, and translate.

1. *In cibo et potu Carolus (temperans) erat quam céteri.*

2. *Ebrietatem (multum, superlative) abominabatur.*

3. *Saepe dicebat nóxia córpori suo (sum) ieiúnia.*

4. *Convivabatur (raro, superlative), sed cum magno hóminum número.*

5. *Erat eloquéntia copiosus poteratque quod volebat apertíssime (exprimo).*

6. *Nec (pátrius) tantum sermone contentus, étiam peregrinis linguis óperam inpendit.*

7. *Latinam (bene, superlative) dídicit et aeque illa ac pátria lingua orabat.*

8. *In céteris disciplinis Alcoinum, virum undecumque (doctus, superlative), praeceptorem hábuit.*

9. *Et rhetóricae et dialécticae, praecípue tamen astronómiae (multum, superlative) témporis et laboris impertivit.*

HOUR 18

The Subjunctive Mood, Present and Imperfect Tenses; Exhortation; Purpose Clauses; Indirect Commands

CHAPTER SUMMARY

LESSON PLAN:
In this hour you will learn about ...

- How to form the *subjunctive* mood in the present and imperfect tenses
- How to use this mood in independent clauses for exhortations and certain types of commands
- How to use the subjunctive in subordinate clauses expressing purpose and indirect commands

So far, you have been working with verbs in the indicative mood (for statements and questions), in the imperative (for commands), and in the infinitive.

INTRODUCTORY READING

To get started, have a look at these famous love lyrics, sent by the Roman poet Catullus (who died in 54 B.C.) to his mistress before their affair turned sour.

CATULLUS TO HIS GIRLFRIEND

*Vivamus, mea Lésbia, atque **amemus,***
Rumoresque senum severiorum
Omnes unius aestimemus assis.
Nobis, cum semel óccidit brevis lux,
Nox est perpétua una dormienda.
Da mi básia mille, deinde centum;
Dein mille áltera, dein secunda centum,
Dein usque áltera mille, deinde centum,
Dein, cum mília multa fecérimus,
*Conturbábimus illa, **ne sciamus,***
Aut ne quis malus invidere possit,
Cum tantum sciat esse basiorum.

Let us live, my Lesbia, and **let us love,** and let us count the rumors of grouchy old men as worth a penny. Once the brief sunlight has gone down, we must sleep one eternal night.

Give me a thousand kisses, then a hundred, then another thousand, then another hundred, then another thousand and a hundred. Then, when we have produced many thousands, we will mix them up, **that we may not know,** and so no wicked person can begrudge us when he knows, how great is the number of our kisses.

The famous opening line contains two verbs with slightly unusual forms: *vivamus* (not *vívimus*) and *amemus* (not *amamus*). By changing the middle vowel, Latin-speakers indicate a shift from the statements "we live" and "we love" to the *exhortations* "let us live" and "let us love."

These new forms are in the *subjunctive* mood. Toward the end of the poem, we see another example of the subjunctive mood. The verb *sciamus,* after the conjunction *ne,* means "so that we may not know" or "in order that we may not know." This clause tells the reason or *purpose* of mixing up the kisses. This is one of the subordinate clause types that regularly contain a subjunctive verb.

FORMS OF THE SUBJUNCTIVE MOOD

The subjunctive is usually indicated by a change in the stem of the verb. How the stem changes depends on the conjugation to which it belongs.

THE PRESENT SUBJUNCTIVE

To learn the stems of the present subjunctive, study the following table.

Present Subjunctive Stem

	I	II	III
Indicative	*amat*	*docet*	*mittit*
Subjunctive	*amet*	*dóceat*	*mittat*

	III –io	IV
Indicative	*capit*	*audit*
Subjunctive	*capiat*	*audiat*

TIME SAVER

The stem of the present subjunctive has traditionally been learned with devices like this:

WE HEAR A LIAR.

This sentence contains the stem vowels of the four conjugations in numerical order. Remember that third conjugation *–io* verbs have the same stem as the fourth conjugation.

CONJUGATING THE PRESENT SUBJUNCTIVE

Once you have the right stem, conjugating the present subjunctive is a simple matter. Just add the appropriate person/number endings for the active or passive voices. Study the following tables.

Conjugating the Present Subjunctive

I	II	III	IV
love	*teach*	*send*	*hear*

Active Voice

Singular

ame-m	*dócea-m*	*mitta-m*	*aúdia-m*
ame-s	*dócea-s*	*mitta-s*	*aúdia-s*
ame-t	*dócea-t*	*mitta-t*	*aúdia-t*

Plural

ame-mus	*docea-mus*	*mitta-mus*	*audia-mus*
ame-tis	*docea-tis*	*mitta-tis*	*audia-tis*
ame-nt	*dócea-nt*	*mitta-nt*	*aúdia-nt*

Passive Voice

Singular

ame-r	*dócea-r*	*mitta-r*	*aúdia-r*
ame-ris	*docea-ris*	*mitta-ris*	*audia-ris*
ame-tur	*docea-tur*	*mitta-tur*	*audia-tur*

Plural

ame-mur	*docea-mur*	*mitta-mur*	*audia-mur*
ame-mini	*docea-mini*	*mitta-mini*	*audia-mini*
ame-ntur	*docea-ntur*	*mitta-ntur*	*audia-ntur*

IRREGULAR VERBS IN THE PRESENT SUBJUNCTIVE

A few common verbs in Latin do not follow the "We Hear a Liar" pattern. Instead, they form the present subjunctive with a stem in –*i*.

Irregular Verbs in the Present Subjunctive

sum	possum
(be)	**(be able)**

Singular

si-m	possi-m
si-s	possi-s
si-t	possi-t

Plural

si-mus	possi-mus
si-tis	possi-tis
si-nt	possi-nt

TASK 1: CONVERTING INDICATIVE TO SUBJUNCTIVE

Convert the following verbs from the indicative to the subjunctive mood.

1. *ámbulat*
2. *suscípimus*
3. *videntur*
4. *audiris*
5. *estis*
6. *potes*
7. *timémini*
8. *surgo*
9. *scitur*

IMPERFECT SUBJUNCTIVE

In the imperfect tense, the subjunctive mood is usually indicated by a stem ending in *–re*. Study the following table.

Imperfect Subjunctive Stem

	I	*II*	*III*
Indicative	*amabat*	*docebat*	*mittebat*
Subjunctive	*amaret*	*doceret*	*mítteret*

	III –io	IV
Indicative	*capiebat*	*audiebat*
Subjunctive	*cáperet*	*audiret*

Notice that the *–re* infix is added to the stem vowel proper to each conjugation.

JUST A MINUTE

The stem of the imperfect subjunctive is virtually identical with the present active infinitive:

- *amare* (to love) becomes *amare-*
- *videre* (to see) becomes *videre-*
- *cápere* (to catch) becomes *cápere-t*

To this stem, we add the usual personal endings for the active and passive voices.

Conjugating the Imperfect Subjunctive

I	II	III	IV
love	*teach*	*send*	*hear*
Active Voice			
Singular			
amare-m	*docere-m*	*míttere-m*	*audire-m*
amare-s	*docere-s*	*míttere-s*	*audire-s*
amare-t	*docere-t*	*míttere-t*	*audire-t*
Plural			
amare-mus	*docere-mus*	*mittere-mus*	*audire-mus*
amare-tis	*docere-tis*	*mittere-tis*	*audire-tis*
amare-nt	*docere-nt*	*míttere-nt*	*audire-nt*
Passive Voice			
Singular			
amare-r	*docere-r*	*míttere-r*	*audire-r*
amare-ris	*docere-ris*	*míttere-ris*	*audire-ris*
amare-tur	*docere-tur*	*míttere-tur*	*audire-tur*
Plural			
amare-mur	*docere-mur*	*mittere-mur*	*audire-mur*
amaré-	*doceré-mini*	*mitteré-mini*	*audiré-mini*
amare-ntur	*docere-ntur*	*mittere-ntur*	*audire-ntur*

Irregular verbs also follow the rule that the imperfect subjunctive stem resembles the present active infinitive.

Irregular Verbs in the Imperfect Subjunctive

sum	possum
(be)	**(be able)**
Singular	
esse-m	posse-m
esse-s	posse-s
esse-t	posse-t
Plural	
esse-mus	posse-mus
esse-tis	posse-tis
esse-nt	posse-nt

TASK 2: CONVERTING INDICATIVE TO SUBJUNCTIVE

Convert the following verbs from the indicative mood to the subjunctive.

1. *parabat*
2. *mittebamur*
3. *placebant*
4. *audiris*
5. *eras*
6. *poteramus*
7. *manducabatis*
8. *quaerebam*
9. *praebebatur*

THE SUBJUNCTIVE IN INDEPENDENT CLAUSES

In Latin, the subjunctive mood is used in a number of ways. English, on the other hand, has retained only traces of the subjunctive (as in "God **bless** you," "if this **be** treason," and "lest he **come**"). The meaning of the Latin subjunctive is usually conveyed in English by helping verbs, which vary according the context.

Exhortations

One common use of the present subjunctive is to *exhort* a group, of which the speaker is a part, to do something. We can think of these as "first person commands." They are expressed in English with the helping verb "let":

- *Vivamus atque amemus:* **Let us live** and **love.**
- *Procedamus in pace:* **Let us go forth** in peace.
- *Studeamus diligenter:* **Let us study** hard.

Task 3: Translating Exhortations

Turn the statements in bold into exhortations, and retranslate into English.

1. *Véniunt hippopótami! Celériter **natamus** (nato, –are):* The hippos are coming! **We are swimming** quickly.

2. *Amici nostri in perículo sunt. **Monemus** eos:* Our friends are in trouble. **We warn** them.

3. *Alexander nos in proélium vocat. **Pugnamus:*** Alexander calls us into battle. **We fight.**

4. *Caesar venit. **Interfícimus** eum:* Caesar is coming. **We kill** him.

5. *Gaudemus ígitur, iúvenes dum sumus:* **We rejoice** then, while we are young.

Polite and Negative Commands

We have seen that ordinary commands are given in the imperative mood; negative commands are formed with the imperative forms *noli/nolite* and the infinitive:

- *Ambulate et **nolite cúrrere!:*** Walk and **don't run!**

Sometimes, however, commands are made more polite by using the present subjunctive:

- *Veni, veni, **vénias!:*** Come! Come! **Please come!**

The subjunctive with *ne* is also regularly used as an alternative to *noli* + infinitive. There is no difference in meaning between these constructions.

- *Noli timere!* Do not be afraid!
- *Ne tímeas!* Do not be afraid!

THIRD PERSON COMMANDS

The subjunctive is also used in "third person commands." Like exhortations, these normally appear in modern English with the helping verb "let" (or, rarely, "may"):

- *Caesar venit! **Véniat:*** Caesar is coming! **Let him come.**
- *Deus te **benedicat:*** (May) God **bless** you!

TASK 4: TRANSLATING COMMANDS WITH THE SUBJUNCTIVE

Turn the statements in bold into second and third person commands, and retranslate.

1. ***Dicit,*** *quicquid vult:* **He says** whatever he wants.
2. *Et Deus ait, "**Fit** lux"* (*fio, fíeri;* conjugate as a III –*io* verb): And God said, "There **is** light."
3. ***Est*** *pax in terra, et mecum **íncipit:*** There **is** peace on earth, and **it begins** with me.
4. *Placentam **manducant:*** **They are eating** cake.
5. *Non **ámbulas:*** **You are** not **walking.**

WISHES

The idioms we have been working with so far are technically called *jussive* (from *iubeo, –ere, iussi, iussus,* for "command") because they are expressions of the speaker's will.

A similar, but semantically distinct, situation occurs when the speaker *wishes* for something to happen. To indicate this, English relies on various, somewhat convoluted, expressions:

- If only he would come!
- I wish he would come!
- Would that he would come!
- May he come!

In Latin, it is sufficient to say *véniat,* using the subjunctive mood. If you want to distinguish a wish from a third person command (as in, "let him come"), you may add *ut, uti,* or *útinam.* Negative wishes are preceded by *ne.*

- *Véniat!:* If only he would come! May he come!
- *Ut véniat!:* May he come!
- *Ne véniat!:* May he not come!

The examples so far contain wishes for something in the future—that is, to be fulfilled *after* the wish. Sometimes, though, we wish that something *were* happening *now*. Such wishes are expressed in Latin in the imperfect subjunctive. The negative is *non*.

- *Ut veniret!:* If only he were (now) coming!
- *Ut non veniret!:* Would that he were not (now) coming!

Note that the Latin imperfect subjunctive is analogous to the English verb "were ... –ing."

TASK 5: TRANSLATING WISHES

Translate the following sentences into English as wishes.

1. *Útinam Caesar in theatrum ne intret!*
2. *Útinam nox esset brevior!*
3. *Vivat rex!*
4. *Utinam víveret rex!*
5. *In perículum ne vénias!*

THE SUBJUNCTIVE IN SUBORDINATE CLAUSES

So far, you have been working with the subjunctive mood in clauses that stand by themselves. More often than not, however, you will find subjunctive verbs in subordinate clauses indicating such things as the purpose or result of an action, its time or circumstances, or the conditions under which it may be performed. The term *subjunctive* (Latin *subiunctivus*), in fact, refers to the way in which these clauses are "subjoined" or subordinated to others.

PURPOSE CLAUSES

One common type of subordinate clause requiring the subjunctive mood is called a *final clause* or *purpose clause* (Latin *enuntiatum finale*). Such clauses state the purpose or end of the main verb:

- *Latinae stúdeo **ut** divítias innumerabiles **obtíneam:** I study Latin **in order that** I **may obtain** countless riches.

- *Caesar Gálliam invasit **ut** divítias **obtineret:*** Caesar invaded Gaul **in order** that he **might obtain** riches.

Notice that purpose clauses contain two identifying elements: the conjunction *ut* (in order that) and a subjunctive verb. In English, the verb is rendered with the helping verbs "may" or "might."

JUST A MINUTE

English allows great flexibility in expressing purpose:

- I study Latin in order that I may get rich.
- I study Latin so that I may get rich.
- I study Latin that I may get rich.
- I study Latin to get rich.

All of these are possible translations of a Latin purpose clause with *ut* and the subjunctive:

Latinae stúdeo ut dives fiam.

Purpose clauses become negative when *ut* is replaced with *ne*:

- *Latinae stúdeo **ne pauper fiam:*** I study Latin **in order** that I **may not become** poor.
- *Brutus Caésarem interfecit, **ne tyrannidem instítúeret:*** Brutus killed Caesar, **in order that he might not establish** a tyranny.

SEQUENCE OF TENSES

We have seen in the previous examples that purpose clauses are sometimes rendered with "may …" and sometimes with "might …." Your translation depends on the tense of the subjunctive verb:

- *ut … **obtíneam*** (present subjunctive): in order that I **may obtain**
- *ut … **obtinerem*** (imperfect subjunctive): in order that I **might obtain**

The shift that occurs in both languages is due to a phenomenon called *sequence of tenses.* According to this rule, the tense of a subordinate verb must harmonize with the tense of the main verb. The rule as it applies to purpose clauses may be set out as follows:

- If the main verb is in a non-past tense, the subjunctive verb must be in the present tense, and is translated "may …."
- If the main verb is in a past tense, the subjunctive verb must be in the imperfect tense, and is translated "might …."

Task 6: Translating Purpose Clauses

Translate the clauses in bold.

1. *Multi hómines vivunt,* ***ut manducent:*** Many people live, ….

2. *Cucurri ad flúvium,* ***ut mílites monerem:*** I ran to the river, ….

3. *Básia confundamus,* ***ne sciant númerum basiórum:*** Let us mix up the kisses, ….

4. *Haec rogo,* ***ut veritatem sciam:*** I ask these things, ….

5. *Mílites fugerunt,* ***ne caperentur:*** The soldiers fled, ….

6. *Festinábimus,* ***ut draconem fugiamus:*** We shall hurry, ….

7. *Philosóphiae studebam,* ***ut naturam rerum intellégerem:*** I studied philosophy, ….

Indirect Commands

Another type of subordinate clause requiring the subjunctive is called an indirect command (Latin *mandatum obliquum*). Indirect commands are like indirect statements, except that they depend on verbs of commanding or requesting:

- *Ímpero* ***ut*** *quam primum* ***vénias:*** I command **that you come** as quickly as possible. (I order you to come as quickly as possible.)

- *Rogo* ***ut*** *quam primum* ***vénias:*** I ask **that you come** as quickly as possible. (I am asking you to come as quickly as possible.)

Note that in Latin, indirect commands are set up in the same way as purpose clauses (*ut* + subjunctive verb). In English, however, they are usually rendered with an infinitive (as in "I order you **to come** …").

Negative indirect commands are likewise introduced by *ne:*

- *Rogo* ***ne*** *vénias:* I am asking you **not** to come.

Latin indirect commands also follow the rule of sequence of tenses. If the verb in the main clause is in a past tense, the tense of the subjunctive verb must be imperfect. However, this shift will not affect your English translation.

- *Rogabam* ***ne venires:*** I asked you **not to come.**

Task 7: Translating Indirect Commands

Translate the clauses in bold.

1. *Móneo (vos)* **ne in urbem intretis:** I warn (you) ….

2. *Alexander (eos) hortabatur* **ut fórtiter pugnarent:** Alexander encouraged them ….

3. *Imperator Domitianus ómnibus imperavit* **ut eum "Dominum" vocarent:** The emperor Domitian commanded everyone ….

4. *Rogo (vos)* **ne crocodillos alatis:** I am asking … *(alo, –ere* means "feed").

5. *Cur ímperas (mihi)* **ut haec fáciam?:** Why do you command me …?

ESSENTIAL VOCABULARY

The following common words should be committed to memory.

Essential Vocabulary

Latin	Meaning	Related Word
Nouns		
argentum, –i (neuter)	silver, money	Argentina
aurum, –i (neuter)	gold	
consuetudo, consuetúdinis (feminine)	custom, habit	
mos, moris (masculine)	custom, way	mores, moral
natura, –ae (feminine)	nature	
nomen, nóminis (neuter)	name	nominal
via, –ae (feminine)	way	
vulgus, –i (neuter)	the common people	
Pronoun		
áliquis, áliquid	something	
Verbs		
cáreo, –ere, cárui (+ ablative)	lack, be without	
conspício, –ere, conspexi, conspectus	see	conspectus
convénio, –ire, conveni	fit, agree with	convenient
gaúdeo, –ere, gavisus sum	rejoice (in), enjoy	

Latin	Meaning	Related Word
Verbs		
hortor, –ari, hortatus sum	encourage	exhortation
pono, –ere, pósui, pósitus	put, place	position
sequor, sequi, secutus sum	follow	consecutive
stúdeo, –ere, –ui	study	
Adjectives		
communis, –e	common	communal
dissímilis, –e	dissimilar	
fácilis, –e	easy	facility
símilis, –e	similar	
Adverbs		
cotídie	every day	
intus	inwardly	
Preposition		
secundum	according to	
Conjunctions		
ne	not	
ne ... quidem	not even	
nempe	for	
ut, uti	as; (in order) that	

RECOGNITION VOCABULARY

Go through this list once or twice, and then look for these words in the Reading Exercise.

Recognition Vocabulary

Latin	Meaning	Related Word
descéndo, –ere, –scendi	descend	
promitto, –ere, –misi, –missus	promise	
admirátio, admirationis (feminine)	admiration, wonder	
áppeto, –ere, –ivi, –itus	seek, desire	appetite
congregátio, congregationis (feminine)	coming together	congregation
contrárius, –a, –um	contrary, opposite	
frugálitas, –tatis (feminine)	frugality	
humánitas, humanitatis (feminine)	humanity	
imitor, –ari, –atus sum	imitate	
luxúria, –ae (feminine)	luxury	
neglegens, negligentis (adjective)	negligent	
notábilis, –e	notable	
odiosus, –a, –um	hateful, odious	
ódium, –ii (neuter)	dislike, hatred	
persérvero, –are, –avi, –atus	persevere	
perverse	perversely	
philosóphia, –ae (feminine)	philosophy	
proféssio, professionis (feminine)	profession	
públicus, –a, –um	public	
ridículus, –a, –um	laughable, ridiculous	
sensus, –us (masculine)	sense	

Latin	Meaning	Related Word
separo, –are, –avi, –atus	separate	
solidus, –a, –um	solid	
squalor, squaloris (masculine)	filth, squalor	
tempero, –are, –avi, –atus	temper, moderate	
toga, –ae (feminine)	toga	

SUMMARY

In this hour, you have learned how to conjugate verbs in the subjunctive mood, in the present and imperfect tenses. You have also learned how to use these forms independently in exhortations, commands, wishes, and subordinate clauses expressing purpose and indirect commands.

Knowing these things will be especially useful when you read Latin philosophical literature, which is full of exhortation and advice. The writings of Seneca are a case in point.

READING EXERCISE

The Roman statesman Lucius Annaeus Seneca (who died in 65 A.D.) lived in turbulent times. Exiled under the emperor Claudius, he returned as one of the chief advisors of the young emperor Nero. This, alas, was not a position anyone could have held for long. Knowing that his career (and life) could end at any minute, he consoled himself with the tenets of the Stoic philosophy. Among his surviving writings we have a volume of letters addressed to a young (and perhaps fictitious) friend, who was just beginning his own philosophical studies. In the following letter, Seneca warns his friend not to "show off" his newly acquired self-discipline. (Slightly adapted)

AN EXHORTATION TO MODEST PHILOSOPHY

Quod pertináciter studes et, ómnibus omissis, hoc unum agis, ut te meliorem cotídie fácias, et probo et gaúdeo; nec tantum hortor ut persérveres, sed étiam rogo. Illud autem te admóneo: ne eorum more, qui non profícere sed cónspici cúpiunt, fácias in hábitu tuo aut génere vitae aliquid notábile. Ásperum cultum et intonsum caput et neglegentiorem barbam et indictum argento ódium et cubile humi pósitum, et quicquid áliud ambitionem perverse séquitur, evita. Satis ipsum nomen philosóphiae, etiamsi modeste tractatur, invidiosum est: quid si nos hóminum consuetúdini coepérimus excérpere? Intus ómnia dissimília sint, frons pópulo nostro convéniat. Ne spléndeat toga: ne sórdeat quidem. Ne habeamus argentum in quod sólidi auri caelatura descénderit, sed ne putemus frugalitatis indícium (esse) auro argentoque caruisse. Meliorem vitam sequamur quam vulgus, sed non contráriam: alioquin eos, quos emendari vólumus, fugamus a nobis et avértimus. Nihil enim imitari volunt nostri, dum putant imitanda esse ómnia. Hoc primum philosóphia promittit: sensum communem, humanitatem et congregationem. Ab hac proféssione dissimilitudo nos separábit. Nempe propósitum nostrum est secundum naturam vívere: hoc contra naturam est, tórquere corpus suum et fáciles odisse mundítias et squalorem appétere et cibis non tantum vílibus uti, sed taetris et hórridis. Quemádmodum desiderare delicatas res luxúriae est, ita usitatas et parábiles fúgere, deméntiae (est). Frugalitatem éxigit philosóphia, non poenam: potest autem esse non incompta frugálitas. Hic mihi modus placet: temperetur vita inter bonos mores et públicos; suspíciant omnes vitam nostram, sed agnoscant.

Reading Vocabulary

admóneo, admonere, admónui, admónitus	advise, warn
agnosco, –ere, agnovi	recognize
alioquin	otherwise
ambítio, ambitionis (feminine)	vainglory, showiness
asper, –a, –um	harsh, unpleasant
averto, –ere, averti, aversus	turn away
barba, barbae (feminine)	beard
caelatura, –ae (feminine)	concealment
coepi, –isse (perfect of *incípio*)	begin
cubile, cubilis (neuter)	bed, couch
cultus, cultus (masculine)	dress, appearance
delicatus, –a, –um	soft, delicate
deméntia, –ae (feminine)	madness
desídero, –are, –avi, –atus	desire
dissimilitudo, –dinis (feminine)	unlikeness
emendo, –are, –avi, –atus	amend, change

etiamsi	even if
évito, –are, –avi, –atus	avoid
excérpo, –ere, –excerpsi	cut out from, remove from
éxigo, –ere, exegi, exactus	require
frons, frontis (feminine)	forehead, expression
fugo, –are, –avi, –atus	put to flight, chase away
hórridus, –a, –um	rough, tacky
humi	on the ground
incomptus, –a, –um	unkempt
indícium, indícii (neuter)	sign, indication
indico, –ere, indixi, indictus	declare (war)
intonsus, –a, –um	uncut
invidiosus, –a, –um	suspect, unpopular
ipse, –a, –um	the very ...; the ... itself
modeste	modestly, moderately
modus, –i (masculine)	way, limit, moderation
mundítiae, –arum (feminine)	cleanliness, neatness
noster, nostra, nostrum	our
odi, odisse (perfect only)	dislike, hate
omitto, omíttere, omisi, omissus	omit, set aside
parábilis, –e	(easily) obtainable
pertináciter	tenaciously, assiduously
primum	first
profício, profícere, profeci	make progress, improve
propósitum, –i (neuter)	plan
quemádmodum	just as
quicquid	whatever
quidem	with *ne,* means "not even"
sórdeo, sordere	be grubby
spléndeo, splendere	shine
suspício, suspícere, suspexi, suspectus	look up to; suspect
suus, sua, suum	one's own
taeter, taetra, taetrum	foul, yucky
tórqueo, torquere, torsi	twist, torture
tracto, tractare, tractavi, tractatus	handle

continues

Reading Vocabulary   (continued)

usitatus, –a, –um	usual, common
vílis, vile	cheap, vile
vólumus	we wish

QUIZ

A

Translate the following verbs (translate all subjunctives as wishes).

1. *hábitat*
2. *cápiat*
3. *videt*
4. *ámbulet*
5. *mittet*
6. *desíderet*
7. *moneret*
8. *esset*
9. *dúbitat*
10. *fúgiat*

B

Choose the form in the parentheses that best fits the sentence, and translate.

1. *Pertináciter (studes/stúdeas), ut te meliorem cotídie (facis/fácias).*
2. *Intus ómnia dissímilia (sint/essent), frons pópulo nostro convéniat.*
3. *Ne (putamus/putemus) frugalitatis indícium esse auro argentoque caruisse.*
4. *Meliorem vitam (sequemur/sequamur) quam vulgus, sed non contráriam.*
5. *Ab hac professióne dissimilitudo nos (separabit/separet).*
6. *Nempe propósitum nostrum est secundum naturam (vívere/vivamus).*
7. *Frugalitatem éxigit (philosóphia/philosóphiam), non poenam.*
8. *(Suspíciat/suspíciant) omnes vitam nostram.*

Perfect and Pluperfect Subjunctive; Indirect Questions

CHAPTER SUMMARY

LESSON PLAN:

In this hour you will learn about ...

- Conjugating subjunctive verbs in the perfect and pluperfect tenses
- Using all four tenses of the subjunctive to form indirect questions

So far, you have learned how to conjugate subjunctive verbs in the present and imperfect tenses and how to use these forms in certain clauses.

INTRODUCTORY READING

Look for new forms and constructions in this famous poem by the Roman poet Horace (who died in 8 B.C.):

SEIZE THE DAY!

*Tu **ne quaesíeris** (scire nefas) quem mihi, quem tibi*
*Finem di **déderint,** Leuconoe; nec Babylónios*
***tenta(ve)ris** números. Ut mélius, quicquid erit, pati!*
Seu plures híemes, seu tríbuit Iúpiter últimam,
Quae nunc oppósitis debílitat pumícibus mare
Tyrrhenum. Sápias, vina liques, et spátio brevi Spem
longam réseces. Dum lóquimur, fúgerit ínvida Aetas;
carpe diem, quam mínima crédulapóstero.

Don't ask (for it is unlawful to know) what end the gods **have given** to me, or to you, Leuconeoe; and **don't play** with Babylonian numbers. How much better (it is) to endure whatever will be—whether Jupiter (will grant) more winters, or has given the last, which now fatigues the Tyrrhenian Sea with opposing cliffs of pumice. Be smart: pour the wine, and in this brief time put away hope of a long life. While we speak, our short span of life will have fled away. Seize the day, trusting as little as you can in the future.

At the beginning of this poem, we find negative commands (*ne quaesíeris, nec tentáveris*) that are not conjugated, as in the previous chapter, in the present subjunctive. Instead, we encounter forms of the *perfect* subjunctive.

We also find another use of the perfect subjunctive in the sentence *Ne quaesíeris, quem … finem di* **déderint** (Don't ask, what … end the gods **have given**). The verb *déderint* occurs in a question that has been subordinated to the "asking" verb *quaesíeris*. *Indirect questions* regularly contain verbs in the subjunctive mood.

Two New Tenses of Subjunctive Mood

The subjunctive occurs in four tenses: the present, imperfect, perfect, and pluperfect. There are no subjunctive forms in the future or future perfect tenses, because the other tenses already have a note of possibility or "futurity."

The Perfect Subjunctive, Active Voice

The perfect tense of the subjunctive is formed in a manner analogous to the perfect indicative. This means, first of all, that active and passive forms have different stems.

To form the perfect subjunctive, active, take the stem derived from the third principal part, and add new endings with the infix *eri*.

Perfect Subjunctive Active of *Amo*

Singular	Plural
amáv-eri-m	*amav-éri-mus*
amáv-eri-s	*amav-éri-tis*
amáv-eri-t	*amáv-eri-nt*

The same endings are added to all perfect active stems, regardless of the conjugation the verb belongs to, as in *monú-erim, dúx-erim,* and *fú-erim*.

PROCEED WITH CAUTION

The endings for the perfect subjunctive, active, closely resemble those of the future perfect indicative. The one exception is the form in the first person, singular: *amávero* (future perfect indicative) becomes *amáverim* (perfect subjunctive). To distinguish the other forms, you will need to consider the context:

- *Si haec **féceris**, laudáberis:* If **you will have done** this, you will be praised.
- *Ne haec **féceris**!* Don't **do** this!

In this and subsequent lessons, you will learn which clauses require a subjunctive verb.

TASK 1: CONVERTING INDICATIVE TO SUBJUNCTIVE

Convert the following verbs from the indicative to the subjunctive mood.

1. *amaverunt*
2. *monuistis*
3. *misi*
4. *audívimus*
5. *dedisti*
6. *fuit*

THE PERFECT SUBJUNCTIVE, PASSIVE VOICE

The perfect subjunctive, passive, is formed analogously with the indicative mood. It is a periphrastic (two-part) form, consisting of the perfect passive participle (the fourth principal part) and the present subjunctive of the verb *sum*.

Perfect Subjunctive Passive of *Amo*

Singular	Plural
amatus, –a, –um sim	*amati, –ae, –a simus*
amatus, –a, –um sis	*amati, –ae, –a sitis*
amatus, –a, –um sit	*amati, –ae, –a sint*

TASK 2: CONVERTING ACTIVE TO PASSIVE

Convert the following verbs from the perfect subjunctive, active to the perfect subjunctive, passive.

1. *laudáveris*
2. *víderim*
3. *interfecérimus*
4. *míserint*
5. *légerit*
6. *mutavéritis*

THE PLUPERFECT SUBJUNCTIVE, ACTIVE VOICE

The pluperfect subjunctive, active, is formed by combining the perfect active stem with endings built on the infix *isse*.

Pluperfect Subjunctive Active of *Amo*

Singular	Plural
amav-isse-m	amav-isse-mus
amav-isse-s	amav-isse-tis
amav-isse-t	amav-isse-nt

In the same way, we come up with the forms *monuissem, duxissem,* and *fuissem.*

TIME SAVER

Remember that the imperfect subjunctive stem resembles the present active infinitive (as in *monere-m* and *esse-m*). In the same way, the pluperfect subjunctive active stem resembles the perfect active infinitive: *amavisse* (to have loved) becomes *amavissem.*

TASK 3: CONJUGATING THE PLUPERFECT SUBJUNCTIVE ACTIVE

Fully conjugate the following verbs in the pluperfect subjunctive, active.

1. *dóceo, docere, dócui, doctus*
2. *possum, posse, pótui*

THE PLUPERFECT SUBJUNCTIVE, PASSIVE VOICE

The pluperfect subjunctive, passive, consists of the perfect passive participle (the fourth principal part) and the imperfect subjunctive of the verb *sum.*

Pluperfect Subjunctive Passive of *Amo*

Singular	Plural
amatus, -a, -um essem	amati, -ae, -a essemus
amatus, -a, -um esses	amati, -ae, -a essetis
amatus, -a, -um esset	amati, -ae, -a essent

TASK 4: CONVERTING ACTIVE TO PASSIVE

Convert the following forms from the active to the passive voice.

1. *docuissent*
2. *misissem*
3. *laudavisset*

4. *intellexissemus*

5. *amavissetis*

6. *habuisses*

OVERVIEW OF FORMS IN THE SUBJUNCTIVE MOOD

Congratulations! You have now learned the entire regular verb system of the Latin language! Because we have covered the subjunctive mood at an accelerated pace, it may help to scan the following table of subjunctive stems.

Overview of Subjunctive Stems

Tense	Stem
Present	*WE BEAT A LIAR*
Imperfect	*–ere–* (same as present active infinitive)
Perfect active	perfect active stem + *–eri–*
Perfect passive	perfect passive participle + *sim*
Pluperfect active	perfect active stem + *–isse–* (same as perfect active infinitive)
Pluperfect passive	perfect passive participle + *essem*

TASK 5: IDENTIFYING TENSE AND VOICE

Identify the tense and voice of the following subjunctive verbs; then indicate whether the subject would be "I," "you," "he/she/it," "we," "y'all," or "they."

1. *amarem*

2. *monuisset*

3. *misérimus*

4. *audiamur*

5. *dati sitis*

6. *fúerint*

7. *laudarentur*

8. *mónita esset*

9. *esses*

10. *monearis*

11. *ductus sit*

12. *oremus*

PERFECT SUBJUNCTIVE IN COMMANDS

As you saw in the Introductory Reading, the perfect subjunctive can by used interchangeably with the present subjunctive in polite and negative commands. There is no change in meaning.

- *Quid agis? **Ne quaesíeris!*** How are you doing? **Don't ask!**

INDIRECT QUESTIONS

Subjunctive forms regularly show up in *indirect questions*. A question becomes indirect when it is subordinated to a "head" verb, usually one of asking or answering:

- Who is coming?
- I am asking you who is coming.

In the first sentence, the question is posed directly; in the second, it is subordinated to the verb "I am asking."

In English, it is usually not necessary to change the mood of the verb in an indirect question. In Latin, however, such verbs always go into the subjunctive mood:

- *Quis **venit?**:* Who **is coming?**
- *Rogo (te) quis **véniat:*** I am asking you **who is coming.**

Note again that *véniat* is translated "is coming"; there is no need here for the helping verbs encountered in other uses of the subjunctive mood ("may," "might," and so on).

SEQUENCE OF TENSES IN INDIRECT QUESTIONS

We saw in the last lesson that subjunctive verbs generally must harmonize with the tense of the verb in the main clause. This is called the rule of *sequence of tenses*. When it comes to indirect questions, however, this rule should pose no difficulties in translation.

Follow this rule of thumb: translate subjunctive verbs in indirect questions as if they were indicative, keeping the same tense:

- *Rogo quid **fácias:*** I am asking what **you are doing.**
- *Rogabam quid **fáceres:*** I asked what **you were doing.**
- *Rogo quid **féceris:*** I am asking what **you did/have done.**
- *Rogabam quid **fecisses:*** I asked what **you had done.**

Note, for example, that you translate the present subjunctive *fácias* as if it were present indicative (you are doing).

TASK 6: TRANSLATING INDIRECT QUESTIONS

Translate the verbs in bold.

1. *Pópulus rogabat quo Sanctus Geórgius draconem **dúceret:*** The people asked where St. George … the dragon.
2. *Néscio ubi argentum **posúerim:*** I do not know where … the money.
3. *Imperator fíliam regis rogavit, quem cóphinum **elegisset:*** The emperor asked the king's daughter, which casket …. (*élego* means "choose")
4. *Iudith dubitabat, an Holofernem interfícere **posset:*** Judith doubted whether she … to kill Holofernes.
5. *Quaerebamus, quae urbes a Caésare **captae essent:*** We were asking what cities … by Caesar.
6. *Séneca docet quómodo philósophus vívere **débeat:*** Seneca teaches how a philosopher … to live.
7. *Mirabamur, cur mílites in flúvium **mitterentur:*** We wondered why the soldiers … into the river.

"FUTURE" SUBJUNCTIVES

So far, we have been dealing with indirect questions about events occurring before or at the same time as the "head" verb in the main clause.

What happens if the question is about an event *subsequent* to the main verb? Here Latin-speakers found themselves in a bind, for they had not developed a future subjunctive. Luckily, they could sometimes fall back on the active periphrastic construction, which you learned in Hour 15.

If the main verb is in one of the "nonpast" tenses, a "future subjunctive" can be created for the indirect question by combining the future active participle and the present subjunctive of *sum.*

- *Rogo quid facturus sis:* I am asking (you) what **you are going to do** (what you will do).

If the main verb is in a past tense, the same construction is used with the imperfect subjunctive of *sum:*

- *Rogavi quid facturus esses:* I asked what **you were going to do** (what you would do).

In the last example, note the tense shift in English from "will" to "would."

TASK 7: TRANSLATING INDIRECT QUESTIONS II

Translate the verbs in bold.

1. *Augustinus rogabat, quómodo Deum **inventurus esset:*** Augustine asked how … God.

2. *Néscimus, quid in hoc libro **inventuri simus:*** We don't know what … in this book.

3. *Alexander nesciebat, quid milítibus **dicturus esset:*** Alexander did not know what … to the soldiers.

4. *Caesar Brutum rogat, quid illo pugione **facturus sit:*** Caesar asks Brutus, what … with that dagger.

ESSENTIAL VOCABULARY

The following common words should be committed to memory.

Essential Vocabulary

Latin	Meaning	Related Word
Nouns		
médium, –i (neuter)	middle	
puer, –i (masculine)	boy	puerile
Verbs		
egrédior, égredi, egressus sum	go out	egress
ingrédior, íngredi ingressus sum	go in	ingress
loquor, loqui, locutus sum	speak	locution
progrédior, prógredi progressus sum	step forward	progress
quaero, –ere, quaesivi	ask, seek	question
signífico, significare, significavi, significatus	mean	signify
táceo, –ere, tácui	be silent	taciturn
Adjective		
útilis, –e	useful	utility

Latin	Meaning	Related Word
Adverbs		
ántea	before, previously	
póstea	afterward	
posthac	after this	
postrídie	next day	
Preposition		
ob (+ accusative)	on account of	
Conjunctions		
an	whether; or	
priusquam	before	
utrum	whether	

RECOGNITION VOCABULARY

Go through this list once or twice, and look for these words in the Reading Exercise.

Recognition Vocabulary

Latin	Meaning
delíbero, –are, –avi, –atus	deliberate
inquiro, inquíere, inquisivi, inquisitus	inquire
matrona, matronae (feminine)	matron
parens, parentis (common)	parent
prudéntia, prudéntiae (feminine)	prudence
secretum, secreti (neuter)	secret
senator, senatoris (masculine)	senator
senatus, senatus (masculine)	senate
siléntium, siléntii (neuter)	silence
violenter	violently
úrgeo, urgere	urge

SUMMARY

In this hour, you have learned the perfect and pluperfect tenses of the subjunctive mood, and you have learned how to use the subjunctive in indirect questions. You will find this helpful when reading Roman historians and story-tellers, who are notoriously fond of "indirect" constructions.

READING EXERCISE

As part of their training in rhetoric, young Romans acquired a repertory of stories from Greek and Roman history illustrating the civic virtues. The following story, set in the early Roman Republic, is related by the Roman encyclopedist, Aulus Gellius (who died in the late second century A.D.). (Adapted)

A CLEVER ROMAN BOY

Mos ántea senatóribus Romae fuit, in cúriam cum praetextatis fíliis introire. Tum, cum in senatu res maior quaedam consultata eaque in diem pósterum prolata est, ita decreverunt: "nemo rem tractatam enúntiet, priusquam decreta sit." Mater vero Papírii pueri, qui cum parente suo in cúria fúerat, percunctata est fílium, quidnam in senatu patres egissent. Puer respondit, id tacendum esse, neque dici licere. Múlier fit audiendi cupídior; secretum rei et siléntium pueri ánimum eius ad inquirendum incendit; quaerit ígitur violéntius. Tum puer, matre urgente, lépidi atque festivi mendácii consílium capit. Deliberavisse senatum dixit, utrum videretur utílius rei públicae, ut unus vir duas uxores haberet, an ut una fémina duobus viris núberet. Hoc illa ubi audivit, compavescit, et domo trépidans egréditur ad céteras matronas. Pervenit ad senatum postrídie matronarum caterva. Lacrimantes atque obsecrantes orant, ut una pótius duobus nupta fíeret, quam ut uni duae. Senatores ingredientes in cúriam, quae esset illa mulíerum intempéries et quid postulátio ista significaret, mirabantur. Puer Papírius, in médium cúriae progressus, quid mater audire institisset, et quid ipse matri dixisset, denarravit. Senatus fidem atque ingénium eius approbat et consultum facit: "Ne post hac púeri cum pátribus intróeant, praeter ille unus Papírius." Huic púero póstea cognomen honoris grátia índitum est "Praetextatus," ob tacendi loquendique in aetate togae praetextae prudéntiam.

Reading Vocabulary

approbo, –are, –avi, –atus	approve
caterva, catervae (feminine)	crowd
cognomen, cognóminis (neuter)	surname
compavesco, –ere, –pavi	blanche, become pale
consulto, –are, –avi, –atus	consult, consider
consultus, –us (masculine)	decree
cúpidus, –a, –um	desirous
cúria, cúriae (feminine)	senate house

decerno, –ere, –crevi, decretum	decide, decree
denarro, –are, –avi, –atus	tell, relate
domo	from home
duo, duae, duo (dative case: *duobus, duabus*)	two
enúntio, –are, –avi, –atus	tell
festivus, –a, –um	smart, neat
fides, fídei (feminine)	faith
grátia (+ genitive)	for the sake of
incendo, –ere, –cendi	fire up, inflame
indo, –ere, índidi, inditus	endow, bestow
ingénium, –i (neuter)	intelligence, character
insisto, –ere, ínstiti	insist (+ infinitive)
intempéries, –ei (feminine)	outrageous conduct
intróeo, –ire, –ii (present subjunctive: *intróeam*)	go in
ipse	he himself
lácrimo, –are, –avi	weep
lépidus, –a, –um	clever
licet, licere, lícuit	be permitted
mendácium, –ii (neuter)	lie, deceit
miror, –ari, –atus sum	wonder
nubo, núbere, nupsi, nuptus	marry
nupta, nuptae (feminine)	married woman, wife
óbsecro, –are, –avi, –atus	beseech
oro, –are, –avi, –atus	beseech, speak, pray
Papírius, –i (masculine)	Papirius
pater, patris (masculine)	father; senator
percunctor, –ari, –atus sum	ask
pervénio, –ire, perveni	arrive
pósterus, –a, –um	later
postulátio, –ionis (feminine)	demand
pótius	rather, instead
praetexta, –ae (feminine)	bordered toga (worn by Roman boys)

continues

Reading Vocabulary (continued)

praetextatus	wearing the bordered toga (of boys)
prófero, –ferre, –tuli, –latus	put forth, extend
quaedam	a certain
quidnam	what (in the world)
suus, –a, –um	his, her, its, their (own)
tracto, –are, –avi, –atus	discuss, treat,
trépido, –are, –avi	tremble, shake

QUIZ

A

Translate the following sentences. Remember that the way you translate the subjunctive depends on whether it appears in an exhortation, command, wish, purpose clause, indirect command, or indirect question.

1. *Latine discamus!* (*disco, díscere, dídici* means "learn")

2. *Ne Latine discas!*

3. *Rogas, cur Latine discam.*

4. *Útinam Latine discam!*

5. *Hoc librum emi, ut Latine díscerem.*

6. *Móneo te ne Latine discas.*

7. *Nesciebam, cur Latine didicisses.*

8. *Rogabam ne Latine dísceres.*

B

Answer the following questions, which are based on the Reading Exercise, in Latin.

1. *Qui mos antiquis Romanis fuit?*

2. *Quid mater Papírii eum rogavit? Quid ille respondit?*

3. *Cur mater violéntius quaerebat?*

4. *Quale consílium puer capit?*

5. *De qua re, secudum Papírium, deliberavit senatus?*

6. *Hoc audito, quid fecit mater?*

7. *Quid mulíeres senatum oraverunt?*

8. *Cur póstea Papírio índitum est nomen "Praetextatus"?*

HOUR 20

Result, Temporal, Causal, and Concessive Clauses

CHAPTER SUMMARY

LESSON PLAN:

In this hour you will learn about …

- How to construct subordinate clauses indicating result (so that …), fear (lest …), time (when, as …), cause (since …), and concession (although …)

- How to distinguish between overlapping uses of the same conjunction (for example, *ut* and *cum*)

So far, you have learned to use the subjunctive in various independent and subordinate clauses, including clauses of purpose, indirect command, and indirect question.

INTRODUCTORY READING

Some of the complexities of this lesson will be apparent in the following extract of a medieval drinking song. After passing out in a tavern, the author has a vision in which Lyeus and Thetis, the personifications of water and wine, debate before the throne of God.

WINE AND WATER DEBATE

Cum sederet síquidem in excelsis Deus et cepisset spíritus trepidare meus, statim in iudício Thetis et Lyeus intrant et altéruter actor fiet et reus.

AQUA

Meum decus admodum Deus ampliavit, quando me de púteo potum postulavit: de torrente, síquidem, attestante David bibit et proptérea caput exaltavit.

VINUM

Te quamvis aquáticus bibat Nazareus, quantum salutíferus sit effectus meus patet, dum Apóstolus mandat, immo Deus, ut me propter stómachum bibat Timótheus.

When God was sitting on high, and my spirit began to tremble, Thetis and Lyeus enter into court and become prosecutor and defendant by turns.

WATER

God greatly increased my prestige when he asked to drink me from the well; and from the torrent, as David attests, he drank and raised his head.

WINE

Although the teetotaling Nazarene drinks you, it is clear how healthful my effect is, when the Apostle, nay God himself, commands Timothy to drink me for the sake of his stomach.

In this extract, you will notice that there are three ways of saying "when" in Latin: *cum, quando,* and *dum.* Moreover, *cum* takes the subjunctive mood (*sederet, cepisset*), but *quando* and *dum* are followed by indicative verbs (*postulavit, mandat*). You also encountered a concessive clause (*quamvis … bibat,* meaning "although … he drinks"), a type that may also be found either with the indicative or subjunctive mood. Let's sort out a few of these finer points of Latin syntax.

Temporal Clauses: *Cum*

A temporal clause indicates the time of the event in the main clause:

- *Cum Caesar senatum **intraret,** omnes senatores surrexerunt:* **When** Caesar **entered** the Senate, all the senators rose.
- *Quando **vídeo** opera Dei, gaúdeo:* **When** I **see** the works of God, I rejoice.
- *Ut haec **dicebat,** mortuus est:* **As** he **was saying** these things, he died.
- *Postquam ábiit, cervísiam deprómpsimus:* **After** he **left,** we opened a beer.

Most temporal conjunctions (such as *quando,* "when"; *ut,* "as"; and *postquam,* "after") are followed by verbs in the indicative mood. One of the exceptions is *cum,* which may take either the indicative or the subjunctive mood.

The rules for choosing between them are a little fluid, especially in postclassical Latin. In general, though, *cum* (when) is followed by the subjunctive if 1) the main verb is in a past tense, and 2) the speaker is interested in the general circumstances, rather than the precise time, of the main verb:

- *Cum iuventus floreret, gaudebam:* When my youth bloomed, I enjoyed it.

Notice that the subjunctive *floreret* is translated as though it were an imperfect indicative (bloomed, was blooming).

On the other hand, a Latin writer will use the indicative to define a point in time:

- *Cum sol occidit, urbem oppugnávimus:* When the sun set (at sunset), we attacked the city.

TASK 1: TRANSLATING TEMPORAL CLAUSES

Translate the following sentences.

1. *Postquam Iudith Holofernem interfecit, omnes eam laudaverunt.*
2. *Cum argentum invenérimus, gavísi sumus.*
3. *Ut mílites in flúvio natabant, hippopótami in aqua iacebant.*
4. *Cum urbs arderet* (burned)*, Nero gaudebat.*

OTHER TEMPORAL CONJUNCTIONS

There are other temporal conjunctions that can appear with either mood, with a slight difference in meaning. Consider the following set:

- *dum:* while, until, as long as
- *donec:* while, until

When these words introduce clauses that merely signify the time of the main verb, the indicative is used:

- *Dum licuit, urbem despoliaverunt:* While it was permitted, they looted the city.

The subjunctive, however, may be used to indicate something "unreal" (that is, conditional or merely anticipated) about the verb in the subordinate clause:

- *Oderint, dum metuant:* Let them hate, as long as they fear (provided that they fear).
- *Expectábimus donec véniant:* We will wait until they come.

The same distinction applies to the conjunctions *antequam* and *priusquam* (before). They are used with the indicative to indicate a point in time, but with the subjunctive to refer to anticipated events:

- *Bárbari fugerunt priusquam Romani advenerunt:* The barbarians fled before the Romans arrived.
- *Fugiamus priusquam Romani advéniant!* Let's get out of here before the Romans arrive!

Despite the difference in meaning, subjunctive verbs in these clauses are translated the same way as indicative verbs.

Task 2: Translating Temporal Clauses II

Complete the translations of the following sentences.

1. *Nero se interfecit, priusquam cives eum apprehénderent:* Nero killed himself ....

2. *Laboremus, dum vita gaudeamus* (enjoy): Let us work ....

3. *Dum senatus deliberabat, pueri tacebant:* ..., the boys kept silent.

4. *In urbe manebamus, donec exercitum vidimus:* We waited in the city ....

Causal Clauses

A causal clause is one that explains the cause or motive of the event in the main clause. The following are the common causal conjunctions:

- *quod:* because
- *quia:* because
- *quóniam:* because
- *síquidem:* because
- *cum:* since, because

In causal clauses, *cum* regularly takes the subjunctive mood:

- *Quae cum ita sint, fúgere débeo:* Since these things are so (this being the case), I must flee.

The other conjunctions are regularly followed by the indicative if the clause refers to an *actual* cause. If the speaker relates a cause as *alleged,* without endorsing the allegation, the subjunctive is used:

- *Caesar interfectus est **quod** rem públicam **abóluit:*** Caesar was killed because he abolished the republic.

- *Caesar interfectus est, ut coniurati asseruerunt, **quod** rem publicam **aboluisset:*** Caesar was killed, as the conspirators claimed, because he had abolished the republic.

Note that in the second sentence, the speaker does not vouch for the conspirators' motives; he merely reports what *they* say. This subtlety of Latin syntax is not directly translatable into English: the subjunctive form *aboluisset* is rendered "had abolished."

PROCEED WITH CAUTION

Keep in mind that, depending on the context, *quod* can mean "what," "that/which," "that" (introducing indirect statements), and "because." Context is your best guide here:

- *Quod periculum imminet?:* What danger threatens?
- *Non vidit periculum, quod imminebat:* He did not see the danger which/that threatened.
- *Milites aiebant, quod periculum imminebat:* The solders said that danger threatened.
- *Fugerunt milites, quod periculum imminebat:* The soldiers fled, because danger threatened.

TASK 3: TRANSLATING VERB FORMS

Choose the form of the verb in parentheses that best completes the sentence, and translate.

1. *Caesar spem deponebat* (gave up), *cum Brutum inter coniuratos (videbat/videret).*
2. *Latina difficilis est quod Romani insani* (crazy) *(fuerunt/fuerint).*
3. *Romani urbem ceperunt, ut aiunt, quod hostes (imminebant/imminerent). Noli eis credere!*
4. *Laudemus Deum, quia ipse* (he) *nos (fecit/fecerit).*

TASK 4: TRANSLATING *QUOD*

Complete the translation of the following sentences, using the correct translation of *quod.*

1. *Periculum, quod omnes timebant, Sanctus Georgius ridebat:* Saint George laughed at the danger … everyone feared.
2. *Georgius draconem vicit, quod in Deum credebat:* George conquered the dragon … he believed in God.
3. *Populus Georgium rogavit, quod consilium haberet:* The people asked George … plan he had.
4. *Georgius proclamabat, quod urbem liberare volebat:* George proclaimed … he wished to free the city.

CONCESSIVE CLAUSES

Another type of clause is called concessive; these are marked in English with the conjunctions "although," "even though," and "even if." In Latin, the most common conjunctions are these:

- *etsi:* even if
- *etiamsi:* even if
- *quamquam:* although
- *quamvis:* although
- *cum:* although

In Latin, the first three conjunctions (*etsi, etiamsi, quamquam*) are usually followed by verbs in the indicative mood. Clauses with *quamvis* and the ubiquitous *cum,* on the other hand, regularly take a subjunctive verb:

- *Quamquam saepe monuisti, in flúvio me lavi:* Although you often warned me, I bathed in the river.
- *Cum multum studuissem, nihil tamen dídici:* Although I had studied a lot, I still learned nothing.

TASK 5: WORKING WITH CONCESSIVE CLAUSES

Choose the form of the verb that best completes the sentence, and translate.

1. *Quamquam multa (sciebat/sciret), abbas latine loqui non póterat.*
2. *Quamvis saepe (pugnáverat/pugnavisset), miles timebat.*
3. *Etsi Caesar in bello (vincebat/vínceret), eum non sequebamur.*
4. *Cum fortis (erat/esset), Holofernes tamen périit* (perished).

OVERVIEW OF THE CONJUNCTION *CUM*

You have probably noticed that *cum* (like *quod*) is an all-purpose Latin conjunction, meaning "when," "since," and "although." It can also be confused with the preposition *cum* (with). The following table may help you keep its meanings distinct, with the help of certain contextual clues.

Overview of *Cum*

Clause Type	Meaning	Mood	Context
temporal	when	indicative subjunctive	past main verb
causal	since	subjunctive	
concessive	although	subjunctive	*tamen* or similar expression in main clause

TASK 6: TRANSLATING *CUM*

Complete the translations of the following sentences with the correct rendering of *cum*.

1. *Cum ad urbem advenissemus, draconem vídimus:* … we saw a dragon.

2. *Timebamus, cum draconem numquam vidissemus:* We were afraid ….

3. *Cum draconem numquam vidissemus, ália tamen monstra conspexeramus:* … we had (nevertheless) spotted other monsters.

4. *Cum Seneca eum monebat* (advised), *Nero bonus erat imperato ….* Nero was a good emperor.

RESULT CLAUSES

In the last lesson, we saw that the conjunction *ut* can be used to introduce clauses of purpose (in order that …) and indirect commands (to …). In certain contexts, though, it may indicate a clause of *result*. Study the following:

- *Tam diligenter studúimus **ut** omnia facile disceremus:* We studied **so** diligently **that** we learned everything easily.

- *Ita vivamus, **ut** omnes nos laudemus:* Let us live in **such a way that** all people praise us.

Notice that, unlike purpose clauses, result clauses are not translated with special helping verbs in English.

TIME SAVER

Result clauses are often set up in the main clause by expressions meaning "so." The most common are: *tantus, –a, –um* (so great, such); *tam* (so); *ita* (so); and *adeo* (so). For example, *Lux vestra **ita** spléndeat **ut** hómines Deum gloríficent* means "Let your light so shine that people glorify God."

Negative result clauses are always introduced by *ut … non*. This distinguishes them from other negative *ut* clauses in the subjunctive, which replace *ut* with *ne:*

- *Ita vivamus, **ut** nemo nos **non** laudet:* Let us live in **such a way that** no one fails to praise us.

- *Laboremus, **ne** fame pereamus:* Let us work, **that** we may not die of hunger.

If the main clause is negated, a negative result clause may begin with *quin* (that):

- **Nullus** *liber tam malus est,* **quin** *áliquo modo lectori prodeat:* No book is so bad that it does not help the reader in some way.

Latin result clauses also admit a greater range of tenses than do purpose clauses (which normally appear only in the present and imperfect):

- *Ita laboravi ut me saepe laudáveris:* I have worked in such a way that you have often praised me.

- *Ita timet, ut numquam íterum pugnaturus sit:* He is so afraid that he is never going to fight (never will fight) again.

PROCEED WITH CAUTION

Spoken English tends to blur the distinction between purpose and result clauses, which are close in meaning:

We work so that people will praise us.

We work, so people will praise us. (result)

Latin is generally more finicky about this distinction:

Laboramus, ut hómines nos laudent. (purpose)

(Ita) laboramus, ut hómines nos laudaturi sint. (result)

TASK 7: TRANSLATING RESULT CLAUSES

Complete the translations of the following sentences.

1. *Hoc tam parvum est, ut inveniri non possit:* This is so small ….

2. *Iudith adeo fórtiter egit, ut omnes eam laudarent:* Judith acted so bravely ….

3. *Alexander ita ímperat, ut mílites eum timeant:* Alexander commands in such a way ….

4. *Tantum erat perículum, ut ex urbe fugerim:* The danger was so great ….

NOUN CLAUSES OF RESULT

Sometimes a result clause functions as the subject of an "impersonal" verb. Such verbs are these:

- *fit* (perfect: *factum est*): it happens

- *áccidit:* it happens

- *évenit:* it happens
- *fíeri potest:* it may be, it is possible

Study the following examples:

- *Fit ut domum iam vénerim:* It happens that I have just come home.
- *Fíeri potest ut hippopótami hómines edant:* It is possible that hippos eat people.

Task 8: Translating Noun Clauses of Result

Turn the following sentences into noun clauses of result, depending on the verb in parentheses. Then retranslate.

1. *Matrem tuam vidi (Fit …):* I saw your mother.

2. *Cibus paratus est (Fíeri potest …):* The food is ready.

3. *Mulíeres consílium senatorum audíverant (Evenit …):* The women had heard the senators' plan.

4. *Aliquid dídici (Fíeri potest …):* I have learned something.

Clauses of Fearing

Another kind of dependent clause comes after verbs indicating fear or apprehension:

- *Tímeo ne Romani véniant:* I am afraid that the Romans are coming.
- *Tímeo ut Romani véniant:* I am afraid that the Romans are not coming.

The verb in a clause of fearing takes the subjunctive mood. The present and imperfect subjunctive refer to actions that take place at the same time or after the verb of fearing:

- *Tímeo ne Romani véniant:* I am afraid that the Romans are coming/will come.
- *Timebam ne Romani venirent:* I was afraid that the Romans were coming/would come.

JUST A MINUTE

In fear clauses, the conjunction *ne* means "that"; the conjunction *ut* means "that … not." One can also express "negative" fears with *ne … non:*

- *Tímeo ne Romani non véniant:* I fear that the Romans are not coming.

TASK 9: TRANSLATING FEAR CLAUSES

Translate the fear clauses in the following sentences.

1. *Tímeo **ne Holofernes pópulum Ísrael vincat:*** I fear ....

2. *Tímeo **ut Iudith Holofernem occiderit:*** I fear ....

3. *Timebam **ne coniurati Caesarem non occidissent:*** I was afraid ....

OVERVIEW OF THE CONJUNCTION *UT*

Like *cum*, *ut* is a highly ambiguous conjunction in Latin. Here is an overview of its uses.

Overview of *Ut*

Clause Type	Meaning	Mood	Negative
temporal	as, when	indicative	*non*
purpose	(in order) that	subjunctive	*ne*
indirect command	to	subjunctive	*ne*
result	although	subjunctive	*non*
fear	that (*ne*)	subjunctive	*ut, ne non*

TASK 10: TRANSLATING *UT* CLAUSES

Translate the *ut* clause (in bold) so that it fits the rest of the sentence.

1. *Alexander mílites hortabatur, **ut fórtiter pugnarent:*** Alexander urged his soldiers ....

2. *Alexander eis pecúniam promittebat, **ut fórtiter pugnarent:*** Alexander promised them money ....

3. *Alexander ita eos confortavit, **ut fórtiter pugnarent:*** Alexander encouraged them so much ....

4. ***Ut fórtiter pugnabant,** Alexander eos laudabat:* ... Alexander praised them.

5. *Alexander timebat **ut fórtiter pugnarent:*** Alexander feared ....

ESSENTIAL VOCABULARY

These common words should be committed to memory.

Essential Vocabulary

Latin	Meaning	Related Word
Nouns		
codex, codicis (masculine)	book	codicil
ignis, –is (masculine)	fire	igneous
iudex, iudicis (masculine)	judge	judicial
lumen, luminis (neuter)	light	luminous
parens, parentis (common)	parent	
peccatum, –i (neuter)	sin	
regna, –orum (neuter)	kingdom	reign
sermo, –onis (masculine)	speech, language	sermon
sol, solis (masculine)	sun	solar
Verbs		
aúdeo, –ere, ausus sum	dare	audacious
éruo, –ere, erui, erutus	rescue, draw out	
interrogo, –are, –avi, –atus	ask	interrogate
invado, –ere, –vasi	come in, enter	invade
méntior, –iri, mentitus sum	lie	
pergo, –ere, porrexi	go on, continue	
rápio, –ere, rapui, raptus	seize, snatch	rapacious
sumo, –ere, sumpsi, sumptus	take up	assume
Adjectives		
creber, –ra, –rum	frequent	
miser, –ra, –rum	wretched	
Adverbs		
ferme	almost	
umquam	ever	

RECOGNITION VOCABULARY

Go through this list once or twice, and look for these words in the Reading Exercise.

Recognition Vocabulary

Latin	Meaning	Related Word
antiquus, –a, –um	ancient	antique
Christianus, –i (masculine)	Christian	
confíteor, –eri, confessus sum (+ dative)	confess, praise	
exhaustus, –a, –um	exhausted	
propheta, –ae (masculine)	prophet	
resono, –are, –avi, –atus	resound, echo	
saeculáris, –e	secular	
serpens, –ntis (masculine)	serpent (the Devil)	
spíritus, –us (masculine)	spirit	
tribunal, –is (neuter)	judgment seat	tribunal
versículum, –i (neuter)	short verse	

SUMMARY

In this hour, you have learned how to construct and translate temporal, causal, concessive, result, and fear clauses. These are some of the most common examples of subordination in Latin, and they play a big part in the "periodic" (some would say "long-winded") style of classical Latin oratory.

You are now ready to meet a famous Latin writer and translator who gave up everything for God—except his Ciceronian prose style. For this reason, you may want to check the translation first so that you don't get lost in the Latin.

READING EXERCISE

St. Jerome (*Didymus Hieronymus,* ca. 345–420 A.D.), whom we have already met as the translator of the Vulgate Latin Bible, was also a champion of the ascetic movement in the Christian West. As a young man, he renounced the pleasures and ambitions of the world and embraced the rigorous disciplines of the desert fathers. However, he did not give up his love of secular Latin literature. In a famous letter, he describes a vision in which God rebuked him for his literary preoccupations. (Notice, however, that he tells the story in a style suspiciously redolent of the author he renounces.) (Slightly adapted)

St. Jerome's Vision

Cum, ante annos plúrimos, castrassem me domo, paréntibus, sorore, cognatis et (quod his difficílius est) consuetúdine lautioris cibi propter regna caelorum, et Hierosólymam militaturus pérgerem, bibliotheca, quam mihi Romae summo stúdio ac labore conféceram, carere non póteram. Ítaque miser ego ieiunabam lecturus Túllium; post nóctium crebras vigílias, post lácrimas quas recordátio praeteritorum peccatorum ex imis viscéribus eruebat, Plautus sumebatur in manibus. Si quando prophetam legere coeperam, sermo incultus horrebat, et quia lumen caecis óculis non videbam, non putabam culpam esse oculorum, sed solis. Dum ita me antiquus serpens illudebat, in média ferme quadragésima febris corpus exhaustum invasit.

Tum súbito raptus in spíritu ad tribunal iúdicis pertrahor, ubi tantum lúminis et tantum fulgoris erat ex circumstántium claritate, ut, proiectus in terram, sursum aspícere non auderem. Interrogatus condicionem, respondi me esse Christianum: et ille qui residebat, "Mentiris," ait, "Ciceronianus es, non Christianus; ubi thesaurus tuus, ibi et cor tuum." Ilico obmútui et inter vérbera (nam caedi me iússerat) magnis igne consciéntiae torquebar, illum versículum réputans: "In inferno autem quis confitébitur tibi." Clamare tamen coepi et éiulans dícere: "Miserere mei, dómine, miserere mei." Haec vox inter flagella resonabat .... Deiurare coepi et nomen eius obtestans dícere: "Dómine, si umquam hábui códices saeculares, si légi, te negavi."

Reading Vocabulary

aspício, –ere, –pexi, –spectus	see, look upon
bibliotheca, –ae (feminine)	library
caecus, –a, –um	blind
caedo, –ere, cécidi, caesus	beat, cut, kill
castro, –are, –avi, –atus	castrate, cut off
Ciceronianus, –i (masculine)	Ciceronian, devotee of Cicero

continues

Reading Vocabulary   (continued)

circumsto, –are, –steti	stand round, surround
cláritas, –tatis, (feminine)	brilliance, clarity
cognatus, –a, –um	related, kin
condício, –ionis (feminine)	religious profession, faith
consciéntia, –ae (feminine)	conscience
deiuro, –are, –avi, –atus	swear, make a vow
domo	from home
dum	while; provided that
éiulo, –are, –avi, –atus	cry out
febris, –is (feminine)	fever
flagellum, –i (neuter)	whip
fulgor, –oris (masculine)	brightness
Hierosólyma, –ae (feminine)	Jerusalem
hórreo, –ere, horrui	be rough; make one shudder
ieiuno, –are, –avi	fast
ilico	straightaway, immediately
illudo, –ere, illusi	play with, delude
imus, –a, –um	deep, low; the depths
incultus, –a, –um	uncultured, simple
infernum, –i (neuter)	hell
lácrima, –ae (feminine)	tear
lautus, –a, –um	elegant, tasty
mílito, –are, –avi	serve (as a soldier)
miséreor, –eri, misertus sum	have pity
obmúto, –ere, –ui	be silent
obtestor, –ari, –atus sum	swear, take an oath
pértraho, –ere, –traxi	drag
Plautus, –i (masculine)	Plautus, a Roman comedian
praeteritus, –a, –um	past

proiectus, –a, –um	cast down
quadragésima, –ae (feminine)	Lent
recordátio, –ionis (feminine)	recollection
réputo, –are, –avi, –atus	recall
resídeo, –ere, –sedi	sit
Romae	at Rome
si quando	if ever
stúdium, –i (neuter)	zeal, effort
súbito	suddenly
sursum	up
thesaurus, –i (masculine)	treasure
tórqueo, –ere, torsi	twist, torment
Túllius, –i (masculine)	Tully (M. Tullius Cicero, a Roman orator)
vérbera, –um (neuter)	blows
vigília, –ae (feminine)	vigil
víscera, –um (neuter)	innards, heart

Quiz

A

Identify the following verbs by tense, mood, and voice. Ambiguous forms are marked by a number in parentheses.

1. *amáveram*
2. *amávero*
3. *amáverim*
4. *monerent*
5. *monuerunt*
6. *monúerint* (2)
7. *fuisses*
8. *fuisti*
9. *fúeras*

10. *fúeris* (2)

11. *auditus es*

12. *auditus esses*

13. *auditus eris*

14. *auditus sis*

B

Choose the form that best completes the sentence, and translate.

1. *Cum Hierosólymam (pergebam/pérgerem), bibliotheca carere non póteram.*

2. *Dum ita me antiquus serpens (illudebat/illuderet), in média ferme quadragésima febris corpus invasit exhaustum.*

3. *Tantum lúminis erat ut sursum aspícere non (audebam/auderem).*

4. *Interrogatus condícionem, Christianum me (esse/fuisse) respondi.*

5. *"Mentiris," ait, "Ciceronianus (es/est), non Christianus; ubi thesaurus tuus, ibi et cor tuum."*

6. *(Clamans/clamare) tamen coepi et éiulans dícere: "Miserere mei, dómine, miserere mei."*

7. *"Dómine, si umquam habúi códices saeculares, te (negavi/negavit)."*

HOUR 21

Relative Clauses with the Subjunctive; More Pronouns

CHAPTER SUMMARY

LESSON PLAN:
In this hour you will learn about ...

- The indefinite pronouns (such as *quidam,* "a certain one," and *áliquis,* "some one") and their related adjective forms

- Forming relative clauses in the subjunctive mood to characterize a noun, or to indicate purpose, result, cause, or concession

- Relative clauses that may be "attracted" into the subjunctive mood by other subjunctive verbs

So far, you have encountered a number of pronouns, which may be classified as personal (*ego,* "I"; *tu,* "you"), demonstrative (*hic,* "this one"; *ille,* "that one"), interrogative (*quis,* "who?"; *quid,* "what?"), and relative (*qui, quae, quod,* "who," "which," "that"). Up to this point, relative clauses have contained verbs in the indicative mood.

INTRODUCTORY READING

Look for these new items in the introductory reading, from Cicero's dialogue *On Friendship.* Here, one of Cicero's characters argues that friendship is based on affection rather than self-interest.

THE TRUE BASIS OF FRIENDSHIP

Quapropter a natura mihi videtur pótius quam ab indigéntia orta amicítia, applicatione magis ánimi cum quodam sensu amandi quam cogitatione quantum illa res utilitatis esset habitura. Nihil est enim amabílius virtute, nihil quod magis adlíciat ad diligendum, quippe cum propter virtutem et probitatem étiam eos quos numquam vídimus quodam modo diligamus. Quis est qui C. Fabrícii, M. Cúrii nondum caritate áliqua et benevoléntia memóriam usurpet, quos numquam víderit.

And so, friendship seems to me to have arisen from nature rather than need, by an attachment of the soul with a certain feeling of love, rather than by a calculation of how much utility the thing is going to have.

For there is nothing more lovable than virtue, nothing that attracts (one) more to loving, since it is on account of virtue and probity that we somehow love even those whom we have not yet seen. Who is there, who does not still take up the memory of Gaius Fabricius or Manius Curius with some kind of affection and good feeling, (although these are men) whom he has never seen?

In the reading passage, you notice the expressions *cum quodam sensu* (with a certain sense) and *aliqua caritate* (some kind of affection). These show how pronouns and adjectives built on the *qu–* stem can be used in an indefinite sense.

We also notice three relative clauses that contain verbs in the subjunctive mood. As we will see, this can occur when the relative clause generalizes or characterizes (as in *nihil est quod,* which means "there is nothing that …").

It also sometimes happens that an ordinary relative clause, which should be in the indicative, is attracted to the subjunctive by another subjunctive verb. An example is *quos numquam víderit,* which means "whom he has never seen"; it is attracted to the subjunctive by the verb *usurpet.* Let us look at these rules in turn.

INDEFINITE PRONOUNS AND ADJECTIVES

Sometimes we want to talk about something generically, but not as if it were "any old" item. In English we convey this notion with the adjective "certain":

- On **certain** days, we meet and drink coffee.

Here the speaker does not specify the days of the meeting (such as "Tuesdays"), but intimates that he *could* name the days if he chose. A speaker who wishes to be less definite might say this:

- On **some** days, we meet and drink coffee.

Here, the speaker merely indicates that the meeting takes place on some days and not others. One could imagine a statement that is still less specific:

- On **any day** of the week, you can find us in the coffee shop.

These English expressions coincide with the indefinite pronouns and adjectives in Latin grammar. The typically combine *quis* or *qui* with a suffix that indicates the degree of "indefiniteness" intended.

QUIDAM

The most "definite" of the indefinite pronouns is *quidam*, which means "a certain one." This pronoun is formed by combining the interrogative pronouns *quis* with the suffix *–dam*.

Declension of Pronoun *Quidam*

	Masculine/Feminine	Neuter
Nominative	qui-dam	quid-dam
Genitive	cuius-dam	cuius-dam
Dative	cui-dam	cui-dam
Accusative	quen-dam	quid-dam
Ablative	quo-dam	quo-dam

In conjunction with a noun (or sometimes as an alternative pronoun), you will also find the following adjective forms, based on *qui*.

Declension of Adjective *Quidam*

	Masculine	Feminine	Neuter
Singular			
Nominative	quidam	quaedam	quoddam
Genitive	cuiusdam	cuiusdam	cuiusdam
Dative	cuidam	cuidam	cuidam
Accusative	quendam	quandam	quoddam
Ablative	quodam	quadam	quodam
Plural			
Nominative	quidam	quaedam	quaedam
Genitive	quorundam	quarundam	quorundam
Dative	quibusdam	quibusdam	quibusdam
Accusative	quosdam	quasdam	quosdam
Ablative	quibusdam	quibusdam	quibusdam

The plural forms of this adjective also serve as the plural of the pronoun *quidam*, given previously.

- ***Quosdam** in via vídimus:* We saw **certain** (**people**) on the road.

Note that agreement between noun and adjective must be accomplished in the *qui* element:

- *Quosdam libros non ápprobo:* I do not approve of **certain** books.
- *Quaedam casae ardent:* **Certain** houses are burning.

Task 1: Working with *Quidam*

Choose the form of the pronoun or adjective *quidam* that best completes the sentence, and translate.

1. *(Quidam) amicorum argentum habemus.*
2. *Illa fémina (quidam) res me dócuit.*
3. *In (quidam) urbe terríbilis draco hábitat.*
4. *(Quidam) non sunt iusti.*
5. *(Quidam) matris vocem audivi.*
6. *Cum (quidam) régibus imperator bellum gerebat (bellum gerebat* means "waged war").

Aliquis

Another pronoun, which is still less definite, is *aliquis* (someone). It is formed by adding the prefix *ali–* to forms of the pronouns *quis* and *quid*.

- *Áliquis pulmentum meum manducavit:* Someone has been eating my porridge.
- *Áliquid me turbat:* Something is bothering me.
- *Áliquem in via vidi:* I saw someone in the street.

A corresponding adjective is formed by adding *ali–* to *qui, quae,* and *quod*:

- *Áliquos hómines in via vidi:* I saw some people in the road.

Note that the form aliqua is used for both the feminine singualar nominative and the neuter nominative/accusative plural:

- *Áliqua fémina nos salutat:* Some woman is hailing us.
- *In schola aliqua didici, quae iam oblitus sum:* In school I learned a few things, which I have already forgotten.

Task 2: Working with *Aliquis* and *Aliqui*

Choose the form of the pronoun *aliquis* or the adjective *aliqui* that best completes the sentence, and translate.

1. *(Áliquis) in via vídeo.*
2. *(Áliqui) mílites gládios non habent.*
3. *(Áliqui) fémina cibum parat.*
4. *(Áliqui) clamantes audivi.*
5. *(Áliqui) naves in perículum venerunt.*
6. *(Áliquis) illud argentum dedi.*

OTHER FORMS WITH THE *ALI–* PREFIX

Other words can be rendered "indefinite" by adding the prefix *ali–:*

- *alícubi:* somewhere
- *alicunde:* from somewhere
- *áliquot:* some, a number of
- *aliquando:* sometime
- *áliquo:* to someplace
- *aliquámdiu:* for some time
- *aliquantus, –a, –um:* some

TASK 3: TRANSLATING FORMS WITH *ALI–*

Complete the translation of the following sentences.

1. *Aliquando, princeps meus véniet:* … my prince will come.
2. *Ille sonus alicunde venit:* That noise is coming ….
3. *Áliquot hómines bonos quaérimus:* We are looking for ….
4. *Aliquámdiu magistrum blatterantem audívimus:* We listened to the teacher babble ….

SHORTENED FORMS OF *ALI–* PRONOUNS, ADJECTIVES, AND ADVERBS

The *ali–* prefix is dropped if the indefinite word follows the words *nisi* (unless), *si* (if), *num* (surely not, whether), and *ne* (not). This leaves an unprefixed form of the *qu–* word, which nevertheless retains its indefinite value and is usually translated "any."

- *Si quis móverit, sagittam emitte!:* If anyone moves, shoot!
- *Si quando te adiuvi, nunc mihi succurre!:* If ever (at any time) I helped you, now help me!

TIME SAVER

For years, Latin students have been learning this rule by reciting the following verse: "After *nisi, si, num* and *ne, ali–* takes a holiday."

TASK 4: TRANSLATING INDEFINITE PRONOUNS

Translate the clauses in bold.

1. ***Ne quis dicat,*** *latinam esse facilem:* … that Latin is easy.
2. ***Si quem*** *in foro* ***víderis,*** *noli cum eo cólloqui:* … in the forum, don't speak with him.
3. ***Nisi quis vénerit,*** *iánuam claudam:* … I will close the door.
4. ***Nisi quas res paravérimus,*** *navigare non potérimus:* … we will not be able to sail.

OTHER COMPOUNDS WITH *QUIS*

Other indefinite pronouns are created by adding suffixes to *quis* or *qui*. The following are common:

- *quisquis:* whoever
- *quisquam:* anyone
- *quispiam:* someone, anyone
- *quivis:* anyone, any
- *quilibet:* anyone, any
- *quicumque:* whoever

These also have corresponding adjective forms with *qui.* In the pronoun *quisquis,* both elements are declined:

- *Quemquem vides, amicus esse debet:* Whomever you see must be a friend.

Before the elements *–quis* and *–quam, quid* becomes *quic–:*

- *Quicquid féceris facílius erit quam hoc:* Whatever you do will be easier than this.

TASK 5: TRANSLATING COMPOUND PRONOUNS

Translate the words or clauses in bold.

1. *Quóslibet víderis, noli argentum eis dare:* ... don't give them money.

2. *Quémpiam in theatro quaerebamus:* We were looking for ....

3. *Quemquem amas, te redamare debet.* ... should love you in return.

4. *Numquam **quicquam** in illa casa invénimus.* We never found ... in that house.

RELATIVE CLAUSES WITH THE SUBJUNCTIVE

In Hour 6, you first encountered clauses that define or describe a noun in another clause:

- *Ecce pausa **quae** récreat ...:* Here is the pause **that** refreshes ...

- *Pater noster, **qui** es in caelis ...:* Our Father, **who** art in heaven ...

Normally, relative clauses make specific assertions that require an indicative verb. Occasionally, however, the verb in the relative clause has overtones of hypothesis or intentionality, and the subjunctive is used.

CLAUSES OF CHARACTERISTIC

As an example of the distinction just mentioned, consider these two sentences:

- *Ea est quae heri me **salutavit:*** She is the one who **greeted** me yesterday.

- *Is est qui alas muscarum **abrípiat:*** He is the (kind of) guy who **tears** the wings **off** flies.

In the first sentence, the relative clause identifies "her" in terms of a real event; thus, the indicative mood (*salutavit*) is employed. In the second sentence, however, the relative clause is used to characterize the antecedent as the "type" who does such things. Hence, the subjunctive (*abrípiat*) is used. Notice, however, that the verb is translated into English as if it were indicative (tears).

As you have already seen in the Introductory Reading, relative classes of characteristic are apt to occur after negative and interrogative clauses, such as the following:

- *nemo est qui:* there is no one who/that

- *nihil est quod:* there is nothing that

- *quis est qui:* who is there who/that

- *quid est quod:* what is there that

TASK 6: TRANSLATING RELATIVE CLAUSES

Translate the following sentences.

1. *Fortis miles est, qui perículum numquam fúgiat.*

2. *Nemo est, qui perículum numquam fúgiat.*

3. *Quis est qui haec intéllegat?*

4. *Haec sunt témpora, quae ámimas hóminum probent* (*probent* means "test").

RELATIVE CLAUSES OF PURPOSE

Occasionally, a relative clause of characteristic has overtones of purpose:

- *Alexander quosdam mílites elegit, qui contra hippopótamos pugnarent:* Alexander chose certain soldiers who might fight (to fight) against the hippos.

- *Da mihi aliquid quod bibam:* Give me something that I may drink (to drink).

Notice that English usually avoids this construction, replacing it with an infinitive phrase (such as "to fight").

TASK 7: TRANSLATING RELATIVE CLAUSES II

Translate the following sentences.

1. *Quaero áliquid, quod fáciam.*

2. *Non hábui quicquam, quod dícerem.*

3. *Caesar misit mílites, qui regem cáperent.*

4. *Elegi servum, cui argentum darem.*

OTHER RELATIVE CLAUSES WITH THE SUBJUNCTIVE

More rarely, a relative clause may contain the notion of result:

- *Hic liber dignus est qui eiiciatur:* This book is worthy that it be thrown out (is worthy of being thrown out, deserves to be thrown out).

In other contexts, the relative clause may imply cause (since, because) or concession (although):

- *Me míserum, qui órphanus nunc factus sim:* Poor me, who have now become an orphan (because I have become …).

- *Ego, qui multas Linguas didícerim, Latine haud scio:* I, who have learned many languages (although I have …), hardly know Latin.

When translating sentences like these, it is often better to replace the relative pronoun with the appropriate adverbial conjunction (such as "because" and "although").

Task 8: Translating Relative Clauses III

Translate the clauses in bold.

1. *Geórgius, **qui multos dracones vícerit,** martyr tamen óbiit:* George … nevertheless died as a martyr.

2. *Nomen Dei dignum est, **quod in honore habeatur:*** The name of God is worthy ….

3. *Caesar, **qui Romanum impérium régeret,** de multis rebus sollicitabatur:* Caesar … was concerned about many things.

Relative Adverb Clauses

In some of the examples you have just studied, a relative clause is used as the equivalent of an "adverbial" clause indicating the purpose, result, or cause of the main verb. By extension of this principle, certain forms of the relative pronoun become outright adverbial conjunctions:

- *quátenus:* in order that
- *quóminus:* in order that … not

Clauses of this type require the subjunctive mood:

- *Latine studemus quátenus dívites **fiamus:*** We study Latin in order that **we may become** rich.

There are also adverbs that function in the same way as relative pronouns and set up adverbial clauses with the subjunctive:

- *Quaérimus locum **unde** ómnia videre possimus:* We are looking for a place **from which** we may be able to see everything.
- *Quaérimus locum **ubi** bene nos habeamus:* We are looking for a place **where** we may enjoy ourselves.
- *Quaérimus locum **quo** parentes invitemus:* We are looking for a place **to which** we may invite our parents.

TASK 9: TRANSLATING RELATIVE ADVERBS

Translate the clause in bold.

1. *Invénimus casam,* **ubi fílios educaremus:** We found a house ….

2. *Imitemus Christum,* **quátenus fílii Dei simus:** Let us imitate Christ, ….

3. *Legit libros philosophorum,* **unde sapiéntiam dísceret:** She read the books of philosophers, ….

4. *Terram quaerebant,* **quo pópulum dúcerent:** They were looking for a land ….

SUBJUNCTIVE BY ATTRACTION

Finally, verbs that would normally be in the indicative mood are sometimes "attracted" or drawn into the subjunctive. This happens if they occur in clauses that are logically dependent on other subjunctive verbs:

- *Qui est tam stultus, ut oppugnet eum, qui amicus* **sit?:** Who is so dumb that he attacks the one who **is** his friend?

Normally one would say *qui amicus est,* because the relative clause defines the antecedent pronoun, *eum.* In this case, however, it is closely tied to the result clause *ut oppugnet eum.* Thus, the verb is attracted to the subjunctive mood.

If an ordinary relative clause is not logically bound to another subjunctive verb, but merely is added parenthetically, the verb will be the indicative:

- *Hanc pugionem fero ut Caésarem, qui Gallos* **vicit,** *interfíciam:* I am carrying this dagger that I may kill Caesar, who **conquered** the Gauls.

TASK 10: TRANSLATING THE SUBJUNCTIVE

Complete the translation of the following sentences.

1. *Hunc librum scribo ut eos dóceam, qui Latine légere cúpiant:* I am writing this book that I may teach those ….

2. *Ne credatis ómnibus qui bene loquantur:* Don't trust all people ….

3. *Miror an omne, quod spléndeat* (*splendeo* means "glitter"), *re vera sit aurum:* I wonder whether everything … is really gold.

4. *Speramus ne orbis terrarum, qui est tértius* (third) *a sole, omnino péreat:* We hope that the Earth … may not be utterly destroyed.

ESSENTIAL VOCABULARY

The following common words should be committed to memory.

Essential Vocabulary

Latin	Meaning	Related Word
Nouns		
grátia, –ae (feminine)	favor, grace; thanks	gracious
grátias ago, –ere, egi	give thanks	
magister, –tri (masculine)	teacher, master	schoolmaster
píetas, pietatis (feminine)	devotion	piety
spes, spei (feminine)	hope	
Verbs		
ago, ágere, egi, actus	do, drive; plead (a case) (legal)	action
fero, ferre, tuli, latus	carry, bear	
formo, –are, –avi, –atus	form, set	
instítuo, –ere, –ui, institutus	establish; teach	institute
váleo, –ere, válui	be well, take care	valediction
Adjectives		
aetas, aetatis (feminine)	age, time of life	
causa, –ae (feminine)	cause; case	
certus, –a, –um	certain, fixed, definite	
noster, –ra, –rum	our	
próximus, –a, –um	near	proximate

continues

Essential Vocabulary   (continued)

Latin	Meaning	Related Word
Adverbs		
dénique	finally	
ínvicem	in turns; each other	
paulatim	gradually	
Conjunctions		
cum	when, since, although	
quasi	as if	
verum	but	

RECOGNITION VOCABULARY

Go through this list once or twice, and then look for these words in the Reading Exercise.

Recognition Vocabulary

Latin	Meaning	Related Word
acumen, acúminis (neuter)	shrewdness	acumen
adfício, –ere, –feci, –fectus	affect, touch	
ártifex, artíficis (masculine)	artist	artificial
canto, –are, –avi, –atum	sing	chant
cáritas, –tatis (feminine)	love, charity affection	
cástitas, –tatis (feminine)	chastity	
clamor, –oris (masculine)	shout(ing)	clamor
concórdia, –ae (feminine)	concord, harmony	
educo, –are, –avi, –atus	bring up	educate
exemplum, –i (neuter)	example	
éxcito, –are, –avi, –atus	arouse, excite	
frugálitas, –tatis (feminine)	frugality	
glória, –ae (feminine)	glory	

Latin	Meaning	Related Word
líttera, –ae (feminine)	letter	literature
perpétuus, –a, –um	endless	perpetual
praeceptum, –i (neuter)	teaching	precept
récito, –are, –avi, –atus	recite, perform	
solicitudo, –túdinis (feminine)	concern	solicitude
versus, –us (masculine)	verse, line	

SUMMARY

In this hour, you have learned how to translate indefinite pronouns and clauses combining relative pronouns, adjectives, and adverbs with the subjunctive mood. This knowledge is critical when reading the more polished Roman authors, especially in the Imperial Period. A good example of their style is found in this hour's reading.

READING EXERCISE

Under the "good" emperors Nerva and Trajan, C. Plinius Caecilius Secundus (Pliny, 61–113 A.D.), held important financial and administrative posts. He also earned a reputation for public speaking and *belles-lettres*. Posterity has saved a collection of his letters, which often amount to short essays on Roman life and literature. The following note is addressed to the aunt of his third wife, Calpurnia. Pliny, who in middle age is considerably older than his bride, gives us a good idea of what a Roman statesman and literary figure looked for in a mate. (Slightly adapted)

PLINY'S WIFE

Cum sis pietatis exemplum, fratremque óptimum et amantíssimum tui pari caritate diléxeris, filiamque eius ut tuam díligas ..., non dúbito, máximo tibi gaúdio fore, cum cognóveris, (eam) dignam patre, dignam te, dignam avo evádere. Summum est (ei) acumen, summa frugálitas; amat me, quod indícium est castitatis. Accedit his stúdium litterarum, quod ex mei caritate concepit. Meos libellos habet, léctitat, ediscit étiam. Qua illa solicitúdine (adfícitur), cum videor acturus; quanto, cum egi, gaúdio adfícitur! Disponit (aliquem), qui núntiet sibi, quem adsensum, quos clamores excitáverim, quem eventum iudícii túlerim. Éadem, si quando récito, in próximo sedet, discreta velo, laudesque nostras avidíssimis aúribus éxcipit. Versus quidem meos cantat étiam, formatque cíthara, non artífice áliquo docente, sed amore, qui magister est óptimus.

His ex causis in spem certíssimam adducor, perpétuam nobis maioremque in dies futuram esse concórdiam. Non enim díligit aetatem meam aut corpus, quae paulatim occidunt ac senescunt, sed glóriam. Nec aliud decet (puellam) tuis mánibus educatam, tuis praeceptis institutam, quae nihil in contubérnio tuo víderit, nisi quod sit sanctum honestumque, et quae dénique amare me ex tua praedicatione consuéverit. Nam, cum matrem meam parentis loco verereris, a puerítia statim formare me solebas, talemque fore ominari, qualis nunc uxori meae vídeor. Certatim ergo tibi grátias ágimus: ego, quod illam mihi, et illa, quod me sibi déderis, quasi nos ínvicem elegáveris. Vale.

Reading Vocabulary

accedo, –ere, accessi	come to, go to
adduco, –ere, –duxi, –ductus	lead, bring
adsensus, –us (masculine)	assent, approval
amantíssimus, –a, –um	superlative of *amans*
auris, auris (feminine)	ear
ávidus, –a, –um	eager, avid
avus, –i (masculine)	grandfather
certatim	in competition
cíthara, –ae (feminine)	lyre
concípio, –ere, –cepi, –ceptus	conceive, create
consuesco, –ere, –suevi	be accustomed
contubérnium, –i (neuter)	dwelling; company
decet, decere, décuit	befits, suits
díligo, –ere, dilexi, –lectus	love, esteem
discerno, –ere, –crevi, –cretus	set apart, discern
dispono, –ere, –pósui, –situm	assign
edisco, –ere, edídici	learn by heart
élego, –ere, –legi, –lectus	choose
evado, –ere, evasi	evade, escape, turn out
eventus, –us (masculine)	outcome, event, happening
excípio, –ere, excepi, exceptus	take up
fore	will be (= *futurum esse*)

gaúdium, –ii (neuter)	joy
honestus, –a, –um	honorable, respectable
idem, éadem, idem	the same (one)
indícium, –i (neuter)	indication, sign
léctito, –are, –avi, –atus	read often, read over and over
libellus, –i (masculine)	(small) book, notebook
núntio, –are, –avi, –atus	announce, tell
óccido, –ere, óccidi	die
óminor, –ari, –atus sum	predict
óptimus, –a, –um	best
par, paris (adjective)	equal, comparable
praedicátio, –ionis (feminine)	telling, preaching
puerítia, –ae (feminine)	boyhood
senesco, –ere, sénui	grow old
sibi	to her
velum, –i (neuter)	veil, curtain
véreor, vereri, véritus sum	honor, respect; fear

Quiz

A

Convert the following verbs to the corresponding form of the subjunctive. Keep the same person, number, tense, and voice.

1. *amat*
2. *videbamus*
3. *monuistis*
4. *sunt*
5. *eram*
6. *ducímini*
7. *laudata es*
8. *míserat*
9. *hortati eramus*
10. *audiebatis*

B

Complete the sentences with the correct form of the verb in parentheses, and translate.

1. *Cum tu (sum) pietatis exemplum, non dúbito, hoc máximo tibi gaúdio fore.*

2. *Amat me, quod indícium est (cástitas).*

3. *(Meus) libellos habet, léctitat, ediscit étiam.*

4. *Qua illa (sollicitudo) adfícitur, cum vídeor acturus.*

5. *Disponet áliquem, qui (núntio) sibi, quem adsensum, quos clamores ego (éxcito).*

6. *Versus quidem (meus) cantat étiam, formatque cíthara, non artífice áliquo (docens), sed amore, qui magister est óptimus.*

7. *Non enim díligit (aetas) meam aut corpus, quae paulatim óccidunt, sed glóriam.*

8. *Nec aliud decet puellam tuis mánibus educatam, quae nihil in contubérnio tuo (video), nisi quod (sum) honestum.*

9. *Certatim ergo tibi grátias ágimus: ego, quod illam mihi, et illa, quod me sibi (do).*

QUIZ

The Potential Subjunctive; Conditions

CHAPTER SUMMARY

LESSON PLAN:
In this hour you will learn about ...

- The subjunctive used in main clauses to talk about potential actions
- Forming conditions, or structures marked by the conjunction *si* (if)

So far, you have learned how to use the subjunctive independently to express such things as commands and wishes and in various subordinate clauses.

INTRODUCTORY READING

Look for conditions in the following extract from a medieval *pastourelle*. This was a genre of popular song in which an amorous nobleman meets a beautiful shepherdess. These lines occur after their inevitable union:

DON'T TELL MY FAMILY

Quid fecisti, inquit, prave!
Vae vae tibi! Tamen ave!
Ne reveles ulli cavae
ut sim domi tuta!

Si sénserit meus pater
vel Martinus maior frater,
erit mihi dies ater;
vel si sciret mea mater,
cum sit angue peior quater,
virgis sum tributa!

She said, "You scoundrel, what have you done! Woe, woe to you! But hey! Don't reveal (this) to any cave, that I may be safe at home!

If my father finds out, or my big brother, Martin, it will be a black day for me! Or if my mother knew, who is four times worse than a snake, I am doomed to a flogging!"

The girl is afraid of what *will* happen to her *if* her father and the formidable Martin *find out*. This is a typical *future condition*. These are often (as here) set up in Latin with the indicative mood in both the main clause and the *si* clause (*sénserit,* "will have found out"; *erit,* "will be").

When speaking of her mother, though, she switches to a different construction: "If my mother *knew* …." This indicates a condition that is unreal in the *present* time; hence, the imperfect subjunctive (*sciret*) must be used.

Let us look now at the various types of conditional sentences in Latin.

CONDITIONS

A conditional sentence is one that contains an "if" clause:

- If you **study** hard, you **will learn** a lot.

Conditional sentences have two parts: the conditional clause (Latin *enuntiatum condicionale,* the "if" clause) and the main or "conditioned" clause (*enuntiatum condicionatum*). Certain rules govern the tense and mood of both the main and conditional clauses.

SIMPLE CONDITIONS

A simple condition is one that has indicative verbs in both clauses:

- *Frater, si rogare* **debes, nescis:** Brother, if you **have** to ask, you **don't know.**
- *Si Romae* **habitabas,** *multa* **sustinebas:** If you **lived** in Rome, you **endured** a lot.

The implication of these sentences is that the main clause is the natural or inevitable consequence of the conditional: if A, then (necessarily) B.

FUTURE "MORE VIVID" CONDITIONS

The most common type of simple condition, however, relates to future time. This is called the future "more vivid" condition, because it conveys a definite expectation of what will happen:

- *Si Latinae studúeris, dives fies:* If you will have studied Latin (if you study Latin), you will become rich.
- *Si in cúriam véneris, óccides:* If you will have come into the Senate house (if you come into the Senate house), you will die.

These conditions are most commonly set up with the future perfect indicative (*studúeris*) in the conditional clause, and the future indicative (*fies*) in the main clause.

JUST A MINUTE

In English, future "more vivid" conditions are usually set up with the present tense in the conditional (if) clause:

- *Si haec **féceris,** laudabo te:* If you **do** these things, I will praise you.

The same construction sometimes occurs with other conjunctions, such as *cum* (when):

- *Cum mater haec cognóverit, púniet me:* When Mother finds out about these things, she will punish me.

Task 1: Translating Conditions

Translate the following sentences.

1. *Si Romam iter fecisti, multa vidisti.* (*iter* means "a journey")
2. *Si Romam iter féceris, multa videbis.*
3. *Si feminae libros legerint, doctae fient.*
4. *Si gládium invénerit, Iudith Holofernem interfíciet.*
5. *Si hódie dies Martis est, in Italia sumus.* (*dies Martis* means "Tuesday")
6. *Si Geórgius draconem céperit, pópulus in Deum credet.*

Future "Less Vivid" Conditions

Future more vivid conditions, like other simple conditions, indicate a firm conviction about what *will* happen if some condition is met. Sometimes, however, we speak of the future in more hypothetical terms:

- If you **should ask** me, I **would answer** truthfully.

Latin grammarians termed these "should/would" conditions "less vivid." They are easily recognized in Latin because the present subjunctive occurs in both the main and the conditional clauses:

- *Si **roges** me, ego veráciter **respóndeam:*** If you **should ask** me, I **would answer** truthfully.

Occasionally, the conditional clause contains a perfect subjunctive:

- *Si **díxeris**, Latinam esse difficilem, **rídeam:*** If you **should have said** (should say) that Latin is difficult, I **would laugh.**

TIME SAVER

Think of future less vivid conditions as "should/would" conditions.

TASK 2: TRANSLATING CONDITIONS II

Translate the following sentences.

1. *Si quis hoc roget, non respóndeam.*
2. *Si populus in Deum credat, ego hunc draconem interfíciam.*
3. *Si rex fíliam ad imperatorem mittat, pacem hábeat.* (*pax* means "peace")
4. *Si Caesar flumen tránseat, mílites sequantur.*
5. *Si urbem Romam cápias, tota Itália vincatur.*

CONTRAFACTUAL CONDITIONS

A different type of hypothetical condition has to do with the present or past:

- If I **were** rich, I **would** not **be working.**
- If I **had known** better, I **would** not **have left** home.

Conditional sentences like these are called "contrafactual" or "unreal," because they describe situations that are not taking place or that did not take place. In Latin, these are indicated by the imperfect or pluperfect subjunctive in both clauses:

- *Si dives **essem**, non **laborarem:*** If I **were** rich, I **would** not **be working.**
- *Si **sapuissem**, domo non **discessissem:*** If I **had known better,** I **would** not **have left** home.

Note that the imperfect subjunctive is used for present contrafactual conditions, and the pluperfect for past contrafactual conditions. Occasionally you will see these forms in a *mixed* condition, such as the following:

- *Si Latinae **studuissem**, dives **essem:*** If I **had studied** Latin (then), I **would be** rich (now).

TASK 3: TRANSLATING CONDITIONS III

Translate the following sentences.

1. *Si mílites non pugnavissent, urbs capta esset.*
2. *Nisi te amarem, hoc tibi non darem.*
3. *Si perículum esset verum, ex urbe fugeremus.*
4. *Si rústicus mus in urbe habitavisset, non diu ibi vixisset.* (*vivo, vívere, vixi* means "live")
5. *Si haec fecissem, Deum nunc orarem.*

SUMMARY OF CONDITIONAL SENTENCES

To keep the various types of conditional sentences straight, the following table may be helpful.

Overview of Conditions

Type	Conditional Clause	Main Clause
Simple	*Si* + indicative	indicative
	Si hoc fecisti, If you did this,	*te laudavi.* I praised you.
Future More Vivid	*Si* + future perfect	future indicative
	Si hoc féceris, If you do this,	*te laudabo.* I will praise you.
Future Less Vivid	*Si* + present/perfect subjunctive	present subjunctive
	Si hoc fácias, If you should do this,	*te laudem.* I would praise you.
Present Contrafactual	*Si* + imperfect subjunctive	imperfect subjunctive
	Si hoc fáceres, If you were doing this,	*te laudarem.* I would be praising you.
Past Contrafactual	*Si* + pluperfect subjunctive	pluperfect subjunctive
	Si hoc fecisses, If you had done this,	*te laudavissem.* I would have praised you.

TASK 4: TRANSLATING CONDITIONS IV

With the help of the previous table given, translate the following sentences.

1. *Si Latinae studes, omnes te laudant.*
2. *Si Latinae studúeris, omnes te laudabunt.*
3. *Si Latinae stúdeas, omnes te laudent.*
4. *Si Latinae studeres, omnes te laudarent.*
5. *Si Latinae studuisses, omnes te laudavissent.*
6. *Si Latinae studuisses, omnes te laudarent.*

"IMPLIED" CONDITIONS: PRESENT AND PAST

The main clauses of contrafactual conditions may be used by themselves to indicate hypothetical situations in the present and the past:

- *Latinae **studerem**, sed ótium non hábeo:* I **would study** Latin, but I don't have the time.
- *Romam **venissem**, sed non póteram:* I **would have come** to Rome, but I was not able.

In sentences such as these, there lurks an "implied" condition: *I would have come to Rome, **if** I had been able.* You will also see implied conditions of the future less vivid type:

- *Caésarem interfícere **aúdeas?**:* **Would** you dare to kill Caesar (if you should get the chance)?
- ***Velim** (ut) mecum vénias:* I **would like** you to come with me (if you should be so kind).

In English, we often speak of future possibility using the helping verbs "may," "might," or "could":

- *Dicat áliquis, hoc esse impossíbile:* Someone **may** say that this is impossible.
- *Dicas hoc esse impossíbile:* You **could** say that this is impossible.

PROCEED WITH CAUTION

Expressions of future possibility with "may" or "could" should not be confused with expressions of liceity (to be permitted) or possibility (to be able). These are expressed differently in Latin:

Licet (alícui) hoc fácere: One **may** do this. (One is permitted to do this.)

Póteras hoc dícere: You **could** say this. (You were able to say this.)

Task 5: Translating Implied Conditions

Translate the following sentences.

1. *Caesar impérium prudenter rexisset; sed a senatóribus interfectus est.*
2. *Díxeris draconem Geórgium timere.*
3. *Velim ut fratrem meum invénias.*
4. *Geórgius in Deum credebat; áliter* (otherwise) *draconem non vicisset.*

Essential Vocabulary

These common words should be committed to memory.

Essential Vocabulary

Latin	Meaning	Related Word
Nouns		
donum, doni (neuter)	gift	donate
salus, salutis (feminine)	salvation, health	salutary
templum, templi (neuter)	temple	
virtus, virtutis (feminine)	virtue	
Verbs		
advénio, –ire, –veni	arrive, come	advent
curo, –are, –avi, –atus	care for	cure
effício, –ere, effeci, –fectus	make	effect
elabor, elabi, elapsus sum	slip away	elapse
ignoro, –are, –avi, –atus	not know	be ignorant
iuvo, –are, iuvi	help	
sérvio, –ire, servii, –itus	serve	
téneo, –ere, ténui, tentus	hold	tenacious
trado, –ere, trádidi, tráditus	hand over	trade
tríbuo, –ere, tríbui, tributus	give, allot	tribute

continues

Essential Vocabulary   (continued)

Latin	Meaning	Related Word
Adjectives		
brevis, –e	short	brief
cálidus, –a, –um	hot	
mélior, mélius	better	ameliorate
novus, –a, –um	new	
Adverbs		
mox	soon	
pótius	rather	
Conjunction		
unde	whence; hence	

RECOGNITION VOCABULARY

Go through this list once or twice, and look for these words in the Reading Exercise.

Recognition Vocabulary

Latin	Meaning
aeternus, –a, –um	eternal
altare, –is (neutral)	altar
anáthema, –atis (neutral)	anathema
appáreo, –ere, –ui	appear
consiliárius, –ii (masculine)	councilor
cultus, –us (masculine)	cult, worship
dígnitas, dignitatis (feminine)	dignity
doctrina, –ae (feminine)	doctrine, teaching
fructus, –us (masculine)	fruit, profit
minister, ministri (masculine)	minister
momentum, –i (neuter)	moment
praesens, praesentis	present
profíteor, –eri, professus sum	profess
relígio, –ionis (feminine)	religion
sénior, –ioris (masculine)	elder, senior

Latin	Meaning
serénitas, serenitatis (feminine)	serenity
spátium, spatii (neuter)	space
utílitas, utilitatis (feminine)	utility, usefulness

Summary

In this hour, you have learned how to form and translate Latin conditional sentences and implied conditions. These constructions occur frequently in deliberative contexts, such as the momentous decision that follows.

Reading Exercise

The following story is told by St. Bede ("the Venerable," 672–735), an English monk who recorded the history of his church not long after its founding. The Anglo-Saxon king, Edwin, wishes to convert from paganism to Christianity, but waits to make a decisive step until he confers with his nobles and priests at Witan. The first speaker in this passage is Coifi, a pagan priest who notes the shortcomings of the old religion.

Why Be Christians?

"Tu vide, rex, quale sit hoc, quod nobis modo praedicatur; ego autem tibi verissime, quod certum dídici, profíteor: quia nihil omnino virtutis habet, nihil utilitatis, relígio illa, quam hucusque tenúimus. Nemo autem studiósior est quam ego culturae deorum nostrorum; et nihilominus multi sunt, qui ampliora a te benefícia accípiunt quam ego et maiores dignitates, magisque prosperantur .... Si autem dii aliquid valerent, me pótius iuvarent, qui illis impénsius servire curavi. Unde restat ut, si perspéxeris ea, quae nunc nobis nova praedicantur, meliora esse et fórtia, festinemus absque ullo cunctámine illa suscípere."

(Another noble continues:) *"Talis mihi videtur, rex, vita hóminum praesens in terris, quale cum, te residente ad cenam cum dúcibus ac ministris tuis témpore brumali, accenso quidem foco in médio et cálido effecto cenáculo, advéniens unus passer domum citíssime pervoláverit. Is, cum témpore quo intus est hiemis tempestate non tángatur, sed tamen, parvíssimo spátio serenitatis ad momentum excusso, mox de híeme in híemem regrédiens, tuis óculis elábitur. Ita haec vita hóminum ad breve tempus apparet; quid autem sequatur, quidve praecésserit, prorsus ignoramus. Unde, si haec nova doctrina cértius áliquid áttulit, mérito esse sequenda videtur." His simília céteri seniores ac consiliárii divínitus admóniti adde-bant.*

(Coifi wraps up the meeting:) *"Iam olim intelléxeram nihil esse, quod colebamus, quia quanto studiósius in eo cultu veritatem quaerebam, tanto minus inveniebam. Nunc autem aperte profíteor, quia in hac praedicátione véritas claret illa, quae nobis vitae salutis et beatitúdinis aeternae dona valet tribúere. Unde súggero, rex, ut templa et altária, quae sine fructu utilitatis sacrávimus, ócius anathémati et igni tradamus."*

Reading Vocabulary

absque	from, without
accendo, –ere, –cendi, –census	burn
admóneo, –ere, –ui, –itus	advise, warn
amplus, –a, –um	ample
aperte	openly
áffero, afferre, áttuli	bring (to, forth)
beatitudo, –inis (feminine)	blessedness, happiness
benefícium, –ii (neuter)	benefit
brumalis, –e	of winter
cenáculum, –i (neuter)	dining room
cena, –ae (feminine)	dinner
cito	quickly
cláreo, –ere, clárui	be clear
colo, –ere, cólui, cultus	worship
cultura, –ae (feminine)	cultivation
cunctamen, –minis (neuter)	hesitation, delay
dii, deorum (masculine)	gods
divínitus	divinely, from above
excútio, –ere, –cussi, –cussus	shake out, stop
focus, –i (masculine)	fire, hearth
hiems, hiemis (feminine)	winter
hucusque	this far
impense	diligently
mérito	deservedly
modo	just now
nihilominus	nevertheless
ócius	more quickly

passer, –is (masculine)	sparrow
perspício, –ere, –spexi	see, perceive
pervolo, –are, –avi	fly through
praecedo, –ere, –cessi	precede
praedicátio, –ionis (feminine)	preaching
praedico, –are, –avi, –atus	preach
prorsus	thoroughly
prósperor, –ari, –atus sum	prosper
quanto	(with *tanto,* the more … the more …)
quidve	*quid + ve,* or what
regrédior, –i, regressus sum	go back
resídeo, –ere, –sedi	sit down
resto, –are, –avi	remain
sacro, –are, –avi, –atus	dedicate, make sacred
studiósior, –ius	more zealous
studiósius	more zealously
súggero, –ere, –gessi, –gestus	suggest
tango, –ere, tétigi, tactus	touch
tempestas, tempestatis (feminine)	storm, weather
vere	truly

QUIZ

A

Complete the following verb synopsis. All forms should be in the same person and number.

Review Exercise A

Indicative	*Active*	*Passive*
Present	*mittit*	*míttitur*
Imperfect	_____	_____
Future	_____	_____
Perfect	_____	_____
Pluperfect	_____	_____
Future Perfect	_____	_____

Review Exercise A (continued)

Indicative	Active	Passive
Present	_____	_____
Imperfect	_____	_____
Perfect	_____	_____
Pluperfect	_____	_____

B

Choose the form of the word in parentheses that best completes the sentence, and translate.

1. *Tu vide, rex, quale (sum) hoc, quod nobis modo praedicatur.*

2. *Ego autem (tu) verissime, quod certum dídici, profíteor.*

3. *Quia nihil omnino virtutis habet, nihil (utilitas), relígio illa, (qui) hucusque tenúimus.*

4. *Si autem dii áliquid (váleo), me pótius iuvarent, qui illis impénsius servire curavi.*

5. *Unde restat ut (festino) absque ullo cunctámine novam religionem suscípere.*

6. *Ita haec vita hóminum ad breve tempus apparet; quid autem (sequor), quidve praecésserit, prorsus ignoramus.*

7. *Unde, si haec nova doctrina cértius áliquid (áffero), mérito esse sequenda videtur.*

The Subjunctive in Indirect Statements; Reflexive Pronouns

LESSON PLAN:
In this hour you will learn about ...

- How to use the indicative and subjunctive moods in clauses that depend on indirect statements
- How to decline and translate reflexive pronouns (himself, herself, itself)

So far, you have learned how to construct indirect statements with the infinitive mood, as well as various ways of using the indicative and subjunctive moods in subordinate clauses. You have also encountered a number of personal pronouns.

INTRODUCTORY READING

A good place in which to look for these constructions is the cerebral "reflection" of René Descartes (1596–1650). Here is an extract from the Latin synopsis of his famous *Meditations*.

DESCARTES AND DOUBT

> *In secunda (meditatione), mens quae, sua libertate utens, supponit ea ómnia non exístere, de quorum existéntia vel mínimum potest dubitare, animadvertit fíeri non posse, quin ipsa ínterim existat. Quod etiam summae est utilitatis, quóniam hoc pacto fácile distinguit quaenam (pertíneant) ad se, hoc est, ad naturam intellectualem, et quaenam ad corpus pertíneant. Sed quia forte nonnulli rationes de ánimae immortalitate illo in loco expectabunt, móneo eos me conatum esse nihil scríbere quod non accurate demonstrarem.*

In the second meditation, the mind, which, using its own liberty, supposes that all the things, about the existence of which it can have even the least doubt, do not exist, notices that it is impossible that *it* (the mind) does not exist. This (point) is also very useful, for in this way it (the mind) easily determines what things pertain to itself, that is, to the intellectual nature, and what pertain to the body. But since some people, perhaps, will expect in this place arguments about the immortality of the soul, I advise them that I have tried to write nothing which I (could) not precisely demonstrate.

In Descartes' philosophy, the reflective soul must distinguish "itself" (*se*) from other concepts by using "its own" (*sua*) freedom of thought. Here we see that forms referring back to the subject of the sentence are built on an *s–* stem.

The reading also contains an example of indirect statement: *móneo eos me conatum esse nihil scríbere* ... ("I advise them that I have tried to write nothing ..."). Occasionally, other clauses depend on this construction, requiring shifts of tense and/or mood (as in *quod ... demonstrarem*).

REFLEXIVE PRONOUNS

In English, we often find that the person or thing identified as the subject has another function in the same clause:

- I can see **myself.**
- **You** should give **yourself** a pat on the back.
- **He** will tell us about **himself.**

In the first example, the person represented as the subject (I) is also the object of the verb "see." In the second example, the same person is both subject and indirect object. In the third, the antecedent of "he," the subject, is also the object of the preposition "about."

In these situations, the second pronoun is said to *reflect* back on the subject, and *reflexive* forms are used. In English, reflexive pronouns are regularly marked by the suffix *–self.*

REFLEXIVE PRONOUNS: FIRST AND SECOND PERSONS

In older English texts, however, we find that the element *–self* was sometimes optional:

- Get **thee** to a nunnery! (Get yourself to a "nunnery"!)
- Hie **thee** hence! (Get yourself out of here fast!)

These older usages resemble Latin reflexive constructions when the subject is "I," "you," "we," or "y'all":

- *Duc te abhinc!:* Hie thee hence! (Scram!)

In other words, if the subject is in the first or second persons, the personal pronouns *ego*, *tu*, *nos*, and *vos* can have a reflexive sense:

- *Me tibi committo:* I entrust **me** to you. (I entrust **myself** to you.)
- *Hoc **mihi** promitto:* I promise this to **me**. (I promise this to **myself**.)

Certain idioms that are not reflexive in English may require a reflexive pronoun in Latin:

- *Nos lavamus:* We wash (**ourselves**).
- *Vos paratis:* You get (**yourselves**) ready.

PROCEED WITH CAUTION

The forms *nos* and *vos* can be understood as nominative or accusative, depending on the context. Be careful, then, not to confuse emphatic subject pronouns with reflexive objects:

- ***Vos** mammonae servitis, **nos**, Deo:* **You** serve mammon; **we** serve God.
- *Hostes véniunt! Servate **vos**!: The* enemies are coming! Save **yourselves**!

TASK 1: TRANSLATING REFLEXIVE PRONOUNS

Translate the following sentences.

1. *Haec mihi verba saepe dico.*
2. *Levate vos a terra!* (*levo* means "raise")
3. *Saepe nobis mentimur.*
4. *Cur te non servas?* (*servo* means "save")
5. *Suasi mihi hoc esse fácile.*

REFLEXIVE PRONOUNS: THIRD PERSON

The simple expedient of using a personal pronoun for the reflexive would not work, however, when the subject is in the third person. Consider the following sentence:

- *Illum vidit:* He saw **him**.

Our assumption here is that the subject and object are two different people. To make the object reflexive, a special pronoun was required:

- *Se vidit:* He saw **himself.**

The form *se* indicates that the object pronoun reflects back on the subject.

On the other hand, Latin-speakers did not consider it necessary to distinguish the singular forms of this pronoun from plural, since the number of the antecedent was already indicated by the verb:

- *Se vidit:* He saw **himself.**
- *Se viderunt:* They saw **themselves.**

Moreover, there is no distinction in gender, since that also could be guessed from the context:

- *Caesar se vidit:* Caesar saw **himself.**
- *Calpúrnia se vidit:* Calpurnia saw **herself.**

FORMS OF THE THIRD PERSON REFLEXIVE PRONOUN

Having eliminated both number and gender from the paradigm, the Romans required only five forms for the third person reflexive pronoun. They resemble those of *ego* and *tu:*

Third Person Reflexive Pronoun

Singular and Plural, All Genders	
Nominative	—
Genitive	*sui*
Dative	*sibi*
Accusative	*se*
Ablative	*se*

Note that there is no nominative case form, since this pronoun is used only to "reflect" on the subject.

TRANSLATING REFLEXIVE PRONOUNS

You have already seen that your translation of such forms as *sui* and *se* will depend on the context:

- *Calpúrnia se crúciat:* Calpurnia torments **herself.**
- *Caesar se décipit:* Caesar deceives **himself.**
- *Calpúrnia Caesarque se decípiunt:* Calpurnia and Caesar deceive **themselves.**

There are also times when the suffix *–self* will not be appropriate, even when the reflexive pronoun is used. Consider, for example, the following sentence:

- *Caesar mílites iubet **sibi** parere:* Caesar commands the soldiers to obey **him.**

The complicating factor here is that two verbs are involved: "commands" and "to obey." In Latin, the reflexive form is used whenever a pronoun reflects back on the subject of the whole clause (in this case, Caesar). In English, however, *–self* is used only to reflect back on the implied subject of the nearest verb. For this reason, *sibi* is rendered here with the personal pronoun, "him."

Another wrinkle is that in Latin, reflexives are often used in dependent clauses to reflect upon the subject of the main clause:

- *Caesar milítibus ímperat, ut **sibi** páreant:* Caesar commands the soldiers to obey **him** (that they obey **him**).

This tends to happen in indirect commands and questions, purpose clauses, and wishes:

- *Rogavit illos quid **sibi** déderint:* He asked them what they had given to **him.**
- *Laboravit, ut omnes se laudarent:* He worked, in order that all might praise **him.**

TASK 2: TRANSLATING REFLEXIVE PRONOUNS AND *SUI*

Translate the reflexive pronoun in bold.

1. *Sapientes numquam se decípiunt:* Wise people never deceive ….
2. *Imperator Nero, turba appropinquante, se interfecit:* As the mob approached, the emperor Nero killed ….
3. *Pauci **sibi** non credunt:* Few people do not trust ….
4. *Cícero de se semper loquebatur:* Cicero was always talking about ….
5. *Christianus omnem **sui** amorem depónere debet:* The Christian should give up all love ….

6. *Alexander mílites se sequi iussit:* Alexander ordered the soldiers to follow ….

7. *Fília regis Geórgium rogavit, ut se a dracone servaret:* The king's daughter begged George to save … from the dragon.

8. *Mens nescit, quid sensus sibi praesentent:* The mind does not know, what the senses present ….

THE ADJECTIVE *SUUS*

The pronoun *sui* has a corresponding adjective, *suus, –a, –um.* It indicates possession that refers back to the subject:

• *Miles gládium suum portat:* The soldier carries **his** sword.

Like all adjectives, *suus* must agree in gender, number, and case with the noun that it modifies, regardless of the gender or number of the possessor:

• *Fémina gládium suum portat:* The woman carries **her** sword.

• *Fémina gládios suos portat:* The woman carries **her** swords.

Thus, your English translation of *suus* (his, her, its, their) will depend on the context:

• *Mílites gládios suos portant:* The soldiers carry **their** swords.

Like the pronoun *sui, suus* "reflects" on the subject of the whole clause; in dependent clauses, it may reflect on the subject of the main clause:

• *Caesar mílites ímperat ut currum suum trahant:* Caesar orders the soldiers to draw **his** chariot.

Note also that with *suus,* Latin is able to avoid ambiguities that are inescapable in English. Consider the following sentence:

• Marcus carries **his** book.

Out of context, you cannot tell whether the book belongs to Marcus or to some other "he." In Latin, however, the difference is plain:

• *Marcus librum suum portat:* Marcus carries **his** (own) book.

• *Marcus librum eius portat:* Marcus carries **his** (another's) book.

• *Romani linguam suam docent:* The Romans teach **their** (own) language.

• *Romani linguam eorum discunt:* The Romans learn **their** (another nation's) language.

Task 3: Translating *Suus*

Translate the adjective *suus* in context.

1. *Féminae illae líberos* **suos** *a perículo defendunt:* Those women are defending … children from danger.

2. *Alexander mílites* **suos** *ab hippopótamis defendit:* Alexander defends … soldiers from the hippos.

3. *Mágdala libros* **suos** *saepe legit:* Magdala often reads … books.

4. *Iudith Deum orat ut vires* **suos** *aúgeat:* Iudith begs God to increase … strength.

5. *Mens nescit quae* **suarum** *impressionum falsae sint:* the mind does not know which of … impressions are false.

The Intensive Pronoun/Adjective *Ipse*

Another pronoun/adjective in Latin has the intensifying effect sometimes found in forms with the suffix *–self*:

- *Cícero* **ipse** *venit:* Cicero **himself** is coming.
- **Ipsa** *haec dixit:* **She herself** said this.
- *Mens non dúbitat quin* **ipsa** *existat:* The soul does not doubt that **it** (itself) exists.

Note that these sentences do not contain reflexive situations; the pronoun or adjective merely draws attention to a noun. However, *ipse* can also be used to emphasize the idea of reflexive action:

- *Te* **ipsum** *nóscito:* Know thyself.

Sometimes the reflexive pronoun and *ipse* are linked by the infix *–met–:*

- **Nosmetipsos** *ignoramus:* We do not know **ourselves.**

The forms of the pronoun/adjective *ipse* resemble those of the other personal and demonstrative pronouns.

The Pronoun/Adjective *Ipse*

Singular	Masculine	Feminine	Neuter
Nominative	*ipse*	*ipsa*	*ipsum*
Genitive	*ipsius*	*ipsius*	*ipsius*

continues

The Pronoun/Adjective *Ipse*   (continued)

Singular	Masculine	Feminine	Neuter
Dative	*ipsi*	*ipsi*	*ipsi*
Accusative	*ipsum*	*ipsam*	*ipsum*
Ablative	*ipso*	*ipsa*	*ipso*

Plural	Masculine	Feminine	Neuter
Nominative	*ipsi*	*ipsae*	*ipsa*
Genitive	*ipsorum*	*ipsarum*	*ipsorum*
Dative	*ipsis*	*ipsis*	*ipsis*
Accusative	*ipsos*	*ipsas*	*ipsa*
Ablative	*ipsis*	*ipsis*	*ipsis*

TASK 4: TRANSLATING *IPSE*

Translate the following sentences.

1. *Pythagorei dícere solebant, "Ipse dixit."* (*Pythagorei* means "the Pythagoreans")
2. *Mágdala ipsa habet libros quos numquam legit.*
3. *Romani ipsi nos iusserunt se iuvare.*
4. *Omne ánimal se ipsum amat.*
5. *Memetipsum in spéculo vídeo.* (*speculum* means "mirror")

DEPENDENT CLAUSES IN INDIRECT STATEMENTS

You have already seen that in Latin, indirect statements are usually set up with the verb in the infinitive mood and the subject in the accusative case:

- *Dixit **Caésarem venire:*** He said **that Caesar was coming.**

Sometimes an indirect statement will have other clauses depending on it. Depending on the type of clause involved, either the indicative or the subjunctive will be used:

- *Dixit Caésarem, qui Gallos **vícerat**, Romam venire:* He said that Caesar, who **had conquered** the Gauls, was coming to Rome.
- *Dixit Caésarem, ut urbem **régeret**, Romam venire:* He said that Caesar was coming to Rome that **he might rule** (to rule) the city.

Relative clauses that would ordinarily be in the indicative mood may switch to the subjunctive when they are attached to an indirect statement. This shows that the relative clause belongs to the reported statement, and has not been added by the speaker:

- *"Caesar, qui Gallos **vicit**, Romam venit"*: "Caesar, who **has conquered** the Gauls, is coming to Rome."

- *Dixit Caésarem, qui Gallos **vicisset**, Romam venire:* He said that Caesar, who **had conquered** the Gauls, was coming to Rome.

However, if information is added or simply endorsed by the person who reports it, the indicative is used:

- *"Caesar Romam venit"*: "Caesar is coming to Rome."

- *Dixit Caésarem, qui Gallos **vícerat**, Romam venire:* He said that Caesar, who **had conquered** the Gauls, was coming to Rome.

SEQUENCE OF TENSES IN INDIRECT STATEMENTS

If the verb in a dependent clause is in the subjunctive mood, its tense is usually determined by the "head" verb that governs the indirect statement. Study the following two sentences:

- *"Abire debemus, ut ad tempus **veniamus**"*: "We must go, in order that we **may arrive** on time."

- ***Dixit** nos abire debere, ut ad tempus **veniremus**:* He said that we must go, that we **might arrive** on time.

In the first sentence, the verb *veniamus* is in the present tense because the main verb (*debemus*) is a non-past verb. In the second example, however, an imperfect subjunctive (*veniremus*) is required because the new main verb is *dixit*, in the perfect tense.

TASK 5: WORKING WITH THE SEQUENCE OF TENSES

Translate the clauses in bold.

1. *Imperator puellae dixit unum cophinorum, **quos spectaret**, ánulum continere:* The emperor told the girl that one of the caskets ... contained a ring.

2. *Geórgius asséruit se draconem interfecturum esse, **ut pópulus in Deum créderet**:* George declared that he would kill the dragon ....

3. *Mens credit ea **quae víderit** non esse vera:* The mind believes that the things ... are not true.

4. *Augustinus crédidit ómnia, **quae fecisset,** vana fuisse:* Augustine believed that all the things ... had been meaningless.

CONDITIONS IN INDIRECT STATEMENTS

The rules for sequence of tense get a little more complicated when the dependent clause is a condition. Study the following examples.

- *"Si hoc féceris, laudabunt te":* "If you do (will have done) this, they will praise you."
- *Dicit eos laudaturos esse me, si hoc fécerim:* He says that if I do this, they will praise me.
- *Dixit eos laudaturos esse me, si hoc fecissem:* He said that if I did this, they would praise me.

The original condition had a future perfect indicative (*féceris*) in the "if" clause and a future indicative in the main clause: a future "more vivid" condition.

In an indirect statement, the future perfect indicative becomes a perfect subjunctive (*fécerim*) after a non-past verb (*dicit*), and a pluperfect subjunctive (*fecissem*) after a past verb (*dixit*).

Note that the subjunctive verbs are translated "I do" and "I did" (not "I have done" and "I had done") because they occur in a future condition.

If the original sentence is a future less vivid condition, the subjunctive verb follows the rule for sequence of tenses:

- *"Si hoc fácias, laudent te":* "If you should do this, they would praise you."
- *Dicit eos laudaturos esse me, si hoc fáciam:* He says that they would praise me, if I should do this.
- *Dixit eos laudaturos esse me, si hoc fácerem:* He said that they would praise me, if I should do this.

Note that the present subjunctive in the *si* clause becomes imperfect if the "head" verb is past (*dixit*). The English translation of the condition remains unchanged.

Now look at some examples of contrafactual conditions:

- *"Si hoc fáceres, laudarent te":* "If you were doing this, they would be praising you."
- *Dicit eos laudare me, si hoc fácerem:* He says that they would be praising me, if I were doing this.
- *Dixit eos laudare me, si hoc fácerem:* He said that they would be praising me, if I were doing this.

In these examples, the original condition belongs to the present contrafactual type. Note that both Latin and English keep as much of the original syntax as possible. In Latin, the correspondence of present infinitive to imperfect subjunctive indicates that you are dealing with this type of condition.

Now look at what happens to past contrafactual conditions in indirect statement:

- *"Si hoc fecisses, laudvissent te":* "If you had done this, They would have praised you."
- *Dicit eos laudavisse me, si hoc fecissem:* He says that they would have praised me, if I had done this.
- *Dixit eos laudavisse me, si hoc fecissem:* He said that they would have praised me, if I had done this.

As was the case with present contrafactuals, the syntax of past contrafactual conditions is retained in indirect discourse, except that the main verb goes into the perfect infinitive.

The foregoing rules can be reduced to the following table.

Conditions in Indirect Statements

	Future More Vivid	*Future Less Vivid*
Direct Statement	*Si hoc féceris, laudabunt te.*	*Si hoc fácias, laudent te.*
	If you do this, they will praise you.	If you should do this, they would praise you.
Indirect Statement *(Non-past)*	*Dicit eos me laudaturos esse, si hoc fécerim.*	*Dicit eos me laudaturos esse, si hoc fáciam.*
	He says that they will praise me, if I do this.	He says that they would praise me, if I should do this.

continues

Conditions in Indirect Statements (continued)

	Future More Vivid	Future Less Vivid
Indirect Statement *(Past)*	*Dixit eos me laudaturos esse, si hoc fecissem.*	*Dixit eos me laudaturos esse, si hoc facerem.*
	He said that they would praise me, if I did this.	He said that they would praise me, if I should do this.

	Present Contrafactual	Past Contrafactual
Direct Statement	*Si hoc faceres, laudarent te.*	*Si hoc fecisses, laudavissent te.*
	If you were doing this, they would be praising you.	If you had done this, they would have praised you.
Indirect Statement *(Non-past)*	*Dicit eos me laudare, si hoc facerem.*	*Dicit eos me laudavisse, si hoc fecissem.*
	He says that they would be praising me, if I were doing this.	He says that they would have praised me, if I had done this.
Indirect Statement *(Past)*	*Dixit eos me laudare, si hoc fácerem.*	*Dixit eos me laudavisse, si hoc fecissem.*
	He said that they would be praising me, if I were doing this.	He said that they would have praised me, if I had done this.

TASK 6: TRANSLATING CONDITIONS IN INDIRECT STATEMENTS

Translate the words in bold.

1. *Imperator promittit se fílium puellae in matrimónium **daturum esse,** si illa cophinum sapienter **elégerit:** The emperor promises that he … his son to the girl in marriage if she … a casket wisely ….*

2. *Iudith constítuit se Holofernem **interfecturum esse**, si ille multum **bíberet:*** Judith decided that she ... Holofernes, if he ... a lot.

3. *Hierónymus pollícitus est se saeculares libros **reiecturum esse** (reício* means "reject"), *si Deus sibi pepercisset (parco, –ere, péperci* means "forgive"): Jerome promised that he ... secular books, if God ... him.

4. *Mens scit se nihil **intellégere**, si ómnia **dubitaret:*** The mind knows that it ... nothing, if it ... all things.

5. *Alexander intellexit se omnes mílites **perdidisse**, nisi hippopótamos **vicisset:*** Alexander understood that he ... all his soldiers, if he ... not ... the hippos.

ESSENTIAL VOCABULARY

These common words should be committed to memory.

Essential Vocabulary

Latin	Meaning	Related Word
Nouns		
motus, –us (masculine)	motion	
sensus, –us (masculine)	sense	
Pronouns		
qui–, quae–, quodcumque	whatever	
sui, sibi, se, se	him, her, it (-self), them (-selves)	
Verbs		
fallo, –ere, fefelli, falsus	deceive	false
nego, –are, –avi, –atus	deny, say no	negate
néscio, –ire, –ii	not know	
néscio quis	someone, anyone (I don't know who)	
persuádeo, –ere, persuasi	persuade	
prófero, –ferre, –tuli, –latus	utter, bring forth	
státuo, –ere, státui, statutus	establish	statute

continues

Essential Vocabulary (continued)

Latin	Meaning	Related Word
Adjectives		
falsus, –a, –um	false	
mínimus, –a, –um	least	minimal
potens, potentis	powerful	potent
Adverbs		
dénique	finally	
plane	plainly, obviously	
quare	why?	
quóties	as often (as)	quotient
saltem	at least	
summe	supremely	
super	more, above	

RECOGNITION VOCABULARY

Go over this list once or twice, and look for these words in the Reading
Exercise.

Recognition Vocabulary

Latin	Meaning
auctor, –oris (masculine)	author
diversus, –a, –um	different from
existo, –ere, éxstiti	exist
figura, –ae (feminine)	figure
memória, –ae (feminine)	memory
occásio, –ionis (feminine)	occasion
repraesento, –are, –avi, –atus	represent
suppono, –ere, suppósui, supósitus	suppose

SUMMARY

In this hour, you have learned how to decline reflexive and intensive pronouns, and how to translate subordinate clauses in indirect statement. Now
you are ready for the heart of Descarte's *Meditations on First Philosophy*, in
which he makes his famous argument for his own existence.

READING EXERCISE

René Descartes had the benefit a traditional humanistic and philosophical education from the French Jesuits. However, he revolutionized philosophy by devising an inductive method, based on radical doubt, for the theory of knowledge and being. Here is the key passage from his second meditation, in which he founds his philosophy on the certainty of his own consciousness.

DO I EXIST?

Suppono ígitur ómnia quae vídeo falsa esse; credo nihil umquam extitisse eorum quae mendax memória repraesentat; nullos plane hábeo sensus; corpus, figura, exténsio, motus, locusque sunt chímerae. Quid ígitur erit verum? Fortassis hoc unum: nihil esse certi.

Sed unde scio nihil esse diversum ab eis ómnibus quae iam recénsui, de quo ne mínima quidem occásio sit dubitandi? Numquid est áliquis Deus (vel quocumque nómine illum vocare possum) qui mihi has ipsas cogitátiones immittit? Quare vero hoc puto, cum forsan ipsemet illarum auctor esse possim? Numquid ergo saltem ego aliquid sum? Sed iam negavi me habere ullos sensus, et ullum corpus. Haéreo tamen; nam quid inde? Sumne ita córpori sensibusque alligatus, ut sine illis esse non possim? Sed mihi persuasi nihil plane esse in mundo, nullum caelum, nullam terram, nullas mentes, nulla córpora; nonne ígitur étiam me non esse? Immo certe ego eram, si quid mihi persuasi. Sed est deceptor néscio quis, summe potens, summe cálidus, qui de indústria me semper fallit. Haud dúbie ígitur ego sum, si me fallit; et cum fallat quantum potest, nunquam tamen effíciet, ut nihil sim, quámdiu me áliquid esse cogitabo. Ádeo ut, ómnibus satis superque pensitatis, dénique statuendum sit hoc pronuntiatum: "Ego sum, ego existo," quóties a me profertur vel mente concípitur, necessário esse verum.

Reading Vocabulary

alligo, –are, –avi, atus	bind to
cálidus, –a, –um	clever
chímera, –ae (feminine)	chimera, illusion
cogitátio, –ionis (feminine)	thought
concípio, –ere, –cepi,–ceptus	conceive
deceptor, –toris (masculine)	deceiver
dúbie	doubtfully (*haud dúbie:* "without a doubt")
effício, –ere, –feci	bring it about (*ut:* "that")

continues

Reading Vocabulary (continued)

exténsio, –ionis (feminine)	extension
forsan	perhaps
fortassis	perhaps
haéreo, –ere, haesi	hesitate
iis	(same as *eis*)
immitto, –ere, –misi,–missus	put in
immo	on the contrary, indeed
indústria, –ae (feminine)	purpose;
de indústria	on purpose
ipsemet	(same as *ipse*)
mendax, –acis (adjective)	lying, deceiving
necessário	necessarily
pénsito, –are, –avi, –atus	think about, ponder
pronuntiatum, –i (neuter)	statement
quámdiu	how long
quantum	as much (as)
recénseo, –ere, –ui	survey

QUIZ

Choose the form in parentheses that best completes the sentence, and translate.

1. *Suppono ígitur ómnia (qui/quae) vídeo falsa esse.*
2. *Credo nihil umquam (extitisse/extiterunt) eorum quae mendax memória repraesentat.*
3. *(Nulli/Nullos) plane hábeo sensus; corpus, figura, exténsio, motus, locusque sunt chímerae.*
4. *Sed unde scio nihil (esse/fuisse/futurum esse) diversum ab iis ómnibus quae iam recénsui?*
5. *Sumne ita córpori sensibusque alligatus, ut sine illis esse non (possum/possim)?*
6. *Immo certe ego eram, si (quem/quid) mihi persuasi.*
7. *"Ego sum, ego existo," quóties a me profertur vel (mentis/mente) concípitur, necessário est verum.*

Gerundive and Supine Constructions; More Pronouns; Numbers

CHAPTER SUMMARY

LESSON PLAN:

In this hour you will learn about …

- Forming two other types of verbal noun and adjective: the gerundive and the supine
- Using these forms to express purpose
- Declining and translating pronouns/adjectives relating to the concept of duality, and those which have unusual suffixes
- Reading Latin numbers

So far, you have learned how to use verbal adjectives (participles) as clause-substitutes, and also how to decline and translate various kinds of pronouns.

INTRODUCTORY READING

Look for these features in the following essay on the value and purpose of human life, by Giovanni Pico della Mirandola (1463–1494). According to Pico, learning Latin is just the first step; our goal is to be like the angels.

HUMAN DESTINY

Invadat ánimum sacra quaedam ambítio ut, mediócribus non contenti, anhalemus ad summa, adque illa consequenda (quando póssumus, si vólumus) totis víribus enitamur. Dedignemur terréstria, caeléstia contemnamus, et quicquid mundi est denique posthabentes, ultramundanam cúriam eminentíssimae divinitati próximam advolemus. Ibi, ut sacra tradunt mystéria, Séraphim, Chérubim, et Throni primas póssident; horum et dignitatem et glóriam emulemur. Érimus illis, cum voluérimus, níhilo inferiores.

Let a holy ambition invade our souls, that, not content with mediocre things, we may strive for the highest, and let us strive to obtain them (when we can and if we wish it) with all our might. Let us disdain earthly things and reject even those above, and finally, counting as less valuable whatever belongs to the world, let us fly to the court that is closest to the supreme divinity. There, as the holy mysteries relate, the Seraphim, Cherubim, and Thrones hold the first (places); let us emulate their dignity and glory. When we wish, we will be not at all inferior to them.

Notice that Pico urges us to struggle with all our might "to obtain those things" (*ad illa consequenda*). This phrase includes a form that resembles a future passive participle (*consequenda*), This word modifies *illa,* but is translated as though it were active, and took *illa* as its object. This form is called a *gerundive*.

GERUNDIVES

A gerundive (Latin *gerundivum*) is a type of verbal adjective, which has no equivalent in English. The Romans thought of the gerundive as a "gerund turned into an adjective," because it is used in the same constructions as the gerund:

- *Legendo multa díscimus:* We learn a lot by reading. (*legendo* is a gerund)
- *Libris legendis multa díscimus:* We learn a lot by reading books. (*legendis* is a gerundive)

The difference is that the gerund (*legendo*) is a verbal noun, which stands on its own in the sentence, whereas the gerundive (*legendis*) is a verbal adjective, agreeing with a noun (*libris*).

The form of the gerundive is identical with the future passive participle.

Formation of the Gerundive

Conjugation	Stem	Endings
I	*amand–*	*–us, –a, –um*
II	*timend–*	*–us, –a, –um*
III	*ducend–*	*–us, –a, –um*
III –io	*capiend–*	*–us, –a, –um*
IV	*audiend–*	*–us, –a, –um*

Note that the gerundive is declined as an adjective of the first/second declension type.

SYNTAX OF THE GERUNDIVE

The tricky thing about the gerundive is that it relates to the noun it modifies as a verb to its object:

- *Libris legendis multa díscimus:* We learn much **by reading books.**
- *Sciéntia **reipúblicae regendae** perútilis est: The science of **governing a state** is very useful.*
- *Óperam navemus **grammáticae ediscendae:** Let us devote our energy to learning grammar.*

Note that the gerundive is translated as if it were a gerund; the noun with which it agrees is treated as its object.

The really bizarre thing about this construction is that the noun "object" takes the case that would be required for the gerund. Suppose, for example, that you want to say this:

- By waging war, we will have peace.

"By waging" is an expression of *means* requiring the ablative case. If we use the gerundive construction, we will have to put "war" (*bello*) in the ablative case and make "waging" (*gerend–*) agree with it:

- ***Bello gerendo,*** *pacem obtinébimus.*

Similarly, if you want to say, "The idea of learning grammar gives me the willies," the expression "of learning" points to the genitive case. This is the case you will use for "grammar" (*grammática, –ae* [feminine]), making the gerundive agree with it:

- *Nótio grammáticae discendae me terret.*

TASK 1: TRANSLATION

Translate the phrases in bold.

1. *Alexander **belli gerendi** opportunitatem numquam omisit:* Alexander never omitted an opportunity ….
2. ***Dracónibus vincendis** Sanctus Geórgius pópulum ad fidem Christianam convertit:* St. George converted the people to the Christian faith ….
3. ***Linguis discendis** óperam raro damus:* We rarely devote our time ….

EXPRESSIONS OF PURPOSE WITH GERUND AND GERUNDIVE

You have already learned that the gerund after *ad* and *causa* can be used to express purpose:

- *Edo ad **vivendum:** I eat for living (I eat to live).*
- *Edo **vivendi** causa: I eat for the sake of living.*

The same constructions appear with the gerundive:

- *Caesar ad **Gallos vincendos** processit:* Caesar went forward **to beat the Gauls.**
- *Caesar processit **Gallorum vincendorum** causa:* Caesar went forward for the sake **of beating the Gauls.**

Note that when *ad* is used, the noun "object" of the gerundive goes into the accusative case; after *causa* or *gratia* ("for the sake ..."), it goes into the genitive. As usual, the gerundive agrees with this noun in gender, number, and case.

TASK 2: TRANSLATING GERUNDIVES

Translate the phrases in bold.

1. *Iudith Holofernem decapitavit **ad pópulum Israelíticum liberandum** (libero* means "free")*:* Judith beheaded Holofernes ....

2. *Hierónymus in desertam successit **carnis domandae causa** (caro, carnis* [feminine], "flesh"; *domo* means "tame"): Jerome withdrew into the desert ....

3. *Árabis fílius vítulum in saccum pósuit **ad amicos probandos** (probo* means "test"): The Arab's son put a calf in a sack ....

THE SUPINE

There is yet another way of expressing purpose or intention in Latin, although its use is more restricted. It involves a type of verbal noun called the supine. This form is related to the fourth principal part of the verb.

Formation of the Supine

Principal Parts	Supine
*núntio, ... **nuntiat-us***	***nuntiat-um, nuntiat-u***
*vídeo, ... **vis-us***	***vis-um, vis-u***
*fácio, ... **fact-us***	***fact-um, fact-u***

The stem of the supine is identical to that of the perfect participle. (Indeed, many grammars and dictionaries give the *–um* form of the supine, rather than the perfect participle, as the fourth principal part.)

The *–um* (accusative) form is used after verbs of motion to indicate purpose or intention:

- *Eo cúbitum* (from *cubo, –ere*): I am going to lie down.
- *Caesar ábiit piscatum* (from *pisco, –are*): Caesar went fishing.
- *Romani véniunt urbem captum:* The Romans come to capture the city.

Note that in the last example, the supine *captum* takes a direct object (*urbem*). Remember that the supine also shows up in the future passive infinitive (as in *amatum iri,* meaning "to be about to be loved").

The *–u* form of the supine covers some usages associated with the dative and ablative cases. It occurs after adjectives and certain stock phrases:

- *Mirábile dictu!:* (It is) wonderful to tell (in the telling)!
- *Haec sunt difficília memoratu:* These things are hard to relate.
- *Si hoc fas est dictu ...:* If it is permissible to say this ....
- *Hic frater est maior natu:* This brother is older (greater in birth).

Notice that this form is often, but not always, translated by the English infinitive (as in *dictu,* meaning "to tell" or "to say").

TASK 3: TRANSLATION

Translate the words in bold.

1. *Difficile est **dictu** quam iucundum sit Latine díscere:* It is difficult … how much fun it is to learn Latin.
2. *Legati pacem nos **rogatum** venerunt:* The ambassadors came … for peace.
3. *Venerunt Hierosólymam sacra loca **visum**:* They came to Jerusalem … the holy places.
4. *Libri Latini fáciles sunt **lectu**:* Latin books are easy ….

REVIEW OF EXPRESSIONS INDICATING PURPOSE

You have probably noticed that Latin has various ways of expressing the purpose of an action. They can be set out in a table.

Expressions of Purpose

Purpose Clause	*Caesar venit ut urbem cáperet.* Caesar came that he might capture the city.
Gerund	*Caesar venit ad pugnandum.* Caesar came to fight (for fighting).
	Caesar venit pugnandi causa. Caesar came for the sake of fighting.
Gerundive	*Caesar venit ad urbem capiendam.* Caesar came to capture the city.
	Caesar venit urbis capiendae causa. Caesar came for the sake of capturing the city.
Supine	*Caesar venit urbem captum.* Caesar came to capture the city.

TASK 4: WORKING WITH PURPOSE CONSTRUCTIONS

Convert the purpose clauses in the following sentences first into constructions with the gerund/gerundive, and then into the supine. Then translate.

1. *Alexander ad Índiam venit ut loca mirabília videret:* Alexander came to India to see amazing places.
2. *Caesar Romam rédiit ut repúblicam régeret:* Caesar returned to Rome to govern the state.

MORE PRONOUNS

You have already seen that pronouns not only serve to link one clause with another, but also can add shades of meaning, such as definiteness and indefiniteness. In this last lesson, we will have a look at a few other pronouns/adjectives with semantic peculiarities.

PRONOUNS/ADJECTIVES OF "DUALITY"

The early Indo-European languages often have special forms and words for "two" of something. These have disappeared from English, apart from a few words such as "pair," "either," "neither," and "both." Latin also has a few words that are used only when two objects are involved.

Pronouns/Adjectives of Duality

uter, utra, utrum	which (of two)?
neuter, neutra, neutrum	neither (of two)
alter, áltera, álterum	one, the other (of two)
uterque, utraque, utrumque	either, both

All of these words are declined in the same way as first/second declension adjectives, except that the genitive singular ending for all genders is *–ius,* and the dative singular ending for all genders is *–i:*

- *Áltera manus alterius negótia nésciat:* Let one hand not know the other's business.
- *Neutri candidato confídimus:* We trust neither candidate.

As the first example illustrates, the combination *alter ... alter* means "one ... the other":

- *Alter dives, alter pauper natus est:* One (man) was born rich, the other poor.

The pronoun/adjective *uterque* is declined in the first part (*uter–*). It is always singular in Latin, but can be translated as "both":

- *Utraque manu scríbere possum:* I can write with **both hands.**
- *Duo consília hábeo;* **utrumque** *me terret:* I have two plans; **both** scare me.

TASK 5: TRANSLATING PRONOUNS/ADJECTIVES OF DUALITY

Translate the phrases in bold.

1. *Utra manu scribis: déxtera an sinistra?:* ... do you write: the right or the left?
2. *Áltera manu scribo;* ***áltera** (manu) número:* I write ...; I count ....
3. *Utraque manu libros porto:* I carry books ....
4. *Neutra manu scríbere possum:* I can write ....

INDECLINABLE SUFFIXES

As you saw in the case of *uterque,* some pronouns have suffixes that change the meaning of the root. Here are some common suffixes of this type:

- *–que:* every ...
- *–cumque:* –ever, every, any
- *–vis:* –ever, every, any
- *–libet:* –ever, every, any

We have already seen (in Hour 21) that these suffixes can be tacked onto pronouns and adjectives such as *quis* and *qui:*

- *Quocumque témpore vénies, ego tibi convéniam:* At whatever time you come, I will meet you.

- *Quódlibet ánimal vitam suam servare conatur:* Every animal tries to save its own life.

They can also appear with adverbs, such as *ubi:*

- *Lingua Latina **ubicumque** intellégitur:* Latin is understood **everywhere.**

JUST A MINUTE

The suffix *–vis* comes from the verb *volo* and means "you want"; the suffix *–libet* is actually the impersonal verb "it pleases." The sense is "any … that pleases you":

- *Quaélibet mínima res est consideranda:* Every little thing (any little thing you like) must be considered.

TASK 6: WORKING WITH SUFFIXES

Translate the words in bold.

1. ***Quicumque*** *in Deum credíderit, habebit vitam aeternam:* … believes in God, will have eternal life.

2. ***Quicquid*** *audívero tibi nuntiabo:* I will tell you … I hear.

3. ***Quovis modo*** *operare potes, sed hanc régulam observa:* You can work …, but keep this rule.

4. ***Quandocumque*** *haec verba lego, lacrimo:* I weep … I read these words.

REVIEW OF Q-WORDS

As you first get used to reading Latin, you may find that you are often hung up on "those Q-words." Keep this list for handy reference:

Q-Words

qua	by what way? as
qualis, quale	what kind of …?, such as
quam	than, as … as possible

quamobrem	why? wherefore
quando	when
quantus, −a, −um	how much
quapropter	why? wherefore
quare	why? wherefore
qui, quae, quod	who, which; what?
quia	because
quidam	a certain …
quidem	indeed
quis, quid	who? what? someone, something
quin	why not? but that, from … *−ing*
quod	that, because
quómodo	how
quóminus	that not, from … *−ing*
quóniam	because, that
quoque	also
quo	to where?
quot	how many

Numbers

Finally, it will be handy when reading to know something about numbers. These occur in various kinds, but the two most common kinds of numbers are called *cardinal* (the counting numbers: "one, two, three") and *ordinal* (used for ranking: "first, second, third").

The Basic Numbers

Here is how you count to 10 in Latin.

Numbers 1 to 10

	Cardinal	Ordinal
I	*unus* (one)	*primus, −a, −um* (first)
II	*duo*	*secundus, −a, −um*
III	*tres*	*tértius, −a, −um*
IV	*quattuor*	*quartus, −a, −um*
V	*quinque*	*quintus, −a, −um*

continues

Numbers 1 to 10   (continued)

	Cardinal	Ordinal
VI	sex	sextus, −a, −um
VII	septem	séptimus, −a, −um
VIII	octo	octavus, −a, −um
IX	novem	nonus, −a, −um
X	decem	décimus, −a, −um

The cardinal numbers *unus*, *duo*, and *tres* are treated as adjectives and are declined in case and gender.

Declining *Unus, Duo,* and *Tres*

	Masculine	Feminine	Neuter
Nominative	unus	una	unum
Genitive	unius	unius	unius
Dative	uni	uni	uni
Accusative	unum	unam	unum
Ablative	uno	una	uno

	Masculine	Feminine	Neuter
Nominative	duo	duae	duo
Genitive	duorum	duarum	duorum
Dative	duobus	duabus	duobus
Accusative	duo(s)	duas	duo
Ablative	duobus	duabus	duobus

	Masculine/Feminine	Neuter
Nominative	tres	tria
Genitive	trium	trium
Dative	tribus	tribus
Accusative	tres	tria
Ablative	tribus	tribus

The other cardinal numbers are indeclinable (they never change their form). All ordinal numbers are declined as first/second declension adjectives.

TASK 7: ADDITION

Do the following addition problems, using this formula: *Unus et unus sunt duo* (One and one are two).

1. II + IV =
2. III + V =
3. I + III =
4. VI + II =
5. VII + I =

HIGHER NUMBERS

Cardinal numbers between 10 and 20 usually add the indeclinable suffix *–decim*; the ordinal form is *–decimus*.

Numbers 10 to 20

XI	*úndecim*	*undécimus*
XII	*duódecim*	*duodécimus*
XIII	*trédecim*	*tértius décimus*
XIV	*quattuórdecim*	*quartus décimus*
XV	*quíndecim*	*quintus décimus*
XVI	*sédecim*	*sextus décimus*
XVII	*septéndecim*	*séptimus décimus*
XVIII	*duodeviginti*	*duodevicésimus*
XIX	*undeviginti*	*undevicésimus*
XX	*viginti*	*vicesimus*

Note that *duodeviginti* (eighteen) literally means "two from twenty"; *undeviginti* (nineteen) means "one from twenty."

Multiples of 10 are marked with the suffixes *–ginta* (which is also indeclinable) and *–gésimus*.

Numbers 20 to 90

XX	*viginti*	*vicésimus*
XXX	*triginta*	*tricésimus*
XL	*quadraginta*	*quadragésimus*
L	*quinquaginta*	*quinquagésimus*
LX	*sexaginta*	*sexagésimus*
LXX	*septuaginta*	*septuagésimus*
LXXX	*octoginta*	*octogésimus*
XC	*nonaginta*	*nonagésimus*

Multiples of 100 are formed with the suffixes *–centi* or *–genti* for cardinal numbers, and *–centesimus* for ordinals.

Numbers 100 to 900

C	centum	centésimus
CC	ducenti	ducentésimus
CCC	trecenti	trecentésimus
CD	quandringenti	quadringentésimus
D	quingenti	quingentésimus
DC	sescenti	sescentésimus
DCC	septingenti	septingentésimus
DCCC	octingenti	octingentésimus
DCCCC	nongenti	nongentésimus

Cardinal numbers with the suffixes *–centi* and *–genti* are declined as plural adjectives of the first and second declensions (for example, *ducentae puellae* means "two hundred girls").

PROCEED WITH CAUTION

The suffixes for multiples of 10 and 100 in the cardinal numbers are easily confused. It may help to remember that the latter always contain an element derived from *centum,* "one hundred." Look especially for the *e* in the root: *quadraginta* means "forty"; *quadringenti* means "four hundred."

When deciphering ordinal numbers, remember that multiples of 100 have the longer suffix *–centésimus* or *–gentésimus: quadragésimus* means "fortieth"; *quadringentésimus* means "four-hundredth."

Multiples of *mille* (one thousand) are formed simply by combining the basic counting numbers with the plural form, *mília.*

Numbers 1,000 to 3,000

M	mille	millésimus
MM	duo milia	bis millésimus
MMM	tria milia	ter millésimus

The ordinal number *bis millésimus* literally means "twice one-thousandth." *Bis* is a *numeral adverb,* which is used to indicate multiplication. The numeral adverbs for the first 10 numbers are as follows.

Numeral Adverbs

I	*semel* (once)
II	*bis* (twice)
III	*ter*
IV	*quater*
V	*quínquiens*
VI	*séxiens*
VII	*séptiens*
VIII	*óctiens*
IX	*nóviens*
X	*déciens*

TASK 8: WORKING WITH ORDINAL AND CARDINAL NUMBERS

Read the following numerals as both cardinal and ordinal numbers.

1. XVI (16)
2. XXX (30)
3. CD (400)
4. MM (2000)

COMBINING NUMBERS

The numbers in between multiples of 10, 100, and 1,000 are formed pretty much as in English:

- *viginti (et) unus:* twenty-one
- *quadraginta quattuor:* forty-four
- *centum viginti duo:* one hundred twenty-two
- *mille centum quadraginta tres:* one thousand, one hundred forty-three

Ordinal numbers are similarly formed:

- *vicésimus primus:* twenty-first
- *millésimus centésimus quadragésimus tértius:* one thousand, one hundred forty-third

Note that in Latin, all numbers in an ordinal combination must be declined as adjectives. You will most often see these longer numbers in dates:

- *Anno Dómini millésimo quadringentésimo quadragésimo secundo, Christóphorus Columbus ad Americam pervenit:* In the year of our Lord 1492 (the one thousand four hundred ninety-second year of our Lord), Christopher Columbus discovered America.

TASK 9: WORKING WITH ORDINAL AND CARDINAL NUMBERS II

Read the following numerals as both cardinal and ordinal numbers.

1. XVIII (18)
2. XXXV (35)
3. DXXIV (524)
4. MDCLXXVIII (1,678)
5. MMMCCCXCVIII (3,398)

ESSENTIAL VOCABULARY

The following common words should be committed to memory.

Essential Vocabulary

Latin	Meaning	Related Word
Nouns		
dígnitas, dignitatis (feminine)	dignity	
gradus, gradus (masculine)	steps, grade	gradual
praeceptum, praecepti (neuter)	precept	
régula, regulae (feminine)	rule	regular
vis, vis (feminine) (plural: *vires*)	force, strength	violence
Verbs		
admóneo, –ere, –ui, –itus	warn, advise	admonish

Essential Vocabulary

Latin	Meaning	Related Word
Verbs		
appello, –are, –avi, –atus	call	appeal
éxcito, –are, –avi, –atus	rouse	excite
fingo, –ere, finxi, fictus	make (up), form	fiction
pervénio, –ire, –veni	arrive	
scribo, –ere, scripsi, scriptus	write	scripture
Adjective		
tres, tria	three	triple
Adverbs		
postremo	finally	
primo	(at) first	
prius	first, beforehand	
recte	rightly	rectitude

Recognition Vocabulary

Go through this list once or twice and look for these words in the Reading Exercise.

Recognition Vocabulary

Latin	Meaning
Apollo, –inis (masculine)	Apollo, a Greek god
Christianus, –a, –um	Christian
disputátio, –ionis (feminine)	disputation
dialéctica, –ae (feminine)	dialectic, a branch of philosophy
Graecus, –a, –um	Greek
interpretátio, –ionis (feminine)	interpretation, translation

continues

Recognition Vocabulary   (continued)

Latin	Meaning
liberalis, –e	liberal
moralis, –e	moral
mystérium, –ii (neuter)	mystery
naturalis, –e	natural
necessárius, –a, –um	necessary
norma, –ae (feminine)	norm, rule
philósophus, –i (masculine)	philosopher
Plato, –onis (masculine)	Plato, a Greek philosopher
praescribo, –ere, praescripsi	prescribe
praesens, –ntis (adjective)	present
sacer, –ra, –rum	sacred, holy
sacrosanctus, –a, –um	sacrosanct
secretus, –a, –um	secret
significántia, –ae (feminine)	significance, meaning
theológia, –ae (feminine)	theology
theológicus, –a, –um	theological

SUMMARY

In this hour, you have tied up a number of loose ends: the gerundive and supine, dual pronouns, special suffixes, and numbers. You have now covered all the essentials of Latin grammar. Congratulations! For advice on what to do next, see the Postscript. In the meantime, celebrate your admission to the ranks of the *humanissimi* by reading a snippet from the great Italian humanist Pico.

READING EXERCISE

The Renaissance was an exciting time to be a Latin scholar. Many of the works now considered classics had been newly discovered (or rediscovered), just as the horizons of European culture expanded to include the Near East. An extraordinary document of this period is the *Orátio de dignitate Hóminis*, delivered by the young humanist Giovanni Pico della Mirandola. Pico promised to show that the ancient philosophies of Persia, Israel, Greece, and Rome agreed in all essential matters with each other and with Christianity. The vehicle of this massive (if improbable) synthesis was to be Pico's elegant Ciceronian Latin. Unfortunately, he died not long after this programmatic address, leaving the project of a unified "humanism" to Latin students of the future.

In the following passage, Pico compares Greek religious rites and the inscriptions on Apollo's temple at Delphi to the branches of philosophy. (Adapted)

The Unity of Human Wisdom

Verum enimvero, nec Mosáica tantum aut Christiana mystéria, sed priscorum quoque theológia liberálium ártium et emolumenta nobis et dignitatem ostendit.

Quid enim áliud significant in Graecorum arcanis gradus initiatorum? Qui primo purificati per illas quasi "februales" artes, moralem et dialécticam, ad mysteriorum pervenerunt susceptionem? Haec quid aliud esse potest, quam secretioris per philosóphiam naturae interpretátio?

... Sacra Apóllinis nómina, si quis eorum significántias et latitántia perscrutetur mystéria, satis ostendunt Deum illum non minus esse philósophum quam vatem. Hoc Ammónius iam satis est executus; sed súbeant ánimum, Patres, tria Délphica praecepta necessária his, qui non ficti sed veri Apóllinis (qui "illúminat omnem ánimam venientem in hunc mundum") sacrosanctum et augustíssimum templum ingressuri sunt. Vidébitis nihil áliud illa praecepta nos admonere, quam ut tripartitam hanc, de qua est praesens disputátio, philosóphiam totis víribus amplectamur.

Illud enim MEDEN AGAN, id est "nequid nimis," virtutum ómnium normam et régulam per mediocritatis rationem, de qua moralis agit, recte praescribit. Tum illud GNOTHI SEAUTON, id est "cognosce te ipsum," ad cognitionem totius naturae, cuius interstítium est natura hóminis, nos excitat et inhortatur. Qui enim se cognoscit, in se ómnia cognoscit, ut Zoroaster prius, deinde Plato in Alcibiade scripserunt. Postremo hac cognítione per naturalem philosóphiam illuminati iam Deo próximi, EI, id est "es" dicentes, theológica salutatione verum Apóllinem familiáriter proindeque felíciter appellábimus.

Reading Vocabulary

ago, ágere, egi, actus	*with de: deal with*
Alcibiades, –is (masculine)	Alcibiades, a dialogue written by Plato
Ammónius, Ammónii (masculine)	Ammonius, a Greek philosopher
amplector, –ari, amplectatus sum	embrace
arcanus, –a, –um	secret
arcanum, –i, (neuter)	secret rite
augustus, –a, –um	venerable
cognítio, cognitionis (feminine)	knowledge
Délphicus, –a, –um	Delphic, of Delphi
EI	you are (in Greek)
emolumentum, –i (neuter)	profit, benefit
enimvero (after *verum*)	but surely, indeed
éx(s)equor, –i ex(s)ecutus sum	follow up on, explain
familiáriter	familiarly, as a friend
februalis, –e	purifying
felíciter	happily
GNOTHI SEAUTON	know yourself (in Greek)
illúmino, –are, –avi, –atus	illuminate, enlighten
inhortor, –ari, –atus sum	exhort, urge
inítio, –are, –avi, –atus	initiate
interstítium, –ii (neuter)	interval, space between, midpoint
látito, –are, –avi	lie hidden
MEDEN AGAN	nothing in excess (in Greek)
Mediócritas, mediocritatis (feminine)	moderation
Mosáicus, –a, –um	Mosaic
nequid	nothing
perscrutor, –ari, perscruatus sum	search through

priscus, −a, −um	original, ancient
proinde	(and) so, accordingly
puríficо, −are, −avi, −atus	purify
salutátio, salutationis (feminine)	greeting
suscéptio, susceptionis (feminine)	undertaking, reception
tripartitus, −a, −um	three-part
vates, −is (masculine)	prophet
Zoroaster, −ri (masculine)	Zoroaster (Zarathustra), a Persian prophet

Quiz

Choose the form in parentheses that best completes the sentence, and translate.

1. *Priscorum theológia liberálium ártium (dígnitas/dignitatem) ostendit.*

2. *Quid enim áliud (significat/significant) in Graecorum arcanis gradus initiatorum?*

3. *Iniati, purificati per (illos/illas) quasi "februales" artes, ad mysteriorum pervenerunt susceptionem.*

4. *Sacra Apóllinis nómina satis ostendunt Deum illum non minus (est/esse) philósophum quam vatem.*

5. *Quicumque enim se cognoscit, in (sibi/se) ómnia cognoscit.*

Postscript

WHERE TO GO FROM HERE?

You have now seen the basic forms and rules of Latin grammar, and you have a sense of what it is like to read Latin texts. How should you continue your study of Latin?

In reading a foreign language, as in all things, practice makes perfect. As soon as you can, find a text that appeals to you and work through it. At first, you will make the most headway with an easy text, such as the *Vulgate Bible* or the *Carmina Burana*. Plan to read a little at a time. It will also help you to have an English translation handy, to smooth over rough spots or to give you an idea of the context before you start.

Many of the ancient Latin classics are available in bilingual editions in the Loeb Classical Library (Harvard University Press) or in other collections. Furthermore, a number of texts and translations from all periods are currently available on the World Wide Web. Using a standard search engine, type in the name of your author and see what you find; alternatively, you can visit the Bibliotheca Latina site at http://polyglot.lss.wisc.edu/classics/biblio.htm. You will also find a weekly news bulletin in Latin on the Web site of Radio Finland at www.yle.fi/fbc/latini/index.html.

There are a number of good pocket and mid-sized dictionaries available for Latin students. At some point, you should also acquire a standard Latin grammar. That of J. H. Allen and J. B. Greenough is readily available; it can also be accessed online through the Perseus site at http://perseus.csad.ox.ac.uk.

Finally, keep your eyes and ears open. Latin turns up in all sorts of places where people hoped to be heard across the centuries. They are now speaking to you!

APPENDIX
Answer Key

ANSWERS TO EXERCISES IN HOUR 1

TASK 1

Latin was a widely spoken language. It was spoken throughout the territory of the Roman Empire. It gradually evolved into the romance languages. An example is Spanish, which is the primary language of Spain and Central and South America. Latin is considered an important part of a liberal education. To paraphrase a Spanish philosopher: "A gentleman or lady is someone who has forgotten Latin and Greek."

TASK 2

All eastern peoples, however—such as Hebrews and Syrians—make sounds in the throat. All Mediterranean peoples, such as Greeks and Asians, form words on the palate. All Western people, such as Italians and Spaniards, make words on the teeth. Syrian or Chaldean is close to Hebrew in speech and the sound of the letters. Some, however, think the Hebrew language is the same as the Chaldean because Abraham was from Chaldea. But if this is accepted, how are Hebrew boys in the Book of Daniel ordered to be a taught a language which they do not know?

TASK 3

1. people: noun, from: preposition
2. neighboring: adjective
3. spoke: verb, when: conjunction
4. they: pronoun
5. soon: adverb, all: adjective
6. to: preposition, Western: adjective, in: preposition
7. language: noun, but: conjunction
8. joined: verb

Task 4

1. *servi*
2. *manus*
3. *féminae*
4. *casae*
5. *linguae*
6. *dies*
7. *horti*
8. *spes*
9. *mulíeres*
10. *coloni*
11. *urbes*
12. *hómines*

Task 5

1. *via:* feminine
2. *exércitus:* masculine
3. *spécies:* feminine
4. *modus:* masculine
5. *spes:* feminine
6. *casa:* feminine
7. *fides:* feminine
8. *hortus:* masculine

Task 6

1. *perícula*
2. *génua*
3. *génera*
4. *verba*
5. *lítora*
6. *spátia*
7. *saxa*
8. *ópera*

Task 7

1. The Romans invade …
2. Hannibal lives …
3. Roman soldiers are …

Task 8

1. *Dómini vivunt:* The masters live.
2. *Féminae docent:* Women teach.
3. *Verba evéniunt:* Words come forth.
4. *Puella ámbulat:* The girl walks.

Task 9

1. *lingua Latina*
2. *dómini multi*
3. *verba Latina*
4. *res bona*
5. *currus novi, currus novus*
6. *múlier romana*
7. *poetae latini*
8. *puellae bonae*
9. *res áliae, res alia*

Reading Exercise

There were various languages after the flood, when the Tower of Babel was built. For in the beginning there was one language, Hebrew, which the patriarchs and prophets spoke. In the beginning there were as many languages as peoples, and then more peoples than languages, because from one language many peoples come forth.

There are three sacred languages: Hebrew, Greek, and Latin, which especially stand out throughout the whole world. In these languages the accusation of the Lord was written over his cross. Thus, and because the Holy Scriptures are obscure, these languages are useful a lot.

ANSWERS TO EXERCISES IN HOUR 2

TASK 1

1. *linguae omnes*
2. *nómina ómnia*
3. *res fáciles*
4. *lingua difícilis*
5. *reges fortes*

TASK 2

1. *útilis, –e:* third declension
2. *térritus, –a, –um:* first/second declension
3. *grácilis, –e:* third declension
4. *honestus, –a, –um:* first/second declension

TASK 3

1. *verba utília*
2. *nomen honestum*
3. *reges térriti*
4. *féminae graciles*
5. *poeta honestus*
6. *res útiles*

TASK 4

1. *boni, mali, deformes*
2. *bona, mala*
3. *formosae, damnatae*
4. *difficília*

TASK 5

1. *ámbulat:* he walks
2. *ámbulant:* they walk
3. *ámbulat:* she walks
4. *ámbulat:* it walks

READING EXERCISE

The Greek language is considered more illustrious than the rest. For it is better-sounding than Latin and all (other) languages. This language is divided into five varieties. The first is *koine,* that is mixed or common, which all people use. The second is Attic, that is, Athenian, which all Greek authors write. The third is Doric, which the Egyptians and Syrians have. The fourth is Ionic, and the fifth is Aeolic.

There are four Latin languages: the original, Latin, Roman, and mixed. The original is the language that the most ancient Italians under Janus and Saturn spoke. They spoke Latin when Latinus and the Etruscans were kings. Roman is the language that the poets Naevius, Plautus, Ennius, and Vergil, and the orators Gracchus, Cicero, and the rest spoke. They spoke the mixed after the empire was more widely spread, and it was corrupt.

Now every language, whether Greek, Latin, or another, can be learned either by hearing or because a teacher teaches (it). Although there is no one to whom all languages are known, yet no one is so lazy that he does not know the language of his people. For what else is he to be regarded, except worse than brute animals?

QUIZ

1. *Latina "mixta" est corrupta:* Mixed Latin is corrupt.
2. *Ex una lingua multae gentes evéniunt:* Out of one language many peoples come forth.
3. *Tres sunt linguae sacrae: Latina, Graeca, Hebraea:* There are three sacred languages: Latin, Greek and Hebrew.
4. *Graeca est sonántior quam Latina et multae linguae:* Greek is better sounding than Latin and many languages.
5. *Omnis lingua discíbilis est audiendo, aut quia praeceptor docet:* Every language can be learned by hearing, or because a teacher teaches (it).
6. *Nemo est, cui omnes linguae notae sunt:* There is no one to whom all languages are known.

ANSWERS TO EXERCISES IN HOUR 3

TASK 1

1. beast: nominative
2. Macedonians: accusative
3. Indians: nominative
4. animal: nominative
5. horns: accusative
6. water: accusative
7. Alexander: nominative
8. men: accusative

TASK 2

1. *reginam*
2. *dóminos*
3. *patrem*
4. *manum*
5. *diem*
6. *spes*
7. *linguas*
8. *mílitem*

TASK 3

1. *hippopótamos*
2. *mílites*
3. *puellam*
4. *rem*
5. *manus*

Task 4

1. *fortes*
2. *magnus*
3. *omnem*
4. *magnum*
5. *bona* or *bonae* or *bonas*
6. *fortes*
7. *fácilem*
8. *boni* or *bonos*
9. *magna*

Task 5

1. *Macédones trans flúvium natant:* The Macedonians swim across the river.
2. *Rex circum urbem ámbulat:* The king walks around the city.
3. *Mílites propter terrorem clamant:* The soldiers shout because of fear.
4. *Aves ad terram cadunt:* The birds fall to the earth.
5. *Puella in casam currit:* The girl runs into the house.
6. *Pulla trans viam ámbulat:* The chicken walks across the road.

Task 6

1. The soldier is not able to say.
2. The hippos begin to shout.
3. The king orders the people to walk.
4. Alexander is not willing to be brave.
5. He would like to be able to teach Latin.

Task 7

1. *Alexander hippopótamos non timet:* Alexander does not fear the hippos.
2. *Hómines hippopótamos non cómedunt:* People do not eat hippos.
3. *Mílites ignes non accendunt:* The soldiers do not light fires.
4. *Alexander mílites non confortat:* Alexander does not comfort the soldiers.

Reading Exercise

Circling the river, around the eleventh hour they come to a lake which is sweet and like honey, and they pitch camp. Then Alexander orders the soldiers to cut the forest which is around the lake. And it is a spacious lake (covering) up to one mile. Then Alexander commands them to light many campfires. And when the moon begins to shine, suddenly scorpions come to the same lake to drink. Then serpents begin to come, and big and variously colored dragons, and the whole earth resounds on account of their hissing. For the same dragons have crests, and they carry their breasts erect (and have) open mouths; their breath is mortal, and through their eyes shines venom. Seeing them, the terrified soldiers think that (they) all are about to die. Then Alexander begins to comfort them, saying, "O brave fellow soldiers, do not let your mind be troubled, but just as you see me do, so do!" And saying this he immediately seizes a spear and shield and begins to fight against the dragons and serpents that come over them. Seeing this, the soldiers are very comforted, and seizing arms they similarly begin to fight against them. They kill some at (with) arms, but others with fire; and twenty soldiers perish because of the dragons, and thirty slaves. Alexander and all the army endure many difficulties, and he immediately commands them to light many fires outside the army itself.

Then from the thicket come mice bigger than foxes, and they eat the dead bodies. Bats like doves fly there, having teeth like human teeth, and they strike (them) in their faces and hit them: they rip off nostrils to (from) some, and the ears from others. As light approaches, birds big as vultures come; they have a red color, (and) they have black feet and beaks; and they do not harm them (the soldiers), but fill the whole river and begin to drag fish and eels from there and eat them.

Then (the Macedonians) leave the dangerous lands and they come into the Bactrian lands, which have gold and other riches; men receive them kindly there, and they stay for twenty days. And they find people there who are called Chinese. And there are trees there that drop leaves just like wool, which the same tribe collects and makes vestments from them. The soldiers begin to have a brave attitude because of the victories and prosperous circumstances which they have after such great misfortunes.

Quiz

A

Singular

Nominative	*puella fortis*	*rex bonus*	*nomen magnum*
Accusative	*puellam fortem*	*regem bonum*	*nomen magnum*

Plural

Nominative	*puellae fortes*	*reges boni*	*nómina magna*
Accusative	*puellas fortes*	*reges bonos*	*nómina magna*

B

1. *Alexander iubet mílites incídere silvam:* Alexander orders the soldiers to cut down the forest.
2. *Stagnus est spatiosus ad unum miliárium:* The lake is spacious (covering up) to one mile.
3. *Tota terra résonat propter síbilos eoru:* The whole earth resounds because of their hissing.
4. *Mílites pertérriti exístimant quod omnes sunt morituri:* The terrified soldiers think that (they) all are about to die.

5. *Tunc Alexander íncipit confortare eos:* Then Alexander begins to comfort them.
6. *Et statim apprehendit scutum et íncipit pugnare contra dracones:* And he immediately seizes a shield and begins to fight against the dragons.
7. *Ut lux appropinquat, véniunt aves magnae ut vúltures:* As light approaches, birds big as vultures come.
8. *Deinde invéniunt gentes quae nominatae sunt Seres:* Then they find people who are named Chinese.
9. *Sunt ibi árbores quae mittunt ipsa fólia velut lana:* There are trees there which drop leaves just like wool.
10. *Mílites habent fortem ánimum propter victórias:* The soldiers have a brave attitude because of the victories.

ANSWERS TO EXERCISES IN HOUR 4

TASK 1

1. 3rd person plural	3. 1st plural	5. 3rd singular
2. 2nd plural	4. 1st singular	6. 2nd singular

TASK 2

1. *ámbulant*	3. *ambulamus*	5. *ámbulat*
2. *ambulatis*	4. *ámbulo*	6. *ámbulas*

TASK 3

1. they ask	4. they listen	7. y'all ask
2. he/she/it listens	5. you ask	8. y'all listen
3. we ask	6. I listen	

TASK 4

1. *iubere:* II	4. *custodire:* IV	6. *salire:* IVII
2. *cantare:* I	5. *interfícere:* III	7. *monere:*
3. *scríbere:* III		

TASK 5

I	II	III	IV
ask	warn	say	find
Singular			
rogo	*móneo*	*dico*	*invénio*
rogas	*mones*	*dicis*	*ínvenis*
rogat	*monet*	*dicit*	*ínvenit*

continues

Plural

rogamus	*monemus*	*dícimus*	*invenimus*
rogatis	*monetis*	*dícitis*	*invenitis*
rogant	*monent*	*dicunt*	*invéniunt*

TASK 6

1. *rogamus*   **4.** *móneo*   **7.** *ínvenis*
2. *rogant*   **5.** *dicunt*   **8.** *ínvenit*
3. *monet*   **6.** *dícitis*

TASK 7

1. he/she/it asks   **5.** they warn   **9.** they say
2. I ask   **6.** he ... warns   **10.** they find
3. we ask   **7.** you say   **11.** y'all find
4. we warn   **8.** he ... says   **12.** you find

TASK 8

Catch	Kill
Singular	
cápio	*interfício*
capis	*intérficis*
capit	*intérficit*
Plural	
cápimus	*interfícimus*
cápitis	*interfícitis*
cápiunt	*interfíciunt*

TASK 9

1. *ámbulo, ambulare*, I   **5.** *incípio, incípere*, III *–io*
2. *dico, dícere*, III   **6.** *invénio, invenire*, IV
3. *dóceo, docere*, II   **7.** *vénio, venire*, IV
4. *fácio, fácere*, III *–io*   **8.** *vivo, vívere*, III

TASK 10

1. deprive: infinitive   **4.** help: imperative
2. went: indicative   **5.** belong: indicative
3. raise: infinitive

TASK 11

1. *roga, rogate*
2. *íncipe, incípite*
3. *mone, monete*

4. *ínveni, invenite*
5. *vive, vívite*

TASK 12

1. Begin!
2. Live!
3. Y'all warn!

4. Find!
5. Lead!
6. Ask!

7. Y'all do!
8. Y'all say!

TASK 13

1. *Noli rogare!* Do not ask!
2. *Nolite incípere!* Do not begin!
3. *Noli monere!* Do not warn!
4. *Nolite invenire!* Do not find!
5. *Noli vívere!* Do not live!

TASK 14

1. The supermarket is open for twenty-four hours.
2. We work for many days.
3. We wait for the whole day.
4. They play for three hours.
5. They beseige Troy for many years.

TASK 15

1. *sumus*
2. *sum*
3. *est*

4. *estis*
5. *sunt*

6. *est*
7. *es*

TASK 16

1. *potestis*
2. *póssumus*

3. *prosum*
4. *prodest*

5. *potest*
6. *prosunt*

7. *potes*
8. *prodestis*

TASK 17

1. he, she, it is
2. y'all are useful
3. you are able
4. he ... is able
5. they are
6. y'all are

7. he ... is useful
8. they are able
9. I am useful
10. they are useful
11. I am
12. you are

READING EXERCISE

A certain bowman catches a small bird, called a nightingale. When he wishes to kill her, the nightingale begins to speak, and says, "What is the use, O man, if you kill me? For you are not able to fill your stomach with me. But if you are willing to send me away, I have three commands; if you keep them carefully, you can get a great advantage from it." But he, astounded by her speech, promises to send her away, if she should pronounce these three useful commands. But she says, "Hear me! Do not try to seize the thing that you are not able to get! This is the first. Hear the second! Do not be sad because of a lost and irrecoverable thing. Hear the third! Do not believe an incredible word! Keep these three (rules), and it is well to you." But he, according to the promise, lets her fly away. The nightingale sings sweetly, flying through the air.

After the song she says: "Woe to you, man: you have a bad idea and you lose a great treasure today! For there is a pearl in my stomach, which is larger than an ostrich's egg." Hearing these things, he is very saddened. He stretches out his net and tries to catch her, saying, "Come into my house; I wish to feed you. You can fly at will." To him the nightingale (says), "Now I know for certain that you are foolish. Of the things that I said to you, you indeed keep none, since you are sad about me, lost but irrecoverable, and you try to catch me with your net even if you are not able to catch me, and, moreover, you believe that so big a pearl is in my stomach, even if I am, on the whole, not able to equal the measure of an ostrich's egg. You are stupid, and in stupidity you will always remain." The man returned to his home, sorrowing.

Quiz

A

1. *margaritae grandes*
2. *fortunas meliores*
3. *consílium forte*
4. *res pérditae*
5. *margaritam grandiorem*

B

1. *Sagittárius avículam parvam capit, nómine philomelam:* The bowman catches a little bird, called a nightingale.
2. *Philomela íncipit dícere, et ait, "Quid prodest, o homo, si me occidis?"* The nightingale begins to speak, and says, "What's the use, O man, if you kill me?"
3. *Non enim ventrem tuum de me implere potes:* You can not fill your stomach from (with) me.
4. *Audi me! Noli rem, quae apprehéndere non potes, apprehéndere temptare!:* Listen to me! Don't try to seize something that you cannot get!
5. *Vae tibi, homo, malum consílium habes!* Woe to you, man, you have a bad idea!
6. *Nunc pro certo scio, quod fátuus es:* Now I know for sure that you are stupid.
7. *Ego tota ad modum ovi stuthionis non possum attingere:* I, as a whole, cannot equal the size of an ostrich's egg.

ANSWERS TO EXERCISES IN HOUR 5

TASK 1

1. *fémina, féminis*
2. *equo, equis*
3. *perículo, perículis*
4. *dracone, dracónibus*
5. *exércitu, exercítibus*
6. *re, rebus*

TASK 2

1. nominative singular
2. accusative singular
3. ablative singular
4. nominative or ablative singular
5. nominative plural
6. nominative or accusative plural
7. ablative singular
8. accusative singular
9. nominative or ablative singular
10. nominative singular, nominative or accusative plural
11. accusative plural
12. ablative plural
13. accusative singular
14. ablative singular
15. nominative or accusative singular

TASK 3

1. *fémina tristi*
2. *rege magno*
3. *rebus ómnibus*
4. *cúrribus magnis*
5. *die tristi*
6. *dóminis fórtibus*

TASK 4

1. with the horse
2. under the sea
3. on the table
4. in the house
5. over the land
6. out of the city
7. (down) from the mountains
8. out of the place
9. from the chariot
10. with the king
11. in front of the city
12. from the sea

TASK 5

1. with a sword.
2. from Rome.
3. with great diligence.
4. with fire and the sword.
5. on that day.
6. in/with a loud voice.
7. with hammer and nails.
8. from their country.

READING EXERCISE

St. George finds a girl sitting near the lake and weeping a lot. And he says to her, "Woman, why are you weeping? Why do you sit in this awful place?" And the girl responds, "Sir, this is the city of Lisia, which is very good and excellent, and filled with all good things. But it has in it one very great evil, which overcomes every evil. In the water dwells a very cruel dragon, who comes out of the water every day and fights against the emperor and against the people and devours all [the people]. All the citizens have already given up their sons; my father gives up his only daughter. There, you have everything. Go then in peace."

But St. George, raising his eyes to heaven, calls upon God, saying, "Show a sign now through your great mercy, and send this evil beast beneath my feet." Then a voice from heaven comes to him, saying, "O George, I do as you ask. Do what you will; I am with you."

After this a great bellowing comes from the water. The girl exclaims in a great voice, "Sir, flee quickly; look, the evil dragon is coming." St. George, hastening to it, makes the sign of the Holy Cross, saying, "Lord God, give me power against this dragon." When he says this, the dragon suddenly falls before his feet. He says to the girl: "Untie your belt and my bridle and bring them to me." She unties and hands over her belt and the bridle. St. George says, "Take hold of the dragon and walk with it through the middle of the city."

When the people see this great miracle, the holy man exclaims with a great voice, "Do not fear! Believe in the living God and in Jesus Christ, his Son, and I will kill the dragon." The people shout, "We believe!" Then St. George cuts off the head of the dragon.

QUIZ

A

1. we see
2. they say
3. y'all give
4. I have
5. you sit
6. he … fears
7. they come
8. you are
9. y'all can
10. he/she/it goes

B

1. *pro casa:* in front of the house
2. *ad casam:* to the house
3. *per casam:* through the house
4. *super casa:* over the house
5. *in casa:* in the house
6. *a casa:* from the house
7. *de casa:* (down) from the house
8. *e casa:* out of the house
9. *sub casa:* under the house

C

1. *Sanctus Geórgius ínvenit puellam sedentem prope lacum:* St. George finds a girl sitting near the lake.
2. *"Múlier, cur ploras?"* "Woman, why are you crying?"
3. *"Cur sedes in indigno loco?"* "Why do you sit in an awful place?"
4. *Lísia est cívitas óptima, omnibus bonis repleta:* Lisia is an excellent city, filled with all good things.

5. *In aqua hábitat draco tetérrimus, qui cotídie dévorat cives multos:* In the water lives a very cruel dragon, who devours many citizens every day.

6. *Sanctus Geórgius élevat óculos ad caelum et Deum ínvocat:* St. George raises his eyes to heaven and calls upon God.

7. *"Ostende signum nunc, et mitte hanc béstiam sub pédibus meis":* "Show a sign now, and send this beast under my feet."

8. *Puella exclamat voce magna, "Dómine, fuge velóciter":* The girl exclaims in a great voice, "Sir, flee quickly."

9. *"Dómine, da mihi virtutem contra draconem istum":* "Lord, give me power against this dragon."

10. *Puella ámbulat cum eo per médiam cívitatem:* The girl walks with it through the middle of the city.

11. *Omnes viri, ubi hoc magnum miráculum vident, exclamant, "Crédimus!"* All the men, when they see this great miracle, exclaim, "We believe."

ANSWERS TO EXERCISES IN HOUR 6

TASK 1

1. Who captures a small bird? (nominative)
2. Whom does St. George find near the river? (accusative)
3. What does the nightingale say? (accusative)
4. About what is the bowman sorry? (ablative)
5. What is on the table? (nominative)

TASK 2

1. *Qui homo avículam capit? Sagittárius:* Which man captures a small bird? The bowman.

2. *Quam avículam sagittárius capit? Philomelam:* Which/what small bird does the bowman catch? The nightingale.

3. *Quae puella draconem expectat? Imperatoris fília:* Which girl does the dragon wait for? The emperor's daughter.

4. *Quod monstrum Sanctus Geórgius occidit? Draconem:* Which monster does St. George kill? The dragon.

5. *Quam ob rem dolet sagittárius? Ob magaritam pérditam:* Because of what thing is the bowman sad? Because of a lost pearl.

6. *In qua urbe hábitat puella? Lísia:* In which city does the girl live? Lisia.

TASK 3

1. How many soldiers do the hippos devour?
2. In how much danger are we?
3. What kind of books do you read?
4. How many monsters has St. George overcome?
5. With what kind of men do we live?

Task 4

1. *Qualis avícula est philomela?* What kind of bird is the nightingale?
2. *In quali casa hábitas?* In what kind of house do you live?
3. *Qualem librum in manu habes?* What kind of book do you have in your hand?
4. *Quales féminae latine discunt?* What sort of women learn Latin?
5. *Quália verba dicit pópulus?* What sort of words does the people say?
6. *Quale monstrum terret civitatem?* What sort of monster terrifies the city?
7. *De quálibus libris sapiéntiam díscimus?* From what kind of books do we learn wisdom?

Task 5

1. *Quid Mágdala in manu tenet? Librum latinum:* What does Magdala have in her hand? A Latin book.
2. *Cur Mágdala libros legit? Sápiens esse cupit:* Why does Magdala read books? She wants to be wise.
3. *Quando draco Lísiam terret? Cotídie:* When does the dragon terrify Lisia? Every day.
4. *Quis imperatoris fíliam servat? Georgius:* Who saves the Emperor's daughter? George.
5. *Quómodo Latinam díscimus? Celériter:* How do we learn Latin? Quickly.
6. *Quando hanc lectionem complemus? Mox:* When do we finish this lesson? Soon.
7. *Quo instrumento Geórgius caput draconis ámputat? Gládio:* How (with what instrument) does G. cut off the dragon's head? With a sword.

Task 6

1. *Terrentne hippopótami mílites?* Do the hippos terrify the soldiers?
2. *Sapiuntne féminae?* Are women wise?
3. *Caditne draco ante Sanctum Geórgium?* Does the dragon fall before St. George?
4. *Doletne sagittárius?* Is the bowman sad?
5. *Discimusne velóciter?* Do we learn Latin quickly?

Task 7

1. Does St. George fight with the dragon?
2. Is Lisia a very good city?
3. Does the girl sit near the water?
4. Do the people fear the dragon?
5. Are the dragons large?

Task 8

1. Doesn't the abbot drink wine? (The abbot drinks wine, doesn't he?) The abbot doesn't drink wine, does he?

2. Don't the hippos eat people? The hippos don't eat people, do they?

3. Isn't St. George afraid? St. George isn't afraid, is he?

4. Don't the people believe in God? The people don't believe in God, do they?

5. Aren't the hippos friendly? The hippos aren't friendly, are they?

TASK 9

1. The hippos don't scare the soldiers, do they?

2. Aren't women wise?

3. We don't learn Latin quickly, do we?

4. Isn't the bowman sad?

TASK 10

1. No, (he isn't).

2. No; (rather,) the dragon is afraid.

3. No, (not at all).

4. You bet it is! (Yes!)

TASK 11

Once upon a time two clerics were walking outside the city at nightfall. Soon they came to a place **where ruffians were known to meet.** One cleric said, "Let us go another way. **As the philosopher says,** 'Do not pass through an unjust nation.'" The other said, "It won't hurt to pass through." Then they heard a sweet song **that came from a nearby inn.** One of the clerics went his way, but the other, **because he was pleased by the song,** entered and sat down. Suddenly, the sheriff entered the house and arrested all those present, **because the inn was a notorius den of thieves. Although he protested,** the cleric was led with the rest to execution.

TASK 12

1. *Populus timet, quia draco dévorat multos.*

2. *Ubi/cum Georgius haec dicit, cadit draco ante pedes eius.*

3. *Si créditis in Deum, nolite timere draconem!*

4. *Puella manet prope flúvium, ubi draco hábitat.*

TASK 13

1. a girl

2. the horse

3. people

TASK 14

1. whom

2. who

3. whom

4. who

5. whom

Task 15

1. *quae*   **5.** *quibus*
2. *quod*   **6.** *quam*
3. *qui*   **7.** *quae*
4. *quem*   **8.** *quos*

Reading Exercise

An. I put up with books; I do not put up with Latin ones.

Ma. Why?

An. Because that language does not suit women.

Ma. Isn't it appropriate, if a woman born in Germany learns French?

An. Yes.

Ma. Why?

An. She can have a conversation with people who know French.

Ma. And do you think that it is inappropriate if I learn Latin, and I have a conversation every day with so many authors, with such eloquent, such learned, such wise, such faithful advisers?

An. Books absorb much of women's brains ("take away much of the brain from women").

Ma. How much brains you have, I do not know; I certainly would prefer to consume the little that I have in good studies, rather than in nocturnal parties, in drinking up large cups.

An. I indeed do not want a learned wife.

Ma. But I rejoice that I have a husband unlike you. For he loves me more because I am learned, whom I also love on account of (his) learning.

An. I hear it frequently said, that a wise woman is twice stupid.

Ma. Indeed, people who are stupid say that. A woman who is truly wise does not think herself wise. On the other hand, she who thinks herself wise is twice stupid. What do you think about the Virgin Mary? About Paula and Eustochium? They read sacred books, didn't they?

An. But that is now rare.

Ma. Once an ignorant abbot was rare like that; now nothing is more common. Once princes and Caesars were not less learned than powerful. Nor is a learned woman so rare as you think; there are not a few thoroughly noble women, who are able to contend with any man. Therefore, beware! We will preside in theological schools; we will preach in churches!

Quiz

1. *Fero libros, non fero Latinos:* I put up with books; I don't put up with Latin ones.

2. *Quápropter? Quia non cónvenit féminis:* Why? Because it is not appropriate for women.
3. *Nonne decorum est, si fémina discit Gállice?* Isn't it fitting, if a woman learns French?
4. *Ego nolo uxorem doctam:* I do not want a learned wife.
5. *Fémina quae vere sapit, non putat se sapientem:* A woman who is truly wise does not think herself wise.
6. *Neque ádeo rara est fémina docta, ut tu putas:* Nor is a learned woman as rare as you think.
7. *Sunt in Itália non paucae mulíeres adprime nóbiles, quae cum quovis viro possunt conténdere:* There are in Italy not a few very noble women, who can compete with any man.

ANSWERS TO EXERCISES IN HOUR 7

TASK 1

1. used to fight: past habitual
2. made: past simple
3. will decide: future simple
4. killed: past simple
5. were coming: past progressive
6. are running: present progressive
7. will be falling: future progressive
8. turned: past simple

TASK 2

1. *ambulabat*
2. *ambulabatis*
3. *ambulabam*
4. *ambulabamus*
5. *ambulabant*
6. *ambulabas*

TASK 3

1. y'all walked
2. I was walking
3. we were walking
4. he was walking
5. they were walking
6. you were walking

TASK 4

1. *docebam*
2. *docebamus*
3. *docebatis*
4. *mittebas*
5. *mittebat*
6. *mittebant*
7. *audiebant*
8. *audiebam*
9. *audiebamus*

TASK 5

1. we were teaching
2. you were teaching
3. they were teaching
4. I was sending
5. y'all were sending
6. he was sending
7. you were hearing
8. he was hearing
9. y'all were hearing

TASK 6

1. *ambulabo*
2. *ambulabis*
3. *ambulabunt*
4. *docebit*
5. *docébimus*
6. *docébitis*

TASK 7

1. *mittam*
2. *mittemus*
3. *mittent*
4. *mittetis*
5. *aúdiet*
6. *aúdies*
7. *aúdiam*
8. *aúdient*

TASK 8

1. *ambulabit*
2. *aúdiam*
3. *amabo*
4. *mittet*
5. *ducent*
6. *iubébitis*
7. *fáciet*
8. *capiemus*
9. *vénient*
10. *docebit*
11. *iubebis*
12. *cápies*

TASK 9

1. *est, erat:* he was; *erit:* he will be
2. *estis, eratis:* y'all were; *eritis:* y'all will be
3. *sunt, erant:* they were; *erunt:* they will be
4. *sum, eram:* I was; *ero:* I will be
5. *sumus, eramus:* we were; *erimus:* we will be
6. *es, eras:* you were; *eris:* you will be

TASK 10

1. y'all are able
2. y'all were useful
3. you were able
4. I will be useful
5. we will be able
6. they will be useful
7. they are able
8. I am useful

READING EXERCISE

Honorius, a very rich man, who had an only son whom he loved a lot, was the ruler. The reputation of the emperor spread through the world, because he was in all things upright and just. Nevertheless, he was waging a war against a king and he was devastating him. At length the king thought: "I only have one daughter, and my adversary, one son. If in some way I will be able to join my daughter to his son in matrimony, I will obtain lasting peace." He sent his daughter to the emperor in a ship with a treasure and five soldiers, with handmaidens.

The emperor, when he saw her, said, "Dearest daughter, before you will have my son as husband, I will test you through one act." While he was saying this, he bought out three caskets. The first was (made) of the purest gold and precious stones. And over the casket was an inscription like this: "Who(ever) will open me, will find in me what he deserves." And the whole casket was filled with the bones of dead people. The second was made of the purest silver, and of gems from (in) every part, which had an inscription like this: "Who(ever) chooses me, will find in me what nature gives." This casket was filled with earth. The third casket was made of lead, having an inscription like this: "I choose rather to be and to rest here than to remain in the treasure of the king." In this casket were three precious rings.

Then the emperor said to the girl: "Dearest one, here are three caskets; choose whichever you wish; and if you (will) choose well, you will obtain my son as husband." She inspected the three caskets closely and said in her heart: "God, who sees all things, give me the grace of so choosing that I will not fail him, for whom I have labored much." Then she touched the first casket and read the inscription: "Whoever (chooses) me ...." She thought, "The outside of the casket is precious, but what lies hidden inside, I do not know at all; thus I do not wish to choose it." Then she read the second. She said: "Nature never grants that the daughter of my father should marry the son of the emperor. And so ...." She read the third casket saying, "It is better for me to rest with the son of the emperor than in my father's treasures." And she shouted with a loud voice: "I choose this third casket." The emperor said: "Good girl! You choose prudently enough. In that casket are three of my precious rings; one for me, one for my son, and the third for you as a sign of engagement." Immediately he celebrated the wedding, and handed his son to her, and thus they ended their life in peace.

QUIZ

A

1. imperfect; they were shouting
2. present; they have
3. present; you open
4. imperfect; he was able
5. future; he ... will test
6. future; he ... will say
7. present; they think
8. future; we will come

B

1. *Honórius unicum fílium habebat:* Honorius had one son.
2. *Fama imperatoris per mundum volabat, quod in ómnibus probus erat et iustus:* The reputation of the emperor spread through the world, because in all things he was upright and just.
3. *Misit fíliam suam ad imperatorem in nave cum thesauro:* He sent his daughter to the emperor in a ship with treasure.
4. *Primus cóphinus erat de auro puríssimo et lapídibus pretiosis:* The first casket was (made) of purest gold and precious stones.

5. *"Qui me apériet, in me invéniet quod méruit."* "Whoever will open me, will find in me what he deserves."

6. *Secundus habebat talem superscriptionem:* The second had an inscription like this ….

7. *Pótius éligo hic esse quam in thesauris regis permanere:* I choose rather to be here than to remain in the treasures of the king.

8. *In cóphino sunt tres ánuli:* In the casket are three rings.

ANSWERS TO EXERCISES IN HOUR 8

TASK 1

1. *féminae, feminarum*
2. *equi, equorum*
3. *perículi, periculorum*
4. *draconis, draconum*
5. *manus, mánuum*
6. *spei, sperum*
7. *generis, generum*
8. *mílitis, mílitum*

TASK 2

1. *finis, fínium*
2. *animalis, animálium*
3. *civis, cívium*

TASK 3

1. genitive singular, nominative plural
2. genitive singular
3. accusative plural
4. genitive plural
5. accusative singular
6. ablative singular
7. genitive plural
8. genitive singular
9. nominative singular, ablative singular
10. genitive singular
11. nominative singular, accusative singular
12. nominative singular, genitive singular, nominative plural, accusative plural
13. accusative singular
14. nominative plural, accusative plural

TASK 4

1. *féminae omnis*
2. *regis magni*
3. *rerum ómnium*
4. *cúrruum magnorum*
5. *diei omnis*
6. *dominorum fórtium*

TASK 5

1. *equus Geórgii:* the horse of George, George's horse
2. *fília regis:* the daughter of the king, the king's daughter

3. *mílites Alexandri:* the soldiers of Alexander, Alexander's soldiers
4. *libri féminae:* the books of the woman, the woman's books
5. *lingua Romanorum:* the language of the Romans, the Romans' language
6. *dentes hippopotamorum:* the teeth of the hippos, the hippos' teeth

TASK 6

1. *multi mílitum:* many of the soldiers
2. *timor hippopotamorum:* fear of the hippos
3. *fémina magnae sapiéntiae:* a woman of great wisdom

TASK 7

1. *áquila:* 1, *aquil-*
2. *celéritas:* 3, *celeritat-*
3. *cibus:* 2, *cib-*
4. *scelus:* 3, *sceler-*
5. *fácies:* 5, *faci-*
6. *latratus:* 4, *latrat-*

TASK 8

1. *fémina audax, audaci*
2. *monstrum ingens*
3. *feminarum audácium*
4. *monstris ingéntibus*
5. *féminae audacis, audaces*
6. *monstrorum ingéntium*

TASK 9

1. *puellas paúperes*
2. *puellarum paúperum*
3. *úbium pauperum*
4. *dómino paúpere*
5. *regis paúperis*
6. *res pauper, paúperes*
7. *féminae paúperis, paúperes*
8. *dómini: paúperis, paúperes*

READING EXERCISE

THE CROW AND THE WOLF

A crow was eating cheese (which he had) snatched from a window, sitting in a high tree. A wolf, seeing him, begins to praise the shine of his wings and the beauty of his head, and the elegance of his entire body. He says, "One thing is lacking, a sonorous voice. If he had this (which), he would outdo all birds easily." But the crazy crow wished to show that he had a voice (that was) both pleasant and suave. And while he gets ready for singing, he lets the cheese go from his beak, which the sneaky wolf quickly snatches with his eager teeth.

Moral: He who listens to flatterers willingly ought to listen to this fable.

THE TORTOISE AND THE EAGLE

A tortoise takes up a contest with an eagle covering a certain space. He proposes a place and says, "Whichever (of us) arrives first at this place on the third day will be the victor." The eagle, holding the slowness of the tortoise in contempt, begins to fly ahead, and to rest often, to do other things, and finally to rest the whole night and not to fly off very early. But the tortoise does not let up at all on the trip, and goes on day and night, and marches straight to the destined place. And so, with his diligence, he arrived first to the destined place, and beat the eagle.

Moral: The motion of zeal and mind is more effective for speed, than (movement) of the body.

THE CITY MOUSE AND THE COUNTRY MOUSE

Once upon a time, a country mouse receives a city mouse into his poor cave. The latter, however, does not want the slight food that his host offers: chickpeas and oats. "Why," he says, "do you live so? Don't you wish to come with me to the city, where we will be better off?" The country mouse agrees. From there both continue to the city in the middle of the night, until they come to a rich home. There are many scraps left over from a large dinner there, placed in large baskets. There the city mouse seats his friend and sets a continuous feast (before him). The latter, eating eagerly, rejoices over his changed fortune. Suddenly, however, a huge noise shakes (them) both: they are scared out of their wits and run scared through the whole house. The house rings with the deep barking of Molossian dogs.

Then the country mouse says this:

"I hardly need this kind of life. Farewell: the forest and my cave, safe from attack, will relieve me with their slender seed."

QUIZ

A

1. *amicorum véterum*
2. *domus altae*
3. *rex audax*
4. *fília tristis*
5. *nocti longo, nocte longo*
6. *mílitem bonum*
7. *corpus ingens*
8. *úbium optimarum*
9. *diebus bonis*

B

1. *Corvus raptum de fenestra cáseum comedebat:* The crow ate cheese (that he had) snatched from the window.
2. *Vulpes laudare íncipit pennarum nitorem:* The wolf begins to praise the sheen of his feathers.
3. *At corvus demens, cupiebat ostendere quod vocem habebat canoram:* But the crazy crow wanted to show that he had a pleasant voice.
4. *Dum se ad canendum cómparat, cáseum emittit rostro:* While he prepares himself to sing, he drops the cheese from his beak.
5. *Testudo ait, "uter prior ad hunc locum pervéniet die tertio, victor erit":* The tortoise says, "whichever (of us) will come first to this place on the third day will be the winner."

6. *Itaque sedulitate sua ad locum designatum prior advenit:* And so, with his diligence, he came first to the designated place.

7. *Mus urbanus "Cur" inquit, "ita vivis? Nonne vis mecum ad urbem venire?"* The city mouse says, "Why do you live this way? Don't you wish to come with me to the city?"

8. *Multa ibi fercula de magna cena supersunt, in magnis canistris posita:* Many scraps from a big dinner were left over there, placed in big cannisters.

9. *Exánimes trepidant et pávidi per totam domum currunt:* They are scared out of their wits and run terrified through the whole house.

10. *Pérsonat domus alta latratu canum Molossiorum:* The house resounds with the deep barking of Molossian dogs.

ANSWERS TO EXERCISES IN HOUR 9

TASK 1

1. *ambulávimus*
2. *ambulaverunt*
3. *ambulavit*
4. *ambulavi*
5. *ambulavisti*
6. *ambulavistis*

TASK 2

1. *apéruit*
2. *accepisti*
3. *dedisti*
4. *iússimus*
5. *vicistis*
6. *didícimus*
7. *dixerunt*
8. *cucurri*
9. *cepit*

TASK 3

1. *cuccurrit:* perfect
2. *dicit:* present
3. *réddidit:* perfect
4. *vincit:* present
5. *dixit:* perfect
6. *videt:* present
7. *hábuit:* perfect
8. *fecit:* perfect
9. *habet:* present
10. *amat:* present
11. *dedit:* perfect
12. *vidit:* perfect

TASK 4

1. Once upon a time, a father summoned his son.
2. "Now you have spoken truly, father."
3. Then my friends said, "We already have wandered the entire night."
4. Then we returned home.

TASK 5

1. *iuste:* justly
2. *nobíliter:* nobly
3. *certe:* certainly
4. *aeque:* equally
5. *rationáliter:* rationally
6. *gráviter:* gravely

TASK 6

1. *ibam:* I was going
2. *ite!* Go!
3. *ferunt:* they carry
4. *iisti:* you went
5. *tulerunt:* they carried

6. *feram:* I will carry
7. *ferent:* they will carry
8. *eo:* I go
9. *ibis:* you will go
10. *tulit:* he, she, it carried

READING EXERCISE

An Arab who was about to die called his son and said: "Say, son: how many friends have you obtained while I have been alive? In answer, the son said, "I have obtained one hundred friends, I think." The father said, "The philosopher says: 'Do not praise a friend until you will have tested him.' I indeed am old and I have acquired scarcely half a friend. How, then, have you acquired one hundred? Go therefore and test them all, and learn if any of them at all will be a complete friend to you!" The son said, "How will I test them?" The father said, "Kill a calf and put (it), (after it has been) cut into pieces, into a sack, and the sack will be dyed with blood on the outside. And when you (will) come to a friend, say: "Dear friend of mine, I have killed a man by accident; bury him, I ask you; for no one will hold you under suspicion, and thus you will be able to save me." The son did just as the father ordered. However the first friend to whom he came said, "Take the dead guy with you over your own neck! As you have done evil, so pay the penalty! You will not enter into my home." As he did this (going) through all (his friends) one by one, they all responded in the same way. And so, returning to his father, he announced what he had done. His father said,"(What) happened to you (is) what the philosopher said: 'Friends are many while they are counted, but in necessity, they are few.' Go to the half-friend I have and see what he says!" (The son) went and spoke to this one just as he had done to the others. (The other) said, "Enter my house! We ought not to spread this secret abroad!" And so, he sent out his wife with all his family, and dug a grave. However, when he saw all things prepared, (the son) explained the matter, just as it was, and gave thanks. Then he returned to his father and told him all about it. The father said, "Regarding such a friend the philosopher says, 'He is truly a friend who helps you when the world fails you.'"

QUIZ

A

1. *Vade ígitur et proba omnes amicos:* Go therefore and test all (your) friends.
2. *Quómodo probabo eos?* How shall I test them?
3. *Fecit fílius sicut pater imperavit:* The son did just as the father ordered.

4. *Sicut tu fecisti malum, poenam da! In domum meam non intrabis:* Just as you have done evil, pay the penalty! You will not enter into my house!

5. *Ad patrem rédiit et ómnia narravit:* He returned to his father and told (him) all.

6. *Vade ad amicum quam ego hábeo dimídium:* Go to the half friend that I have.

7. *Fílius ad patrem rédiit et ómnia narravit:* The son returned to his father and told (him) all.

B

1. *Fílius centum amicos acquisivit.*
2. *Noli laudare amicos donec probabis eos.*
3. *Arabs dimídium amicum habet.*
4. *Fílius vítulum interfecit.*
5. *Amici fílium non acceperunt.*
6. *Amici sunt pauci in necessitate.*
7. *Verus amicus est qui te adiuvat, cum saéculum tibi déficit.*

ANSWERS TO EXERCISES IN HOUR 10

TASK 1

1. *dómino, dóminis*
2. *exercítui, exercítibus*
3. *féminae, féminis*
4. *hómini, homínibus*
5. *mánui, mánibus*
6. *luci, lúcibus*
7. *mundo, mundis*
8. *speciei, speciebus*

TASK 2

1. *consílio, consíliis*
2. *córpori, corpóribus*
3. *fini, fínibus*
4. *animali, animálibus*

TASK 3

1. *féminis:* dative or ablative plural
2. *dómino:* dative or ablative singular
3. *corpóribus:* dative or ablative plural
4. *fíliae:* genitive or dative singular, nominative plural
5. *mari:* dative or ablative singular
6. *rei:* genitive or dative singular

TASK 4

1. The boys walk with the girls.
2. The boys give flowers to the girls.
3. The girls receive flowers from the boys.
4. The father hears the voice of (his) daughter.
5. The father gives an answer to (his) daughter.
6. The daughters love their dad.

Task 5

1. *féminae omni*
2. *cúrrui magno*
3. *consílio omni*
4. *regi magno*
5. *diei omni*
6. *rei magnae*
7. *rebus ómnibus*
8. *mari magno*
9. *dóminis fórtibus*

Task 6

1. *exércitu omni:* ablative singular
2. *regis magni:* genitive singular
3. *hómini omni:* dative singular
4. *hómines magni:* nominative plural
5. *animali forti:* dative or ablative singular

Task 7

1. I will show the book to Caesar.
2. We cooked a delicious meal for mother.
3. Arsenic is dangerous to people.
4. This solution is evident to all.
5. That film is not suitable for children.

Task 8

1. We serve a just master.
2. The Latin language was useful (for use) to the Romans.
3. The flowers, which I gave, do not please the girl.
4. We study many things in school.
5. Sons always ought to obey their fathers.
6. Brutus met Caesar in the city.

Task 9

1. *linguae omnes:* nominative plural
2. *regum bonorum:* genitive plural
3. *perícula grándia:* nominative or accusative plural
4. *draco péssimus:* nominative singular
5. *naves multas:* accusative plural
6. *urbi magnae:* dative singular
7. *manus una:* nominative singular
8. *manus dextrae:* genitive singular or nominative plural
9. *res pública:* nominative singular
10. *dómini fortis:* genitive singular
11. *féminae omni:* dative singular
12. *viro paúpere:* ablative singular

Task 10

1. *Non nobis, sed nómini tuo da glóriam!*
2. *Vídeo te; potesne me videre?*
3. *Timor vestri non movet me, sed amor.*
4. *Numquam mihi flores das exinde.*
5. *Grátias ágimus tibi, quia nos adiuvisti.*
6. *Magna pars mei cupit hoc exercítium pergere.*

Reading Exercise

Nero, (being) very similar to Caligula, his uncle, suceeded Claudius; he both deformed and diminished the Roman empire, (being) a man of unusual luxury and extravagance. He killed an incalculable portion of the senate; he was an enemy to all good (people). To the end, he prostituted himself most disgracefully, for he used to dance and sing on stage in burlesque or tragic clothing. He committed many acts of parricide, killing his brother, wife, sister, and mother. He burned the city (of) Rome, because he wished to see a spectacle such as that in which captured Troy once burned. Having dared nothing at all in warfare, he almost lost Britain. For under him (his rule) enemies captured and sacked two noble towns. The Parthians took away Armenia and sent the Roman legions into slavery.

(When) because of all these things (he had become) detestable to the Roman world, all people deserted him and the senate judged him an enemy. They sought him for punishment, and the punishment was such: to flog him, having been led through public naked and carrying a fork, and to throw him from a rock. Therefore he fled from the Palatine and killed himself in the suburban villa of his freedman. He built the Roman baths, which before (we called) "Neronian," (but) now we call "Alexandrian." He died in his thirty-second year, the fourteenth of his rule, and the whole family of Augustus died in him.

Quiz

A

	I	II	III	IV	V
	girl	*master*	*king*	*chariot*	*thing*
Singular					
Nominative	*puell-a*	*domin-us*	*rex*	*curr-us*	*r-es*
Genitive	*puell-ae*	*domin-i*	***reg-is***	*curr-us*	*r-ei*
Dative	***puell-ae***	*domin-o*	*reg-i*	*curr-ui*	***r-ei***
Accusative	*puell-am*	*domin-um*	*reg-em*	*curr-um*	*r-em*
Ablative	*puell-a*	***domin-o***	*reg-e*	***curr-u***	*r-e*

Plural

Nominative	*puell-ae*	*domin-i*	*reg-es*	*curr-us*	*r-es*
Genitive	*puell-arum*	*domin-orum*	*reg-um*	*curr-uum*	*r-erum*
Dative	*puell-is*	*domin-is*	*reg-ibus*	*curr-ibus*	*r-ebus*
Accusative	*puell-as*	*domin-os*	*reg-es*	*curr-us*	*r-es*
Ablative	*puell-is*	*domin-is*	*reg-ibus*	*curr-ibus*	*r-ebus*

B

1. *Successit Nero, Calígulae simíllimus:* Nero succeeded, being very similar to Caligula.
2. *Infinitam senatus partem interfecit; bonis ómnibus hostis fuit:* He killed an incalculable portion of the senate; he was an enemy to all good people.
3. *Nam saltabat et cantabat in scaena:* For he danced and sang on the stage.
4. *Parricídia multa commisit, fratrem, uxorem, sororem, matrem interfíciens:* He committed many acts of parricide, killing his brother, wife, sister, and mother.
5. *Urbem Romam incendit, quia spectáculum cérnere cupiebat:* He burned the city of Rome, because he wished to see the spectacle.
6. *In Brittánia hostes duo óppida ceperunt:* In Britain, (our) enemies took two towns.
7. *Nero e Palátio fugit:* Nero fled from the palace.

Answers to Exercises in Hour 11

Task 1

1. *aperúerat*
2. *iusseramus*
3. *díxerant*
4. *accéperas*
5. *viceratis*
6. *cucúrreram*

Task 2

1. *déderis*
2. *didicérimus*
3. *céperit*
4. *obíero*
5. *potuéritis*
6. *fúerint*

Task 3

1. The boy will do just as his father will have ordered (orders).
2. When you had killed the king, you fled the city.
3. He told his father everything that he had done.
4. When Caesar had conquered the enemy, he acted more insolently.
5. The city mouse said, "If you will have come (come) with me, you will eat well."

Task 4

1. *ea*	**4.** *id*	**7.** *eis*	**10.** *ei*
2. *ei*	**5.** *eius*	**8.** *(cum) eo*	**11.** *eius*
3. *eorum*	**6.** *eum*	**9.** *is*	**12.** *eas*

Task 5

1. Honorius waged war against a king and was clobbering him.
2. George said, "God, grant me power against that dragon. With your help, I will overcome it."
3. The king thought, "I have one daughter. If I marry her to Honorius' son, I will have peace."
4. My house is burning! I will hasten to it.
5. We are hastening to that city, in which the dragon lives.
6. We all praise those who know Latin.

Task 6

1. The abbot calls Magdala; she answers him.
2. That book does not please me.
3. At that time, Nero fought against the senate; it denounced him.
4. George hurried to the dragon; it shouted mightily.
5. Those men do not fear the hippos; they, however, devour the men.

Reading Exercise

On the fourth day Holofernes made dinner for his servants, and said to Vagao, his eunuch: "Go, and persuade that Hebrew woman to live with me voluntarily. For it is unseemly among the Assyrians if a woman mocks a man and passes from him unscathed."

Then Vagao went in to Judith, and said: "Don't fear, good girl. Go in to my master; he will honor you and you will eat with him, and you will drink wine in enjoyment." Judith responded to him, "Surely I will not contradict my master? All that shall be good and best before his eyes I will do; and whatever pleases him, will be best to me all the days of my life." And she rose, and adorned herself with her clothing; and having entered she stood before his face. Now, the heart of Holofernes was stricken, for it was burning in desire for her. And Holofernes said to her, "Drink now, and recline in enjoyment, because you have found favor before me." And Judith said, "I will drink, master, because today my spirit is elated more than all of my days." And she took, and ate, and drank before him that which her handmaiden had prepared for her. And, having been made merry toward her, Holofernes drank a great deal of wine, as much as he had never drunk in his life.

However, when it was late, his servants hurried to their lodgings, and Vagao closed the doors of the bedroom and went away. All were tired from the wine; and Judith was alone in the bedroom. Holofernes was lying in the bed, asleep with excessive drinking. Judith stood before the bed, praying with tears and with movement of her lips in silence, saying, "Strengthen me, O Lord, the God of Israel, and look upon the works of my hands in this hour, and just as you promised, raise up Jerusalem, your city; and I will accomplish this thing, which I have believed could be done through you." And when she had said these things, she went to the column which was at the head of his bed and untied his dagger, because it was hanging (there), tied to it. And when she had drawn it, she seized the hair on his head, and said, "Strengthen me, O Lord God, in this hour." And she struck at his neck twice and cut off his head, and took away his canopy from the columns, and rolled his headless body away.

Quiz

A

Verb Synopsis Table

Present	*amant*	*míttimus*
Imperfect	*amabant*	*mittebamus*
Future	*amabunt*	*mittemus*
Perfect	*amaverunt*	*mísimus*
Pluperfect	*amáverant*	*miseramus*
Future Perfect	*amáverint*	*misérimus*
Present	*cápio*	*est*
Imperfect	*capiebam*	*erat*
Future	*cápiam*	*erit*
Perfect	*cepi*	*fuit*
Pluperfect	*céperam*	*fúerat*
Future Perfect	*cépero*	*fúerit*

B

1. *In quarto die Holofernes fecit cenam servis:* On the fourth day Holofernes made dinner for his servants.
2. *Dixit Vágao ad Iudith: "Noli timere, bona puella":* Vagao said to Judith: "Don't fear, good girl."
3. *Honorificabit te et manducabis cum eo:* He will honor you and you will eat with him.
4. *Quicquid Domino meo placúerit, hoc mihi erit óptimum:* Whatever will have pleased my master, this will be best to me.

5. *Holofernes erat ardens in concupiscéntia eius:* Holofernes was burning in (with) desire of her.
6. *Et dixit ad eam "Bibe nunc, quóniam invenisti grátiam coram me":* And he said to her, "Drink now, because you found favor before me."

ANSWERS TO EXERCISES IN HOUR 12

TASK 1

1. *accípiens*   3. *ostendens*   5. *sciens*
2. *parans*   4. *placens*   6. *putans*

TASK 2

1. *puellas ambulantes*
2. *puellae ambulantis, ambulanti, ambulantes*
3. *puella ambulans, ambulante*
4. *virum ambulantem*
5. *viro ambulanti, ambulante*
6. *viri ambulantis, ambulantes*
7. *mánui ambulanti*
8. *mánuum ambulántium*
9. *manus ámbulans, ambulantis, ambulantes*

TASK 3

1. George, hurrying/as he was hurrying to the city, saw the girl.
2. To the girl weeping/who was weeping, he said "Don't be afraid."
3. He did not fear the dragon exhaling/although he was exhaling fire.
4. "God will save you believing/if you believe."
5. The people praised George leading/because he was leading the dragon.

TASK 4

1. With Cleopatra urging/since Cleopatra urged (it), Marc Antony started a civil war.
2. With the people asking/when (since) the people asked, George killed the dragon.
3. With the nightingale singing/when the nightingale was singing, the bowman stretched his bow.
4. With the hippos devouring the Macedonians/because the hippos were devouring the Macedonians, Alexander was sad.
5. With Holofernes sleeping/while Holofernes was sleeping, Judith drew her sword.

Task 5

1. By drinking Holofernes lost his life.
2. St. George entered the church for the sake of praying (to pray).
3. Now we give some time to thinking.
4. All criminals have a mode of operating.
5. Many people do not eat for living (to live), but live for eating (to eat).

Reading Exercise

Literate men, who, as Ficino said, "are as much unoccupied with the body, as they are occupied with the mind and the brain," practically all endure the problems of a sedentary life ….

In general, intellectuals tend to suffer from every weakness of the stomach. Nearly all who seriously give attention to the study of literature suffer from languor of the stomach; for when the brain digests the things that a lust of knowledge and an appetite for literature ingest, they can only digest badly the food that is taken in …. Therefore, from this (condition) arise the indigestion, the chronic flatulence, the pallor and leanness of the whole body, the (private) parts deprived of reproductive fluid: in sum, all the injuries that are the consequences of bad humors. Thus, little by little, the studious, although endowed with the temperament of Jupiter, become saturnine and melancholic. We are accustomed to say that the melancholic are clever, but perhaps (we would say) more appropriately that the clever become melancholic, because the more spiritual part of the blood is absorbed with the works of the mind, while the more earthly part is left inside …. Therefore, professors of literature are especially subject to the melancholic passions, all the more if they have such a temperament from the beginning. Thus they tend to be slender in stature, sallow, leaden, cranky, and desirous of a solitary life.

But because the health of the wise is so much in the interest of the Commonwealth, it is right, insofar as it can be done, to preserve and restore it. Therefore they ought to enjoy freer air, and to adopt a varied kind of life …. As far as food is concerned, they should regard as an oracle the saying of Hippocrates: "The object of health is not to be filled with food" …. As for wine, it is preferable to other drinks; we praise undiluted wine, but (it must be) moderate. I know that many literate people, with the counsel of their doctors, make use of light wines, and so they think that they are able to drink as much as they like. But this is not as safe as they think. For these light wines acquire a certain acidity, especially in summer …. As far as the regimen of other things is concerned … they ought to make daily use of moderate exercise of the body, if the air is pure and serene, and the winds are silent …. A bath of sweet (fresh) water is also healthy, especially in summer, when black bile infests learned people.

QUIZ

A

present	infinitive	participle	gerund	perfect
amo	amare	amans	amandi	amavi
laudo	laudare	laudans	laudandi	laudavi
hábeo	habere	habens	habendi	hábui
dico	dícere	dicens	dicendi	dixi
cápio	cápere	cápiens	capiendi	cepi
aúdio	audire	aúdiens	audiendi	audivi

B

1. of the soldier
2. you send
3. kings
4. you see
5. you love
6. girls
7. (by) seeing
8. I show
9. to, for a horn
10. I feared

C

1. *Dum cérebrum cóncoquit ea, quae sciendi libido íngerit, non potest concóquere ea, quae fuerunt ingesta alimenta.*
2. *Melanchólicis.*
3. *Non debent.*
4. *Meracum, sed módicum.*
5. *Non est; quia aciditatem quandam adsciscit.*
6. *Quando aer purus ac serenus est, et venti silent.*
7. *Tempestate; quod atra bilis ibi litteratos infestat.*

ANSWERS TO EXERCISES IN HOUR 13

TASK 1

1. *laudor*
2. *laudantur*
3. *laudámini*
4. *laudatur*
5. *laudamur*
6. *laudaris*

TASK 2

1. you are taught
2. he/she/it is taught
3. he/she/it is sent
4. y'all are sent
5. we are heard
6. they are heard
7. you are caught
8. I am caught

TASK 3

1. they were being taught
2. we were being led

3. y'all were being heard
4. I was being praised
5. he/she/it was being warned
6. they were being killed
7. you were being found
8. he/she/it was being prepared

TASK 4

1. *laudabuntur*
2. *monebor*
3. *laudábitur*
4. *monébimur*
5. *laudabímini*
6. *monéberis*

TASK 5

1. he/she/it is sent
2. he/she/it will be sent
3. they will be sent
4. I am heard
5. I will be heard
6. you will be heard
7. you are captured
8. you will be captured
9. y'all will be captured

TASK 6

1. I will be loved
2. we were being taught
3. we are sent
4. they will be caught
5. he was loved
6. you will be taught
7. you are sent
8. I will be caught
9. I was being loved
10. y'all are taught

TASK 7

1. *laudari:* to be praised
2. *moneri:* to be warned
3. *dici:* to be said
4. *intérfici:* to be killed
5. *sentiri:* to be felt

TASK 8

1. *laudare!* Be praised!
2. *monémini!* Be warned!
3. *accípere!* Be accepted!
4. *audímini!* Be heard!

TASK 9

1. Holofernes is killed by a Hebrew woman.
2. Educated men are often afflicted by diseases of the stomach.
3. We are taught by literate men.
4. We are tormented by the Latin language.

READING EXERCISE

The Chinese people are more or less bronze-colored and white, with simian nostrils, very small eyes, sparse beards, and long hair, which they carefully comb. There is not, however, one kind of hairstyle for all. Unmarried people separate their hair from the forehead, (whereas) married people comb it together. This mark especially distinguishes both classes. The foremost (citizens), rich men, and those who practice military service cover their bodies with multi-colored silk; the lower class and the poor (cover their bodies) with linen or cotton.

Women are diligent about the care of their heads. They bind up their hair, (which has been combed for a long time and arranged) on top with headbands adorned with gems and gold. The ornamentation of the rest of the body is less alluring. They agree that the highest praise for beauty and form is (to be had) in the shortness and slenderness of the foot: and so their delicate feet are bound up with cords from infancy. Modesty has great honor among noble women. They are rarely seen: they do not go forth in public, unless in a hand-carried chair, which is covered with veils.

They calculate years from twelve lunar periods, and every third year they add one to the twelve. The beginning of the year is celebrated on the new moon of the month of March. (They celebrate) that day with public cheer; each person also celebrates his birthday with private festivity. They send gifts and baskets to each other; then they have elaborate banquets, in which most exquisite games are included. Elaborate comedies and tragedies are exhibited, and plays taken from ancient history …. The nature of the parties is this: Many are invited. A personal table, made of wood like the most splendid ebony, is placed before individual guests …. They think it a mark of boorishness to handle food with the fingers.

QUIZ

A

1. *docetur:* he/she/it is taught
2. *cápiunt:* they catch
3. *amabamur:* we were being loved
4. *aúdiet:* he/she/it will hear
5. *monebímini:* y'all will be warned
6. *mittetur:* he/she/it will be sent
7. *audiris:* you are heard
8. *laudo:* I praise
9. *dicebar:* I was said
10. *intérficis:* you kill

B

1. *Mulíeres circa curam cápitis diligentes sunt:* Women are diligent about the care of their heads.
2. *Réliqui córporis ornatus est mínime lascivus:* The ornamentation of the rest of the body is less alluring.
3. *Pedes tenelli ab infántia fásciis constringuntur:* (Their) delicate feet are bound up with cords from infancy.
4. *Magnum apud nóbiles matronas honorem habet pudicítia:* Modesty has great honor among noble women.
5. *Non in públicum pródeunt nisi in gestatória sella, quae velis tégitur:* They do not go out into public except in a hand-held chair, which is covered by veils.
6. *Múnera et spórtulas ínvicem mittunt:* They send gifts and baskets to each other.
7. *Comoédiae ac tragoédiae exhibentur sumptuosae:* Elaborate comedies and tragedies are exhibited.
8. *Conviviorum autem rátio est talis:* The nature of the parties is this (such).
9. *Invitantur multi:* Many are invited.
10. *Cibos dígitis attrectare, notam rusticitatis putant:* They consider it a mark of boorishness to touch food with the fingers.

ANSWERS TO EXERCISES IN HOUR 14

TASK 1

1. present active
2. perfect passive
3. present active
4. perfect passive

TASK 2

1. praised
2. warned
3. spoken
4. made/done
5. heard

TASK 3

1. *addo:* added
2. *suádeo:* persuaded
3. *ago:* done
4. *reddo:* returned
5. *quaero:* sought
6. *invénio:* found
7. *tego:* covered

TASK 4

1. Brutus left Caesar having been killed in the theatre. Brutus left Caesar, who had been killed, in the theatre.

2. Brutus, having been praised by the senators, left Rome nonetheless. Although Brutus had been praised by the senators, he left Rome nonetheless.
3. The husband lifted his wife, having been led to their new home, over the threshold. The husband led his wife to their new home and lifted her over the threshold.
4. The hippos devoured the soldiers having been sent into the river. The hippos devoured the soldiers who had been sent into the river.
5. The king's daughter, having been ordered to choose a casket, chose the third. When the king's daughter was ordered to choose a casket, she chose the third.

TASK 5

1. With the dragon having been killed, George left the city. When the dragon had been killed, George left the city.
2. With my children having been praised, I rejoice. When my children have been praised, I rejoice.
3. With the army having been called together, Caesar cheered up his soldiers. After the army was called together, Caesar cheered up his soldiers.
4. With his daughter having been seen, the king rejoiced. When he saw his daughter, the king rejoiced.
5. With the food having been prepared, we all sat down to the table. When the food had been prepared, we all sat down to the table.

TASK 6

1. I will have been loved
2. they had been loved
3. he/she/it has been/was loved
4. we had been loved
5. y'all will have been loved
6. I have been loved/was loved

TASK 7

1. *Mílites ab Alexandro confirmati sunt.*
2. *Roma a Nerone accensa est.*
3. *Illud consílium a Caésare reiectum erat.*
4. *Sagittárius a philomela reprobatus erit.*
5. *Illa verba numquam audita sunt.*

TASK 8

1. In this building it is not permitted to smoke.
2. It was necessary to study hard.
3. Not by one road does one arrive at so great a secret.
4. There was discussion in the senate about the Gallic war.
5. In (my) youth, it was permitted to play.

READING EXERCISE

When the treaty had been struck, teams of three brothers, just as it had been agreed, took up arms. They promptly stepped forward into the middle, between the two battle lines. The two armies sat down on both sides in front of their camps, intent on this spectacle with their whole minds. The signal is given, and the young men, in groups of three, run together with hostile arms. When they had fought among themselves for a while with equal strength, and the three Albans had been wounded, two Romans fell dying, one above the other. (The Albans) surround the surviving Roman. By chance, he was not wounded. And so he takes to flight, thinking, "They will surely chase me, even if they have been wounded." Now he had fled a little way out of the place where they had fought, when, looking back, he sees them following from great intervals. One was scarcely distant from him; and so he (the Roman) turns back with great force upon him and kills him. Soon he hastens to the second, and likewise gives him to death (kills him). Now, with the battle having been evened, two men survived, equal in number, but far different in strength. Exulting, the Roman said: "I have given two brothers to Hell; now I will give the third." Then he plunges his sword into the (other's) neck, and despoils him as he lies. The Romans received Horatius with cheers and congratulations. And then on either side they bury their own.

QUIZ

A

1. *amáverant:* they had loved; *amati erant:* they had been loved
2. *monúeris:* you will have warned; *mónitus eris:* you will have been warned
3. *reliqui:* I left; *relictus sum:* I have been left
4. *petíveram:* I had asked; *petitus eram:* I had been asked
5. *dixerunt:* they said; *dicti sunt:* they have been said
6. *audivisti:* you heard; *auditus es:* you have been heard
7. *laudavérimus:* we will have praised; *laudati érimus:* we will have been praised
8. *céperint:* they will have caught; *capti erunt:* they will have been caught
9. *monueratis:* y'all had warned; *móniti eratis:* y'all had been warned
10. *dedit:* he gave; *datus est:* he has been given

B

1. *Datur signum, infestisque armis terni iúvenes concurrunt:* The signal is given, and the youths, in groups of three, run together with hostile arms.
2. *Vulneratis tribus Albanis, duo Romani exspirantes corruerunt:* When the three Albans had been wounded, two Romans fell dying.
3. *"Illi me certe petent, etsi vulnerati sunt":* They will certainly chase me, although they have been wounded.

4. *Romanus exultans; "Duos," inquit, "fratrum Mánibus dedi, tértium nunc dabo":* Exulting, the Roman said, "I will have given two of the brothers to Hell; now I will give the third."

Answers to Exercises in Hour 15

Task 1

1. Alexander encouraged his terrified soldiers.
2. Even if we fail, we will try again.
3. The "Roman" dialect is the one that the best writers spoke.
4. Caesar will use both persuasion and force.
5. Haven't you ever tried Chinese food?

Task 2

1. *Horátius hostes se interfecturos fugit:* Horatius fled his enemies (who were) about to kill him.
2. *Geórgius draconem interfecturus pópulum oravit:* George, (when he was) about to kill the dragon, addressed the people.
3. *Pater fílios in perículum ambulaturos prohíbuit:* The father stopped his kids, (who were) about to walk into danger.
4. *Nos morituri te salutamus!* We (who are) about to die salute you!

Task 3

1. *Índicem tibi librorum legendorum dabo:* I will give you a list of books to be read.
2. *Rationem pecúniae expendendae réddidi:* I gave an accounting of money to be spent.
3. *Verba memoriae committenda non multa sunt:* The words to be committed to memory are not many.

Task 4

1. *Romani in Gálliam venturi sunt:* The Romans are about to come to Gaul.
2. *Magister omnes pueros laudaturus est:* The teacher is going to praise all the boys.
3. *Caésare imperante, res pública moritura erat:* When Caesar was in command, the Republic was about to die.
4. *Calpúrnia Caesarem monitura erat, cum Brutus advenit:* Calpurnia was about to warn Caesar when Brutus arrived.

Task 5

1. The Latin language is to be learned by us. (We must learn …).
2. The hippos are not to be feared by the soldiers. (The soldiers should not …).

3. This business was to be taken up by you. (You had to take up …)
4. We have worked enough! Now we must drink some wine!

TASK 6

1. *Exercítia in hoc libro non sunt difficília:* The exercises in this book are not difficult.
2. *Hanc rem non fácile explanare póssumus:* We cannot easily explain this thing.
3. *Haec sunt nonnulla eorum, quae máxime mihi placent:* These are some of my favorite things.
4. *Animália huius géneris extra Índiam ádmodum rara sunt:* Animals of this type are rare outside India.
5. *Hae féminae libros non legunt:* These women do not read books.

TASK 7

1. *Iste catus vasum pretiosum meum fregit!* That cat (of yours) just broke my precious vase!
2. *Istos hómines iuste vituperávimus.* We justly cursed those men.
3. *Ista exercítia me ad insániam ádagunt.* These exercises are driving me nuts.

READING EXERCISE

The use of friendship is varied and multiple, and many pretexts for suspicions and offenses are given. It is the mark of a wise man sometimes to avoid these, sometimes to lighten them, sometimes to bear them. One offense should be endured, if utility in friendship and good faith are to be retained. For friends should often be both warned and reproached; and these things should be received in a friendly spirit, when they are done with good will. Yet what my friend says in the *Andria* is somehow true:

Truth causes hatred, complaisance (makes) friends.

Truth is harmful, if hatred, which is the poison of friendship, is really born from it. But complaisance is much more harmful, because by indulging sins, it allows a friend to go headlong (into ruin). The greatest fault, however, is (found) in the one who both scorns the truth and is driven by complaisance to dishonesty.

Therefore, in every such matter, one must have reason and care. First, if (there is) a warning, it will be without bitterness; then, if (there is) reproof, it will lack insulting language. In complaisance, however, (since we gladly use words of Terrence) courtesy ought to be present; flattery, the helper of vices, should be far removed, (for it) is not only unworthy of a friend, but it is not even worthy of a free man. For one lives one way with a tyrant, and another way with a friend. That (saying) of Cato is clever, as are many (of his): "Bitter enemies render better service to some people than those who seem to be their close (sweet) friends; for the former often speak the truth, the latter, never." And it is absurd that those who are warned do not take the annoyance that thay ought to take, but they take that which they ought to do without. For they are not grieved because they have sinned, but they take it badly that they are reproached. On the contrary, they should have been sorry for their sin, and rejoiced with correction.

QUIZ

1. *Impérium Romanum a Nerone deformatum est:* The Roman empire was damaged by Nero.
2. *Mílites romani a Parthis victi sunt:* The Roman soldiers were conquered by the Parthians.
3. *Princípium anni a Sinis celebratur:* The beginning of the year is celebrated by the Chinese.
4. *Munera ínvicem ab illis mittuntur:* Gifts are sent by them to each other.
5. *Horátius a Romanis ovantibus acceptus est:* Horatius was received by the rejoicing Romans.
6. *Amici ab amicis monendi sunt:* Friends ought to be warned by friends.

ANSWERS TO EXERCISES IN HOUR 16

TASK 1

1. The hippos are said to have swum across the river.
2. Caesar seems to have been killed by Brutus.
3. George is thought to have killed a dragon.
4. Literate people seem to have been afflicted with various diseases.

TASK 2

1. The soldiers are thought to be about to conquer in battle.
2. Brutus seemed to be about to answer Caesar.
3. Many people are said to be going to be saved by God.

TASK 3

1. I think Alexander to be just. I think that Alexander is just.
2. I think Latin to be difficult. I think that Latin is difficult.
3. I think the world to be good. I think that the world is good.
4. I say him to come. I say that he is coming quickly.
5. I hear them to know all things. I hear that they know all things.
6. I see the soldiers to be conquered. I see that the soldiers are being conquered.

TASK 4

1. We often say that literate men are melancholy.
2. The crow thought that his voice was beautiful.
3. We thought that the emperor was (had been) a just man.
4. The abbot thinks that women ought not to learn Latin.
5. The bowman believes that a pearl is in the stomach of the nightingale.
6. Alexander thought that all his soldiers would fight against the hippos.

TASK 5

1. *Marce*		**3.** *puer bone*	
2. *fili*		**4.** *Sili Itálice*	

TASK 6

1. *Milvaukiae*	**4.** *Syracusis*
2. *Detroiti*	**5.** *Parísiis*
3. *Chicágine*	

READING EXERCISE

And then, having been admonished to return to myself, I entered into my intimate places, with you leading, and I was able, since you became my helper. I entered and saw with the eye of my soul above the same eye of my soul, above my mind, an unchangeable light—not this common (light), the one visible to all flesh, nor that which was, as it were, bigger, and of the same kind. This was not that (light), but something else, quite different from all those things. And so it was not above my mind as oil is above water, nor as the sky is above the earth, but higher, because it made me, and I (was) lower, who was made by it. Who-(ever) knows the truth, knows it, and who(ever) knows it, knows eternity. Love knows it. O eternal truth and true love and lovable eternity! You are my God: I sigh for you day and night. And when I first knew you, you took me up, and I saw that there was something that I might see; but I was not yet able to see. And you shook the infirmity of my gaze, shining in me strongly, and I trembled with love and shuddering: and I found that I was far from you in a region of dissimilarity. And I thought that I heard your voice from on high: "I am the food of grown-ups: grow and you will eat me. You will not change me into you, as (you change) the food of your flesh, but you will be changed into me." And I knew that you teach people for (in keeping with) their iniquity. And you made my soul waste away like a spider web, and I said: "Surely the truth is nothing, since it is diffused through neither finite nor infinite spaces?" And you shouted from afar: "I am who am." And I heard, just as it is heard in my heart, and there was no cause whatsover for doubting. And it was easier to doubt that I lived, than that there was no truth, which is seen through the things that are made.

QUIZ

	Active Voice	Passive Voice
Present	*amare*	*amari*
Perfect	*amavisse*	*amatus esse*
Future	*amaturus esse*	*amatum iri*
Present	*míttere*	*mitti*
Perfect	*misisse*	*missus esse*
Future	*missurus esse*	*missum iri*

B

1. *Et inde admónitus redire ad memet ipsum, intravi in loca íntima mea:* And then, having been admonished to return to myself, I entered into my intimate places.
2. *Pótui, quóniam factus es adiutor meus:* I was able, since you became my helper.
3. *Nec lux illa erat supra mentem meam:* And that light was not above my mind.
4. *Qui novit veritatem, novit eam:* Who knows the truth, knows it.
5. *Tu es deus meus, tibi suspiro die ac nocte:* You are my God, I sigh for you night and day.
6. *Et reverberavisti infirmitatem aspectus mei, rádians in me vehementer:* And you shook the infirmity of my gaze, shining in me strongly.
7. *Et putavi me audire vocem tuam de excelso: "Cibus sum grándium: cresce et manducabis me":* And I thought that I heard your voice from on high: "I am the food of grown ups: grow and you will eat me."
8. *Nec tu me in te mutabis sicut cibum carnis tuae, sed tu mutáberis in me:* And you will not change me into you, as (you change) the food of your flesh, but you will be changed into me.
9. *Et cognovi te pro iniquitate erudire hóminem:* And I learned that you teach men for (their) iniquity.
10. *Faciliusque dubitabam vívere me, quam non esse veritatem:* And I more easily doubted that I lived, than that there was no truth.

ANSWERS TO EXERCISES IN HOUR 17

TASK 1

1. *vérior*
2. *brévior*
3. *ingéntior*
4. *lóngior*
5. *audácior*
6. *cárior*

TASK 2

1. *reginam fortiorem*
2. *reginis fortióribus*
3. *reginae fortioris, fortiori, fortiores*
4. *virorum fortiorum*
5. *viro fortiori, fortiore*
6. *vir fórtior*
7. *manu fortiore*
8. *mánui fortiori*
9. *manus fórtior, fortioris, fortiores*

TASK 3

1. *Fémina Israelítica fórtior erat quam rex:* The Israelite woman was braver than the king.

2. *Néminem sanctiorem vidi quam Geórgium:* I saw no one holier than George.
3. *Caésaris mílites fortiores sunt quam Pompeii:* The soldiers of Caesar are braver than those of Pompey.
4. *Nullam viam breviorem vidi quam illam:* I have seen no street shorter than that one.
5. *Quae lingua est facílior quam Latina?* What language is easier than Latin?

Task 4

1. *Caesar nobílior est Bruto:* Caesar is nobler than Brutus.
2. *Hippopótami celeriores sunt mílitibus:* The hippos are faster than the soldiers.
3. *Nullum hóminem laetiorem vidi Marco:* I have not seen a happier man than Marcus.
4. *Nulla res difficílior est illa:* No matter is more difficult than that one.
5. *Illa monstra terribiliora sunt his:* Those monsters are more terrible than these

Task 5

1. *veríssimus*	4. *longíssimus*
2. *brevíssimus*	5. *audacíssimus*
3. *ingentíssimus*	6. *caríssimus*

Task 6

1. *celérior, celérrimus*	3. *humílior, humíllimus*
2. *púlchrior, pulchérrimus*	4. *gracílior, gracíllimus*

Task 7

1. *vérius, veríssime*	4. *áltius, altíssime*
2. *brévius, brevíssime*	5. *humílius, humíllime*
3. *mélius, óptime*	6. *celérius, celérrime*

Task 8

1. The hippos swim faster than the soldiers.
2. The hippos swim as quickly as possible.
3. The king sent his daughter, whom he loved, to the emperor.
4. The king sent as much money as possible (as he could) to the emperor.
5. Magdala was more literate than the abbot.

Reading Exercise

(He was) temperate in food and drink, but in drink more temperate, since he greatly despised drunkenness in any man, not to speak of himself and his own people. He was not so much able to abstain from food, and often complained that fasts were harm(ful) to his body. He feasted very rarely, and this only on the principal feasts, with a great number of people. The daily dinner was served on only four dishes (at a time), except the fried meat, which hunters would bring on stakes; he liked to eat this more than any other food. During the meal he listened either to a performance or to a reader. Histories and the deeds of the ancients were read to him. He also delighted in the books of Saint Augustine, especially the ones that are entitled "(On) The City of God."

He was copious and exhuberant in eloquence, and he could express whatever he wished very clearly. He was not content merely with his native (paternal) language, but he also devoted attention to foreign languages. He learned Latin very well and spoke it as well as his native language. As for Greek, he could understand it better than he could pronounce it. He most studiously cultivated the liberal arts, and he endowed the teachers of these with great honors. In learning grammar he heard (studied under) Peter of Pisa, an elderly deacon; in the other disciplines he had Alcuin, also named Albinus, ... a most learned man in all subjects, as his teacher; with him he also spent a great deal of time and effort on rhetoric and dialectic, but especially on astronomy. He learned the art of arithmetic, and he examined the course of the stars with prudent attention. He tried to write, and he used to travel with tables and notebooks in his bed under the pillows; but this effort, which was begun too late and out of its proper place, had little success.

QUIZ

A

	Positive	Comparative	Superlative
reginarum	*fórtium*	*fortiorum*	*fortissimarum*
amicos	*fortes*	*fortiores*	*fortíssimos*
rege	*laeto*	*laetiore*	*laetíssimo*
cúrrui	*bono*	*meliori*	*óptimo*
rebus	*magnis*	*maioribus*	*máximis*

B

1. *In cibo et potu Carolus temperántior erat quam céteri:* In food and drink Carolus was more temperate than the rest.
2. *Ebrietatem plúrimum abominabatur:* He hated drunkenness very much.
3. *Saepe dicebat nóxia córpori suo esse ieiúnia:* He often said that fasting was harmful to his body.
4. *Convivabatur raríssime, sed cum magno hóminum número:* He feasted very rarely, but with a great number of men.

5. *Erat eloquéntia copiosus poteratque quod volebat apertíssime exprímere:* He was plentiful of (in) speech, and he was able to express what he wished very clearly.

6. *Nec pátrio tantum sermone contentus, étiam peregrinis linguis óperam inpendit:* And being content not only with his native language, he also expended effort on foreign languages.

7. *Latinam óptime dídicit et aeque illa ac pátria lingua orabat:* He learned Latin very well and spoke it as well as his native language.

8. *In céteris disciplinis Alcoinum, virum undecumque doctissimum, praeceptorem hábuit:* In the other disciplines he had Alcuin, a man very learned in all subjects, as his teacher.

9. *Et rhetóricae et dialécticae, praecípue tamen astronómiae plúrimum témporis et laboris impertivit:* He also spent a great deal of time and effort on rhetoric and dialectic, but especially on astronomy.

ANSWERS TO EXERCISES IN HOUR 18

TASK 1

1. *ámbulet*
2. *suscipiamus*
3. *videantur*
4. *audiaris*
5. *siti*
6. *possis*
7. *timeámini*
8. *surgam*
9. *sciatur*

TASK 2

1. *pararet*
2. *mitteremur*
3. *placerent*
4. *audireris*
5. *esses*
6. *possemus*
7. *manducaretis*
8. *quaérerem*
9. *praeberetur*

TASK 3

1. *Véniunt hippopótami! Celériter natemus:* The hippos are coming! Let us swim quickly.

2. *Amici nostri in perículo sunt. Moneamus eos:* Our friends are in trouble. Let us warn them.

3. *Alexander nos in proélium vocat. Pugnemus:* Alexander calls us into battle. Let us fight.

4. *Caesar venit. Interficiamus eum:* Caesar is coming. Let us kill him.

5. *Gaudeamus ígitur, iúvenes dum sumus:* Let us rejoice then, while we are young.

TASK 4

1. *Dicat, quicquid vult:* Let him say whatever he wants.

2. *Et Deus ait, Fiat lux:* And God said, "Let there be light (let light be made).

3. *Sit pax in terra, et mecum incípiat:* Let there be peace on earth, and let it begin with me.

4. *Placentam manducent:* Let them eat cake.

5. *Ne ámbules:* Don't walk.

TASK 5

1. May Caesar not enter into the theater!
2. Would that the night were shorter!
3. May the king live!
4. Would that the king were living!
5. May you not come into danger!

TASK 6

1. Many people live, in order that they may eat (to eat).
2. I ran to the river, that I might warn the soldiers.
3. Let us mix up the kisses, that they may not know the number of the kisses.
4. I ask these things, in order that I may know the truth.
5. The soldiers fled, that they might not be captured.
6. We shall hurry, that we may flee the dragon.
7. I studied philosophy, that I might understand the nature of things.

TASK 7

1. I warn (you) not to enter into the city.
2. Alexander encouraged them to fight bravely.
3. Domitian commanded all to call him "Master."
4. I am asking you not to feed the crocodiles.
5. Why do you command me to do these things?

READING EXERCISE

I approve of and rejoice at the fact that you apply yourself assiduously, and, having set aside all (other) things, you do this one thing, to make yourself better every day. I not only encourage you to persevere, but I also implore you. I give you this warning, however: do not, like those who do not want to improve, but to seem so, make something notable in your dress or style of life. Avoid a harsh appearance and an uncut head, a careless beard, a declaration of war against money, and a bed placed on the ground, and whatever else perversely follows vainglory. The name itself of philosophy, even if it is handled with moderation, is sufficiently suspect: what (will happen) if we begin to remove ourselves from the custom(s) of human beings? Let all things be dissimilar inside, (but) let our expression agree with our people. Let your toga not be bright; but neither let it be grubby. Let us not have silver to conceal our gold, but let us not think that it is a sign of frugality to have done without gold and silver. Let us follow a better life than the common people, but not an opposite (kind of life): otherwise we will chase and turn away those whom we wish to be changed. For they want to imitate nothing we do, when they think that they must imitate everything.

Philosophy promises this first: common sense, humanity, and a coming together (fellowship). Dissimilarity will separate (us) from this profession. For our idea is to live according to nature. It is against nature to torture one's body, to hate simple neatness, to desire filth, and to use foods (that are) not only cheap, but foul and rough. Just as it is madness to desire things that are soft and luxurious, so also it is (madness) to flee ordinary and obtainable (things). Philosophy requires frugality, not punishment. Frugality can, however, be not unkempt (tidy). I like this (kind of) moderation: Let our life be tempered between good habits and those of the people. Let all people look up to our life, but let them (also) recognize (it).

Quiz

A

1. he/she/it lives	**6.** may he desire
2. may he catch	**7.** would that (if only) he were warning
3. he sees	**8.** would that (if only) he might be
4. may he walk	**9.** he doubts
5. he will send	**10.** may he flee

B

1. *Pertináciter studes, ut te meliorem cotídie fácias:* You apply yourself assiduously, that you may make yourself better every day.
2. *Intus ómnia dissimília sint; frons pópulo nostro convéniat:* Let all be dissimilar inwardly, (but) let (our) expression agree with our people.
3. *Ne putemus frugalitatis indícium esse auro argentoque caruisse:* Let us not think that it is a sign of frugality to have been without gold and silver.
4. *Meliorem vitam sequamur quam vulgus, sed non contráriam:* Let us follow a better life than the common people, but not (one that is the) opposite.
5. *Ab hac proféssione dissimilitudo nos separabit:* Unlikeness will separate us from this profession.
6. *Nempe propósitum nostrum est secundum naturam vivere:* For our plan is to live according to nature.
7. *Frugalitatem éxigit philosóphia, non poenam:* Philosophy requires frugality, not punishment.
8. *Suspíciant omnes vitam nostram:* Let all people look up to our life.

Answers to Exercises in Hour 19

Task 1

1. *amáverint*	**4.** *audivérimus*
2. *monuéritis*	**5.** *déderis*
3. *míserim*	**6.** *fúerit*

Task 2

1. *laudatus sis*
2. *visus sim*
3. *interfecti simus*
4. *missi sint*
5. *lectus sit*
6. *mutati sitis*

Task 3

1. *docuissem, docuisses, docuisset, docuissemus, docuissetis, docuissent*
2. *potuissem, potuisses, potuisset, potuissemus, potuissetis, potuissent*

Task 4

1. *docti essent*
2. *missus essem*
3. *laudatus esset*
4. *intellecti essemus*
5. *amati essetis*
6. *hábitus esses*

Task 5

1. imperfect active, I
2. pluperfect active, he/she/it
3. perfect active, we
4. present passive, we
5. perfect passive, y'all
6. perfect active, they
7. imperfect passive, they
8. pluperfect passive, he/she/it
9. imperfect active, you
10. present passive, you
11. perfect passive, he/she/it
12. present active, we

Task 6

1. The people asked where St. George was leading the dragon.
2. I do not know where I have placed the money.
3. The emperor asked the king's daughter which casket she had chosen.
4. Judith doubted whether she was able to kill Holofernes.
5. We were asking what cities had been captured by Caesar.
6. Seneca teaches how a philosopher ought to live.
7. We wondered why the soldiers were being sent into the river.

Task 7

1. Augustine asked how he would find God.
2. We don't know what we will find in this book.
3. Alexander did not know what he would say to the soldiers.
4. Caesar asks Brutus what he will do with that dagger.

READING EXERCISE

Formerly the senators at Rome had the custom of going into the senate house with their underage sons. Then, when a certain weightier matter was considered in the senate and it was carried over onto the following day, they decreed as follows: "Let no one talk about the matter under discussion, before it has been decided." But the mother of the boy Papirius, who had been in the senate house with his father, asked her son what the fathers in the senate had done.

The boy answered that it had to be kept secret, and that he was not permitted to talk about it. His mother became more desirous of hearing it; the secrecy of the matter and the silence of the boy inflamed her mind to inquire, and so she asked him more forcefully. Then the boy, with his mother pressing him, conceived the idea of a smart and clever lie. He said that the senate had deliberated whether it seemed more useful to the republic for one man to have two wives, or for one woman to marry two men. When she heard this, she became pale, and, trembling, she went from her home to the other matrons. She arrived at the senate the next day with a crowd of matrons. With tears and entreaties they urged that one woman belong to two men, rather than two women to one man. The senators, as they were going into the senate house, wondered about the women's outrageous conduct and what this demand meant. The boy Papirius stepped into the middle of the senate house and related what his mother had insisted on hearing, and what he had told his mother. The senate approved his faith and character and made a decree: "After this, boys may not go in with their fathers, apart from Papirius alone." Afterwards the surname Praetextatus was bestowed on this boy as an honor, on account of his prudence in being silent and speaking in the age of the bordered toga.

QUIZ

A

1. Let us learn Latin!
2. Do not learn Latin!
3. You ask why I learn Latin.
4. May I learn Latin!
5. I bought this book that I might learn Latin.
6. I warn you not to learn Latin.
7. I didn't know why you had learned Latin.
8. I asked you not to learn Latin.

B

1. *Mos fuit senatóribus in cúriam cum praetextatis fíliis introire.*
2. *Mater rogavit quid in senatu patres egissent. Ille respondit id tacendum esse, neque dici licere.*
3. *Secretum rei et siléntium pueri ánimum eius ad inquirendum incendit.*
4. *Mendácii lépidi et festivi.*
5. *Utrum videretur utílius ut unus vir duas uxores haberet, an ut una fémina duobus viris núberet.*
6. *Mater trépidans egréditur ad céteras matronas.*
7. *Oraverunt ut una pótius duobus nupta fíeret.*
8. *Cognomen honoris grátia inditum est, ob tacendi in aetate togae pretextatae prudéntiam.*

Answers to Exercises in Hour 20

Task 1

1. After Judith killed Holofernes, all (the people) praised her.
2. When we had found silver, we rejoiced.
3. As the soldiers were swimming in the river, hippos were lying in the water.
4. When the city burned, Nero rejoiced.

Task 2

1. Nero killed himself before the citizens seized him.
2. Let us work, as long as we enjoy life.
3. While the senate deliberated, the boys kept silent.
4. We waited in the city until we saw the army.

Task 3

1. *Caesar spem deponebat cum Brutum inter coniuratos videret:* Caesar gave up hope when he saw Brutus among the conspirators.
2. *Latina difficilis est quod Romani insani fuerunt:* Latin is difficult because the Romans were crazy.
3. *Romani urbem ceperunt, ut aiunt, quod hostes imminerent. Noli eis crédere!* The Romans captured the city, they say, because their enemies were threatening. Don't believe them.
4. *Laudemus Deum, quia ipse nos fecit:* Let us praise God, because he made us.

Task 4

1. Saint George laughed at the danger that all (the people) feared.
2. George conquered the dragon because he believed in God.
3. The people asked George what plan he had.
4. George proclaimed that he wished to free the city.

Task 5

1. *Quamquam multa sciebat, abbas Latine loqui non póterat:* Although he knew many things, the abbot was not able to speak in Latin.
2. *Quamvis saepe pugnavisset, miles timebat:* Although he had often fought, the soldier was afraid.
3. *Etsi Caesar in bello vincebat, eum non sequebamur:* Even if Caesar was winning (in) the war, we did not follow him.
4. *Cum fortis esset, Holofernes tamen périit:* Although he was strong, Holofernes perished nonetheless.

Task 6

1. When we had come to the city, we saw a dragon.
2. We were afraid, since we had never seen a dragon.

3. Although we had never seen a dragon, we had (nevertheless) spotted other monsters.
4. When Seneca advised him, Nero was a good emperor.

TASK 7

1. This is so small that it cannot be found.
2. Judith acted so bravely that all praised her.
3. Alexander commands in such a way that the soldiers fear him.
4. The danger was so great that I fled from the city.

TASK 8

1. *Fit ut matrem tuam víderim:* It happens that I saw your mother.
2. *Fíeri potest ut cibus paratus sit:* It is possible that the food is ready.
3. *Evenit ut mulíeres consílium senatorum audivissent:* It happened that the women had heard the senator's plan.
4. *Fíeri potest ut áliquid didícerim:* It happens that I learned something.

TASK 9

1. I fear that Holofernes will conquer the people of Israel.
2. I fear that Judith has killed Holofernes.
3. I was afraid that the conspirators had not killed Caesar.

TASK 10

1. Alexander urged his soldiers to fight bravely.
2. Alexander promised them money, in order that they might fight bravely.
3. Alexander encouraged them so much that they fought bravely.
4. When (as) they fought bravely, Alexander praised them.
5. Alexander feared that they would not fight bravely.

READING EXERCISE

When, many years ago, I cut myself off from home, from my parents, sister, kin and (something which is more difficult than these) from the habit of more elegant eating, (all) for the sake of the kingdom of heaven, and I went on to Jerusalem with the intention of serving, I was unable to do without the library that I had put together in Rome with great effort and work. And so, wretch (that I was), I fasted before reading Tullius; after frequent nocturnal vigils, after the tears which the recollection of past sins drew from deep inside, I took Plautus in my hands. If ever I began to read a prophet, his uncultivated speech made me shudder, and because I did not see the light with my blind eyes, I did not think that it was the fault of my eyes, but of the sun. And while the ancient serpent was thus deluding me, around the middle of Lent a fever entered my exhausted body.

Then suddenly caught up in the spirit, I was dragged to the tribunal of the Judge, where there was so much light and such brightness from the brilliance of those standing around, that, cast down on the ground, I did not dare to look up. When I was asked about my faith, I answered that I was a Christian. And the one who was seated said, "You lie; you are a Ciceronian, not a Christian; where your treasure is, there your heart is also." Immediately I fell silent and between blows—for he had ordered me to be beaten—I was more tormented by the fire of conscience, recalling that versicle: "Who, then, will confess to you in hell?" Nevertheless, I began to shout, and with a cry I said: "Have pity on me, Lord, have pity on me." These words (this voice) resounded amid the strokes (of the whip) … I began to swear, and calling upon his name to say: "Master, if I ever had secular books, if I read them, I denied you."

QUIZ

A

1. pluperfect, indicative, active
2. future perfect, indicative, active
3. perfect, subjunctive, active
4. imperfect, subjunctive, active
5. perfect, indicative, active
6. future perfect, indicative, active; perfect, subjunctive, active
7. pluperfect, subjunctive, active
8. perfect, indicative, active
9. pluperfect, indicative, active
10. future perfect, indicative active; perfect, subjunctive, active
11. perfect, indicative, passive
12. pluperfect, subjunctive, passive
13. future perfect, indicative, passive
14. perfect, subjunctive, passive

B

1. *Cum Hierosólymam pérgerem, bibliotheca carere non póteram:* When I was going on to Jerusalem, I was unable to do without a library.
2. *Dum ita me antiquus serpens illudebat, in média ferme quadragésima febris corpus invasit exhaustum:* While the ancient serpent was thus deluding me, almost in the middle of Lent a fever entered my exhausted body.
3. *Tantum lúminis erat ut sursum aspícere non auderem:* There was so much light that I did not dare look up.
4. *Interrogatus condícionem, Christianum me esse respondi:* When I was asked about my faith, I answered that I was Christian.
5. *"Mentiris," ait, "Ciceronianus es, non Christianus; ubi thesaurus tuus, ibi et cor tuum":* "You lie," he said. "You are a Ciceronian, not a Christian; where your treasure is, there your heart is also."

6. *Clamare tamen coepi et éiulans dícere: "Miserere mei, dómine, miserere mei."* Nevertheless, I began to shout, and, crying out, to say: "Have pity on me, master, have pity on me."

7. *"Dómine, si umquam habúi códices saeculares, te negavi."* "Master, if I ever had secular books, I denied you."

ANSWERS TO EXERCISES IN HOUR 21

TASK 1

1. *Quorundam amicorum argentum habemus:* We have the money of certain friends.
2. *Illa fémina quasdam res me dócuit:* That woman taught certain things to me.
3. *In quadam urbe terríbilis draco hábitat:* A terrible dragon lives in a certain city.
4. *Quidam non sunt iusti:* Certain people are not just.
5. *Cuiusdam matris vocem audivi:* I heard the voice of a certain mother.
6. *Cum quibusdam régibus imperator bellum gerebat:* The emperor waged war with certain kings.

TASK 2

1. *Áliquem in via vídeo:* I see someone on the road.
2. *Áliqui mílites gládios non habent:* Some soldiers do not have swords.
3. *Áliqua fémina cibum parat:* Some woman is preparing the food.
4. *Áliquos clamantes audivi:* I heard some (people) shouting.
5. *Áliquae naves in perículum venerunt:* Some ships came into danger.
6. *Álicui illud argentum dedi:* I gave that silver to someone.

TASK 3

1. Someday my prince will come.
2. That noise is coming from somewhere.
3. We are looking for some (a number of) good men.
4. We listened to the teacher babble for some time.

TASK 4

1. Let no one say that Latin is easy.
2. If you see anyone in the forum, don't speak with him.
3. Unless someone comes, I will close the door.
4. Unless we prepare some things, we will not be able to sail.

TASK 5

1. Anyone(s) you see, don't give them money.
2. We were looking for someone in the theater.
3. Whomever you love, ought to love you in return.
4. We never found anything in that house.

TASK 6

1. A brave soldier is (one) who never flees danger.
2. There is no one who never flees danger.
3. Who is there who understands these things?
4. These are times that test men's souls.

TASK 7

1. I am looking for something that I may do (to do).
2. I didn't have anything to say.
3. Caesar sent soldiers to capture the king.
4. I chose a servant to whom I might give money.

TASK 8

1. *Geórgius, qui multos dracones vícerit, martyr tamen óbiit:* George, although he conquered many dragons, nevertheless died as a martyr.
2. *Nomen Dei dignum est, quod in honore habeatur:* The name of God is worthy to be held in honor.
3. *Caesar, qui Romanum impérium régeret, de multis rebus sollicitabatur:* Caesar, who ruled (because he ruled) the Roman empire, was concerned about many things.

TASK 9

1. We found a house where we might educate our sons.
2. Let us imitate Christ, that we may be sons of God.
3. She read the books of philosophers, from which she might learn wisdom (that she might learn wisdom from them).
4. They were looking for a land to which they might lead the people.

TASK 10

1. I am writing this book that I may teach those who desire to learn Latin.
2. Don't trust all people who speak well.
3. I wonder whether everything that glitters is really gold.
4. We hope that the earth, which is third from the sun, will not be utterly destroyed.

READING EXERCISE

Since you are an example of devotion, and you loved your best and most loving brother with an affection equal (to his own), and you love his daughter as your own ..., I do not doubt that you will have great joy when you learn that she is turning out worthy of her father, worthy of you, and worthy of her grandfather. She has the greatest shrewdness, the greatest frugality; she loves me—which is an indication of her chastity. In addition to these (qualities) comes a love of literature, which she has conceived out of affection for me. She has my notebooks, she reads them over and over, and she even learns them by heart. What anxiety she feels when it seems that I am about to plead a case; what joy, when I have pled it! She appoints (someone) to announce to her what assent, what shouts I have elicited, what verdict I have obtained. Whenever I recite she sits nearby, set apart by a curtain, and takes up our praises with eager ears. Indeed, she even sings my verses, and sets them to the lyre—not with some artist teaching her, but love, which is the best teacher.

For these reasons I am brought to the sure hope that we will have a perpetual and daily growing concord. For she does not esteem my age and body, which gradually grow old and die, but my glory. Nothing else befits (a girl) educated by your hands, taught by your precepts, one who has seen nothing in your company except what is sacred and honorable, and who, finally, learned to love me from your telling. For, when you honored my mother (by taking) the place of a parent, right from boyhood you used to form me and to predict that I would be the sort of person that I now seem to my wife. Therefore we give thanks to you in competition: I, because you have given her to me, and she because you have given me to her—as if you chose us for each other. Farewell.

QUIZ

A

1.	*amet*	6.	*ducámini*
2.	*videremus*	7.	*laudata sis*
3.	*monuéritis*	8.	*misisset*
4.	*sint*	9.	*hortati essemus*
5.	*essem*	10.	*audiretis*

B

1. *Cum tu sis pietatis exemplum, non dúbito, hoc máximo tibi gaúdio fore:* Since you are an example if piety, I do not doubt that this will be a great (source of) joy for you.
2. *Amat me, quod indícium est cástitatis:* She loves me—which is indication of her chastity.
3. *Meos libellos habet, léctitat, ediscit étiam:* She has my notebooks, she reads them again and again, and she even learns them by heart.
4. *Qua illa sollicitúdine adfícitur, cum vídeor acturus:* What anxiety she feels when it seems that I am about to plead a case.
5. *Disponet áliquem, qui núntiet sibi, quem adsensum, quos clamores ego éxcitaverim:* She will appoint someone to announce to her, what assent, what shouts I have excited.
6. *Versus quidem meos cantat étiam, formatque cíthara, non artífice áliquo docente, sed amore, qui magister est óptimus:* Indeed she even sings my verses, and sets them to the lyre, not with some artist teaching, but love, which is the best teacher.

7. *Non enim díligit aetatem meam aut corpus, quae paulatim óccidunt, sed glóriam:* For she does not esteem my age or my body, which gradually die, but (my) glory.
8. *Nec áliud decet puellam tuis mánibus educatam, quae nihil in contubérnio tuo víderit, nisi quod sit honestum:* Nor does anything else befit a girl educated by your hands, who has seen nothing in your company except what is honorable.
9. *Certatim ergo tibi grátias ágimus: ego, quod illam mihi, et illa, quod me sibi déderis:* Therefore we give thanks to you in competition: I, because you have given her to me, and she, because you have given me to her.

ANSWERS TO EXERCISES IN HOUR 22

TASK 1

1. If you made a journey to Rome, you saw many things.
2. If you will have made (if you make) a journey to Rome, you will see many things.
3. If women read books, they will become learned.
4. If she finds a sword, Judith will kill Holofernes.
5. If today is Tuesday, we are in Italy.
6. If George catches the dragon, the people will believe in God.

TASK 2

1. If anyone should ask this, I wouldn't answer.
2. If the people should believe in God, I would kill this dragon.
3. If the king should send his daughter to the emperor, he would have peace.
4. If Caesar should cross the river, the soldiers would follow.
5. If you should capture the city of Rome, all Italy would be conquered.

TASK 3

1. If the soldiers had not fought, the city would have been captured.
2. I would not give flowers to you, unless I loved you.
3. If the danger were true, we would be fleeing from the city.
4. If the country mouse had lived in the city, he would not have lived there for long.
5. If I had done these things, I would now be praying to God.

TASK 4

1. If you are studying Latin, all people praise (everybody praises) you.
2. If you study Latin, everybody will praise you.
3. If you should study Latin, everybody would praise you.
4. If you were studying Latin, everybody would praise you.
5. If you had studied Latin, everybody would have praised you.
6. If you had studied Latin, everybody would be praising you.

TASK 5

1. Caesar would have ruled the empire prudently, but he was killed by the senators.
2. You would have said that the dragon feared George.
3. I would like you to find my brother.
4. George believed in God; otherwise he would not have conquered the dragon.

READING EXERCISE

"You see, king, what kind of thing this is, that is just now preached to us; but I tell you truly what I have learned for certain: the religion, which we have held until now, has no virtue and no utility. No one is more studious than I in the cultivation of our gods; nevertheless, there are many who receive more ample benefits and greater dignities from you than I do, and who prosper more …. If, however, the gods had some power, they would rather be helping me, who have taken care to serve them more diligently. Hence, if you perceive that the new things that now are preached to us are better and strong, it remains for us to make haste to take these things up without any hesitation."

"Such seems to me, O king, (to be) the present life of men on earth. As you are sitting down to dinner in winter time with your leaders and your ministers, when the hearth has been lit in the middle and the dining room has been made hot, a single sparrow comes and flies quickly through the house. It is not touched by the winter weather while it is inside, but when that brief space of serenity is finished, as it passes from winter to winter, it slips away from your eyes. In this way this life of men appears for a short time, but concerning what follows it, or what has preceded it, we have no idea. Hence, if this new doctrine has brought something more certain, it apparently deserves to be followed." The other elders and counselors, advised by God, added (comments) similar to these.

"For some time I had understood that what we were worshipping was nothing, because the more zealously I sought truth in that cult, the less I found (it). Now, however, I profess openly that in this preaching shines the truth that is able to give us the gifts of eternal salvation and happiness. Hence I suggest, O king, that we quickly consign our temples and altars, which we have dedicated without profit, to anathema and fire.

QUIZ

A

Indicative	Active	Passive
Present	*míttit*	*míttitur*
Imperfect	*mittébat*	*mittebátur*

Indicative	Active	Passive
Future	*mittet*	*mittetur*
Perfect	*misit*	*missus est*
Pluperfect	*miserat*	*missus erat*
Future Perfect	*miserit*	*missus erit*

Subjunctive	Active	Passive
Present	*mittat*	*mittatur*
Imperfect	*mitteret*	*mitteretur*
Perfect	*miserit*	*missus sit*
Pluperfect	*misisset*	*missus esset*

B

1. *Tu vide, rex, quale sit hoc, quod nobis modo praedicatur:* See, O king, what kind of thing this is that is now preached to us.
2. *Ego autem tibi verissime, quod certum dídici, profíteor:* But I tell you truly what I have learned for certain.
3. *Quia nihil omnino virtutis habet, nihil utilitatis, relígio illa, quam hucusque tenúimus:* Because this religion which we have held up to now has no virtue at all, no utility.
4. *Si autem dii aliquid valerent, me pótius iuvarent, qui illis impénsius servire curavi:* If however the gods had some power, they would rather be helping me, who have taken care to serve them more diligently.
5. *Unde restat ut festinemus absque ullo cunctámine novam religionem suscípere:* Hence it remains for us to hasten (that we hasten) to take up the new religion without any hesitation.
6. *Ita haec vita hóminum ad breve tempus apparet; quid autem sequatur, quidve praecésserit, prorsus ignoramus:* In this way this life of men appears for a short time; but concerning what follows, or what has preceded it, we have no idea.
7. *Unde, si haec nova doctrina cértius áliquid áttulit, mérito esse sequenda videtur:* And so, if this new doctrine has brought something more certain, it apparently deserves to be followed (deservedly seems to be followed).

ANSWERS TO EXERCISES IN HOUR 23

TASK 1

1. I often say these words to myself.
2. Raise yourselves (up) from the ground!
3. We often lie to ourselves.

4. Why do you not save yourself?
5. I persuaded myself that this is easy.

Task 2

1. Wise people never deceive themselves.
2. As the mob approached, the emperor Nero killed himself.
3. Few people do not trust themselves.
4. Cicero was always talking about himself.
5. The Christian should give up all love of self.
6. Alexander ordered the soldiers to follow him.
7. The king's daughter begged George to save her from the dragon.
8. The mind does not know what the senses present to it.

Task 3

1. Those women are defending their (own) children from danger.
2. Alexander defends his soldiers from the hippos.
3. Magdala often reads her books.
4. Iudith begs God to increase her strength.
5. The mind does not know which of its impressions are false.

Task 4

1. The Pythagoreans were accustomed to say, "He himself said it."
2. Magdala herself has books that she never read.
3. The Romans themselves ordered us to help them.
4. Every animal loves itself.
5. I see myself in the mirror.

Task 5

1. The emperor told the girl that one of the caskets that she was looking at contained a ring.
2. George declared that he would kill the dragon in order that the people might believe in God.
3. The mind believes that the things that it has seen are not true.
4. Augustine believed that all the things that he had done had been meaningless.

Task 6

1. The emperor promises that he will give his son to the girl in marriage if she chooses a casket wisely.
2. Judith decided that she would kill Holofernes, if he drank a lot.
3. Jerome promised that he would reject secular books, if God forgave him.
4. The mind knows that it would know nothing, if it doubted everything.
5. Alexander understood that he would have lost all his soldiers, if he had not conquered the hippos.

READING EXERCISE

I suppose therefore that all the things that I see are false; I believe that nothing of the things that the lying memory represents has ever existed; I plainly have no senses; body, figure, extension, motion and place are illusions. What then will be true? Perhaps this one thing: nothing is certain.

But how do I know that there is nothing that differs from all the things that I have now surveyed, something about which there is not even the least occasion of doubting? Is there some God, or whatever I can call him, who puts these very thoughts in me? But why do I think this, when perhaps I myself am the author of them? Am I, at least, something? But I have already denied that I have any senses and any body. Nevertheless, I hesitate; for what then? Am I so bound to the senses and body that am I not able to be without them? But I have persuaded myself that there is absolutely nothing in the world: no sky, no earth, no minds, no bodies; therefore haven't (I persuaded myself) that I do not exist? On the contrary, I certainly was (did exist), if I persuaded myself. But there is some deceiver, supremely able, supremely clever, who always deceives me on purpose. Without a doubt, then, I am, if he deceives me; and although he deceives me as much as he is able, he will nevertheless not bring it about that I am nothing, as long as I think that I am something. So much that, when all things have been considered sufficiently and more than sufficiently, this statement must finally be established: as often as (the assertion) "I am, I exist," is uttered by me or is conceived by my mind, it is necessarily true.

QUIZ

1. *Suppono ígitur ómnia quae vídeo falsa esse:* I suppose then that all the things that I see are false.
2. *Credo nihil umquam extitisse eorum quae mendax memória repraesentat:* I believe that nothing of the things that the lying memory represents have ever existed.
3. *Nullos plane hábeo sensus; corpus, figura, exténsio, motus, locusque sunt chímerae:* I plainly have no senses; body, figure, extension, motion and place are illusions.
4. *Sed unde scio nihil esse diversum ab iis ómnibus quae iam recénsui?* But how do I know that there is nothing different from all the things that I have now surveyed?
5. *Sumne ita córpori sensibusque alligatus, ut sine illis esse non possim?* Am I so bound to the senses and body, that I cannot be without these?
6. *Immo certe ego eram, si quid mihi persuasi:* On the contrary, I certainly did exist, if I persuaded myself (of) anything.
7. *"Ego sum, ego existo," quóties a me profertur vel mente concípitur, necessário est verum:* As often as the (assertion) "I am, I exist" is uttered by me or is conceived by my mind, it is necessarily true.

ANSWERS TO EXERCISES IN HOUR 24

TASK 1

1. Alexander never omitted an opportunity of (for) waging war.
2. St. George converted the people to the Christian faith by conquering dragons.
3. We rarely devote our time to learning languages.

TASK 2

1. Judith beheaded Holofernes to free the people of Israel.
2. Jerome withdrew into the desert for the sake of taming his flesh.
3. The Arab's son put a calf in a sack to test his friends.

TASK 3

1. It is difficult to say how much fun it is to learn Latin.
2. The ambassadors came to ask us for peace.
3. They came to Jerusalem to see the holy places.
4. Latin books are easy to read.

TASK 4

1. *Alexander ad Índiam venit ad loca mirabília videnda/loca mirabília visum.*
2. *Caesar Romam rédiit ad rempúblicam regendam/rempúblicam rectum.*

TASK 5

1. With which hand do you write: the left or the right?
2. I write with one hand; I count with the other.
3. I carry books with both hands.
4. I can write with neither hand.

TASK 6

1. Whoever believes in God, will have eternal life.
2. I will tell you whatever I hear.
3. You can work however you wish, but keep this rule.
4. I weep whenever I read these words.

TASK 7

1. *Duo et quattuor sunt sex.*
2. *Tres et quinque sunt octo.*
3. *Unus et tres sunt quattuor.*
4. *Sex et duo sunt octo.*
5. *Septem et unus sunt octo.*

TASK 8

1. *sédecim, sextus décimus*
2. *triginta, tricésimus*
3. *quandringenti, quadringentésimus*
4. *duo mília, bis millésimus*

TASK 9

1. *duodeviginti, duodevicésimus*
2. *triginta quinque, tricésimus quintus*
3. *quingenti viginti quattuor, quingentésimus vicésimus quartus*
4. *mille sescenti septuaginta octo, millésimus sescentésimus septu-agésimus octavus*
5. *tria mília trecenti nonaginta octo, ter millésimus trecentésimus nonagésimus octavus*

READING EXERCISE

But surely, not only the Mosaic or Christian mysteries, but also the theology of the ancients shows the dignity and benefits of the liberal arts. For what else do the grades of initiates in Greek secret rites signify? They came to the undertaking of the mysteries after having first been cleansed through those "purifying" arts, as it were: moral philosophy and dialectic. What else can these be than the interpretation of secret nature through philosophy?

… The sacred names of Apollo, if anyone searches through their meaning and hidden mystery, sufficiently demonstrate that the god is not less a philosopher than a prophet. Ammonius has already sufficiently explained this; but, Fathers, let us call to mind the three Delphic precepts necessary for those who intend to enter the sacrosanct and venerable temple, not of the fictional Apollo, but of the true one (who "illuminates every soul coming into this world"). You will see that those precepts give us no other advice but to embrace this three-part philosophy, with which the present disputation is concerned, with all our might.

For MEDEN AGAN, that is, "nothing in excess," rightly prescribes the norm and rule of all virtue by reason of moderation, with which moral (philosophy) deals. Then GNOTHI SAUTON, that is, "know yourself," encourages and rouses us toward the knowledge of all of nature, whose midpoint is the nature of man. For he who knows himself, knows all things in himself, as Zoroaster first, and then Plato wrote in his *Alcibiades*. Finally, having been enlightened by this knowledge through natural philosophy, and now being next to God, and saying EI, that is, "you are," we will call in a familiar and joyful way upon the true Apollo with a "theological" greeting.

Quiz

1. *Priscorum theológia liberálium ártium dignitatem ostendit:* The theology of the ancients shows the dignity of the liberal arts.
2. *Quid enim áliud significant in Graecorum arcanis gradus initiatorum?* For what else do the grades of initiates in the Greek mysteries signify?
3. *Initiati, purificati per illas quasi "februales" artes, ad mysteriorum pervenerunt susceptionem:* The initiates, having been cleansed through these "purifying" arts, as it were, arrive at the undertaking of the mysteries.
4. *Sacra Apóllinis nómina satis ostendunt Deum illum non minus esse philósophum quam vatem:* The sacred names of Apollo sufficiently demonstrate that the god is not less a philosopher than a prophet.
5. *Quicumque enim se cognoscit, in se ómnia cognoscit:* For whoever knows himself, knows all things in himself.

Index